Political Implications of Economic Reform in Communist Systems

Political Implications of Economic Reform in Communist Systems

Communist Dialectic

Edited by Donna L. Bahry
and Joel C. Moses

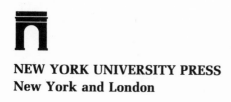

NEW YORK UNIVERSITY PRESS
New York and London

Library of Congress Cataloging-in-Publication Data
Political implications of economic reform in Communist systems:
   communist dialectic / edited by Donna L. Bahry and Joel C. Moses.
      p.   cm.
   Includes bibliographical references.
   ISBN 0-8147-1140-5 (alk. paper) — ISBN 0-8147-1141-3
(pbk. : alk. paper)
      1. Communism—1945–   . 2. Communist countries—Economic policy.
3. Communist countries—Politics and government. 4. Perestroika.
5. Soviet Union—Economic policy—1986–   . 6. Soviet Union—Politics
and government—1985–   . I. Bahry, Donna. II. Moses, Joel C.
HX44.C6438   1990
335.45'09'048—dc20   89-13846
                                                                        CIP

New York University Press books are printed on acid-free paper,
and their binding materials are chosen for strength and durability.

CONTENTS

ILLUSTRATIONS

PREFACE

The dramatic economic experiments and reforms introduced in the socialist world in the 1980s have made the terms *perestroika* and *glasnost'* so well known that they no longer require definition or even translation. They have also stimulated wide-ranging debates in both the East and the West over the political implications of economic change. The essays in this volume, all based on primary sources, present new data on the political fallout in China, the USSR and Eastern Europe.

The chapters highlight alternate but complementary levels of analysis: from changes in the interpretation of Marxism to the specific impacts of reforms on managers, workers, regions, and youth. Some chapters also discuss the political implications of the *limits* to reform, as in Poland and East Germany. Each of the authors thus offers a different perspective on the political economy of reform in centrally planned economies—to show the importance of using multiple levels of analysis for understanding all the political impacts of reform.

In the introductory chapter the editors provide an overview of the reform process, and conclude that the changes represent a quest for a new model of socialism. In true dialectical fashion, however, the new model is not without its own contradictions—which breed new problems for leaders attempting to maintain political stability.

CONTRIBUTORS

Donna L. Bahry is Professor of Political Science at the University of California, Davis, and the author of *Outside Moscow: Power, Politics, and Budgetary Policies in the Soviet Republics* (1987). Her articles have appeared in *Comparative Political Studies, Comparative Politics, Slavic Review,* and the *American Political Science Review.*

Thomas A. Baylis is Associate Professor of Political Science at the University of Texas at San Antonio. He is the author of *The Technical Intelligentsia and the East German Elite* (1974) and *Governing by Committee: Collegial Leadership in Advanced Societies* (1989). He is currently working on a book on Western economic relations with Eastern Europe for the Twentieth Century Fund.

Jack Bielasiak is Associate Professor of Political Science and Director of the Polish Studies Center at Indiana University, Bloomington. He is the coeditor of *Polish Politics: Edge of the Abyss* and the author of numerous articles on Polish politics, the Solidarity movement, and workers' participation in Eastern Europe. He is currently at work on a study of the impact of economic reforms on the working class in socialist countries.

Linda J. Cook holds a Ph.D. from Columbia University and is presently Assistant Professor of Political Science at Brown University. She has conducted research on Soviet workers and the Communist party during the Stalinist period, and is presently working on a study of Soviet social policy, workers, and economic and political reform.

Alfred B. Evans, Jr., received his Ph.D. from the University of Wisconsin (Madison), and is currently Professor of Political Science at California State University, Fresno. His research has dealt with Marxist-Leninist ideology in the USSR and with Soviet rural development policies.

Joel C. Moses is Professor of Political Science, Iowa State University. He is the author of *Regional Party Leadership and Policy-Making in the USSR* (1974), *The Politics of Women and Work in the Soviet Union and the United States* (1983), and several articles on Soviet politics.

Kristen Parris is an ABD in political science at Indiana University. Most recently, she has conducted research in Zhejiang province on the development of private enterprise, for her doctoral dissertation on "Central Authority and Local Society: The Implementation of Private Sector Policy in Contemporary China."

Jean C. Robinson is Associate Professor of Political Science, East Asian Studies, and Women's Studies at Indiana University. She has conducted research in China and Poland, and is completing a book entitled *Alienated Families: Family, State, and Public Policies in Socialist Societies.*

Stanley Rosen teaches political science at the University of Southern California. He is the author of *Red Guard Factionalism and the Cultural Revolution in Guangzhou* (1982), the coauthor of *Survey Research in the People's Republic of China* (1987), and has coedited *On Socialist Democracy and the Chinese Legal System* (1985) and *Policy Conflicts in Post-Mao China* (1986). He edits the journal *Chinese Education.*

Peter Rutland is Assistant Professor of Government at Wesleyan University, and is the author of *The Myth of the Plan: Lessons of Soviet Planning Experience* (1985). He has just completed a manuscript entitled *The Politics of Industrial Stagnation in the USSR.*

Andrea Stevenson Sanjian is Assistant Professor of Political Science at Bucknell University. She received her Ph.D. in political science from Indiana University, and her publications include research on economic management in the USSR and on Soviet social policies and problems.

James Tong is Assistant Professor of Political Science at UCLA. He is the Associate Editor of *Chinese Law and Government*, and his book *Disorder Under Heaven: Rebellions and Banditry in the Ming Dynasty* will be published by Stanford University Press.

1

COMMUNIST DIALECTIC: TOWARD A NEW MODEL OF SOCIALISM?

Donna L. Bahry and Joel C. Moses

Only a little over one hundred years after the death of Karl Marx, his prophetic vision has seemingly come to pass. Internal economic contradictions have led to mounting economic crises. In turn, the economic dilemmas have pressured ruling elites to undertake changes which threaten to erode their own political privileges and promise the transformation of their system. The changes have begun to unleash long-suppressed political demands and in some cases have set into motion what may be irreversible movements for full-scale political and cultural liberation.

Yet the vindication for Marx is an ironic one. During the past decade, it has been not capitalist but Communist states that have found themselves confronting their own classic Marxist dialectic. In response to common economic crises, many Communist countries have been driven to institute reform programs that promise wide-ranging changes in politics and culture as well as economics. Most strikingly evident with the changes in the USSR under Mikhail Gorbachev since 1985, the process has also spread to varying degrees from Budapest to Beijing to Ho Chi Minh City. So similar are some of the cultural, economic, and political trends that the leaders supporting them, such as General Secretary Nguyen Van Linh in Vietnam, have been dubbed "Little Gorbachevs" within their own countries.[1] So parallel are the kinds of economic reforms implemented under the slogan of building "socialism with Chinese characteristics" in China that they seem to have been borrowed from the reform package instituted in Hungary over the last two decades. So similar have the changes in Moscow been to those aborted in the

"Czech spring" of 1968 that some observers wonder whether there is anything other than twenty years separating a Gorbachev from a Dubcek.

In the cultural realm, change has brought wide distribution and critical acclaim for an anti-Stalinist film like *Repentance* throughout the Soviet Union and for the American film *Platoon* throughout Vietnam.[2] It has found theater groups in the USSR choosing their own plays and electing their own artistic leaders, and scientists in China subscribing to Western journals without interference.[3] In the economic realm, change has found newly legitimized capitalist forms in China from free-trade private enterprise zones to a stock market, and Chinese consumers accumulating newly available consumer goods. In the USSR, change has found the legalization of new cooperative enterprises and the beginnings of a capital market. In the political realm, change has brought multicandidate elections for a new Soviet congress, and voter rejection of many candidates supported by the Communist party. And change has found tens of thousands of Chinese students mounting open protests in December 1986, and again in the spring of 1989, for Western-style democratic reforms.[4] In Hungary, change has found the Communist party (HSWP) endorsing a multiparty system, adopting new guarantees on civil liberties and transforming itself into the Hungarian Socialist party; and in Poland it has found the regime legalizing Solidarity, opening up part of the national legislature to competitive election and appointing a premier from Solidarity's ranks.[5] Most dramatic of all, change has brought the overthrow of the Ceaucescu regime in Romania and the fall of the Berlin Wall.

The drama is undeniable, but the real issue in all these changes is their long-term implication for socialism itself as a viable system of rule. At stake in the emergence of this Communist dialectic is whether new political leaders can survive the transformations without unraveling the foundations that have kept political order. The eleven essays presented here address this question, exploring the political impacts of economic restructuring in China, the USSR, and Eastern Europe.

The essays span a diverse set of topics, and highlight the diversity of the reform experience—from the dramatic changes in Hungary and the USSR, to the resistance to reforms in China and parts of

Eastern Europe. Our goal is to emphasize the very different implications of reform for different groups, and at different levels of analysis, from the central level to the individual.

THE COMMON THREADS OF REFORM

One might wonder, along with Peter Rutland (chapter 3) about the ability of political leaders to carry out reforms logically repudiating the entrenched tenets of centralized economic planning.[6] Even where a strong commitment to change exists, reformers in some cases have been more willing to experiment with the new economic mechanisms than with new political forms. Thus while China's economy has undergone substantial revamping since 1978, and public discussions in China have focused on political liberalization, China's leaders have also been quick to clamp down on political demands, as in the winter of 1987 and the spring of 1989.

Moreover, it would be as myopic to underestimate the powerful ideological and vested interests opposed to any real economic and political reform as it would be to dismiss the potential of the changes that are now under way in many Communist states. The uneven pace of reforms and in some instances open reversals attest to the obstacles on the political landscape. The year 1987 alone saw two highly visible advocates of liberalization in the ruling establishments of China and the USSR both fall victim to conservative opposition and to dismissal from the central party apparatus — Hu Yaobang removed as the CPC's general secretary in January and Boris El'tsin as CPSU secretary in November.[7] In the Soviet Union, Gorbachev increasingly has concentrated his speeches on opponents of his triad of perestroika, glasnost' and democratization within party and state organs.[8] Major journals now publish articles seeking to analyze the "braking mechanism" that has set in to slow or obstruct the progress of economic reform.[9]

Yet the common threads of economic reform are more than simple cosmetic changes and more than just isolated and unrelated movements. Judging from stated intentions and policy initiatives, many political leaders have set out to revise the most sacrosanct tenets of Communist theory and practice from the past seven decades.

Oleg Bogomolov, a prominent Soviet academic widely reputed to be among the four closest advisers to Gorbachev,[10] characterized the reform process unfolding simultaneously in several Communist nation states as a "collective search for a new model of socialist society."[11] Despite national differences among Communist systems, and despite variation in the timing and specific nature of their reforms, Bogomolov contends that they share certain common tendencies: decentralizing economic management and diversifying the ownership of productive resources; introducing more democratic forms of participation and decision-making; and expanding economic ties with the nonsocialist world.

THE ECONOMIC DIMENSION

By a "new model of social economics," Bogomolov characterizes a common tendency in many Communist states to rethink centralized state planning and management.[12] Planning and operational authority for economic decision-making are being devolved to state enterprises, local authorities, and farms—and within farms, to contractual family and cooperative units. The long-term trend, Bogomolov explains, should find many Communist nations transferring effective decision-making from the state to the local manager. The main means of production may continue to be state-owned, but they will be leased to industrial enterprises. Within firms, worker participation will become more commonplace. Labor collectives and their councils will set policy for their production units, elect their administrative superiors from foremen or shop supervisors to the actual enterprise managers (or, at least, confirm by vote of the workers the person whom the ministry formally appoints), and own the resources and retain the profits from goods manufactured and sold by the enterprise.[13]

Bogomolov also emphasizes that the state's monopoly over economic activities, entire economic sectors, and resources is increasingly being narrowed. Privately and family-owned enterprises and producer cooperatives have been expanded in agriculture, services, and trade to compete with state enterprises in a less tightly regulated market. By directly combining the producers and owners of the means of production in the workplace, producer cooperatives have been especially lauded as a resuscitation of true socialist principles.[14] In this view, the owner-entrepreneur in a socialist producer cooperative is not conceived to be an exploiter like the capitalist owner, because the socialist-entrepreneur actually participates in production.

In general, the spread of producer cooperatives may presage the evolution of a mixed socialist-capitalist economy in many Communist systems.[15] It may become commonplace for worker-shareholders in producer cooperatives to receive stock in their own companies, for cooperatives to buy and sell shares in each other's company, and for cooperatives to participate in joint ventures with firms in other socialist or even capitalist countries.[16]

The ultimate goal of the economic reforms, according to Bogomolov, is "economic democracy": direct workers' ownership of their own products and direct worker retention of profits as the principal incentive to produce. As state management of the economy is reduced, state enterprise under joint worker-management councils, family-owned enterprises, and producer cooperatives will all be competing for the same market. Through competition, they and not the state will be setting prices and wages and determining the mix of products by responding to consumer demand. For Bogomolov, the new socialist economics embraces the "laws of the market" as universal and consistent with Marxism-Leninism—competition among producers, real consumer choice, and a true interplay of supply and demand.[17]

THE POLITICAL DIMENSION

All these steps toward economic democracy for the producer and the consumer will remain at best good intentions, Bogomolov writes, unless they are directly reinforced by a corresponding tendency toward political democratization. That would allow the innovation, competition, entrepreneurship, risk-taking, and flexibility essential for the reforms to take root in the workplace.[18] Soviet leaders and academics have referred to this broadly as activating the "human factor," by engendering a sense of personal commitment, initiative, and responsibility among officials and private citizens alike. Openly critical of authoritarian values and institutions in the Soviet system and of the apathy and cynicism they have spawned, Gorbachev contends that the human factor can only exist under the right set of objective circumstances. Those objective circumstances must foster democratic norms and expectations between leader and led throughout society—from the workplace to party and state institutions. To implement economic reforms in the spirit intended, the new slogan in the Soviet Union under Gorbachev urges everyone to "learn democracy and public openness."

On the societal level, open discussion and debate now rages over previously sacred or taboo issues. Public attention has focused on the plight of religious believers, ethnic hatreds and conflicts, widespread abuses and injustices in the legal system, and the realities of homelessness, unemployment, drug-abuse, prostitution, and suicide.[19]

As the principles and practices of central planning have come under attack, so, too, have censorship and political controls over scientific and cultural creativity. The degree of candor and freedom allowed the intelligentsia in some Communist countries over recent years is without precedent.[20] In the Soviet Union, as an example, some reformers urge the elimination of "forbidden zones" and "blank spots" from public discussion, and proclaim that "everything is permitted, unless it is prohibited by law." The loosening of political controls has meant a cultural renaissance in the public realm, blurring the distinction between what is now openly published and what was previously limited to samizdat and the political underground.

On the level of state and government, reforms have varied from the revolution in Romania, the opening of East Germany and creation of a multiparty system in Hungary to a more cautious and uneven liberalization in China. Polish authorities in the spring of 1989 reached accords that would legalize Solidarity and provide for limited pluralization of the national assembly, leading to the appointment of a Solidarity leader as Poland's premier; the Soviet Union ran contested elections for a new national Congress of People's Deputies. In China, voters have been offered a choice of candidates for the national people's congress, whose sessions reflect limited openness to debate and criticism of public officials. But the scale of coercion after student demonstrations in 1989 serve as a reminder of how easily liberalization can be reversed.

Experiments elsewhere over the past decade have also included other initiatives to enhance the professional status and influence of deputies as full-time elected representatives.[21] The reforms aim at transforming governmental assemblies into a more effective public forum and a counterweight to the dictates of state officials, reducing direct party controls over the selection and removal of state officials, and expanding the control of local governments over economic policy in their area.

Advocates of reform also propose that open and competitive nationwide debates over public policies should take place before decisions are made by party and state.[22] Laws affirming the right of the public to information reflect a new concern with institutionalizing these principles. Thus, for instance, Hungary's Socialist Workers' party adopted a plan in the spring of 1989 for a new press law, to allow private citizens to set up papers, television and radio stations, to have printing equipment, and to distribute printed materials.[23] And in the Soviet Union, a proposed and highly controversial law on freedom of information and the press would revise the traditional role of the media as an extension of the party.[24] As Bogomolov explains, socialism needs an independent press, because "only a completely and objectively informed person can be a conscientious and active participant of political and economic life and make responsible decisions in self-government structures."[25]

New concepts like "socialist pluralism" and the "dialectics of socialism" have achieved a certain legitimacy in several Communist countries. The concepts assume that a diversity of opinions and alternatives is healthy in socialist society, which is now recognized as inevitably containing distinct and even contradictory groups and interests.[26] The old orthodoxy of a socialist society converging on social and political homogeneity has been challenged, as has the arbitrariness of past decisions. According to Bogomolov, the "socialist states are striving to find mechanisms capable of considering the pluralism of interests, leading them to a certain common denominator, and broadening the base of public consensus."[27] No longer should Communist systems "drive underground the social contradictions" which contributed to their "crisis situations" of the past. Such contradictions, Bogomolov relates, require a normal and healthy outlet, such as the new political movements, informal associations, funds, and political clubs outside the formal channels of party control but for the most part recognized and accepted by the authorities.[28]

THE INTERNATIONAL DIMENSION

A third and closely related common tendency in the new model of socialism Bogomolov describes has found Communist countries "opening up to the outside world."[29] In the economic realm, nations that have traditionally been wary of extensive trade and investment in an international economy dominated by capitalism are now moving more into the world market. Although they account for only 12 percent of world trade, Communist countries have set out to remove the administrative, economic, and political barriers which have limited their involvement in the international economy. Two long-term measures to internationalize will include the eventual elimination of the state's monopoly on foreign trade and the transfer of currencies to convertibility. In the short term, enterprises and producer cooperatives have already been granted legal rights to trade and elicit foreign investment and joint ventures; in China, joint manufacturing and marketing with foreign firms has been promoted by the creation of special economic zones and "open cities." In some countries, foreign investment provisions and tax policies have been liberalized to the point where foreign firms may now own the majority share of joint ventures.

Bogomolov contends that success in domestic economic reform will hinge on success in these efforts to expand trade and international ties. On the one hand, the socialist economies cannot produce many technologically sophisticated goods required for their own expansion as efficiently or cheaply as those marketed elsewhere. On the other hand, the socialist economies can only afford to import these goods if domestic reform efforts succeed in making their products competitive on the world market. The interdependence of the domestic and foreign market is thus both a challenge and a necessity.

THE DILEMMAS OF REFORM

The effort to rethink old economic doctrines has scored some notable successes. Hungary, which has gone through several phases of reform and retrenchment since 1968, has seen its domestic consumer goods develop and its foreign trade expand. Chinese economic reform has yielded even more dramatic results: from 1978 to 1987, direct controls over supplies and production diminished in both industry and agriculture; the cooperative sector expanded; consumer goods production witnessed major increases, foreign trade tripled, and gross farm output per capita more than doubled.[30]

Yet reform experiments in Hungary and China reflect a cycle of liberalization and retrenchment, as decentralization creates imbalances that central authorities counter with a reimposition of central controls. More recent experiments with market-type mechanisms, as in the USSR, have yet to yield results; but here, too, there have been calls to contain some of the early side effects of reform (e.g., inflation, decreased industrial output), by strengthening central direction.

The reform platforms that Bogomolov describes have thus bred common dilemmas in the design and implementation of economic restructuring. Despite an emerging consensus over the *need* to restructure, few leaders have developed a clear or consistent model for achieving the new-style socialism. The now open political maneuvering and the debates in Beijing, Moscow, Budapest, and other capitals in the bloc confirm that there is anything but agreement over how, or how much to reform. The conflicts are most open in the political sphere, but conflicts over economic reform are hardly less divisive. The economists and politicians involved in the debate may often use the same terms, but they seldom agree on what the terms mean in practice.

The resulting compromises make for a less than coherent economic and political blueprint. Reforms have thus been introduced piecemeal, creating multiple contradictions and more than occasional reversals. In China, for example, food prices in the countryside rose with the introduction of market-oriented reforms, while urban food prices remained subsidized. The gap led in 1987 to a run on urban stores and the imposition of rationing for some food items.[31]

In the USSR, the introduction in 1988 of the new law on state enterprises put Soviet firms on formal cost-price accounting *(khozraschet)* and instituted the election of managers by workers— but central planners nevertheless continued to control output and supply plans through state orders taking as much as 100 percent of a firm's output. And managers nominally elected by their own workers could not assume their position without confirmation from ministerial superiors.[32] In Poland, as in several other centrally planned economies, state enterprises may now be declared bankrupt, but in an environment where continued reliance on administrative prices makes it difficult to determine an enterprise's real profits and losses.[33]

As Andrea Stevenson Sanjian notes (chapter 2), the contradictions in the first rounds of economic reform should not be surprising. Some changes are simply easier to implement than others and have come early in the process; some—such as comprehensive price reform—are both more complicated and more politically sensitive and have yet to be fully addressed. Some reformers themselves do not appear to have a consistent platform for economic change. Sorting through the radically different diagnoses and cures that are put forward (see Peter Rutland's review of the Soviet reform debate in chapter 3) may only be possible through an extended period of experimentation. There is also something of a paradox in the notion of a centralized state planning apparatus undertaking decentralization. If the economy of developed socialism has grown too complex to allow effective central balancing of production, services, labor, technological innovation, and the like, then it can hardly be easy for reformers at the center to implement a comprehensive yet balanced reform package.

Political leaders have attempted to skirt some of these problems by relying on experiments to test new economic forms in selected regions and economic branches. Yet the careful trial runs have often been followed by abrupt and wholesale adoption, without fully specifying how they are to work in practice and without fully considering the likely impact of sectoral and regional differences.

Often the goals of the reforms are themselves contradictory. Reformers call for accelerated growth rates and better quality output while drastically reorganizing factories and farms. They have promised an economic environment of stable norms and expectations for producers, to eliminate the disincentives created by the ratchet principle; but central planners and ministries are taken to task for not revising the norms and expectations quickly enough. Enterprise managers and local officials have been given a larger share of investment funds, as an incentive to be more productive and efficient; but the devolution of investment disperses resources among many small projects, and thus exacerbates the investment hunger characteristic of centrally planned economies. Central governments have responded by trying to reabsorb funds that were supposed to be left in local hands.

Reforms have thus reduced at least some central economic controls, but as Jan Prybyla notes, they have yet to fill the vacuum with effective market alternatives.[34] Describing China's experience up through 1989, he concluded that a decade of reforms had created an "in-between construct," one that is neither plan nor market.

For the people and the institutions at the grassroots, the effort to combine the two models poses an array of contradictions and "perverse incentives." Managers, local officials, workers, and private entrepreneurs all find themselves encouraged to take new initiatives while confronting many of the old constraints.

THE MANAGERIAL LEVEL

For managers of state enterprises, the reforms promise greater autonomy, and greater responsibility, but in a less certain environment. Firms are to operate on the basis of profitability, yet without the accurate pricing information necessary to make optimal decisions. In China, for example, the decentralization of investment led local firms and local governments to rush into the production of goods that the state has priced high, such as wine and cigarettes. Few producers moved into the market for products that have traditionally been underpriced. Thus supplies of such goods remained low, with the price system reinforcing shortages by offering end users little incentive to conserve their consumption of such items.[35]

The reforms also give managers more latitude in making decisions about what to produce, but offer far less control over inputs. The supply problems endemic to central planning thus continue to be a major bottleneck. In the Soviet Union, many state enterprises have lobbied central planners to include the supplies they need in mandatory state orders.[36] Some managers have complained that they are forced to agree to fulfill state orders and the corresponding directives from above just to be sure that they will receive needed inputs. Supply problems also continue to plague Chinese managers, since decentralization heightened demand for, and thus intensified, shortages of capital goods. Many new projects begun with local investment funds have thus been left uncompleted, while enterprise managers and local authorities hoard unused supplies as a hedge against future shortfalls.[37]

Managers also find themselves still facing the problems of the ratchet even in the new economic environment. Reform models envision a set of stable guidelines for output, productivity, and taxes, but central authorities are under pressure to change them to fit the prevailing economic climate and the circumstances of individual enterprises. In place of negotiations over output targets, firms and planners find themselves haggling over how much each enterprise will spend on inputs, retain from its earnings, and surrender to higher authorities.

Central governments' penchant for soaking up enterprise earnings also remains strong as long as capital markets remain underdeveloped. Individual enterprises often collect too little in their profit retention schemes to invest themselves on an efficient scale.[38] "Retained" funds thus sit idle, or, if an enterprise does invest, it is often in small and duplicative projects that end up dispersing funds, as the Chinese experience demonstrates. China's granting of more powers to enterprises had led to complaints that investment resources have been spread too thin, with enterprises and local authorities bidding up demand for capital goods and taking resources away from central priorities.[39] The new enterprises created with local funds frequently duplicate each other, operating below capacity because of limited demand and/or lack of supplies and equipment. Hence reforms have created a tension between the incentive effects of allowing enterprises to accumulate funds at the plant level, and the economies of scale and concentration of resources that can accrue from more centralized investment planning. And the tension has turned the quest for stable norms into a constantly changing set of new directives.[40]

Managers face a different bind in dealing with the new campaign to democratize the workplace. Andrea Stevenson Sanjian notes in chapter 2, for example, that while managers are being given enhanced authority and responsibility to run their enterprises on a profit and loss basis, they have now become more subject to the countervailing influence of their own workers through labor councils and worker elections of managers. Management's dilemma is to promote higher productivity without the previous support of central authorities and policies.

Yet as Joel Moses emphasizes (chapter 8), industrialized Communist systems like the USSR may have little alternative to democratizing labor-management relations. The impetus for democracy may not be the fear of another Solidarity movement, but the rapidly advancing revolution in technology. As the Western movement since the 1970s to democratize the workplace suggests, rigid hierarchical divisions between management and labor associated with Taylorism and mass assembly-line procedures of the past may be transformed under the technological imperative of microelectronics.

In a more democratic workplace, managers have stronger incentives to play for workers' support by manipulating wages, bonuses, and collective goods.[41] To a degree, their options are limited, since wage scales and enterprise wage funds continue to be regulated from above in many enterprises. Yet experiments with new forms of labor organization in China and the USSR reveal that managers have been willing to bid up bonuses and benefits to workers even in the absence of rises in labor productivity—thus adding to inflationary pressures.[42] The expansion of cooperative and private economic activity, offering higher earnings to enterprising employees, puts even more pressure on state enterprises to offer competitive wages. Many managers have also been loath to fire workers, because of social pressures in the work collective itself and also because credit restrictions and supply bottlenecks mean that it can still pay to hoard labor as "insurance" against shortages of other inputs.[43]

Certainly a less rigid system of labor-management relations is bound to improve worker morale. There is no guarantee, however, that the interests of worker, manager, and firm will coincide. Workers who gain more of a say in enterprise decisions are likely to have their own priorities and their own perspective on enterprises' decisions. A worker's interest (and that of the state as well) would lie in having a degree of job mobility, in being able to change places of employment as the job market shifts and as labor resources need to be redistributed. A mobile labor force, in turn, is most likely to respond to immediate and individual incentives (wages, bonuses, benefits) rather than to the expansion or profitability of the firm over the long haul, which they may not be around to see. Thus from a worker's perspective, the best strategy for managing an enterprise may be one emphasizing short-term gains rather than long-term growth.

THE REGIONAL AND LOCAL LEVEL

For local officials, especially in China and the USSR, the reforms have brought a new mandate to strengthen government and especially economic decision-making at the grassroots. Reform packages have focused on reinforcing local tax bases, providing more stable revenues, and offering new incentives for localities to spur local economic growth. Local officials have been told to give up their "dependency" on higher authorities and to become entrepreneurs themselves. Local cadres in the Soviet Union have been encouraged to foster new forms of local production and cooperative trade.[44] And, as one Western analyst notes, rural officials in China have gone "from cadres to middlemen," directing the new system of family and contract farming and promoting rural development.[45]

Yet the decentralization of decision-making to enterprises, and the new emphasis on allowing factories and farms to retain more of what they earn, has meant a smaller share of funds available to local budgets (and to national ones as well). In China's villages, the change in finances has made it difficult for local authorities to raise their own capital for the public services and infrastructure needed to promote further local growth.[46] Some urban areas (aside from those in the Special Economic Zones) have fared better, though their success in part has hinged on moving into the production of consumer goods with artificially high administered prices. In the USSR, reforms leaving a larger share of enterprise proceeds in the manager's hands have also eaten into the government budget, and have led in some cases to conflict between enterprises and local officials over taxes.[47] And governments at all levels find themselves further strapped for funds as traditional tax sources such as alcohol sales and profits and retail sales of consumer goods have declined.

Decentralization has also increased the potential for competition and conflict among regions. Faced with heightened responsibility for local development, China's local leaders have attempted to block outside industries from gaining access to local markets, to protect their own local products and thus bolster revenues and employment.[48] Price differentials between raw materials and industrial goods have added to the competition, making raw materials regions reluctant to ship to more industrialized areas.[49] In the USSR, the uneven pace of economic reform among different regions, the worsening shortages of consumer goods, and the overtaxed social infrastructure in more developed regions have fed a wave of regional protectionism, with the Baltic republics erecting barriers against in-migration and against the sale or shipping of scarce goods outside regional borders.[50] Openly acknowledged budget deficits have given rise to a debate among republic spokesmen over the wisdom of continued redistribution from more to less developed areas. And republic and local leaders have advocated "self-financing," which in its most radical form—in the Baltic republics—has been interpreted to mean virtual independence from the central government.

THE PRIVATE SECTOR

For the private sector, the reforms thus far also have created a set of perverse incentives. Potentially, the opportunities for new "socialist entrepreneurs" are extraordinary in the new round of economic reforms, especially given the pent-up demand for consumer goods and services among the mass public. Yet cooperative and individual ventures are often hemmed in by a formidable array of bureaucratic obstacles. As Peter Rutland notes in the Soviet case (chapter 3), simply gaining permission can be an expensive struggle. Licensing requirements often impose stiff fees and bureaucratic rules that discourage all but the most persistent new private businesses. Nor does permission guarantee that the new business will obtain needed supplies, equipment, or space, all of which represent chronic deficit items.[51] For those new businesses that do succeed, public resistance can prove to be another obstacle. Private producers face a deeply held antipathy to free enterprise and the accumulation of wealth. Soviet cooperatives have become the natural scapegoats for exposes in the Soviet press that blame them for shortages in the state stores, price-gouging, and collusion with criminals.[52]

As China's experience shows, developing private or family economic activity has been somewhat easier in the rural sector, where initial capital requirements are lower, where space may be easier to find, and where prices have been allowed to rise to provide incentives for private producers. Still, there have been barriers to entry in the Chinese countryside, too, with some local officials giving short shrift to individuals and small-scale producers.[53] And price differentials between city and countryside led some enterprising rural officials to profiteering, buying food in the towns and reselling it at higher prices in the villages.

As Anders Aslund suggests, the structural constraints on and ambivalence toward private enterprise can create a cycle of expansion and contraction in the cooperative/private sector. Firms are initially allowed to grow in order to reduce the chronic deficit of consumer goods and services, but are then cut back as opposition mounts. Given the limited scope for such enterprises, and the continuing problems they face in securing supplies, equipment, and even space, opportunities to reinvest are limited. And even if capital goods were more readily available, reinvestment might not be attractive in any event, given fears that the state might reverse its policy and seize cooperative and private assets. The more attractive options might be either to operate in the second economy and avoid state regulation, or to channel newly earned income into wages, salaries, and private amenities such as housing.

Since the higher wages, new products, and rivalry for supplies put pressure on state enterprises, state industries are liable to lobby for restrictions to keep the competition at bay. The high wages and the competition with state firms can thus create a public backlash, fueling public demands for a clampdown on cooperative/private enterprise. In these conditions, new cooperative and private enterprises would have strong incentives to look for quick profits (rather than long-term growth), thus adding even more weight to the charges of greed, speculation, and corruption.[54]

THE SOCIAL COSTS OF REFORM

One of the most striking elements of the current reform process has been the increasing willingness of political leaders to broach openly the dislocations and costs that market-type economic reforms can bring. Discussions have focused on the prospects for workers to lose jobs, for firms to go bankrupt, for differentials in incomes to grow, and for prices to rise. As Alfred Evans (chapter 6), Linda Cook (chapter 7), and Joel Moses (chapter 8) demonstrate for the Soviet case, the promise of job security is no longer part of the social contract, although many reformers assume that there will be more of a redistribution of labor rather than outright layoffs. Similarly, Hungary and China have begun to move away from job guarantees, looking for ways to reallocate labor to more productive jobs. China's reform package, for example, envisions an end to the "iron rice bowl," the guarantee of job security, by introducing a contact system in which workers will be employed only for a specified period rather than for life.

In addition, where once equalization of wages was treated as a critical goal in the post-Stalin era, now "wage leveling" evokes denunciations for undermining the incentive structure of socialist society. Reliance on social consumption funds to even out real incomes is supposed to decline, since there is now less emphasis on achieving redistribution of consumption according to need. Housing shortages are to be addressed through more cooperative and private financing. The stability of prices for staples such as milk and meat is no longer quite so sacred. And personal taxes, long viewed as largely insignificant, are now to become more important and more progressive.

There is still, however, a concern with social justice, broadly defined. Along with calls for reducing traditional social guarantees, many reform advocates also press for elimination of special privileges and corrupt practices that undermine equal opportunity. Many also support a restructuring, rather than a dismantling, of the social contract, so that the disadvantaged in socialist society will be guaranteed state assistance.

The net social costs of reform thus far appear to be mixed. On one hand, analysts have been quick to point out the implications for increased stratification. Yet policies that would fundamentally alter social guarantees have been slow to develop and have for the most part been limited in their impact. Certainly reforms that emphasize rewards based on skill and performance should benefit the highly educated, the intellectual and professional workers, and the young. The reform of consumer prices would fundamentally alter patterns of real income and consumption, especially for unskilled workers.

Some signs of changes in stratification are already visible in changing wage patterns in the USSR and income distribution in China. For the USSR, Gertrude Schroeder reports, the reforms have meant that "the lion's share of wage increases planned for 1986–90 (fifteen percent) will accrue to white-collar workers, who comprise about one-fifth of the total in the productive sectors. Blue-collar workers, long nurtured on egalitarian values, well may consider those developments to be unfair, even though wider differentials may be needed to improve incentives."[55] For China, the emphasis on agricultural reform has meant that overall income inequality decreased from 1978 to 1983, while it increased *within* rural areas: the top 1 percent of the population in the countryside received a larger share of income and the bottom 40 percent received less.[56]

In addition to the changing reward structure, dislocations created by worker layoffs have already been felt: workers released from jobs in the USSR have experienced downward mobility and loss of benefits; some have simply opted for early retirement rather than face the rigors of the job market. Others have responded to the loss of their jobs by turning to the legal system to appeal (Cook, chapter 7). A new network of employment services may eventually ease such transitions, but it has been slow to develop.

Yet despite the more open discussion of these issues, most leaders have moved rather cautiously in attempting to redefine the social and welfare guarantees built up by their predecessors. Policies on unemployment, prices, social consumption, and other elements of the old social contract for the most part have remained very conservative. Consumer subsidies still account for a large share of the Soviet and Chinese budgets, and most political leaders have been extremely reluctant to raise state prices for basic consumer goods even though costs have continued to climb.[57] In fact, inflationary pressures seem to create even more of a premium for maintaining price stability on at least some basic products. The inflation rate in China's urban areas, though officially pegged at 21 percent for 1988, has been estimated to be closer to 40 percent.[58] And the Soviet inflation rate seems to be rising, though it too is still subject to varying estimates.[59]

Conservatism also seems evident in employment policies. As of mid-1989, the bulk of Soviet personnel cuts have been visible—as in reducing the staffs of government ministries—but limited in their overall impact on other occupations. To offset any massive layoffs for Soviet industry in the next decade, Soviet planners propose to eliminate first the jobs of older workers about to retire. Soviet planners also count on an expanded pool of part-time jobs and new employment opportunities in the private and cooperative sectors that will compensate for the positions to be eliminated in the state sector (Moses, chapter 8). China's labor policies have also been relatively conservative: only 8 percent of the work force had been brought under the contract system by the end of 1988, and the new system of social services designed to cushion the effects of unemployment had yet to develop.[60] As noted earlier, the conservatism on labor policy may also be reinforced by managers in state enterprises, who still have incentives to hoard labor in order to counteract the uncertainties in the production cycle (Cook, chapter 7).

Many leaders also seem to retain some commitment to regional equality. As James Tong shows (chapter 4), regional redistribution persisted in China despite the efforts to decentralize after 1978. By 1984, for example, health care still showed evidence of substantial equalization among China's provinces. The Maoist system of adhering to basic norms in providing medical services continued well after post-Mao reforms granted more planning and fiscal autonomy to local governments. Tong finds that interprovincial inequality may actually have lessened in the new economic conditions, even in the face of growing regional differences in productivity and revenues.

Given the shorter time span since the implementation of Soviet reforms, regional differences in the USSR under Gorbachev are more difficult to assess. Nonetheless, it is interesting to note that Gorbachev's critiques of the paralyzing dependency among regional and local officials coincided with the granting of substantial overt budget subsidies to less-developed Soviet regions. The 1988 and 1989 state budgets of the USSR allotted subsidies of up to 25 percent of revenues to five republics: Kazakhstan, Uzbekistan, Tadzhikistan, Turkmenistan and Kirgizia.[61] The overt admission of redistribution has been controversial, however: better-off regions, as in the Baltic, have complained about the enforced taxation to finance less productive areas and have advocated regional self-sufficiency. Central Asian leaders have countered by asking for additional help to correct the economic dislocations caused by misguided central planning.[62]

In addition, open ethnic conflict must provide a sobering object lesson for political leaders not to move too quickly in decentralizing or in eliminating budget subsidies for their less-developed regions. Escalating violence in 1988 and 1989 in Armenia, Azerbaidzhan, Georgia, and Uzbekistan may represent only the first manifestation of the Yugoslav problem spreading to other Socialist nations. While many factors have contributed to the violence, the new round of territorial economic wrangling in an era of scarcity and rationing can hardly help to ease the tensions.

THE POLITICAL COSTS OF REFORM

Decentralization and democratization have also bred fundamental changes in politics as usual for ruling Communist parties. Greater reliance on elections, reductions in the scope of nomenklatura lists, and downsizing of the party apparat mean less direct controls over personnel, and thus less leverage for party officials in their dealings with other institutions.[63] Greater emphasis on openness, public debate and official accountability demands a new style of party work and new skills for party officials. As party leaders note, reliance on market mechanisms suggests the need to curb party interference in managerial decisions. And the campaigns for economic reform and democratization also suggest a change in the mix of incentives for people to join and serve in party organizations.[64]

At the same time, party officials still face pressure from above to insure that the local economy prospers, to keep the political peace in their area, and to see that the masses develop the appropriate political values. As Sanjian points out (chapter 2), local apparatchiki may be told to stop interfering in economic management, but they face rebukes from higherups if the potatoes are not harvested or the new construction project is not completed on schedule.[65] Critical comments in the press accuse them of footdragging in developing new electoral procedures and new opportunities for public debate, but they can be ousted when new political demands erupt into public unrest. They are supposed to foster a public spirit and collective values among constituents, but rapid social changes have fostered more private values.

Thus party officials are still called upon to intervene, but with a far more delicate touch than in the past and with less than clear guidelines about when to step in. Given the continued concern with maintaining political control, party leaders have been unwilling to forego coercion altogether. Mass protests by Chinese students were suppressed in late 1986, reportedly on the directive of Deng Xiaoping himself.[66] And the crackdown in the spring of 1989 showed how readily demonstrators could be silenced. In the USSR, the response to open protests has been mixed, with officials tolerating some demonstrations but suppressing others—as in Georgia.

Often the official reaction is less direct. Soviet newspapers have reported, for instance, that party leaders have continued to veto educational and career advancement for individuals involved in "unorthodox" activities.[67] Restrictions of the party's personnel function would, of course, make such indirect penalties more difficult to impose, and that is surely one reason why some party agencies appear reluctant to cede personnel powers.

The reform agenda taking shape in Socialist systems also poses another, and longer term dilemma for ruling Communist parties. While leaders talk of the need to encourage grassroots democracy and openness, to allow people to decide things for themselves, they also continue to talk of the need to instill new values. Harry Harding observes, for example, that China's political establishment still accords the state the obligation to promote moral conduct and to educate citizens in an official doctrine believed to be morally valid.[68] Yet Stanley Rosen, in his overview of new Chinese survey research among youth (chapter 9), reports that changing values may be outpacing the state's capacity for socialization. Rosen notes that "political commitment and unquestioning loyalty toward the Communist party have been replaced in the hierarchy of youth values in post-Mao China by independence of thought and judgment, respect for talent, and a patriotism which does not always take its cues from party leadership." Students are now reluctant to join party organizations, and many local cadres are reluctant to take what they fear will be uncooperative and insubordinate new members. Changes in values are also in evidence in the military, where new recruits are very materialistic. Other sources point to similar evidence of change in the Chinese countryside. The decline of officially mandated collectivism has allowed old sources of conflict—based on kinship and communal identities—to reemerge, and old patronage ties openly to replace "socialist" ones.[69] Thus reforms pose a tension between "bringing civil society back in" and reforming the way it thinks.

As the events of 1989 demonstrated, several parties in Eastern Europe have already failed to solve these multiple dilemmas. For ruling Communist parties, as in the USSR, the advent of competition from new rival organizations can hardly make the tasks of adaptation easier.

THE CONTRADICTIONS OF AN OPEN ECONOMY

Expanding foreign trade and opening up the domestic economy to foreign investors pose additional challenges for economic reformers. One is how to reconcile continued controls with enough openness to foster international economic ties. As Hungarian and Chinese leaders discovered, stringent restrictions on the scope of foreign investment and on repatriation of earnings hardly create an attractive market for foreign capital.[70] Another challenge is how to attract advanced technology when the most saleable local products on the international market are relatively unskilled labor and low-technology goods. Foreign firms attracted to investing in Communist countries have often concentrated on labor-intensive operations requiring few skilled workers (see, e.g., Robinson and Parris, chapter 5). In addition, the "internationalization" of the economy poses the question of how to balance surging demand for imports against the capacity to export. With the decentralization of economic decisions, and especially with the reduction of central controls over foreign trade, trade deficits mushroom and hence become more difficult to pare down.

Reformers also confront the question of how to integrate foreign firms into a planned economy, with its plan rhythms, its very different success indicators, and its lingering problems with supplies, transport, communications, and the allocation of labor. And how much protection should be offered to inefficient native industries and their labor forces from the competition of more attractive foreign products in the domestic market? If foreign firms from Japan and Korea build automotive plants in Communist countries but insist on access to the domestic market for their products, Communist consumers are likely to prefer well-built Toyotas and Hyundais —and their ease of providing spare parts—to their own native models.

Finally, rationalizing foreign trade and investment decisions without true market prices poses a dilemma as well. Producers of goods priced too low by central planners will be eager to export, since world market prices will reward them handsomely. However, the combination of increased exports and the excess demand and lack of incentives to conserve on such goods at home exacerbate domestic shortages. Producers of high-priced goods, on the other hand, have little incentive to look for overseas buyers, since they can earn more at home.[71]

China's Special Economic Zones (SEZ) highlight both the successes and the problems. Growth in some areas such as Shenzhen has been especially rapid, with output and incomes rising more rapidly than the national average, and with direct foreign investment reaching $840 million by 1985.[72] Rapid growth, however, also brought with it rapid inflation, rising demand for domestic investment, and a surge of imports that far exceeded exports.

As Robinson and Parris show (chapter 5), there have been social costs as well. Since much of the foreign investment in such areas has concentrated on low-skill industries such as textiles with traditionally high proportions of female workers, the impact of foreign capital has worked against the ideological commitment to equality of the sexes. Robinson and Parris suggest that women's employment in SEZs create expectations that the women will be "patient, dexterous, and imbued with psychological and physiological characteristics that make them productive workers only in certain traditionally female industries."

CONCLUSIONS

Given the complexity of the economic and political issues confronting communist leaders, what Bogomolov characterized as a collective search for a new model of socialism has proved to be very much a dialectical process. Not only does the centralized, command model of economic planning and management have its internal contradictions; so, too, does the quest for economic reform. The very comprehensiveness of the reforms gives rise to a dilemma: the changes may need to be all-embracing to succeed, but the more comprehensive the reforms, the more difficult to design a package that is internally consistent and workable. The question for the reformers is whether leaders possess the political resources to sustain a continuing experiment with the uneven results and the social and political costs that experiments inevitably bring.

If long-term economic success hinges on popular support for political leaders, implementation of democratic reforms, and mass acceptance of democratic norms, these goals, in turn, seem to hinge in part on how well the system performs in the short term. Unemployment, inflation, inequality, and shortages are likely to worsen rather than improve the quality of life and depress expectations for many people in the USSR, China and Eastern Europe in the next decade. A "politics of stringency" can hardly help to foster support for either leaders or for their long-term economic goals. Unless the leadership can allay widespread perceptions of declining economic conditions, they face an uphill battle in instilling attitudes of self-confidence about the future and norms of bargaining, tolerance, and trust in authorities that stable democratic rule requires.[73]

NOTES

1. Barbara Crosette, "Hanoi Leader and One Hundred Artists Trade Complaints," *New York Times* (hereafter NYT), October 27, 1987, 5; idem, "Hanoi Chief Sees Capitalism as Guide," *NYT*, January 22, 1988, A2; idem, "The Mysterious Mr. N. V. L. Pushes Glasnost in Vietnam," *Christian Science Monitor*, August 18, 1987, 1, 9; Steven Erlanger, "Vietnam, Drained by Dogmatism, Tries a 'Restructuring' of Its Own," *NYT*, April 24, 1989, 1, 10.

2. Roland Eggleston, "Tengiz Abuladze Talks About *Repentance*," *Radio Liberty Research Bulletin* (hereafter *RLRB*), 289/87, July 21, 1987; and Crosette, "Hanoi Leader."

3. Burov, 95–96. On the formation of a new union of theater workers, see Julia Wishnevsky, "RSFSR Theatre Workers' Union Publishes Draft Statute," *RLRB*, 108/87, March 16, 1987, and the translations of articles from the Soviet press under the rubric "Giving Soviet Theaters New Independence," in *Current Digest of the Soviet Press* (hereafter *CDSP*) 38, no. 44 (December 3, 1986): 1–7.

4. See, for example, accounts of lobbying efforts in the Ukraine by Bohdan Nahaylo, "Mounting Opposition in the Ukraine to Nuclear Energy Program," *RLRB*, Supplement 1/88, February 24, 1988; idem, "More Ukrainian Scientists Voice Opposition to Expansion of Nuclear Energy Program," *RLRB*, 135/88, April 6, 1988; and Sergei Voronitsyn, "Plans for Nuclear Power Stations Dropped?" *RLRB*, 96/88, March 6, 1988. On the student protests in China, see the front-page articles in the *NYT*, December 14, 21, 22, 23, 24, 26, and 27, 1986.

5. The measures call for the creation of a new second house, a senate, whose members are to be selected by competitive elections. The Sejm, however, will continue to be the dominant chamber of parliament, and only 35 percent of its seats are to be subject to competitive election. Luisa Vinton, "Round-Table Talks End in Agreement," Radio Free Europe Research (hereafter *RFER*) Poland/6 (April 7, 1989): 7–12.

6. Vlad Sobell, "Economic Stability and Communist Conservatism," *RFER*, RAD Background Report/223 November 11, 1988.

7. On the ouster of Hu Yaobang in China, see Edward Gargan, "Secret Chinese Documents Criticize Hu Yaobang, the Ousted Party Leader," *NYT*, March 8, 1987, 14; and Jim Mann, "Five-Year Power Struggle Led to Hu Yaobang's Fall," *Los Angeles Times*, February 9, 1987, 1, 10–11. On the removal of Boris El'tsin, see Alexander Rahr, "The Ouster of Boris El'tsin—The Kremlin's Avant Gardist," *RLRB*, 506/87, December 18, 1987. Another advocate of political reform, Zhao Ziyang, was ousted in China in the spring of 1989. Note, however, that El'tsin managed to return as a popular candidate to the new Congress of People's Deputies in the March 1989 Soviet elections.

8. See, for example, Elizabeth Teague's analysis of Gorbachev's televised speech and of the increasingly open polemics between reformists and conservatives in "Gorbachev Counterattacks in Tashkent," *RLRB*, 154/88, April 13, 1988.

9. Jean C. Robinson discusses similar problems in "Mao After Death: Charisma and Political Legitimacy," *Asian Survey* 28, no. 3 (March 1988): 353–68.

10. On Bogomolov's prominence, see Anders Aslund, "Gorbachev's Economic Advisors," *Soviet Economy* 3, no. 3 (1987): 246–69, as cited in

Philip Hanson, "Ownership and Economic Reform," *RLRB*, 154/88, April 13, 1988.

11. "The World of Socialism on the Path of Restructuring," *Kommunist*, no. 16 (November 1987): 92–102, esp. 93.

12. Bogomolov, "World of Socialism," 93–97. For an overview of the reforms in China, see Elizabeth Perry and Christine Wong, *The Political Economy of Reform in Post-Mao China* (Cambridge: Harvard University Press, 1985); for the USSR, see Gertrude Schroeder, "Anatomy of Gorbachev's Economic Reform," *Soviet Economy* 3, no. 3 (1987): 219–41.

13. Hungary pioneered in allowing collective farmers to elect their own farm chairmen as early as the 1960s. In industry, however, enterprise directors continued to be appointed by their respective ministries; as of 1983, top managerial positions have been advertised nationally, and candidates have been invited to apply (though party clearance is still the norm). And beginning in 1985, new reforms set up enterprise boards composed of management and workers to oversee enterprise operations. Paul Marer, "Economic Reform in Hungary: From Central Planning to Regulated Market," in U.S. Congress, Joint Economic Committee, *East European Economies: Slow Growth in the 1980's*, 3 (Washington, D.C., 1986), 223–97, especially 254.

14. Bogomolov, "World of Socialism," 95.

15. Phillip Hanson, "Ownership and Economic Reform," and idem, "The Draft Law on Cooperatives: An Assessment," *RLRB*, 111/88, March 23, 1988.

16. In the USSR, state farms in Moscow and Sumi provinces have created shareholders' associations, raising capital to finance further expansion (*CDSP* 40, no. 22 [June 29, 1988]). In Hungary, twenty-two financial and banking institutions created a stock exchange in Budapest in January 1988, trading bonds issued by enterprises, local councils, cooperatives, hospitals, and banks. See Karoly Okolicsanyi, "Stock Exchange Opened in Hungary," *RFER*, Situation Report Hungary/4, March 30, 1988, 31–36.

17. Bogomolov, "World of Socialism," 96–97.

18. Ibid., 98.

19. For a discussion of the new openness on social problems, see Andrea Stevenson Sanjian, "Gorbachev's Social Policies" (Paper presented at the 1988 Annual Meeting of the American Political Science Association, Washington, D.C., September 1988).

20. Even in the GDR, where the Honecker regime had been cool to the idea of perestroika (see Thomas Baylis's overview in chap. 10), there were a few indications of a cultural thaw. The November 1987 congress of the Writers' Union featured unusually open criticism, some publications had begun to openly explore previously forbidden topics; and some

writers who had been expelled from the Writers' Union and/or had left the country were afforded new prominence. See Barbara Donovan, "Signs of Cultural Liberalization in the GDR?" *RFER*, RAD Background Report/111, June 21, 1988.

21. See, e.g., Jeff Hahn, "Power to the Soviets?" *Problems of Communism* 38, no. 1 (January–February 1989): 34–46; Werner Hahn, "Electoral Choice in the Soviet Bloc," *Problems of Communism* 36, no. 2 (March–April 1987): 29–39; and Elizabeth Teague, "Soviet Union Experiments with Electoral Reform," *RLRB*, 69/87, February 18, 1987. On the problems of local soviets and the efforts to resolve them through multican-didate elections and related reforms in the Soviet Union, see I. F. Butko and V. A. Perttsik, "The Twenty-seventh Congress of the CPSU and Tendencies in the Development of Soviet System-Building," *Sovetskoe gosudarstvo i pravo* (hereafter *SGiP*), no. 11 (November 1986): 40–48; G. V. Barabashev, "Electoral Campaigns: Goals and Means," *SGiP*, no. 4 (April 1987): 3–12; A. Ya. Sliva, "The Deputy Inquiry: Normative Model and Practice," *SGiP*, no. 4 (April 1987): 29–38; and I. V. Triakov, "Organizational Work with Leading Cadres in the Administrative Staff of Local Sovets," *SGiP*, no. 5 (May 1987): 72–81.

22. In March, 1988, the Chinese Communist party's General Secretary Zhao Ziyang proclaimed to a Central Committee plenum that open dialogue was necessary well before new reforms and new legislation are adopted. See Patrick Moore, "Zhao Calls for Political 'Checks and Balances' " *RFER*, RAD Background Report/49, March 27, 1988.

23. Judith Pataki "The CC Discusses the Role of the Media," *RFER*, Hungary/6, May 9, 1989.

24. Viktor Yasmann, "Soviet Jurists Discuss Draft Press Law," *RLRB*, 208/87, June 1, 1987; M. A. Fedotov, "The Role of the Press in Legislating," *SGiP*, no. 8 (August 1986): 11–19; V. O. Luchin, "The Referendum and the Development of Socialist Self-Government," *SGiP*, no. 12 (December 1986): 43–50; and Ye. M. Kozhevnikov and M. A. Shafir, "Legal Regulation of Nationwide Discussions in the USSR," *SGiP*, no. 1 (January 1988): 3–11; and Vera Tolz, "Controversy over Draft Law on the Press," *RLRB*, 547/88, December 6, 1988. Tatiana Zaslavskaia, one of the most outspoken and visible advocates of democratic political reform in the Soviet Union, was appointed to head a newly created All-Union Center for the Study of Public Opinion; see Sergei Voronitsyn, "When Sociology Connects with Perestroika," *RLRB*, 166/88, April 15, 1988.

25. Bogomolov, "World of Socialism," 99.

26. Thus, for example, General Secretary Zhao told China's Central Committee that even socialist society was subject to conflicting interests, and the goal of government was to "work to coordinate various kinds of interests and contradictions." Cited in Michael Oksenberg, "China's

Thirteenth Party Congress," *Problems of Communism* 36, no. 6 (November–December 1987): 1–17, esp. 13.

27. Ibid., 98–99.

28. Ibid., 99. On the officially sanctioned Soviet conference for all such informal groups, see Vera Tolz, " 'Informal Groups' Hold First Officially Sanctioned Conference," *RLRB*, 380/87, September 23, 1987. For a survey of such groups in Eastern Europe, see Jiri Pehe, "Independent Movements in Eastern Europe (An Annotated Survey)," *RFER*, RAD Background Report/228, November 17, 1988.

29. Bogomolov, "World of Socialism," 101–2.

30. Jan Prybyla, "China's Economic Experiment: Back from the Market?" *Problems of Communism* 38, no. 1 (January–February 1989): 1–18.

31. Edward A. Gargan, "Pork, China's No. 1 Meat, Will Be Rationed," *NYT*, December 3, 1987, A18.

32. *CDSP* 40, no. 22 (June 29, 1988): 10, 24, and "(Roundtable-Conference Proceedings) Electability of Leaders in Enterprises, Establishments and Organizations," *SGiP*, no. 1 (January 1988): 51–69, and no. 2 (February 1988): 39–50.

33. Roman Stefanowski, "Prime Minister Speaks on the Economy," *RFER*, Polish Situation Report 13, no. 26 (July 1, 1988).

34. Prybyla, "China's Economic Experiment," 8–9.

35. Susan Shirk, "The Politics of Industrial Reform," in Perry and Wong, *Political Economy of Reform*, 195–222, esp. 199–200.

36. *CDSP* 39, no. 52 (January 27, 1988): 1–4. Jean C. Oi describes a similar trend in Chinese agriculture, where "the favorable terms of state contracts and the security they offer in the face of increased production—which has increased competition and made it more difficult to sell crops—have made state contracts coveted opportunities." "Commercializing China's Rural Cadres," *Problems of Communism* 35, no. 5 (September–October 1986): 1–15, esp. 8.

37. Shirk, "Politics of Industrial Reform," 201.

38. See, for example, V. G. Tychina et al., "The ministry of the food industry of the Ukrainian SSR in the conditions of the economic experiment," *Finansy SSSR*, no. 9 (1985): 12–16.

39. Christine Wong, "Material Allocation and Decentralization: Impact of the Local Sector on Industrial Reform," in Perry and Wong, *Political Economy of Reform*, 253–80, 265–68, 254–56; Barry Naughton, "False Starts and Second Wind: Financial Reforms in China's Industrial System," in Perry and Wong, *Political Economy of Reform*, 223–252, esp. 246–47.

40. Hungary's experience is telling in this respect. What were originally designed to be fixed parameters for credit and tax policies have, Janos Kornai argues, been transformed into a set of particularistic rules for specific industries and firms at specific times. Thus taxes are unpredict-

able, since the government may raise them to absorb "above-plan" earnings from one enterprise and redistribute them to a less profitable firm. Thus the new planning system still falls subject to the old ratchet principle. Moreover, Kornai reports that the government's redistribution creates levels of investment that are just as high in unprofitable sectors and firms as they are in profitable ones. See "The Hungarian Reform Process: Visions, Hopes, and Reality," *Journal of Economic Literature* 24, no. 4 (December 1986): 1637–1737, esp. 1694.

41. Shirk, "Politics of Industrial Reform," 201–2.

42. Ibid., 202–3; and P. V. Ragauskas, "Some results and problems of work in the conditions of the economic experiment," *Finansy SSSR*, no. 7 (1985): 32–33.

43. See Andrea Stevenson Sanjian's discussion in chap. 2.

44. The new mandate was described in a resolution "On measures for the further expansion of the role and the strengthening of the responsibility of the soviets of peoples' deputies for accelerating social-economic development in light of the decisions of the Twenty-seventh Congress of the CPSU," published in *Sovety narodnykh deputatov*, no. 9 (1986): 5–13.

45. Oi, "Commercializing," 10–11.

46. Harry Harding, *China's Second Revolution: Reform After Mao* (Washington, D.C.: Brookings, 1987), 101–8.

47. M. G. Pabat, "Role of the budget system in the development of the regional economy," *Finansy SSSR*, no. 9 (1985): 41–45.

48. Christine Wong, "Between Plan and Market: The Role of the Local Sector in Post-Mao China," *Journal of Comparative Economics* 11, no. 3 (September 1987): 385–98; Harding, *China's Second Revolution*, 109–10, 115–16; and Dorothy J. Solinger, "China's New Economic Policies and the Local Industrial Political Process: The Case of Wuhan," *Comparative Politics* 18, no. 4 (July 1986): 379–400, especially 395.

49. However, such arguments surfaced in the USSR well before the initiation of perestroika. See the discussion in Donna Bahry, *Outside Moscow: Power, Politics, and Budgetary Policies in the Soviet Republics* (New York: Columbia University Press, 1987), chap. 2.

50. Donna Bahry, "Perestroika and the Debate over Territorial Economic Decentralization," *Harriman Institute Forum* 2, no. 5 (May 1989).

51. CDSP 39, no. 31 (September 2, 1987): 27–28.

52. John Tedstrom, "Soviet Cooperatives: A Difficult Road to Legitimacy," *RLRB*, 224/88, May 31, 1988; and Bill Keller, "Private Soviet Entrepreneurs, Under Fire, Try Closing Ranks," *NYT*, November 14, 1988, 1, 6.

53. Oi, "Commercializing," 10.

54. Anders Aslund, *Private Enterprise in Eastern Europe: The Non-Agricultural Private Sector in Poland and the German Democratic Republic* (New York: St. Martin's Press, 1985). Aslund notes, however, that the

development of the nonfarm private sector has been somewhat different in the GDR. Private businesses in the GDR have tended in recent times to coexist more easily with state enterprises, supplies and equipment have been somewhat less of a problem, and state regulation has been relatively less burdensome than, for example in Poland. However, the private sector in the GDR continues to include only a small fraction of the workforce.

55. Schroeder, "Anatomy of Gorbachev's Economic Reform," 237.
56. Irma Adelman and David Sunding, "Economic Policy and Income Distribution in China," *Journal of Comparative Economics* 11, no. 3 (September 1987): 444–61, especially 449–53.
57. In China, Harding notes that the share of state expenditures for subsidies to consumers and enterprises "was virtually the same in 1986 as it was in 1981." *China's Second Revolution,* 276. On the other hand, Hungary and Poland have of course raised consumer prices several times. See, for example, the description of Hungary's 1985 price hikes in *RFER,* Hungarian Situation Report/1, February 1985. Hungary also raised prices in 1989, to offset subsidies to agriculture, and the Polish government, too, imposed a price hike in December 1988. *RFER,* Poland/3, February 6, 1989.
58. Prybyla, "China's Economic Experiment," 4.
59. Bill Keller, "Soviets Concede the Ill of Inflation Afflicts Their Body Politics as Well," *NYT,* November 3, 1988, 1, 4.
60. Patrick Moore, "Labor Problems in China," *RFER,* RAD Background Report/219 (China), November 4, 1988.
61. *Izvestiia,* October 21, 1987, 1. The allocation of direct subsidies—especially large ones—is unusual, given a long Soviet history of attempting to avoid such outright grants. See Bahry, *Outside Moscow,* chap. 2.
62. Bahry, "Perestroika and the Debate over Territorial Economic Decentralization."
63. Oksenberg, "China's Thirteenth Party Congress"; John P. Burns, "China's Nomenklatura System," *Problems of Communism* no. 5 (1987): 36–51.
64. Donna Bahry and Brian Silver, "Public Perceptions and the Dilemmas of Party Reform in the USSR," *Comparative Political Studies* (forthcoming). Soviet officials have noted declines in the number of applicants to, and resignations of current members from both the Komsomol and the party. And membership in the Hungarian party's youth league, KISZ, dropped by over 50 percent just between 1985 and 1989. Vladimir Kusin and Judith Pataki "A Federation Replaces the Communist Youth League," *RFER,* Hungary/6, May 9, 1989.
65. As Prybyla notes, Chinese Communist party leader Zhao Ziyang called on party organizations in 1988 to mount mass educational drives that

would cure bank runs, hoarding, and panic buying. See "China's Economic Experiment," 13–14.

66. Edward A. Gargan, "Deng's Crushing of Protest Is Described," *NYT*, January 14, 1987, A3.
67. E.g., a group of museum workers, architects, and scientists who demonstrated in Leningrad against the destruction of a local landmark found their prospects for further education and job advancement blocked by party and Komsomol organs who labeled them as "anti-Soviet." "In the Same Boat," *CDSP* 39, no. 31 (September 2, 1987): 24–25.
68. Harding, *China's Second Revolution*, 172–74.
69. Oi, "Commercializing," 13–14; Elizabeth Perry, "Rural Collective Violence: The Fruits of Recent Reforms," in Perry and Wong, *Political Economy of Reform*," 175–94.
70. Harding, *China's Second Revolution*, 159–63.
71. Shirk, "Politics of Industrial Reform," 200–201; and Philip Hanson, "Foreign Trade: The Restructuring of the Restructuring," *RLRB*, 58/88 (February 9, 1988).
72. Harding, *China's Second Revolution*, 164–70.
73. See the discussion in Ronald Inglehart, "The Renaissance of Political Culture," *American Political Science Review* 82, no. 4 (December 1988): 1203–30.

2

IMPLICATIONS OF REFORM:
THE VIEW FROM THE ENTERPRISE

Andrea Stevenson Sanjian

The ultimate fate of the economic reform process currently under-way in the USSR will be decided within the walls of the Kremlin, by those at the very top of the political system. Nonetheless, oppor-tunities exist for others—from planners to ministerial personnel to those down on the shop floor—to have their input into the process as well, albeit an indirect and limited one. It is those who actually implement economic policy, however, who will show elites whether there is any technical merit to the reforms (i.e., whether they are workable from the point of view of economics), and, at least as important, whether they are viable politically.

Certainly, the politics of economic reform are a matter for elites' analyses, and many theoretical and practical aspects of reform have no doubt been debated within the Politburo with little reference to their reception among those working at the ministerial or enterprise level. Yet such impacts cannot be ignored entirely, and any evalua-tion of the reforms' performance must include the response to them at all levels of the economic system. This is so for the simple reason that dissatisfaction with reform at any or all of these strata can be expected to produce, at best, insufficient enthusiasm (and hence effort) in carrying through on changes, and at worst, actual subver-sion of Moscow's orders. Should such behavior occur, the reforms will be incapable of improving actual economic performance, thus undermining their chance of success regardless of their potential benefits. While a well-designed, comprehensive reform may be able to eliminate or alleviate many possible sources of discontent, it is no doubt unreasonable to expect a flawless reform package, and in any case, while "economic man" may be a useful construct, it is not always possible to predict his utilities precisely and completely.

This chapter will examine the political implications of economic reform from the perspective of management and other professional personnel at the level of the economy's basic unit, the enterprise. ("Management" is used loosely here, and includes not only enterprise directors and the directors of other economic units, but also directors of enterprise subunits and other supervisory personnel, as well as specialists affected by reform, such as those responsible for enterprise financial affairs.)

Analysis of these groups is of value for a number of reasons: For one thing, they constitute vital links in the implementation process, with consequently great influence on its outcome. In addition, they are probably the personnel under the greatest pressure, since they are caught between the demands of planners and ministry bureaucrats above them and the needs of the rank and file workers below, for whose performance management is responsible yet who have their own perspectives on reform. Finally, they are by and large an educated and relatively affluent group with much to gain from change, not only in terms of material well-being but in terms of enhanced prestige; by the same token, however, they also have much to lose, given the degree to which they have benefitted from the status quo. Another measure of their importance for the leadership's plans is the introduction of political reforms to complement the economic ones, with the former aimed at satisfying the nonmaterial aspirations of just such well-educated groups as these; in other words, their support is solicited along two separate planes, in the apparent hope that the two will prove mutually reinforcing.

Enterprise management thus finds itself in a very difficult position, caught between countervailing pressures from above and below, in addition to conflicting visions of its own best interest. Is the additional responsibility and, inevitably, stress, worth the promise —but not yet the reality—of higher living standards? Even if more goods and services are forthcoming, will increased comfort at home outweigh the costs of greater tensions at work? And if, as predicted, the short-term effects of reform do advantage the professionals but disadvantage the blue-collar workers they depend on, will not the workers' predictable discontent make long-term improvements unlikely? Also, are the reforms themselves well-designed enough and comprehensive enough to work anyway, and be worth the effort and the costs of vigorous implementation? Or will those higher up the economic ladder, with different interests or perhaps different perceptions of society's needs, be able to weaken the reform provisions, preventing management from making any significant new contributions to economic growth?

All of these questions and more are clearly on the minds of managers, to judge from Soviet press coverage of the course of reform. There are the expected declarations of support for General Secretary Gorbachev's proposals, and complaints against those accused of impeding progress, but there are also expressions of anxiety and dissatisfaction that should be sending warning signals to the reform's architects. The sources of concern are primarily the reforms themselves, but also include misgivings about the post-reform environment in which they, the managers, will have to live and work. While it is far too early to predict their ultimate response to the Gorbachev program—especially since its final outlines are yet uncertain—it's not too soon to discern potential obstacles to its optimization. And while it is probably safe to rule out resistance in the form of both overt protest and covert activity, it is almost certainly the case that passive resistance or even unwilling compliance would be enough to undercut the effects of reform.

ECONOMIC REFORM AND MANAGEMENT OPINION

Under conditions of central planning, the Soviet manager has become in effect a bureaucrat, in that he (or more rarely, she) is primarily responsible for carrying out instructions from above within a set of narrowly defined standard procedures. These procedural constraints constitute the most significant distinction between him and his Western counterparts, for they mean that initiative—a quality supposedly prized for at least upper-level management in the West—is neither required nor welcome. Thus, as Nove points out, the manager has traditionally been rewarded not on the basis of achievement, but on the basis of how well he obeys orders, in the form of various plans.[1] The principle of *edinonachalie*, or one-man management, has guided Soviet management theory since Lenin's day, yet what this has meant in practice is one man's personal responsibility for plan fulfillment, not real authority. If the Gorbachev reforms can be distilled into a single concept, however, from the point of view of management, it is that performance is no longer to be evaluated essentially in terms of obedience, and that "petty tutelage" from above must be replaced by greater responsibility and authority at the enterprise level.

This, of course, has been the message of many would-be reformers, from Liberman to Zaslavskaia, for over twenty years, and was at the core of the abortive Kosygin reforms of the mid-1960s. The failure of those reforms, though, is impressive evidence that expanding managerial autonomy is not in itself the solution to many problems, and may indeed contribute to them. Both Western and Soviet analysts have been quick to draw this lesson from the Kosygin experience, and the former have been especially skeptical in their prognoses for the current attempts at reform. As Hough reminds us, there are important differences between "Kosygin" (i.e., prime ministerial) and "Gorbachev" (general secretarial) reforms in terms of the prestige and political power behind them, and it is certainly unwise to underestimate the general secretary's resources.[2] It is no less a mistake, however, to disregard the fact that real obstacles emerged in 1965, and that many are likely to reappear in the 1990s.

With regard to management's role in restructuring, two separate but related sets of problems are developing. Both concern managerial autonomy: The first is the issue of how much autonomy the reforms will actually produce, and the second is whether managers welcome it. To date, the degree of actual autonomy has been limited in practice, despite much rhetoric to the contrary, and stems from the many internal contradictions that have developed within the reform provisions.[3] These include, for example, the conflict between encouraging enterprises to be more responsive to customer needs while retaining their subordination to various government agencies and party officials; those same agencies and officials are then held "personally" responsible for enterprise performance yet simultaneously warned against interfering in enterprise affairs. (The ministries and other representatives of central authority thus find themselves in an unenviable position: They have been given the authority to carry out reforms designed in large part to sharply reduce their authority, and with cuts in staff and other resources at that.) Similarly, the reforms' stated goal of improving the quality and efficiency of production coexists with an aggressive campaign to increase output. In addition, managers have been given greater responsibility for the enterprise's decision making, but in the absence of the price reforms necessary for realistic financial analysis.[4]

There are multiple causes for these conflicts, including, no doubt, simple caution: There must be very high levels of understandable anxiety, within the Politburo and without, over moving ahead into an economic environment unfamiliar to virtually everyone in the land, and one, moreover, that is well known to have contributed to social unrest in Eastern Europe. While one can sympathize with the fear of the unknown, however, its practical effect is to put brakes upon the rational extension of the reforms, rendering them at times irrational.

In addition to anxiety, there are apparently internal contradictions within the minds of reformers themselves. Gorbachev himself seems torn between recognition of the utility of the market mechanism and the advantages of decentralization, and commitment to centralized coordination of economic development. In a speech to the Central Committee, for example, he declared that "it is impermissible—and virtually impossible—to resolve all questions from the center," but then went on to detail the ways in which central planning alone can insure the success of perestroika.[5]

Finally, the ambiguous nature of many reform measures is a reflection of political realities, for if there are important lessons to be drawn from Kosygin's experience, there are far greater ones to be learned from Khrushchev's, at least for the general secretary who likes his job. With this in mind, the compromises made between the interests of economic efficiency and development and the interests of the status quo's many beneficiaries—in Gosplan, the ministries, the party apparatus, the defense sector and the like—are only prudent, albeit often economically counterproductive;[6] in other words, economic performance counts for little in the face of political unacceptability. Similarly, it must not be forgotten that there is "sincere" opposition to be considered as well, as opposed to that which amounts to defense of vested interests. The social inequities that nearly everyone foresees emerging are more than a potential source of popular unrest; they are in violation of deeply held principles among elites and masses alike. Hence even such outspoken proponents of reform as Zaslavskaia and Aganbegian carefully display great sensitivity to the social issue amid their calls for change.[7] And of course there are those, in the ministries and elsewhere, who know full well that the economy is on a downward course that must be reversed, yet who remain convinced that only strong central direction can accomplish this.

All of these factors constrain the formation of reform measures, in the attempt to satisfy the needs and demands of different sectors of the political and economic systems. Among the supporters of a cautious approach are, of course, many members of the management sector. They are no more a homogeneous group than is Soviet society as a whole, and one would expect to find the same diversity of interests and opinions within the group as one would among groups. For instance, managers in the defense industries and heavy industry in general, the privileged sectors under the status quo, surely view the prospect of greater balance between heavy and light industry less benignly than does consumer goods management. Also, it is unsafe to assume that managers, for all their technical training, have no opinions on more abstract political issues, such as the nature of socialist society, and that they are uniformly unmoved by the possibility of growing inequality and even hardship. By the same token, however, many managers are in fact specialists whose positions rest on their technical expertise, and who thus might prefer to push ahead with the long-term rationalization of the economy despite the presumably short-term social costs incurred.

It is therefore difficult to determine which is the more accurate portrait of the Soviet manager: bureaucratic conservative or technocratic modernizer. Conventional wisdom in the West has for years suggested the former, and the reasoning has been persuasive.[8] In a bureaucratized economy that prefers discipline and obedience to a more entrepreneurial style of leadership to start with, those selected for management positions are likely to resent disruptions in their routine and to resist having greater responsibility thrust upon them, and indeed, over the years the Soviet press has tended to reinforce that image. Other Western observers, however, have long noted the developing "professionalization" of Soviet managers, in terms of a growing preference for technical rationality over political expedience or ideology as their guide to action. This has led to predictions of mounting pressure from the younger, better-educated members of the group for autonomy for themselves and reform for the economy as a whole.[9] This conclusion is also intuitively satisfying, and surely describes the attitudes of many managers (and other professionals and specialists), though the evidence supporting this is at best mixed.

On the one hand, the older studies effectively substantiated their portraits of the conserving manager, and more recent studies continue to suggest that the nature of the Soviet political system tends to compensate for the centrifugal force of professionalization.[10] More compelling, however, is the fact that the Soviet press continues to support this vision of management, frequently blaming managers for impeding perestroika's progress. Though party and ministry officials bear the brunt of the campaign against obstructionists, enterprise management is not immune from attack, and Popov's critique is typical: "Certain enterprise executives are entirely satisfied with the present system, which exempts them from accountability and risk-taking. And passivity in the basic production unit is the base that allows even management personnel who outright retard restructuring to hold onto their jobs."[11] Aganbegian adds that the list of reform opponents must include not only bureaucrats but "those excessively lazy and insufficiently energetic managers who prefer decisions to come from above and who consider the expansion of the sphere of authority and responsibility a nuisance."[12]

Other reports admit that while progressive managers may be the key to successful restructuring, the more traditional sort are at best a handicap and at worst the root cause of many of the system's problems. They are described as arrogant, protective of their privileges, unconcerned with promoting technological progress, caught in "ossified" methods and procedures, and, often, simply incompetent.[13] One study of directors and chief specialists at 120 enterprises reports that when asked to submit proposals for changing the current elaborate reporting system, their proposals were "virtually identical" to the existing system. The sociologist involved did not attempt to explain this response, but he did offer it as evidence that "sluggishness" and "stereotyped thinking" are common among management.[14]

Especially stinging are the commentaries of fellow managers, who are at times harshly critical of their colleagues. One plant director, for example, claims to describe the average director and the typical attitude when he says,

It is better to adopt an easier plan and overfulfill it by one percent than to underfulfill a difficult one by this same one percent. We need economic incentives that force the enterprise to operate at its maximum. Then a difficult plan will not create the possibility of transforming a capable enterprise into one that is not capable of operating.[15]

Thus there is good reason to believe that the combination of sectoral (e.g., light versus heavy industry) interests, social values, systemically induced behavior, and the like have created a bloc of economic administrators who resist, and even fear, reform. On the other hand, there is also evidence that others welcome it, and that growing professionalization can indeed lead to demands for a new, more autonomous and responsible, role for industrial management.

Two surveys of management personnel and other professionals and officials, conducted shortly before Gorbachev introduced his reforms, are of particular interest. The first uses the broader sample, which included state and party officials as well as enterprise managers and specialists; this may explain why its conclusions are somewhat restrained, since party, ministry, and planning officials are reputedly among the least enthusiastic reformers. (In this regard, it is significant that the journal *Planovoe khoziastvo*, the organ of Gosplan, waited until well into 1987 before jumping on the perestroika bandwagon by adding a section called "Problems of Restructuring.") When asked their preferences from among three economic reform programs, 36 percent of the 185 respondents chose a "stabilization" program (supporting the image of management suggested above), but 28 percent chose a "moderate" program and 16.5 percent opted for a "radical" one; a full 19.5 percent, however, were dissatisfied with all three alternatives. As the authors admit, this scarcely constitutes overwhelming support for significant economic reorganization, but it does show that a majority of the sample advocates at least some reform.[16]

While the prospect of radical reform induced resistance in all but a small fraction of the sample, however, the results of questions on specific measures should provide greater comfort to reformers. For instance, 58.5 percent of those surveyed favored stronger economic incentives to develop new technologies, and 49.5 percent favored tighter discipline over the process of introducing new products and methods. ("Tighter discipline" is hardly compatible with greater autonomy, but this response does suggest an awareness that existing conditions have bred stagnation, and that change of some sort is necessary.) On the crucial issue of converting enterprises to full cost-accounting, or self-financing, 39.5 percent of respondents claimed to support this. On the other hand, only 28 percent favored introducing "obsolete production" procedures, to phase out obsolete equipment and procedures; Gosstandart had introduced measures shortly before the survey was conducted that holds managers responsible for eliminating obsolescence, and perhaps this accounts for the notable lack of enthusiasm.

The second survey, appearing a year later, questioned only enterprise directors; the sample included directors of 60 enterprises in fifteen cities across the country.[17] In this case, the support for reform was expressed much more strongly and less ambiguously. When asked whether they supported "the essential expansion" of the enterprise's economic independence, a full 96 percent of the respondents replied in the affirmative, with the remaining 4 percent responding "more yes than no." Nearly half (47 percent) saw economic independence as a "key problem" for improving the economy, and 42 percent saw it as one of the central problems; write-in responses indicate that many managers also see labor discipline as a major problem for economic performance.

Managers were also asked to identify those areas of responsibility where they felt their authority was inadequate: 48 percent named capital construction, 61 percent production planning, and 65 percent labor and wage-setting. In the written comments, however, it was clear that planning problems generated the most discontent, though preferred solutions fell into two categories. There were those that advocated less restrictive planning, with fewer indicators to constrain plant management, and those that simply called for an improved planning mechanism. There is no indication as to which school of thought predominated or to what extent they overlapped.

In addition to formal surveys such as these, expressions of managerial support for reform frequently surface in the professional and scholarly press (as do, of course, critiques of obstructionist managers). The roundtable discussions of managers and other professionals that are a common feature of several journals often indicate a lively interest in reform issues and an awareness that traditional approaches are in need of reformulation. The impression left with the reader is that those managers participating in such discussions and in interviews—who are doubtless among the more successful members of their profession—are in fact committed to economic modernization and have a professional interest in improving economic and administrative mechanisms.

It should be remembered, too, that while the traditional command economy does not explicitly demand entrepreneurial skills of its managers, it does so implicitly. Their primary responsibility may be meeting assigned targets, but under conditions of taut planning and scarce supplies this often requires delicate negotiations with central authorities, finagling additional supplies from a variety of sources, and manipulating everything from assortment targets to fulfillment records.[18] While some of these practices are perhaps more appropriate to the souk than the modern industrial economy, they do indicate that the entrepreneurial spirit—or more simply, a creative response to challenge—has been very much a part of the Soviet manager's job, and may only need refocusing on new requirements.

What conclusions can be drawn from this mixed evidence? Only tentative ones, of course, though it is probably safe to assume that proreform sentiment is strong, if not necessarily dominant, within the management sector, and that if theses on generational politics are correct, the proreform group heavily represents younger managers and hence can be expected to grow.[19] It is also apparent, however, that significant numbers of managers share the objections to many reform provisions that are common in the ministries, in Gosplan, and in parts of the party apparatus. Therefore, much of the vigor and enthusiasm which are essential to reform's success—and the absence of which were partly to blame for the failure of the Kosygin reforms—must come from the group of managers sympathetic to reform, though just how large this group is remains unclear. Nonetheless, they are the ones who must deal with the resistance, if not outright obstruction, of state and party officials above them; with the likelihood that many suppliers in other enterprises will cling to inefficient old habits; and with the distrust of reform that is widespread among the average workers who are their subordinates.

The Politburo's support notwithstanding, this constitutes a powerful array of forces that could easily blunt the edge of any reformer's ardor. Since the objections to reform on the part of the others are politically sound, however, in that they make perfect sense from the perspective of at least their short-term interests, there is probably little the leadership can do to alter this economic "correlation of forces." (Resorting to "administrative measures" might be able to coerce some compliance, but only at the obvious cost of undercutting the spirit of perestroika, with its stress on responsibility and initiative, and the relaxation of controls.) It is clearly in decision-makers' interests, then, to structure the reform program in such a way as to maximize its appeal for the managers, in order to sustain what support exists as well as to convert skeptics.

The political reforms, including glasnost' and competitive elections, are obvious efforts to do this. So are the veiled promises that reform will generate material abundance, since it is the affluent professionals who will be among those best able to take advantage of more and better goods and services. What, however, of the economic reforms themselves? Are they likely to inspire continued and growing management support? Or will the attempts to appease other interests, plus the concessions to caution, have the ultimate effect of alienating those charged with implementing so many reform measures?

MANAGERS AND THE SUBSTANCE OF REFORM

As the numbers of ministries forced to comply with reform measures has gradually expanded, the improvements attributed to the reforms have been impressive. It is claimed that product quality has increased, contractual discipline improved, technological innovation stimulated, and productivity accelerated.[20] (These claims come despite uneven economic performance overall, though apparent poor performance in some areas may well be due to the strains of transition to new practices.[21]) These conclusions are based not only on performance in the period since January 1987, when the initial reforms were extended to most industries in the economy, but on several years' experience with reform experiments in selected ministries. Some of these go back to 1984, others to 1979, and provide most of the background for management's (and others') attitudes toward reform.

While many managers have been willing to give the reforms credit for some improvement, this cannot be interpreted as full satisfaction with them; indeed, it appears that the more managers support reform in general, the more dissatisfied they are with the reforms that have been enacted so far. Unlike their conservative colleagues, who would object to any disruptions of the status quo, the proreform managers object because in their current form the reforms do not go far enough, and leave too much of the status quo intact. Again, this response appears to be based more on experience with the reform experiments than on the actual Gorbachev reforms, and the pessimism generated by these experiments may, in the end, turn out to be unfounded. Nonetheless, the planners' and ministries' past success in diluting the experimental measures, and their continued ability to undercut the effects of the newly-enacted reforms, do constitute reasonable grounds for skepticism. For example, while the reforms call for freeing prices from administrative controls, the fine print specifies that only prices for new products will be freed. Enterprises will thus be forced to operate in two environments simultaneously: one where they must respond to market-type conditions for some products, and a second dominated by central planning for others.

Similarly, a significant share of enterprise production will continue to be planned, with state orders (*goszakazy*) having priority for supplies and other resources over orders for which other enterprises have contracted.[22] And of course, if rigid targets have been eliminated, they have only been replaced by more flexible—but also more unpredictable—"normatives," rather than true market indicators. These not only require the same type of haggling with ministries than the old output targets did (and which managers may consider an increasingly inefficient use of their time), but they are just as vulnerable to being ratcheted upwards when productivity improves.

It is this type of rearguard action that created managerial disenchantment during the experiment stage, and that has survived into the reform era as well. In other words, the negative experience of the experiments remains relevant, and a useful indicator for how measures that are yet to be implemented might be undermined by bureaucratic intervention. For this reason, the following discussion rests as much on actual experience during the course of various experiments as on speculation on how new and future reforms will function in practice.

Among the most common grounds for complaints is the continued extensive intervention of higher organs in enterprise affairs. In some cases the enterprise's relationships with such organs remains untouched by the reforms, while management believes the arrangements are no longer necessary and have become counterproductive. In other cases, the efforts of superior organs to retain some degree of control over enterprise affairs has led to creation of new devices that often counter the supposed intent of various reform measures.

In the former category, for instance, belongs the retention of various organs—such as Metallurgkomplekt, for parts of the metallurgical industries—with the job of filling out, but not actually concluding, delivery agreements between suppliers and consumers. These intermediaries do nothing but transmit paperwork between the two, rather than leaving arrangements to the enterprises involved, and hence contribute nothing to the changing relationship between buyer and seller but delays. That, at least, is the conclusion of some managers who call for their elimination, claiming that, "this system has outlived itself and intermediate stages between suppliers and consumers impede operation," while retaining yet another level of regulatory authority over enterprises and their staffs.[23]

In general, complaints about obsolete instructions, procedures, and structural arrangements are commonplace. A design bureau in Leningrad, for example, was forced to abide by various guidelines first established decades ago even after participating in the reform experiment for several years. As the director has pointed out, such practices continue to inhibit performance, reform or no reform.[24]

Gosplan and Gossnab are also frequent targets of attack. In addition to many specific complaints (such as those described below), at least some managers argue that their traditional role in the economy has become outmoded, and that their continued efforts to regulate production has become a hindrance. Gossnab, for instance, has been accused of taking an "intermediary" role upon itself, to allow itself to control supplier-consumer relations, in which case it is only performing as intended by its own superiors; nonetheless, some managers consider this situation an impossible one, and urge Gossnab to act more as their partners in insuring deliveries and quality control, than as their watchdogs.[25] In short, managers with reform experience often feel that the enterprise is responsible for adapting to new conditions, but that superior organs with significant control over enterprise environments are not. These organs thus not only fail to assist the enterprise in its new tasks, they actually impede it. Complaints surface, too, about the role of local soviets and party officials, who retain too much formal authority over economic affairs and are too willing to exercise it, in the opinion of some plant directors.[26] Since the party's role in the economy has yet to be fully defined in the reforms, intervention on this front could continue to undermine enterprise autonomy.

These conditions have been a part of the manager's environment for decades. For the conservative, they represent a safety net of sorts, an additional layer of security to which the buck can always be passed when problems develop. To the more progressive manager, they are themselves the problem, and the hoped-for objects of reform. It is no wonder that such managers are now expressing frustrations after realizing that intrusive regulation remains part of the reform program, and will until at least the 1990s. The result is a variety of contradictions between the spirit of the reforms and the directives of traditional organs of enterprise control, and sometimes even contradictions between one aspect of the reform and another.

For some industries, for example, the ministries to which they report measure performance in terms of normative net output, while planning agencies and local party bodies use actual sales as their indicator.[27] (This is perhaps a concrete manifestation of perestroika's simultaneous but mutually exclusive campaigns for increased quality and for increased output.) Similarly, enterprise directors with several years' experience with the reform experiments have complained that throughout the experiment they were held increasingly responsible for fulfilling contractual commitments; at the same time, however, they were still bound by taut planning that allowed them no flexibility regarding material reserves, making it very difficult to satisfy consumers. As one manager complained, under traditional conditions a manager could underfulfill one part of his plan in order to concentrate on others, and thus meet at least some targets; under new conditions this becomes impossible.

Also, while managers are urged to innovate and use their experience in the enterprise's interests, there are few opportunities to do so. Besides the examples already given, they are told to make more efficient use of resources, for instance, and then told on which they must economize, even though savings might more productively be made elsewhere.[28] Intervention reaches as high as the Central Committee, which recently decreed that all ministries, irrespective of their special needs, must now adopt rotor conveyor technology.[29] Finally, the question of pricing remains unresolved for the time being, further undercutting managers' ability to optimize decision-making while reinforcing the role of planning agencies and other bodies, and hindering the transition to enterprise self-financing.

Many managers initially approached the experiments as a learning experience for all involved, and so viewed problems such as the above as only to be expected under such circumstances, pointing them out to superiors as areas in need of corrections. The flaws in the experimental reforms did not, then, in and of themselves disillusion them. The response to their suggestions, though, from Gosplan, Gossnab, and the ministries did: They disappeared into forgotten files (*otkladyvaiutsia v dolgii iashchik*) rather than being integrated into the next round of reforms. This has helped breed the attitude that in the end, the reforms will be of superior organs and for superior organs, and that the needs and experience of enterprise personnel actually count for very little.[30] The fact that the ministries have not been absolved of their own responsibilities for overseeing production, investment, and resource management, and thus have no choice but to continue their intrusive practices, does little to relieve managerial frustration, and only adds to disenchantment with the scope of reform.

This sense of distance between enterprises and their controllers is especially strong in discussions of enterprise incentive funds and employment policies. Management's new authority over the distribution of wages has been one of the most highly publicized aspects of the reforms as currently implemented, and is often considered the linchpin of the experiments. In theory, as the enterprise becomes more efficient and productive its wage fund will increase, to be divided among workers and other personnel. The growth will be financed by increasing output and product quality, by releasing surplus labor, and by streamlining enterprise management.[31] The exact formulas according to which wage funds will grow are varied and complex, but they are geared more toward encouraging efficiency and quality than in the past, when gross output was the single most important indicator.[32] Moreover, this is one area where policymakers and managers have actually accumulated a significant degree of experience: Experiments with one set of wage levels began in 1979 and were expanded in 1984, and the now-famous Shchekino method has been applied by different plants in different ways since 1967.[33] Despite the presumed familiarity with manipulating wages as an incentive instrument, though, this remains a source of discontent. (Workers are even more dissatisfied than their superiors, which is yet further cause for concern, and will be further discussed below.)

The problem is, once again, a gap between theory and proclamation, on the one hand, and actual practice on the other. Managers' most common complaint about the new incentive funds is that they are simply too small to have any significant impact on worker behavior; a recent poll of workers themselves shows that 41 percent of the substantial sample considered inadequate material incentives a "decelerating factor" in the reform process.[34] This has been a particular problem in materials-intensive industries, where production costs are largely governed by the quality of the materials used and where workers' efforts cannot alter the size of the incentive fund very much. The deputy director of one plant reports that such constraints mean that in her factory wages cannot rise by more than 5 rubles 40 kopeks per person per year.[35]

Elsewhere, the rise in productivity has far outpaced the rise in wages, raising concerns that workers will soon grow disillusioned with the promise of greater rewards for greater effort. One production association that had been a participant in the experiments since the early 1980s, for example, saw its output increase by 38%, its labor productivity by 37 percent, but its wage fund by 12 percent. The director complains, too, that the ministry and Gosplan are indifferent to the situation and will not adjust the normatives to better reward workers so long as their productivity is still growing.[36]

In general, the basic dispute seems to be over the indicators on which wage increases are based. Some measures benefit, or disadvantage, some enterprises more than others, even within the same industry, and since it is still higher organs that determine these there is still little discretion available to the manager trying to tailor his wage system to the needs of his enterprise. (He does, however, have greater control over the distribution of his bonus fund than in the past, with fewer constraints on how it is to be used as of January 1, 1987.[37] Prior to that, even under experimental conditions bonus funds were still based on plan overfulfillment, despite the fact that wages were no longer dependent on, or even geared toward, this.[38]) Additional criticisms stem from the fact that norm setting has little foundation in empirical research: despite the years of experiments, no systematic approach, no method, to norm setting has been developed.[39]

The result is wage increments too small to overcome existing problems for labor-management relations. In particular, many regions still confront a labor shortage, which is only partially offset by the willingness of some workers to improve their productivity. Hence, even within the confines of the small increments available to them, managers have often been reluctant to pay out too much to top performers for fear of disturbing "customary relations" with more "passive" workers.[40] In other words, managers may approve of greater wage differentials in theory—and in this they now have the support of policymakers—but when given the chance to apply the theory, they have been reluctant to risk alienating their workforce with perceived violations of the socialist social contract.

While it is possible to increase the fund, and hence the incentive, by releasing surplus, and especially unproductive, labor, managers have been reluctant to do this, too. For one thing, it is often impractical to attempt to let go too many workers when enterprises are often short-handed to begin with, and should it become necessary to hire new workers, the pool of applicants will over-represent other enterprises' rejects. For another, the cost and difficulty of obtaining credit means that even under reform conditions it can be more cost-effective to stay with labor-intensive production than to switch to capital-intensive production.[41]

Managers aware of common consequences of applying the Shchekino method will know, too, that the typical pattern of layoffs is that highly-skilled, but older, workers will be retained (the rational short-term strategy), while less experienced, but younger, workers will be let go. The subsequent aging of the skilled workforce will lead to serious long-term problems, but the continued (albeit reduced) pressures of the plans will still be an incentive to concentrate on the near term. An even less attractive lesson of Shchekino, at least for lower- and middle-level managers, is that a quick way to save on wages is to streamline management, where salaries are higher.[42] This, of course, amounts to firing, in the name of reform, some of the very people who are most likely to be supporters of reform, while placing a much heavier workload on the shoulders of those able to retain their jobs.

For those managers still committed to cutting their workforce in the face of these countervailing pressures, there remains an excellent reason for keeping employment levels high: There has been no suggestion whatsoever in any reform proposals of eliminating the time-honored practice of requisitioning labor for special projects. Factory workers are routinely diverted from industrial jobs to help bring in harvests, to assist with major construction projects and municipal service delivery, and often to help with construction or other programs in their own factories. (This latter constitutes yet another class of problem, since enterprises without enough surplus labor to provide help for construction brigades have found their projects bypassed in favor of those of enterprises that can provide extra workers, and thus help the construction brigade fulfill its own contracts more easily.[43]) Since these requisitions are largely unpredictable, they create a dilemma for the manager who sincerely wants to rationalize his workforce. He can streamline it, and risk being unable to fulfill his own contracts when his workers are drafted, or he can retain a surplus kept on his enterprise's payroll for essentially nonenterprise labor. Managers participating in the experiments have urged that requisitioning authorities at least be held accountable for making efficient use of their commandeered workers, but again, this problem has yet to surface in official discussions.[44]

In sum, then, and despite a number of instances where judicious use of incentive funds and layoffs have contributed to higher productivity,[45] many managers have been skeptical about using this as a long-term strategy—including many who admit to using it successfully during the experiments. In the meantime, they must deal with continuing rearguard efforts by central authorities to regain control over wages and salaries: Gosbank, for instance, continues to lobby for tighter central control over wage funds, arguing that this is the only way to insure that reform will be effective.[46]

A similar problem emerges with respect to profit retention. During the experiments and now under the actual reforms, self-financing does not in fact mean that enterprises keep all, or even most, of their profits and then use them as they see fit for investment, incentives, or whatever. The director of a knitwear factory claims that 70 to 80 percent of earnings in light industry return to the state budgets or the ministry, while a spokesperson from heavy industry complains that a smaller share of profits have been retained by his combine after the reforms than before, and even after productivity had increased.[47] The ability of the ministries to appropriate profits even under *khozraschet* is apparently especially irritating since the ministries do not operate under *khozraschet* themselves. There is increasing grumbling about this, and demands that the ministries be made more accountable for their actions, especially financial ones. It has even been suggested that the ministries be "democratized" by creating supervisory branch councils—made up of managers, workers, technicians, and others from industries subordinate to a ministry—which would, among other things, elect some of the ministerial personnel.[48]

Another set of obstacles to the manager trying to increase enterprise efficiency comes from his lack of realistic control over plant modernization. While management's new authority over enterprise investment funds is a much-heralded aspect of self-financing, it appears that enterprise decision-making is still seriously constrained by outside forces. In particular, even if management is free to determine how and how much to invest in upgrades and new technology, there are still no guarantees that new equipment and the like will actually be delivered in the foreseeable future. Enterprises involved in the experiments have typically had to wait several years for deliveries to be made. While this is no different from the wait under normal conditions, it does show that changes in enterprise operations have not been matched with corresponding changes in the ministries, which still process many reequipment requests, or in relations with suppliers.[49]

Producers of new equipment that might modernize production elsewhere continue to be frustrated by scarce, and often substandard, supplies. Thus a machine tool plant in Moscow has complied with all the requirements of perestroika, yet its aging production line continues to turn out unreliable lathes for which there is little demand. Some obsolete plants, such as the Rustavi steelworks, have simply been shut down, but this solution is considered too drastic to be resorted to widely.[50] Construction to house any new equipment presents additional obstacles, since approval from central authorities is still required and not always forthcoming, and in any case, construction backlogs continue to hinder plant modernization. Average construction times may have declined but they still exceed normatives by 2.6 times, and as one author notes, the normatives themselves "cannot be called strict from the perspective of international comparisons."[51] In the end, even the most vigorous supporter of reform, white-collar or blue, cannot expect to have much success working with obsolete plant and equipment.

In a related problem, enterprises that decide to invest have encountered difficulties in raising the necessary funding. The ministries retain control over at least the process through which enterprises obtain much of their bank credit, but so far the ministries have failed to adapt their procedures to new conditions. In fact, during the course of the experiments the use of credit for reequipment actually fell in one ministry, from 33 million rubles in 1983 to 15 million in 1985; similar declines took place in other branches as well. To be sure, the ministries are not entirely to blame for under-utilization of bank credits: Other means of funding are available that do not require ministerial interventon, but enterprises themselves have been very slow to take advantage of them.[52]

The above problems might be considered flaws in the reform program, or flaws uncorrected by the reform. Some may yet be addressed in future modifications, others (such as those related to pricing) should be relieved once the more radical reforms slated for the 1990s are implemented. It may be the case that many managers will be able to retain their patience and optimism and faith in the reform process until that time. Others, though, may find their support eroding under the stress of abiding by what amounts to conflicting directions from above. This is likely to be exacerbated by the additional stress generated by still other new developments that the reform environment will create.

For example, there is increased pressure to adopt new, more modern methods of management, on top of the fundamental reconceptualization of the management function that the reforms already envision. These include the highly sophisticated quantitative approaches to many administrative tasks that economists and management scientists have advocated for years, but that have encountered stiff opposition in the past. Policymakers had resisted the very objectivity of mathematical methods that could solve problems with little reference to political and/or ideological constraints, and there was also implicit recognition of the fact that such methods would require radical reform in order to work effectively; management, for its part, simply disliked the prospect of coping with disruptive new methods that were not even well suited to traditional conditions. Now that reform itself has been introduced, the old advocates of quantification have reemerged, no longer arguing that mathematical models require reform, but instead that reform requires mathematical models.[53] They may have won over many policymakers in both state and party, but management's resistance is unlikely to have abated: It is one thing to take on new responsibilities denied one in the past; it is quite another to have to retool oneself, and undergo training in difficult new fields.

Then, too, there are the various by-products of perestroika that the average manager (or anyone else, for that matter) probably never imagined. The Chief Administration of State Insurance, for instance, will soon be offering such "new services" as industrial risk insurance, to protect enterprises operating under full accountability from the occasional production catastrophe. In the past, losses of plant, equipment, output, and the like were covered by the state; now they are the enterprise's responsibility, and management must decide how to deal with the risk.[54]

(Perestroika is generating a boom in the insurance sector in general: New types of coverage include not only the equivalent of homeowners' policies and accident coverage for auto passengers, but retirement annuities to soak up some of the potential surplus income created by new wage systems, liability insurance for newly-legal private taxis, and coverage for undertakings in the "individual enterprise" sphere. While the insurance administration is no doubt as plagued by conservative management as the rest of the economy, the fact that it has developed all of these innovative types of coverage and more suggests that at least some in this area view reform as a bonanza.)

A development with the potential for a much greater impact on the managerial function owes more to glasnost' than to perestroika. This is the newly invigorated environmentalism that has led to public demands for more stringent regulation of industrial waste and pollutants. The role of industry in ravaging the Soviet environment has been well documented, as has the absence of formal responsibility on the part of management for the pollution their plants generate. Today, however, managers suddenly find that they must not only struggle with adapting to full financial accountability, but with environmental accountability as well. The public pressure, intensified by aggressive media coverage, has created a public relations nightmare for managers who never had to worry about this sort of problem in the past, and in any case, could easily deflect blame upwards. In addition, a remedy denied environmentalists in the past is now being implemented: Offending plants have been charged clean-up costs to be paid out of their own profits, even though, as noted above, profit retention rates have been lower than anticipated. At the same time, central authorities continue to pressure those same enterprises to increase output, and even site new plants with little regard for environmental impact.[55]

Then, on a somewhat more personal level, there is the matter of income taxes, which are slated to become much more progressive in the attempt to balance out some of the anti-egalitarian effects of the reforms' financial incentives. The problem, from management's perspective, is that this might not only further undermine the utility of wage supplements as stimulants to their workers, it might hurt their own pocketbooks as well. According to new bonus and salary directives, the incomes of professionals such as managers will rise disproportionately higher than those of rank and file workers.[56] Under existing tax policy, even the upper range of salaries, such as those managers already receive, have been taxed at relatively low rates compared to those common in the West. Now there is the lure of still higher incomes in compensation for a more difficult and complex job on the one hand, but the possibility of a significantly greater tax bite on the other. (Perhaps it is this concern that was responsible for some budding "supply side" sentiment at the nineteenth Party Conference: One Speaker declared that "taxes enrich the state only to a point, beyond which they are destructive. They destroy both the citizen and the state."[57]

Last, but certainly not least, comes the issue of elections for plant directors and other supervisory personnel. One reads virtually nothing on such proposals beyond occasional mention of the proposals themselves, and this is one area where managers seem extremely reluctant to comment, to judge from the absence of discussion of the issue in the economic press. It is reasonable to assume, though, that intense anxiety is breeding beneath the silence. This is especially likely given the fact that under new conditions, managers will be evaluated in large part on the basis of their ability to get as much as possible out of their workers; doing so, however, is liable to create the kind of friction that rarely translates into electoral support.

THE "RESTRUCTURING" OF LABOR-MANAGEMENT RELATIONS

The final set of complications to be addressed here involves the possibility, even probability, of significant changes in the relationship between management and labor in the postreform enterprise. Reference to one aspect of this—an intensifying need to motivate workers, and the problems of using the new wage systems to do so —has already been made. The fully-accountable enterprise, and all of its managers, are to be rewarded on the basis of its contract fulfillment, its quality-control record, its savings due to enhanced productivity, and so on. The effort to satisfy all of these objectives will not only strain all of management's resources, it will strain the rest of the workforce as well. And should the workers decide that their rewards are not worth the extra stress and effort, there is little that can be done to alter their work habits. Indeed, given the proposals for elections to management posts, the balance of power in this relationship may well start shifting even further away from managers and more in favor of their workers.

This explains management's preoccupation with the problem of labor discipline, which, as noted earlier, is already considered a major obstacle to optimal enterprise of performance. Without the cooperation of his workforce, no manager, however committed to restructuring he may be, is going to be able to succeed under the new conditions. His means of insuring cooperation are too limited, or too unpredictable, to be reliable instruments: wage increments are often too small to be useful, or too irrational, in that the formulas on which they are based do not always take the requirements of a specific industry—let alone enterprise—into account.

Another very serious problem with the new incentive system is that it is based on the promise of a larger pay packet, though the utility of more money in a system that has been starved for consumer goods for decades is questionable. (In 1988, average monthly wages did rise, by almost 8 percent, but savings rose, too, indicating that demand for consumer goods still goes unmet.[58]) Managers, economists, sociologists and others have no doubts that material incentives work, and that they are most effective instruments for motivating workers, party idealists and their normative incentives notwithstanding. However, there is also substantial agreement on the point that "material incentives" does not have to mean "wages," and that under current conditions, they might best mean "non-wage incentives." In other words, rather than rewarding workers with cash, managers should provide upgraded housing, child-care facilities, cultural and other leisure-time activities, and all manner of services to ease and enhance everyday life.

Research on determining the optimal mix of incentives has become something of a growth industry for Soviet social scientists, and interest in this problem has clearly surged in the past several years.[59] Studies emphasize the importance of those facilities and services that are nominally the responsibility of local governments, but that they frequently fail to provide. The Central Committee has recently admitted that "efforts to strengthen physical facilities in the social and cultural spheres have not achieved a fundamental breakthrough."[60] A gap therefore exists that the enterprise is expected and often willing to fill, since doing so is in fact an excellent incentive and recruitment device.

The housing shortage is most commonly singled out for attention, and managers and central authorities are routinely urged to divert incentive funds to improving the situation here. Many young, and even married, workers are still housed in enterprise dormitories, which are invariably considered unsatisfactory: They are crowded, regimented, and often lacking important conveniences and services.[61] The problem is especially critical in the Far East, where housing shortages are joined by poor development of almost all facilities outside the workplace itself, despite the importance of the region for national economic development. All of this contributes to poor worker morale, high turnover rates, absenteeism, reliance on alcohol for entertainment, and other problems that keep productivity low. One study shows a correlation between the decline in growth rates for Far Eastern industrial output and the gap between that region and the RSFSR as a whole in development of their social infrastructures.[62]

Such findings do not come as revelations to managers, who are well aware of the value of such employment benefits, and complain of their inability to provide more of them. It appears, for example, that at least under the conditions of the experiments, management control of material incentive funds extends only to the ability to distribute them in the form of wages: They do not have the authority to spend the funds as they wish on social and cultural facilities and services.[63] Instead, disbursements for such purposes remain closely regulated. Only 36 percent of the fund itself can be used for this, according to one manager, which in practice means that the enterprise must save for seven to eight years in order to accumulate enough money to build a single residential building.[64]

Light industry is even further disadvantaged, despite the fact that the success of wage incentives depends largely on expended production of consumer goods. The general director of a leather goods association complains that his workers get less than those in other industries, and that even during the experiments "there is a tendency toward reduction." His housing fund allows construction of but ten apartments annually, for a work force of fifteen hundred.[65]

The center's apparent unwillingness to complement industrial investment with investments in workers' welfare may turn out to be a severe impediment to restructuring's progress. As Rutgaizer and Zhuravlev point out, the service sector is even more resource-(and especially labor-)intensive than the consumer goods industry, and new economic conditions will create higher demand for them, straining the economy more than will demand for goods. The situation thus calls for more, not less, investment, as well as greater attention to the problems of services administration than this heavy industry-oriented system is accustomed to pay.[66]

The extent to which the newly expanded private sector can take up the slack by providing the goods and services in high demand remains to be seen, especially given the many reports of difficulties encountered by those trying to establish, sustain, and expand businesses. Political opposition to private enterprise remains strong, thanks to such developments as price increases at *kolkhoz* markets when private restaurateurs, denied access to wholesale markets, do their food shipping there.[67] Recent research confirms the persistance of popular antagonism towards those with "unearned incomes," and shows, too, that many view some types of legal private enterprise little more favorably than they do illegal ones.[68]

A case could be made that management has at least one weapon at its disposal, that being the new emphasis on worker participation as a way to enhance motivation through the job itself. There is evidence—both Western and Eastern—that working conditions, including worker input into enterprise affairs, can increase job satisfaction, but it is not yet clear that manipulating such factors constitutes a powerful enough lever in the newly-turbulent Soviet environment. On the contrary, there is a fundamental contradiction in the policy of simultaneously enlarging both management's authority and labor's participation in management.[69]

Managers fear that their restricted ability to satisfy worker aspirations will be inadequate for maintaining a contented workforce, let alone a highly motivated one. Hence their anxiety when they consider other new developments wrought by perestroika, which could agitate workers beyond the incentives' ability to appease them.

The average worker's fear of the likely by-products of reform—which are well known as a result of Hungarian reform experience—has been broadly publicized. These include inflation, particularly in the basic goods and services that still benefit from heavy subsidies; rising tensions between the highly motivated, who may prosper under the new conditions, and those who prefer a more passive, egalitarian society; and perhaps most important, unemployment. As time goes on, moreover, these fears acquire a firmer grounding in reality. Prices of many goods have in fact gone up, for such reform-related reasons as enterprise self-financing: Many managers, for example, have increased their profits by "upgrading" products or by forcing substitutions on buyers; this enables them to circumvent centrally set prices and charge higher prices. At the same time, shortages in many everyday goods persist and even worsen, and the perceived hardship is actually excerbated by higher wages and by the extra disposable income generated for some when their alcohol consumption declined.[70] Also, reform is beginning to create some unemployment. Goskomstat reports that some one million workers lost their jobs in 1988, which may be a minuscule proportion of the total workforce but which must portend higher unemployment in the future to the average citizen.[71] Officials and economists try, apparently in vain, to show that opportunities abound for laid-off workers, that retraining programs will be available for those in need of skills, and that many of those laid off will simply take early retirement, but anxiety persists.

This has not, however, translated into the kind of behavior that suggests submissiveness in the face of job insecurity. Instead, one finds in the press scattered expressions of worker discontent and even obstructiveness. A number of reports describe worker resistance to wage reforms, especially those taking the form of piece-rate systems, out of fear that any surge in productivity will only result in higher norms and/or more demanding pay scales in the future. While it is too early to tell if these fears are unfounded, they are certainly reasonable given the traditional prominence of the ratchet effect.

A new quality control system has also disrupted labor relations in many plants. The system of "state acceptance" (Gospriemka) is administered by Gosstandart, and as of January 1987 has been introduced into some fifteen hundred "important" enterprises. State acceptance staffs are located in each of the enterprises, but are technically employees of Gosstandart and have been granted such broad powers as the authority to forbid shipment of substandard goods. (As Hanson notes, such a system of centralized quality control is uniquely suited to the needs of a centralized economy, especially one already dominated by sellers' markets; since a market reform would make the system superfluous, its introduction suggests a basic reluctance to rely too heavily on markets.[72])

While similar systems have been found useful in the defense industries, workers (and managers) unused to it see it as a drag on production, and view the *znak kachestva* less as an incentive to correct defects than as a threat to plan fulfillment and hence incomes. In many factories wages have in fact fallen by as much as 10 percent because so much of their output was rejected as substandard.[73] Assembly lines have ground to a halt in some plants as defective goods have piled up, leading to unaccustomed tension and anger; in others, Gospriemka teams—which are made up of plant personnel—are too willing to avoid conflict, and so grant the quality seal to substandard output.[74] Economic statistics indicate, however, that for the most part Gospriemka teams do take their jobs seriously, and so far have resisted pressure to accept shoddy goods from former coworkers.[75] When workers express anger, though, at having their output reduced by quality control requirements, they are blamed for lack of zeal, yet it is also the case that they are frequently working with materials that are themselves substandard, or that have been delivered late and hence must be rushed into production. In fact, Gospriemka can sometimes have a snowballing effect on production, and hence tempers: Large-scale rejections at one plant can cause shortages or delays at another, interfering with production there in such a way that its own output cannot meet Gospriemka quality standards.[76]

The constant and growing pressure to raise both output and quality has made the Soviet workplace far more stressful than in the past. The worker is pressured to learn new skills, take new pride in his work, accept a higher level of discipline, resist turning to vodka as relief from all the new tension, and respond positively to the threat of lower wages and even unemployment if he fails to meet the new standards. Managers, meanwhile, are heavily dependent on their workers actually complying with all this if they are themselves to be considered successful. In the past, unsatisfactory performance was easily, and acceptably, blamed on superiors in central organs, since enterprise management had so little control over its inputs and output. One of the objectives of the reform, however, is to eliminate this diffusion of blame, even though in practice enterprises will continue to be dependent upon and subordinate to outside actors.

Somewhat ironically, this would seem to require greater teamwork—a more effective collective of workers and management—within the enterprise itself than was necessary under traditional conditions, since both groups must now rely on their joint action for their well-being and can no longer count on higher organs to pick up the slack and/or blame. Such a relationship may yet develop, given time to get used to the new system and a recognition on everyone's part that doing so is worth the effort. To the average worker, however, the effort could well appear far greater than the rewards would justify. (After several years' experience with experiments and/or reforms, some 51 percent of workers expect that "the amount of individual work under the new system" will increase "drastically."[77] After all, besides the pressures at work described above, inflation will very probably continue to encroach on his wages at the same time (in theory, at least) that consumer goods become more abundant, and thus stay as out of reach as ever; those same managers who make the workplace so stressful, however, will be the ones whose salaries rise high enough to reap the benefits the worker produces. And if those goods do not in fact materialize, then why bother at all?

The blue-collar grumbling reported both in the Soviet press and abroad indicates that officials and managers have yet to persuade workers that future advantages will outweigh today's costs of adapting to a new environment. This in turn will complicate the manager's task enormously, possibly to the point where it overwhelms any gains he may make in his relations with central organs. The very real likelihood of deteriorating labor-management relations, then, still further jeopardizes the development of managerial support for reform.

CONCLUSION

The Gorbachev program of restructuring is more than just a set of economic reforms or even a set of somewhat riskier political reforms. All of the changes taken together call for nothing less than the transformation of the Soviet system, not only with regard to how its government, its ruling party, and its economy operate, but also how its population functions. The Soviet people—both elites and masses—are being told that they must develop new attitudes toward their work, their community, and their role as members of developed socialist society.

As Gorbachev and his allies describe them, these are noble goals, and his vigor in communicating his vision and in attacking those elements responsible for social and economic stagnation have revitalized the Soviet people. Yet there are important differences between accepting a vision and accepting the stress and effort involved in making it a reality. Thus while support for perestroika as an idea is widespread, the many measures and reforms required for its implementation have encountered serious, and predictable, opposition.

To outline the sources of opposition in broad strokes, the existing powers that be distrust any political reform with the potential to undermine their positions. The planners and ministry staffs and other representatives of central control resist even limited devolution of authority to the enterprise level since doing so threatens to render them superfluous. This is true even of the many who recognize the need for, and even irreversibility of, reform, yet who understandably prefer that others shoulder its costs. (And, as noted earlier, it remains their job to continue asserting central direction over the reform process, surely a thankless job under current conditions.)

The blue-collar workers, for their part, are scarcely anxious to give up the security promised by the traditional social contract in exchange for the threat of unemployment, the possibility of declining real income, and the certainty of more rigorous work standards. The citizenry as a whole, independent of any individual's place in the power structure, fears the prospect of higher prices as subsidies are eliminated and supply and demand move prices to their market levels, resents the growth of social tension as income distribution becomes less egalitarian, and protests the weakening of familiar safety nets for the disadvantaged. Though they will also enjoy the fruits of a healthier economy in the long run should the reforms prove effective, it is these short-term costs—together with the absence of any apparent immediate benefits of perestroika—that preoccupy public opinion.

Those who expect to prosper, on the other hand, make up that small core of support on which reform rests. It includes those with the talent and the wherewithal to take full advantage of the new private enterprise opportunities, although these are so limited, and commitment to regulating profits so strong, that the numbers of emerging entrepreneurs will probably remain insignificant. The intelligentsia, too, can be considered beneficiaries, though not necessarily in a material sense. They are, however, being courted with promises of fewer controls and greater access to audiences and information.

Finally, there are the economic managers, a more substantial group in terms of their numbers and their proximity to power by virtue of party membership and ties to central authorities. They have been promised not only greater material well-being, but greatly enhanced prestige: It is they who will fill the vacuum once inhabited by agents of central economic control. All that will be required of them in return is that they successfully adapt to a completely transformed function, becoming independent, assertive, sensitive to the demands of their workers and customers, and wise in the ways of finance, investment, foreign trade, and marketing.

There are unquestionably those who will relish this opportunity to take full advantage of their potential and at the same time perform what is in effect a service to their country. It is they who will bear the burden of executing reform: of resisting attempts to rein their enterprises back under central control; of coaxing the necessary effort out of reluctant workers; of seeking out the best methods and materials and technology in a system that no longer allocates them administratively; of learning the skills and developing the instincts required to compete successfully both at home and in international markets.

However, there are just as certainly many managers who have responded well to the traditional Soviet system and performed commendably, or at least, satisfactorily. What skills they have are those appropriate to centralized direction and bureaucratic decision-making, and may already include well-developed capacities for prospering that might uncharitably be thought corrupt. Even if they have been honest and energetic, fulfilling their duties to the best of their abilities, they may be extremely reluctant to adapt to a radically different environment that demands radically different skills, especially if they are in mid- or later-career. Then, too, they may also disapprove of Gorbachev's new course, believing that centralized direction, for all its faults as currently practiced, is still the superior method, compared to the vagaries and inequities of market relations. Finally, there are the incompetents, who have managed to hold on to their positions through ties to an old-boy network that has been facilitated by bureaucratic (i.e., noncompetitive) processes. Managers such as these will surely have an interest in sabotaging reforms that put their positions at risk.

That leaves the reforms dependent on the enthusiasts, the managers eager to be released from central controls and free to exercise their own capabilities. But as the examples described in this paper have shown, they too are being let down by the reform process: by measures that go only half way, such that centralized constraints continue to frustrate them at the same time that more is being demanded of them. Such managers may remain committed to reform in principle, and refuse to class themselves with more conservative obstructionists, but in the end they, too, may decide that the program is not worth their support and their energies.

Should this happen, and should the reforms themselves fail to be reformed, then the economy will be left without the critical mass of commitment needed to drive it through the major disruptions that restructuring demands. Without sufficient motivation, such managers will refuse to exert themselves; competition may develop as decreed, but if everyone competes at a very low level, it will accomplish little. They will stop fighting to defend enterprise autonomy against centralizers, and bow to the continuing pressure to comply with ministry and planners' directives. The reforms, in short, will have become eviscerated, complied with in a formal sense but not in spirit, while the economy reverts to its prereform practices and performance. Whatever gains restructuring has made will evaporate (though the more costless changes will no doubt be retained and provide some improvement), and the political support needed to insure passage of more extensive reforms planned for the future will evaporate as well.

This is not to suggest that the fate of reform is dependent solely on the support of one segment of the population, and a relatively small one at that. If nothing else, the managers' own level of support is largely a function of the response of other groups with whom they must interact. Management is, however, a vital link in the reform process, and it has the capacity to make up for resistance elsewhere. Moreover, it is one of the few groups with a professional interest in promoting reform, on the part of at least some of its members, and is thus well worth courting. This can only be done, however, if the leadership is willing to risk further alienating those groups already resisting reform, especially those whose centralizing authority will be supplanted by the new autonomy in the enterprise.

NOTES

1. Alec Nove, *The Soviet Economic System,* 3d ed. (Boston: Allen and Unwin, 1986), 325.

2. Jerry F. Hough, "The Gorbachev Reform: A Maximal Case," *Soviet Economy* 2 (October–December 1986): 302–12.
3. This discussion is limited to the reform proposals in effect as of mid-1987, and will not consider the possible effects of the more extensive reforms endorsed by the Central Committee in late June 1987, but not scheduled for implementation until 1990. See M. S. Gorbachev, "On the party's tasks in the fundamental restructuring of economic management," *Pravda*, June 25, 1987, 1–5.
4. Gertrude E. Schroeder, "Gorbachev: 'Radically' Implementing Brezhnev's Reforms," *Soviet Economy* 2 (October–December 1986): 289–301. See also, "Gorbachev's Economic Reform: A *Soviet Economy* Roundtable," *Soviet Economy* 3 (January–March 1987): 40–53; Jan Adam, "Attempts to Improve the System of Management of the Economy of the USSR in the 1980s" (Paper presented to the annual meeting of the American Association for the Advancement of Slavic Studies, New Orleans, November 20–23, 1986); Philip Hanson, "The Shape of Gorbachev's Economic Reform," *Soviet Economy* 2 (October–December 1986): 313–26; Boris Rumer, "The Realities of Gorbachev's Economic Program," *Soviet Economy* 2 (May–June 1986): 20–31.
5. M. S. Gorbachev, "On the five-year plan for the economic and social development of the USSR in 1986–1990 and the tasks of party organizations in its implementation," *Pravda*, June 17, 1986, 1–4.
6. The military's interest in reform is difficult to determine since its spokesmen have been largely silent, beyond depicting reform as a positive development in the military press. On the one hand, the status quo has certainly served it well, but then, too, it would surely benefit from a more competitive, more technologically sophisticated economy. Those in the defense industries, however, might be expected to have a more conservative perspective on the issue than their colleagues in uniform. For several views on this issue, George G. Weickhardt, "The Soviet Military-Industrial Complex and Economic Reform," *Soviet Economy* 2 (July–September 1986): 193–220; Julian Cooper, "Comments on George Weickhardt's Article," *Soviet Economy*, ibid., 221–27; Timothy J. Colton, "The Military and Economic Reform: A Comment," *Soviet Economy*, ibid., 228–32; Russell Bova, "The Soviet Military and Economic Reform," *Soviet Studies* 40 (July 1988): 385–405.
7. See, for example, T. Zaslavskaia, "The human factor and social justice," *Sovetskaia kul'tura*, January 23, 1986, 3; A. G. Aganbegian, interview in *Los Angeles Times*, June 27, 1987, 15. See also Peter Hauslohner, "Gorbachev's Social Contract," *Soviet Economy* 3 (January–March 1987): 54–89.
8. The foundations for this school include such classic studies as John A. Armstrong, *The European Administrative Elite* (Princeton: Princeton University Press, 1973); Jeremy Azrael, *Managerial Power and Soviet*

Politics (Cambridge: Harvard University Press, 1966); Joseph Berliner, *Factory and Manager in the USSR* (Cambridge: Harvard University Press, 1957; David Granick, *The Red Executive* (Garden City, N.Y.: Doubleday, 1960); David Granick, *Managerial Comparisons of Four Developed Countries: France, Britain, United States, and Russia* (Cambridge: MIT Press, 1972); Barry Richman, *Soviet Management* (Englewood Cliffs, N.J.: Prentice-Hall, 1965).

9. See, for example, John V. Hardt and Theodore Frankel, "The Industrial Managers," in *Interest Groups in Soviet Politics,* ed. H. Gordon Skilling and Franklyn Griffiths (Princeton: Princeton University Press, 1971), 171–208; Jerry F. Hough, *Soviet Leadership in Transition* (Washington, D.C.: Brookings Institution, 1980); Robbin F. Laird and Erik P. Hoffmann, "The Competition between Soviet Conservatives and Modernizers: Domestic and International Aspects," in *The Soviet Polity in the Modern Era,* ed. Hoffmann and Laird (New York: Aldine, 1984), 825–40.

10. See especially Seweryn Bialer, *Stalin's Successors: Leadership, Stability, and Change in the Soviet Union* (Cambridge: Cambridge University Press, 1980), which argues that the political system's ability to restrain professionalization in various ways while also taking advantage of it has been a major source of stability for the post-Stalin system. See, too, Mark R. Beissinger, "In Search of Generations in Soviet Politics," *World Politics* 38 (January 1986): 288–314; Marshall I. Goldman, *Gorbachev's Challenge: Economic Reform in the Age of High Technology* (New York: Norton, 1987).

11. G. Popov, "Restructuring in the economy," *Pravda,* Jan. 20, 1987, 2.

12. Quoted in Goldman, *Gorbachev's Challenge,* 255.

13. See, for example, V. Obukhov, "Invent and utilize," *Pravda,* January 7, 1986, 2, and L. Abalkin, "The economic theory of socialism," *Pravda* May 16, 1986, 2–3; V. Shchepotkin, "People, economic accountability, and money," *Izvestiia,* November 1, 1986, 3.

14. V. Ivanov, in *Izvestiia,* May 5, 1987, 2.

15. "Perestroika continues," *Ekonomika i organizatsiia promyshlennogo proizvodstva* (hereafter EKO), no. 3 (March 1986): 26–43.

16. T. M. Dzhafarli, Sh. L. Kistauri, B. P. Kurashvili, and V. P. Rassokhin, "Several aspects of the acceleration of scientific-technical progress" *Sotsiologicheskie issledovaniia,* no. 2 (April 1983): 58–63.

17. E. Kolosova, "Five questions to directors," EKO, no. 12 (December 1984): 72–75.

18. See Susan J. Linz, "Managerial Autonomy in Soviet Firms," *Soviet Studies* 40 (April 1988): 175–95.

19. See Beissinger, "In Search of Generations," for a survey and for his own findings.

20. V. A. Rzheshevskii, 'From the Experiment to Extensive Dissemination

of New Management Methods," *Dengi i kredit*, no. 11 (November 1985): 33–39 (trans. in Joint Publications Research Service [hereafter JPRS], Economic Affairs Reports, April 1, 1986); N. Ragozhina, "Ways of Further Improving the Economic Mechanism," *Ekonomicheskie nauki*, no. 2 (February 1986): 119–23 (trans. in JPRS Economic Affairs Reports, June 27, 1986).

21. "1987 Panel on the Soviet Economic Outlook: Perceptions on a Confusing Set of Statistics," *Soviet Economy* 3 (January–March 1987): 3–39.

22. Initial reform decrees permitted up to one half of an enterprise's production to go to *goszakazy*, but this so distorted the course of perestroika that the state's ability to plan output was reduced and put under Gosplan's exclusive control, to prevent the ministries from issuing *goszakazy* on their own. *Ekonomicheskaia gazeta*, no. 31 (July 1988): 18–20. For a discussion of continued ministerial intervention in enterprises' ability to negotiate and fulfill contracts, see Heidi Kroll, "The Role of Contracts in the Soviet Economy," *Soviet Studies* 40 (July 1988), 349–66.

23. L. Beliaeva, "Laws, restrictions, perspectives," EKO, no. 11 (November 1985): 58–78.

24. "Perestroika continues," 35–36; "Perestroika: Nature and terms," EKO, no. 3 (March 1987): 63–69.

25. Beliaeva, "Laws, Restrictions," 63–65.

26. "Perestroika: Nature and Terms," 59–63.

27. Beliaeva, "Laws, Restrictions," 66–67.

28. Ibid.

29. "Gorbachev's Economic Reform," 43.

30. Ibid., 68.

31. *Ekonomicheskaia gazeta*, no. 43 (October 1986): 6–7.

32. A. Ivanenko, "An increase in the role of economic incentive funds," *Planovoe khoziaistvo*, no. 12 (December 1985): 62–71.

33. Henry Norr, "Shchekino, Another Look," *Soviet Studies* 38 (April 1986): 141–69; Adam, "Attempts to Improve," 14–21.

34. "The reform mirrored in the opinion poll," *Moscow News*, October 4, 1988, 1.

35. Beliaeva, "Law, restrictions," 75.

36. "Perestroika continues," 41.

37. Interview with B. N. Gavrilov, "Earned pay: Reform of the wage system begins," *Izvestiia*, Sept. 26, 1987, 2.

38. Adam, "Attempts to Improve," 21.

39. V. B. Bronshtein, "On norms and incentives," EKO, no. 4 (April 1985): 150–56.

40. Beliaeva, "Laws, restrictions," 72.

41. A. Miliukov, "The problems of radical reform," *Ekonomicheskaia gazeta*, no. 20 (May 1986): 6–8.

42. Norr, "Shchekino," 148–49.
43. Ibid., 149–50.
44. "Perestroika continues," 32.
45. V. Moskalenko, "Self-financing: Principles, further development," *Voprosy ekonomiki*, no. 2 (February 1987): 50–58; Rzheshevskii, "From the Experiment," 33–39.
46. M. I. Volkov, "Control over expenditure of wage funds," *Dengi i kredit*, no. 3 (March 1986): 52–59.
47. Speech by N. K. Emelina, July 1, 1988, 6. Speech by V. A. Iarin, *Pravda*, July 2, 1988, 7–8.
48. V. Tomashkevich, "The ministry and democratization of management," *Ekonomicheskaia gazeta*, no. 16 (April 1988): 5.
49. Ivanenko, "An increase," 65.
50. *Moscow News*, no. 45 (1988), 12.
51. Egor T. Gaidar, "The course of normalization. An economic observation," *Kommunist*, no. 12 (1988): 41–50. See also "Perestroika: Quality and span," EKO, no. 3 (1987): 55–71.
52. "Perestroika: Quality and span,"
53. See, for example, L. Kantorovich, M. Albegov, and V. Bezukov, "Broader utilization of optimization methods in the national economy," *Kommunist*, no. 9 (Sept. 1986): 44–54.
54. *Izvestiia*, April 26, 1987, 3.
55. *Izvestiia*, October 30, 1988; "The Volga itself is in jeopardy," *Pravda*, December 5, 1988, 4.
56. *Izvestiia*, September 26, 1986, 2; *Ekonomicheskaia gazeta*, no. 33 (August 1985): 9–10.
57. Speech by G. Ia. Baklanov, *Pravda*, July 2, 1988, 7.
58. Joel Kurtzman, "Of Perestroika, Prices and Pessimism," *New York Times*, November 6, 1988, C1.
59. See, for example, T. Baranenkova, "Ways of strengthening labor discipline," *Voprosy ekonomiki*, no. 5 (May 1986): 57–67; Bronshtein "On Norms"; E. B. Gorbunov, "The intensity of labor and raising its productivity," EKO, no. 4 (April 1986): 144–50; L. Rzhanitsyna, "Strengthening the incentive for labor effectiveness," *Voprosy ekonomiki*, no. 6 (June 1985): 82–89.
60. In the CPSU Central Committee and the USSR Council of Ministers," *Pravda*, May 5, 1987, 1, 3.
61. B. S. Pavlov, "With sights on tomorrow," EKO, no. 11 (November 1985): 137–47; "How the Workers' Dormitory Operates," EKO, no. 11 (November 1985): 147–54 (trans. in JPRS Economic Affairs Report, April 8, 1986, 109–14).
62. E: Milovanov and N. Singur, "Planning the social development of the Far East," *Planovoe khoziaistvo*, no. 2 (February 1986): 102–8.
63. "Perestroika continues," 42.

64. Beliaeva, "Laws, Restrictions," 75.
65. "Perestroika continues," 42–43.
66. V. Rutgaizer and S. Zhuravlev, "Resources in the sphere of services to the population," *Voprosy ekonomiki*, no. 12 (December 1985): 109–19.
67. I. Kruglianskaia, "One year later: No competition," *Izvestiia*, September 20, 1988, 3.
68. F. N. Il'iasov and O. B. Mukhammetberdiev, "Public opinion on unearned income," *Sotsiologicheskie issledovaniia*, no. 5 (1988): 52–57.
69. A. E. Levin, "Questions on studying the production situation," *Sotsiologicheskie issledovaniia*, no. 3 (July 1985): 113–15; Darrell Slider, "Worker Participation in Socialist Systems," *Comparative Politics* 18 (July 1986): 401–18; Russell Bova, "The Role of Workplace Participation," *Problems of Communism* 36 (July–August 1987): 76–86.
70. For a report on consumer goods production and trade, see Gaidar, "Course of normalization," 42–43.
71. TASS, in *The Soviet Observer*, December 9, 1988, 2.
72. Hanson, "Shape of Gorbachev's Economic Reform," 317.
73. Marshall Goldman, *New York Times*, August 2, 1987, III 3.
74. Iv. Rytov and A. Sabirov, "And then the production line stopped," *Izvestiia*, Dec. 4, 1986, 2.
75. "1987 Panel on the Soviet Economic Outlook," 35.
76. Gaidar, "Course of normalization," 43–44.
77. "The reform mirrored in the opinion poll."

3

THE DYNAMICS OF THE SOVIET ECONOMIC MECHANISM: INSIGHTS FROM REFORM DEBATES, 1977–1987

Peter Rutland

Practical men, who believe themselves to be quite exempt from any intellectual influences, are usually the slaves of some defunct economist.—J.M. Keynes

A. INTRODUCTION

Most discussions of the dynamics of the Soviet economy by Western scholars revolve around the concept of "reform". There is widespread recognition that the Soviet economy has remained trapped in an "extensive" growth path for too long, and that it must be shifted over to an "intensive" path (i.e., using existing labor and capital resources more efficiently) if the economy is to continue to grow into the 1990s. International competitiveness, military prowess and consumer satisfaction are all seen as contingent upon a successful reform of the economic system. Many Soviet economists share this approach, arguing that only far-reaching systemic reforms in the economic structure can rescue the Soviet economy from its downward path. It also appears that General Secretary Gorbachev himself sees the situation in these terms.

It is our view that there is more than one approach that can be taken to the analysis of the reform phenomenon in the USSR, and that concentration on the likely nature of some imminent systemic reform is not the only legitimate intellectual framework at our disposal. In this chapter we will be looking at Soviet economic reform debates as a window through which to explore the way the existing

Soviet economy works, rather than as an exercise in what the future Soviet economy might look like. Much of the current discussion in the West seems to have a prescriptive rather than descriptive feel, with discussion as to which combinations of institutions are feasible in a Soviet context, or which coalitions of social interests are likely to be capable of pushing a radical reform through.[1]

In this chapter we will resist such futurological tendencies. Instead, we will be looking at Soviet reform debates as a commentary on the existing patterns of economic behavior in the USSR. We will not spend much time on the actual history of institutional reforms over the past twenty years (such an exercise would require a book-length study) but will be focusing upon debates about reform proposals between Soviet academics. These debates, irrespective of their merits as predictors of the future, yield up some interesting insights into the dynamics of the current Soviet economy: insights which tend to be overlooked if one adopts a "blueprint" approach to reform discussions.

Three main findings come out of this exercise. First, the fact that key issues such as party control of the economy have mostly been excluded from the debate implies that reform in these areas will be extremely unlikely. If they have not even been allowed on the public agenda, how can a reforming leader hope to think through the implications of reform, still less build a constituency for change? Second, the very fact that certain problems are repeatedly addressed, with little apparent progress (prime examples being the weakness of budgetary discipline and the perseverance of planning by physical targets) implies to us that these facets of the economy are structural features impervious to reform. Third, one should not forget that the reform debate has more than one side; there are opponents, as well as advocates, of reform. These opponents of reform should not simply be dismissed as self-seeking bureaucrats out to preserve their quiet life. Are the advocates of reform themselves devoid of self interest? (For example, reform advocacy has catapulated Aganbegian and Zaslavskaia to the pinnacle of their profession under Gorbachev.[2]) It is our view that some of the opponents of reform have interesting things to say about how the current economy works.

Are we being excessively pessimistic in choosing to write about the Soviet economy *as it is* rather than as it *might be* if only *perestroika* were to succeed? Not necessarily—since skepticism as to the ability of the Soviet economy to transform itself does not necessarily imply an apocalyptic vision of the future for the USSR. It strikes us as perfectly possible that the Soviet economy will muddle through to the twenty-first century in more or less its present institutional form.

Some may suggest that the debates of the pre-Gorbachev period are of only incidental historical interest, since in the past year or two Gorbachev has changed the whole nature of the debate. However, we do not see any radical shift in the way the problems are conceived or the solutions proposed in 1987–89, and the fact that as of early 1989 economic perestroika is very badly stalled suggests to us that the roots may lie precisely in the inadequate and blinkered nature of the reform debate in preceeding years. Despite having established himself in a politically dominant position, and despite having a firm and resolute desire to reshape the Soviet economy, Gorbachev has been unable to bring about the desired transformation. The problem seems to lie in severe "design flaws" at the very heart of the reform program. The economics profession itself, along with planners and managers, are all children of the era of stagnation, and unless they confront the limitations in the intellectual frameworks they inherited from the Brezhnev years they will be unable to come up with a program which will really tackle the ills facing the Soviet economy.

B. THE BACKGROUND TO THE DEBATES

A fairly frank exchange of views has been taking place in the pages of the Soviet press over the last seven or eight years as to the key structural features of the Soviet economy. This dialogue is in large part an extension of a discussion which began in the late 1950s and ran with various interruptions through the 1960s and 1970s. The debate thus predates the arrival of reform-minded general secretaries such as Andropov and Gorbachev (although they have been instrumental in widening the scope of the debate).

The debaters are a mixture of academics, planners, journalists and party theoreticians. In this paper we will be confining ourselves to the public debate. "Private," unpublished debates have no doubt ranged more widely, and may have had considerable influence over policymakers behind the scenes, but the present author has not had widespread access to such deliberations and they must therefore be left out of consideration here. The debates have reached all corners of the Soviet press, and the most radical and blunt critiques have often been published in wide circulation, noneconomic journals such as *Novyi mir* and *Literaturnaya gazeta*. However, reasons of space and time prevent us from covering the debates in the popular press here in this chapter. Instead we will be concentrating our attention on the discussions to be found in the half-dozen key academic and party journals. Apart from practical considerations, the intellectual justification for treating the popular press separately would be that the nature of the audience is very different, and the articles published therein raising economic controversies play a different role to similar articles published in the academic or party press. Interesting and informative though the occasional reform articles in the popular press might be, it is very difficult to assess their significance in terms of the present (and probable future) functioning of the Soviet economy. Articles published in the specialized economic and party journals are presumably more likely to reflect the views of the decision-making and decision-implementing elites, and are therefore a more reliable guide to the nature of present and future policies.

By the early 1960s Soviet economists and party leaders were already voicing concern that the Soviet economy had begun to exhaust the possibilities of growth through the extensive method (drawing more labor and capital into the national economy). The search began for methods to shift the economy onto a more intensive path. The 1965 Kosygin reforms represented the first economywide attempt to put these ideas into practice. Those reforms failed to take root, and were virtually abandoned within a year. The reform debate itself sputtered on in a desultory fashion. The word and concept of *reform* slowly slipped off the political agenda as Brezhnevite conservatism took hold. (For example, *Ekonomicheskaya gazeta* stopped running its "Reform" page in 1973.) However, the industrial stagnation of the late 1970s forced a reopening of the debate from 1980 onwards (although at first the word *reform* remained taboo). The floodgates opened with the arrival of leaders such as Andropov and Gorbachev who were actively interested in promoting reform.

One must exercise caution in utilizing this body of reform literature for analytical purposes. The debates proceed within the confines of a tacit code, under which certain concepts are prohibited (e.g., market socialism), while other concepts are mandatory (e.g., the leading role of the party, the superiority of socialism over capitalism in all but a few isolated areas). To some extent this code exaggerates the degree of *unity* among the debaters, yet at the same time it also portrays a degree of *disunity* that might not actually reflect the views of the participants.

A false *unity* is imposed upon the debates by the obligation placed upon radical reformers to keep their criticisms of socialism within limits, and to be restrained in their praise for various aspects of capitalism. This imposed unity *also* constrains the opponents of reform, however, since even dyed-in-the-wool conservatives are expected to pay lip-service to the need to improve the economy. It seems to be understood by them that they cannot directly spell out the reasons why they consider large-scale reform to be dangerous or risky. Instead, they communicate their skepticism by expounding at length upon the strengths of the present system, while proposing changes of a marginal or superficial nature. (We will be giving examples in subsequent sections.)

On the other side, a false disunity is created by the understanding that a "debate" is in progress. Academics, in the USSR as everywhere else, are prone to form rival teams which then polemicize among themselves (albeit in a decorous manner, mostly through Aesopian language). There may be less to some of these "disagreements" than initially meets the eye. Academics may be using these debates to draw attention to themselves, or may be taking part in some sort of feud between their own institution and its organizational rivals. It is difficult for an outside observer to separate the "real" intellectual arguments from the personal and bureaucratic feuding. After all the effort of wading through anodyne articles in search of signs of a dispute, the reader is reluctant to concede that the debates so painstakingly unearthed may be ersatz and self-serving, telling us little about the actual functioning of the Soviet economy. The clearest examples of such nondebates are to be found in the areas of *scientific communism* and *historical materialism*. Debates over whether one can put a precise date upon the arrival of *developed socialism*, or the interminable arguments over how to characterize the nature of "contradictions" within socialist society, often amount to little more than "scholastic theorizing." (The latter phrase comes from a speech on this issue by M. Suslov, the Politburo's ideology chief, in 1981.[3]) One should beware of the temptation to read real, substantial political differences into such arcane disputes. In some cases there may be a real hidden agenda: for example, some of the debates over contradictions in society seemed to be a vehicle for discussing whether or not the USSR was obliged to tolerate pluralistic forces in Poland.[4]

However, it is our sense that many of these apparently fierce academic debates *can* be taken at face value, and are merely part of the Soviet academic game. One should not be surprised that Soviet academia should involve such debates. After all, the dialectic is supposed to be the core principle of Soviet social science, and the essence of the dialectic is that there are two sides (at least) to every question. Unfortunately, the dialectic also instructs that all sides will be reconciled into an organic unity by the unfolding of historical processes. This imparts a strangely unreal quality to many of these debates, since each side to the argument is essentially reconcilable with the other.

Despite these caveats about the particular codes shaping Soviet academic debates—codes which have shifted their terms in the Gorbachev era, but by no means disappeared—the debates of the last decade offer some important insights into the functioning of the Soviet economy.

C. THE TYRANNY OF VAL

The first point we wish to pull out of the debate is the widespread recognition by many Soviet economists of how resistant their economic system is to structural change. Repeated attempts to reform the economy (1965, 1973, 1979, 1983) have failed to alter the established procedures by which industrial plans are composed and executed.

The chief symbol of systemic continuity is the role played by the gross output indicator when drawing up plan targets for enterprises. (Gross output — *valovaia produktsiia* — is usually referred to as val.)

The 1965 reform tried to make profits the key target variable, the 1979 package tried to introduce "value added" as the primary indicator, and the 1983 "big experiment" focused on sales and contract discipline. Yet it seems that through all these mutations, val retained a primary position when it came to the routine procedures by which the ministries drew up their plans, allocated supplies, and monitored results. Tracking physical flows of goods seems to be the sine qua non of the planned economy.

It is not as if economists had been unaware of this problem. Attacks on val go back at least to 1956: it is recognized to be an extremely crude variable, leaving little scope for considerations of cost and quality. However, thirty years later, in 1986, one can still find economists citing examples of the absurdities wrought by val. For example, while consumers are complaining that they cannot find any thin typing paper in the stores, one of the major paper mills is still churning out unsaleable thick paper (because their output is measured in tons).[5] Gorbachev himself spoke out against the persistence of val in a speech to the June 1986 CC CPSU plenum.[6]

These are not isolated references. In 1985 D. Valovoi described the problem of the shortage of 50-mm pipe for the plumbing industry in Leningrad.[7] The pipe factory is paid twice as much for 100-mm pipe as for 50-mm pipe (net of input costs), but the machine costs for producing the large and small pipe are identical. As a result, there is no 50-mm pipe being produced. One would have thought that in an administrative and technological center such as Leningrad such problems would have been ironed out after twenty years of efforts to "perfect the economic mechanism." That the situation has not altered suggests to us that it is not merely for lack of trying. It is not merely bureaucratic convention that is involved: the economy's political overseers also seem wedded to a gross output approach. Thus, for example, the garbage collectors of Makeevka in the Ukraine were forced by the local party *raikom* to come up with a plan to expand their "output" of trash by 20 percent over five years![8]

The 1979 value-added system was supposed to solve the val problem: that was the precise purpose of moving plan accounting from gross output to value added. This was to be achieved through the calculation of *normative net output* (NNO), with normative ratios of average or expected value added being calculated for each product type.[9] However, the new system proved too complicated for ministerial planners to cope with. For example, while iron and steel plants did have their targets expressed in normative tons, at the level of the all-union production associations, and within the Ministry of Ferrous Metallurgy itself, planning proceeded on the old basis, in *actual* tons.[10] Similar inertia seems characteristic of other sectors. In 1981 light industry in Latvia announced that it was introducing the planning of kitchenware output on the basis of product mix rather than weight—but only on an *experimental* basis.[11] This clearly implied that val continued to be the standard accounting procedure elsewhere. According to esteemed economists such as E. Manevich, examples of this kind are typical rather than exceptional.[12] Planning from the achieved level and reliance on crude output indicators continues to be the norm throughout Soviet industry.

To us this confirms the firmly entrenched character of some of the core routine operating procedures of the planned economy. We do not mean to imply that there have been *no* improvements in the Soviet planning mechanism over the years. Planning techniques at the micro level have become more sophisticated, and there has been a steady process of institutional development, with new agencies emerging to tackle particular problem areas. (For example, measures taken to improve the supply system, materials economy, and quality control have kept up a steady flow since the mid-1960s.) However, it remains the case that the bulk of Soviet economists seem dissatisfied with the pace of change, and seek further, systemic reforms. Thus participants in the Soviet debates by and large agree that the reign of val must be terminated. Rifts start to appear, however, when it comes to discussing the type of measures needed to replace val, and the role which physical indicators will continue to play in any "reformed" system.

D. PROPOSALS FOR REFORM

Since the early 1960s economists have been advocating greater reliance on monetary and financial indicators, which would take the burden off the central planners, diminish the number of direct commands which would have to be issued, and shift the economy onto a more self-regulating basis. Reformers are fond of arguing that this would actually *increase* the effective control exercised over the economy by the central planners.[13] The present system is seen as giving them formal powers while the way the system works in practice makes them hostage to the machinations of enterprise managers. This lack of real control is particularly visible in areas such as efficiency and innovation, where planners have consistently failed to achieve their chosen goals.

This argument is interesting because it illustrates the consensual nature of the Soviet reform debate. The reformers want to find common ground with their conservative opponents, and seem keen to avoid a direct confrontation over the degree of central control possible or desirable in a planned economy. Do the reformers really believe that decentralization would lead to an increase in the effectivity of central control—or are they secretly convinced that the center must yield influence to the market? It is our intuition that at least some, and probably a majority, of the reform economists sincerely believe that it is possible to rescue the virtues of central planning while shedding its vices. For example, even after the leading Polish economist W. Brus had moved into emigration (and therefore presumably freed himself from the strictures of the internal socialist debate) he continued to vigorously argue that partial marketization could preserve and strengthen the desirable aspects of central planning.[14]

The 1965 reforms represented a major attempt to overcome val by moving from physical to monetary indicators, while radically increasing the autonomy of enterprise managers. The reforms failed, for reasons too well-known to bear repeating here.[15] It is curious to note, however, how little reference has been made in subsequent Soviet debates to the reasons for failure in 1965. The official party history journal pointed out in 1981, for example, that of the three hundred or so history Ph.D.s to come out over the preceding year, not one addressed the question of the history of economic reform.[16] Presumably too many sensitive political questions would be raised by such an inquiry.

Apart from trying to abolish val, the 1979 NNO reform also attempted to effect a greater role across the board for financial indicators.[17] The central issue was to put firms onto full cost accounting, meaning that a real attempt would be made to calculate actual profits and losses, and enterprises would for the first time face a hard budget constraint. Making profits rather than gross output the central bonus-determining performance indicator would lock managers into the new cost/revenue awareness.

Reform-minded economists portrayed the introduction of the NNO system in 1979 as a continuation of the spirit of the 1965 reforms, almost as if they had never failed.[18] N. Fedorenko was still propounding the advanced mathematical optimalization techniques which had been widely touted in the discussion preceding the 1965 reform—even though they had remained a paper exercise (it being virtually impossible to imagine how they could be practically administered).[19]

The debate around the 1979 reform did, however, see the introduction of some more controversial ideas. For example, I. Syroekhin advocated using consumer prices *(tseny potrebitelia)* as the basis for planning;[20] while S. Starostin and G. Emdin called for a sharp increase in monetary incentives, and hinted at the need to introduce the mechanism of redundancy to ensure the elimination of unprofitable firms.[21] Novosibirsk economist A. Aganbegian published a book entitled *Managing Socialist Enterprises* in 1979, advocating a general reform program.[22] (Gorbachev brought Aganbegian to Moscow in 1985 to serve as his chief economic adviser.) Unusually, the leading party theoretical journal *Kommunist* published a critical review of the book in 1981.[23] Reviewer (and himself a reform economist of some standing) P. Bunich found the work an "interesting attempt," but criticized the author's "controversial concept of adaptive planning" and a naive belief in the possibilities for advanced mechanization. "The question is, what to do about it now? . . . Unfortunately, the book does not provide an answer."

Generally speaking, however, the 1979 NNO reform was a compromise solution which preserved a reliance on physically-calculated indicators while trying to move away from val by shifting to value-added targets.[24] Unfortunately, NNO failed to take root. Planners found it too complicated to calculate value added, and financial awareness was not significantly augmented by the reform.

After Andropov's arrival as general secretary we see an experiment launched in five selected ministries in January 1984, the thrust of which was to expand enterprise autonomy and drastically reduce the degree of detailed supervision exercised by the planners in the central ministries. A wide-ranging debate over the forms and methods of economic management ensued in the party and economic press, increasing in intensity in 1986 as the Andropov experiment was extended to a wider range of ministries under the new Gorbachev leadership.

The 1983–87 debates ranged over much of the same ground as those of 1964–65 and 1978–81. Again, however, there were relatively few attempts to relate contemporary proposals to the fate of earlier reforms. In a 1986 piece O. Latsis did refer to the seminal 1964 article of mathematical economist V. S. Nemchinov, but the aspirations of the "optimal planning" school now seem to be considered irrelevant.[25] An exception is a curious article by one of the leading early 1960s reform economists, B. M. Smekhov, which rejected the possibility of optimal planning as unrealistic, but still ended up arguing that it is possible to construct an ordinal ranking of use values (which sounds pretty much like optimal planning to this reader).[26]

The general thrust of the reform argument was to advocate, in T. Zaslavskaia's words, a decisive shift from "administrative direction" to "economic regulation."[27] In Marxist terms, the issue was one of expanding the role played by "commodity/money relations" in the Soviet economy.[28]

Many reformers focused on the question of pricing, arguing that prices must be changed more frequently, and must reflect a balance between supply and demand rather than being a summation of arbitrarily chosen production costs. The existing system, for example, allows small, inefficient enterprises to charge more than large, efficient ones, which would normally be considered economically irrational.[29] Some participants in the debate have gone so far as to introduce the question of pricing according to some measure of consumer use value.[30] When Yu. Borozdin of the Central Mathematical Economics Institute (TsEMI) talks of the need for pricing according to the *use result (poleznyi rezul'tat)* it begins to sound suspiciously like the concept of consumer utility (the cornerstone of Western neoclassical economics).[31]

Attention also returned to the question of cost accounting.[32] There was a continual flow of attacks on the existing accounting system, where costs and revenues play a mostly passive role in the economy. Equipment continues to be regarded as a "free gift" from the center, with managers uninterested in cutting back their capital outlays.[33] Introducing techniques such as *functional cost accounting* (roughly akin to cost/benefit analysis) can, it is suggested, knock two-thirds off the cost of new equipment.[34] It is not surprising that technical innovation is sluggish when, for example, a standard economics text lists twenty different ways to calculate the benefits of new technology.[35] (Can they not come up with a single measure?)

Reliance on monetary and financial indicators offers a straightforward, synthetic (i.e., inclusive) measure of economic performance, in place of the plethora of success criteria currently in operation.[36] It offers a way to cut through the organizational confusion that half a century of steady bureaucratic growth has created, and put the economy on a sound footing.[37] After all, one of the key slogans of the 1981 twentieth Party Congress was that "the economy must be economical."[38] The prominent reformer O. Latsis is one of the most ardent advocates of full cost accounting, arguing for "real profits" rather than "profit indicators," and "real rubles, the sort found in cash registers," instead of the purely paper enterprise accounts which are the norm.[39] The problem lies in distinguishing between "false" and "true" cost accounting. Formal cost accounting has been around in Soviet industry since the 1930s, but the sums are usually calculated in a passive, ex post fashion. Financial indiscipline remained rampant, even after the 1965 reforms. (For example, two-thirds of the funds the new 1965 procedures set aside for amortizing capital were in fact used to acquire new capital.[40]) Even back in 1978 some ministries were claiming to be in the process of introducing a system of *branch cost accounting*, but a deputy head of Gosplan stated in 1985 that these experiments (between 1976 and 1980) had been a failure, and that full cost accounting had never been attained.[41]

To what extent have the various reforms introduced since 1983 succeeded in shifting the economy toward full monetary accountability? The experiment with true full cost accounting which began at the Frunze engineering plant in Sumy in 1985 (under the guidance of P. Bunich) seems to have had good results, and indicates the productivity gains which lie in store if the suggested reforms are introduced.[42] Under the Sumy initiative—and unlike in Andropov's big experiment in the five ministries—profit rates and payments into the state budget are fixed in advance, so the firm has a real budget and a real prospect of financial gain as a result of any efficiency improvements they may achieve. The *will* to introduce full cost accounting is clearly present: new rules introduced in 1986 promised to fix enterprise retention rates and taxes in advance, leaving them to maximize net income.[43] It remains to be seen whether or not full cost accounting can be made to work in practice across large numbers of enterprises.[44] Even NNO is not dead: there are still economists who believe that a correctly designed value-added indicator can combine cost consciousness with the advantages of centrally fixed output targets.[45] Thus, for example, two Belorussian ministries reintroduced normative planning of their wages funds for 1987.[46]

Most reform-minded authors shy away from the question of the possibility of introducing automatic, market-driven structural changes in the Soviet economy. V. Kulikov comes close, in that the special procedures he advocates for winding up loss-making firms sound suspiciously akin to bankruptcy.[47]

Some of the reform proposals go beyond the level of calls for more "commodity/money relations," and broach still deeper structural deficiencies of the Soviet economy. T. Zaslavakaia has been putting forward radical reform proposals for several years in the pages of the Novosibirsk journal *EKO*.[48] Since Gorbachev's accession to power, her ideas have received wider circulation, being aired in an article in the authoritative CPSU theory journal, *Kommunist*.[49] Zaslavskaia's ideas are well-known: she questions the nature of the "moral economy" underpinning the system of central planning. She points to the diversity of interests in socialist society; the lack of clear accountability in the economy; and the absence of strong incentives rewarding better performance. The lack of incentives results from various factors: the chaotic state of performance indicators; the dependence on outside suppliers which diminishes the relevance of one's own efforts; the dearth of quality consumer goods for people to buy; and spuriously egalitarian social and wage policies which have squeezed salary differentials and loaded too much distribution into collective forms ("social consumption"). The incentives argument has been popular with labor economists for many years. For example, L. Gol'din argued in 1983 that only a wage rise of 50 to 60 rubles a month (about 20 percent of average income) would be sufficient to stimulate the best workers to achieve their maximum performance.[50]

Some reformers go beyond even this sensitive incentives issue, and raise the more serious question of the set of property relations appropriate to a developed socialist society. E. Iasin suggests that the current system of full-scale public ownership is the root cause of the sort of abdication of responsibility which Zaslavskaia attacks.[51] Commentators therefore advocate expanding alternative forms of ownership in which there is a more intimate link between effort and rewards—cooperatives, private plots, and private activity in the services sphere.[52] Nineteen eighty-seven saw the introduction of a new law promoting a wider range of cooperative activity and expanding private enterprise in certain defined areas.[53] The latter grew out of an experiment which the RSFSR Ministry of Consumer Services introduced in 1984, allowing part-time private work by students, pensioners, and housewives.[54] A decree of July 1985 introduced "youth housing complexes," under which Komsomol volunteer cooperatives will be allowed to build their own apartments.[55]

However, it is unlikely that substantial growth in the private sector will be allowed to occur. Our skepticism stems from three sources. First, one should recall the record of private enterprise in agriculture in the USSR. When the state has needed food, as in 1979–81, then liberal policies have been introduced, and private plots actively encouraged.[56] However, when the wind shifts peasants may find their activities criminalized (as in 1962). Thus, as the chairman of Voronezh *oblispolkom* (regional soviet executive) explained in 1986, "Many people are not hurrying to raise fruit and vegetables on their garden plots because they are scared that the next administrative crackdown *(sharakhan'e)* will lead to their being accused of illegal earnings."[57] Such a fear is not without foundation: June 1986 saw a new decree "on measures to strengthen the struggle with unearned incomes," promising to "strengthen control over *kolkhoz* markets" (where privately grown produce may be sold) and, for example, stipulating a penalty of up to two years corrective labor for those who persist in buying food in state shops and feeding it to their animals.[58]

Second, the new private enterprise rules involve a restrictive licensing procedure and high fees and taxes.[59] The minimum fee is 100 rubles, rising to 560 rubles for private taxis. These measures may persuade many to stay in the black economy rather than seek legal status. The range of activity allowed is also restricted (no private restaurants, for example — only cooperative ones, and a limited number of them). Above all, the entrepreneurs will still be obliged to put in a forty-hour week for the state at their regular job.

Third, one should recall that the East European socialist states have forty years' experience with their own private sectors, and the record there has not been a happy one. A. Aslund has detailed the cycle of liberatization and repression which has characterized state policy toward the private sector in Poland and the GDR.[60] The overall effect in those countries has been to keep the private sector below 5 percent of national income (even though its contribution to individual services such as taxis may be very high).[61] However, Soviet entrepreneurs will be lucky if they are allowed to approach even those modest levels.

Thus a wide range of reform proposals are on the table for consideration. Some have been in circulation for many years, often having received unequivocal official approval. Some of the proposals have been tried in the past, and failed. Some of the new suggestions remain on the drawing board, others have begun partial implementation. The much-awaited radical reform has not yet arrived, however.[62] What are the arguments that have been used against the reformers, and what are the boundaries that they themselves recognize as constraining the feasible scope of their proposed reforms? These topics will be explored in the following section. We should stress that we are confining our discussion to the issues raised by participants in the Soviet academic reform debate, and we are not offering our own interpretation of the forces favoring and opposing reform in the real world as we ourselves see it.

E. THE OPPONENTS OF REFORM

Advocates of increased reliance on "commodity/money relations" have run into strong opposition from ardent defenders of the socialist system in its present form who raise ideological and practical objections to any steps in the direction of "market socialism." In 1983, P. Ignatovskii published a trenchant article in which he quoted Lenin to the effect that "administrative methods are essential here," and attacked enterprises which are only interested in a "pile of money."[63] He argued that there were two paths open for the USSR: "to return to the market mechanism, which is ruled out if you value the fate of socialism, or to strengthen the conscious principles underlying the economy by elevating the rule of politics."

In 1985 the then-head of the State Prices Committee, N. Glushkov, defended his agency's record by arguing that suggested moves toward models of a self-regulating economy would lead the USSR in the direction of "the long-rejected concepts of "price balance" and a market economy."[64] One of his main worries was that a move in the direction of freer prices would enable some firms to take advantage of their monopolistic position, and would therefore lock in existing inefficiencies. This is a curious argument at first glance —to suggest that a market system would be more rigid than the existing set-up—but it does address a real problem. A. Buzgalin makes the same point in his attack on advocates of "indirect methods" of economic management, arguing that an equilibrium based on price changes alone is not a *true* equilibrium because in order to achieve the latter the actual structure of production must change.[65] (These points correspond to a longstanding argument in Western neoclassical economics over whether price or quantity is dominant in moving a market toward equilibrium.) This argument poses a major challenge to the radical reformers: merely choking off demand by allowing prices to rise is not a solution to the problems the economy faces. They must also introduce mechanisms by which price changes actually lead to changes in the structure of the economy, with enterprising firms expanding production of the high-price goods, while other product lines are wound up. Critics of reform are asking whether or not the market will be relied upon to force through these decisions.

V. Cherkovets summarized the virtues of the current economic system as he sees them in a 1986 article.[66] The socialist economy is rooted in public ownership of the means of production, planned development of the economy, and a needs-based approach to resource allocation. These core principles mean that val is "objectively necessary" to the socialist economy—although it can of course coexist with cost accounting, and should itself be calculated in the most effective manner. Concepts of *market socialism* or *cooperative socialism* are to have no place in the USSR. Cherkovets does not see how the system's virtues could be preserved if a large proportion of the nation's economy was to flourish outside the regulatory power of the central planners.

The conservatives often rally around concepts of justice and equality. For example, a reform-minded reviewer criticized a new book entitled *The Justice of Socialism (Spravedlivost' sotsializma)* for ignoring the scope for "a healthy use of commodity/money relations on a socialist basis."[67] Similarly, a conservative skillfully adapted Gorbachev's slogan "the human factor" to give it a Stalinist twist, arguing that an approach based on the human element (in contrast, presumably, to reliance upon the "impersonal" market) can be traced back to the socialist competition movements of the 1930s.[68] Symbolically, the article began with a quote from an old *Pravda* story from the town Stalino (which was renamed Donetsk in 1961). The contributions of Zaslavskaia have provoked much controversy—for example, with critical letters to *Kommunist* and reports of "polemics" breaking out over her views at a roundtable discussion in Leningrad in late 1986.[69]

The reformers have counterattacked on several occasions. L. Abalkin wrote a reply to the Ignatovskii article cited at the beginning of this section.[70] He suggested that the economic problems the nation faces cannot simply be attributed to "a lag in consciousness, inertia in attitudes, inadequate understanding of social responsibilities" and similar phenomena which could be cured through more intensive political education.[71] "In order to change consciousness, in order to shift it to conform with contemporary demands, one must place man in new circumstances," i.e., reform the economic mechanism.

History has become a battleground for the competing factions. An article by E. Bugaev in *Kommunist* in 1984 lambasted a piece by E. A. Ambartsumov which *Voprosy istorii* had just published, in which NEP had been defended as having been on the verge of "becoming an optimal strategy for the transition to socialism."[72] Ambartsumov was also accused of having advocated "a revival of small ownership activity by certain groups." Bugaev made extensive reference to the crises of 1956, 1968 and 1980 in Eastern Europe to illustrate the dangers of such an approach. The editor of *Voprosy istorii* was obliged to send a humbling apology for having published the offending article.[73] A year later, however, reform-minded writers were marshalling their own quotations from the 1920s in support of a reformist interpretation of the period. G. Popov argued that War Communism was only tolerated because the preservation of the state was in danger: outside of such circumstances, one should beware of "barracks communism," as Marx himself warned.[74] P. Bunich quotes Lenin in defense of NEP, arguing that an attempt to continue planning in physical quantities (as opposed to money) in the conditions of the early 1920s would have led to "a defeat more serious than those inflicted on us by Kolchak, Denikin or Pilsudski."[75] He also pulls a quote from the Twelfth Party Congress (1923) to the effect that "a director's striving for profit . . . serves the interests of the working class."[76]

It is difficult to discern the precise position of the top party leadership in these debates. Andropov was very critical of the problems facing the Soviet economy, yet at the same time in a speech to party veterans in 1983 he cautioned that, "In an economy of such size and complexity as our own it is necessary to be extremely careful. Here like nowhere else the saying applies: 'measure seven times, cut once.' "[77] K. Chernenko paid some lip-service to the need for "renewal" (*obnovlenie*) and "a profound qualitative change," but seems to have done little concrete to help the process along.[78] With the arrival of Gorbachev and his commitment to 'radical reform', of course, the debate shifted into higher gear.[79] The journal *Kommunist* in particular blossomed in 1986 under its new liberal editor, I. Frolov, subsequently promoted to be a personal advisor to Gorbachev.

The reform debates in the academic and party press have not been allowed to boil over into an open, direct clash of opposed opinions. The participants seem to share many overlapping concerns and commitments (whether genuine or a reflection of editorial pressure is difficult to say), and most debaters seek to show how the worries of the other side can be incorporated into their model, rather than pushing forward the disagreements until they become matters of principle. Thus, for example, defenders of physical plan indicators will also concede an important role for cost accounting, and vice versa. Concepts such as value-added indicators, or the socialist principle of "distribution according to work," can be twisted by both sides to their own advantage. Some reformers, most notably A. Aganbegian, seem to want to hide behind the issue of technological change, implying that if only the cornucopia of modern technology can be unleashed all social and economic problems will be solved.[80] L. Abalkin seems to agree, arguing that while organizational changes can have a "substantial" effect, the main impact on growth must come through technical change.[81] The all-embracing yet inchoate notion of the scientific-technological revolution seems to be one of the few ideological principles laid down during the Brezhnev era which has continued to prevail in the Gorbachev era. In general, however, Abalkin seems more cautious on these issues than Aganbegian. For example, a year later we find Abalkin criticizing a new textbook for treating technical change as "autonomous" of the economic mechanisms at work in society.[82]

One area of the debate where the battle-lines have been more clearly drawn, and where the political implications are plain for all to see, is the argument over the continued dominant role enjoyed by the branch ministries.

F. DEBATES OVER THE ROLE OF THE BRANCH MINISTRIES

One of the most complex and politically sensitive relationships within the Soviet political system is that between the hierarchy of party organizations and the network of economic administrative agencies, from ministries down to enterprises. It is our impression that during the Brezhnev era the economic agencies both local and national built up a high degree of autonomy vis-à-vis party organs. While party secretaries could always pull rank and insist on a certain course of action by administrative officials on their *nomenklatura*, the complexity and interdependence of economic life (cutting across the clean regional hierarchy of party organs) made it difficult for party officials to guarantee the results they desired. Thus we would argue that the precise distribution of power between party and managerial institutions is something as yet unresolved, and amounts to the major anomaly in an otherwise fairly well-defined and rigid economic system.

In the debates over the role of private property or commodity/ money relations, or over the most suitable mix of target indicators, it is difficult to discern any systematic difference of opinion between party and administrative officials. For the most part in these debates the interests of party and economic officials are congruent: A defense of the existing system of central planning is also a defense of the interests of party organs as presently constituted.

However, when we turn to the question of the role of the branch ministries, each responsible for supervising enterprises across the country within a given industrial sector, the interests of party and administrative officials start to diverge. Given that party organizations are structured on a territorial basis, we can suggest that party officials will in general favor administrative reforms which favor territorially based planning over the current branch ministry system. Any diminution in the power of branch ministries to interfere with and control the activities of their enterprises is likely to lead to an increase in the power of regional supervisory agencies—among which the most important are the republican and provincial *(oblast')* party committees.

The latest round of arguments over the role of the branch ministries began with a couple of critical articles by G. Popov and B. P. Kurashvili in 1982.[83] These gave expression to the widespread feeling that the ministries exercised too much "petty tutelage" over the work of their subordinate firms. The 1973 associations reform was supposed to have tackled this problem by improving the status of the subordinate units, but in the end it seems only to have made matters worse, by adding another layer of bureaucracy to the chain of command. In fact, as far back as 1980 I. Cherevko had been arguing that the ministries deserved a closer look, suggesting that they be grouped into twenty-one "superministries" in order to force them to concentrate on strategic issues rather than mess with detailed routine management decisions.[84] This was also the strategy advocated in Popov's 1982 article.

The ministry system was not without its defenders, however— some cautious, others more forthright. D. Gvishiani conceded that the existing system led to needless duplication and dilution of effort (particularly, for example, in construction), but he thought that the system could be salvaged by transferring more of the functions of the "staff" ministries and state committees (such as supplies) to the branch ministries themselves.[85] This would serve to make them more autonomous, and thus (in theory) more accountable for their actions.

A trenchant defense of the status quo came from the pen of K. Beliak, the minister of Machine Building for the Livestock Industry.[86] He professed himself to be "amazed" by Popov's article, commenting that such critics "only weakly understand the work of ministries and enterprises, to put it mildly." Beliak's ministry had been created in 1973 to tackle the shortage of livestock equipment, whose provision had previously been the responsibility of seventeen different ministries. As no individual ministry was there to be held responsible for the sector before 1973, livestock machinery had been of poor quality and in acutely short supply. Under the new ministry the volume of equipment increased by 280 percent in seven years. This is the way to get things done, says Beliak. The current large number of economic ministries (about 65) is a result of a series of conscious decisions to promote certain sectors by hiving off new ministries. Examples would include the new Ministry for Construction in the Far East and Baikal (1979), or the new State Committee for Material Reserves (1978). Beliak was skeptical as to the likely impact of any decentralization of planning authority to the regions, reminding readers of Lenin's disdain for "regional anarcho-syndicalism." Ideas of setting up a single, unified engineering ministry strike him as nonsense. "Given our country's massive economy, how could such a monster be managed?'

Notwithstanding these objections, the anti-ministry lobby seemed to be winning the arguments. A 1984 article written jointly by an economist and a secretary of Volgograd *obkom* denounced the continuation of "branchism" and made a plea for making the *oblast'* the cornerstone of the managerial system.[87] It is fairly unusual to see a party official entering these debates, and instructive that he comes down on the side of regionalism. The authors go on to suggest that while Khrushchev's *sovnarkhoz* reform was ill-executed, it did have some positive features. For example, after the break-up of the *sovnarkhozy* in 1965 a successful local rubber combine was split up between different ministries, and its performance has never recovered the level attained when it was under unified local supervision.[88]

Another example of party officials criticizing the ministerial system is provided by a forthright article by A. Klautsen, first secretary of Riga *gorkom* (city party committee) in Latvia.[89] He concedes that product quality has been declining over the past fifteen years (but not in Riga itself, he claims!) and lays the blame firmly at the door of the ministries. He argues that "the strength of all-union or union-republican ministries is such that their enormous inertia . . . means that even the most progressive decisions . . . will not prove capable of breaking through the traditional behavioral stereotypes of their staffs which have built up over many years."[90] Even republican ministries can cause problems (for example, the trade ministry forbidding local firms to sell shoes outside of Riga) but they are impervious to party punishments because they are acting on orders from above.[91]

Such complaints are also to be heard from officials within the economic apparatus—particularly, so it seems, from the enterprise directors who seem to bear the brunt of their erratic behavior. In 1984 the *EKO* magazine published a survey which reported that 89 percent of the managers questioned saw insufficient enterprise independence (i.e., excessive ministerial control) as one of the key factors holding them back in their work.[92] A Cheliabinsk survey conducted in 1986 found that the majority of enterprise-ministry interactions were based on personal contacts rather than on objective economic evaluations.[93] A Ministry of Ferrous Metals economist observed that "The main problems with restructuring (perestroika) do not lie at the level of the brigade, or even the enterprise.

They must be resolved . . . at the level of our ministries and departments. . . . The experience of the 1965 reform testifies to this."[94] G. Popov returned to the attack in the pages of *Kommunist* in 1986, suggesting that the ministry branches should be stripped of 90 percent of their functions.[95]

It was less clear, however, who precisely would take over the functions which would be devolved from the ministries. Presumably, the bulk would flow into the hands of the enterprises. However, there is a danger here. Unless market forces are to be used to coordinate enterprise activities, there is a strong possibility that the "departmentalism" of 65 ministries will be replaced by the "sectionalism" of forty thousand enterprises. Some suggest boosting the role of local soviets.[96] This sort of proposal has been around since 1957, and there is little reason for believing that yet another attempt to boost the power of the soviets would be any more successful than previous ones. Other commentators suggest beefing up the coordinating powers of Gosplan, for example through the introduction of a stronger network of regional plenipotentiaries.[97] Some still recommend the old tactic of creating new territorial coordination agencies in response to particular problems (e.g., the creation of special regional interbranch associations to plan the production of consumer goods[98]).

Most of these proposals remain at the discussion stage. The superministry idea has come a step closer to realization, with the creation of a number of coordinating bureaus at USSR Council of Ministers level during 1986—covering engineering, fuel, and energy and social development—together with a special commission on foreign economic relations and a newly strengthened State Committee for Construction.[99] This approach seems to be patterned on the model of the giant Gosagroprom organization, introduced in 1985 to coordinate the agricultural and food industry sectors.

G. THE GORBACHEV REFORM PACKAGE

How, then, have these long-standing reform debates within the Soviet economic establishment influenced the shaping of the program of economic perestroika? It is difficult to come up with a decisive answer to this question, since perestroika has not taken the form of a clear, decisive package of reforms which take an unambiguous position on the various problems discussed above. Rather what we see is an ad hoc collection of policies driven more by short-run pressures than by a clear conception of the long-term structural reforms which the system requires.

At first the top leadership seemed to think that a renewed emphasis on economic acceleration (*uskorenie*) and discipline would suffice to turn the economy around, using the familiar Brezhnevite technique of large, centrally-managed campaigns. Examples would include the anti-alcohol campaign launched in May 1985, and the planting of a new network of externally-appointed quality control inspectors in each factory (*gospriemka*).[100]

By 1986 the emphasis shifted to the question of a more fundamental restructuring of the economic system (perestroika).[101] However, no clear, integrated reform program was articulated. (Aganbegyan's book *The Economic Challenge of Perestroika*[102] is worryingly vague on the specifics.) Policymakers have found themselves in what Gorbachev delicately referred to as a "pre-crisis" situation,[103] and were forced to respond to a number of immediate pressures: widespread consumer unrest; a 40 percent deterioration in Soviet terms of trade (because of falling oil prices); and a yawning budget deficit (amounting to 20 percent of the total budget).[104] Sifting through the broad but uneven flow of policy initiatives of the 1985–88 period, three general directions of reform can be discerned.

1. New Forms of Ownership

First, there has been a renewed emphasis on the role for new forms of ownership in providing greater incentives—leaseholding in agriculture, and private and cooperative activity in the services sector. By the end of 1988, 787,000 people were employed in private and cooperative cafes, boutiques, and repair shops, and Gorbachev was putting more and more pressure on agricultural officials to sign long leases with teams of would-be farmers.[105]

While these developments are noteworthy by the standards of the Brezhnev years, they remain below the level of the private sector in East Europe. They offer a quick and probably limited improvement in the supply of food and consumer services. Leaseholding is proceeding slowly due to resistance from farm managers, who remain under intense pressure from central authorities to meet strict procurement targets "down to the last cucumber."[106] Local officials continue to resort to tried and tested "formalistic" measures, pretending to respond to the leasing campaign while in fact maintaining traditional managerial control. (For example, a *Pravda* journalist found only two functioning lease teams in the Voronezh region, despite a report that fifteen hundred were in operation.[107])

One new—and worrying—development over the last two years has been the emergence of widespread public opposition to these innovations, on the grounds that they charge unfair prices and generate unfairly high incomes for their operators.[108] It is also widely believed that they serve as a front for black marketeers wishing to launder illegally acquired cash. It is unlikely that these innovations will penetrate the manufacturing sector—which has become the greatest brake on Soviet economic growth. The best that one can expect from the cooperative sector is that it may make life a little easier for consumers, and if allowed to spread on a more extensive basis to, say, house construction may help to soak up the stock of excess savings which has built up over the last decade.[109]

2. Opening the Economy to the West

A second issue which has moved to center stage has been that of opening up the Soviet economy to the West. This strategy did not receive much attention in the Soviet economic literature before 1986, and its most vocal advocates are to be found in the popular press rather than in the economic journals.[110] Two arguments are advanced in favor of such a strategy.

First, by introducing joint ventures with Western partners, and by moving towards ruble convertibility, it might be possible to overcome the cost and price imbalances which have built up in the centrally planned economy over sixty years. By turning to world market prices the planners would find guidance as to which sectors are profitable and which need to be wound down. Thus it offers an escape from the "chicken and egg" paradox which planners face in trying to reform the price structure of industrial goods. If they allow prices to float, firms enjoying monopoly positions will enjoy windfall profits. But if they don't let prices float, they will not know which firm's goods are in demand.

The second argument is that imports are vital in the short run to alleviate the dislocations which will occur even under a successful perestroika (firms retooling, workers moving to new jobs, and so forth). The purchase of $5 billion of consumer items announced in April 1989 sounds impressive, until one realizes that this works out at less than $20 per head. The decline in oil prices means that the USSR has run a deficit in its foreign trade account in three of the last four years, and thus has to borrow or dip into its gold and currency reserves to fund imports.[111]

It would be unwise to overestimate the scope for international integration to transform the Soviet economy, as the latter remains highly autarkic.[112] Although foreign trade as a proportion of net material product rose from 3 to 10 percent between 1965 and 1985, two-thirds of this trade is with the socialist bloc.[113] Soviet experience in the 1970s clearly showed how hard it is for the economy to profitably absorb large quantities of Western machinery. The strategy is also politically risky, since Western partners may start attaching conditions, or resort to embargoes if the international climate changes. The main problem restraining this strategy in the long term is the poor quality of Soviet manufactures (even according to official figures, only 14 percent reach world standards), the lack of a sophisticated marketing network and the sluggishness of response to changing Western consumer tastes.[114]

Nevertheless, this has been one of the few areas where perestroika has pressed steadily ahead. Since mid-1987 new regulations have attracted around fifty Western firms into joint ventures, while a complete overhaul of the foreign trade system began in January 1988, giving some one hundred Soviet firms the right to trade directly with Western partners.[115] It is too early to say whether these ventures will succeed in overcoming the problems surrounding them (inability to repatriate profits directly in hard currency, difficulty of finding reliable suppliers within the USSR, and so on).

3. Reforming the Planning Mechanism

The third area of reform, and by far the most important, is the question of a fundamental overhaul of the rules governing the operation of Soviet industrial enterprises. The central measure was the new law on the state enterprise of June 1987.[116] This was yet another attempt to replace crude central directives with autonomous decision-making by financially independent (cost accounting) enterprises. Ministries would stop issuing detailed plan targets, and enterprise budgets would be fixed for several years in advance. Supplies would no longer be centrally allocated, but would be purchased through a wholesale network. The center would gradually relinquish its control over price setting in favor of price agreements between freely contracting enterprises.

However, the 1987 law turned out to be a confused, contradictory measure which was a great disappointment to the reformist camp. Academic B. Kurashvili argued that "with the adoption of this law perestroika lost its first decisive battle, but pretends not to have noticed and takes it instead for victory."[117] P. Bunich concluded that "In its present form the law on state enterprise will continue to impede the reform."[118] The implementation decrees issued over the following months further diluted the thrust of the reform. Firms were still left with a package of five to twelve target indicators, all subject to arbitary manipulation by the supervising ministry. The planning methodology which ministries use has not changed—they continue to rely on *val* and crude cost-outlay pricing procedures *(zatratny metod)*.[119] A major survey of plant directors at the beginning of 1988 revealed that 80 percent did not perceive any slackening in the tautness of plan targets sent down from their ministries. Sixty-five percent considered the measures taken since 1986 inadequate for the avowed goal of "radical reform."[120]

What went wrong? Economic reform was dead on arrival for two reasons—the leadership's fear of consumer unrest, and design flaws in the reform itself.

First, let us consider the undeniable fact that the reform was introduced in very difficult circumstances, after a period of prolonged economic stagnation and increasing shortages of food and consumer goods (over at least a five-year period). This meant that Soviet consumers and workers were in no mood to accept any further assaults on their standard of living. This put Gorbachev under intense pressure to maintain existing production levels. This constraint was communicated from the political leadership to top ministry officials, who thus found themselves under contradictory pressures—to stop micromanaging the economy *and* to produce results! The clearest symbol of the view that perestroika can produce immediate improvements, and is *not* an IMF-style austerity program, are the repeated assurances that price subsidies on food and housing (which cost the state 103 billion rubles a year[121]) will not be cut without full compensation to consumers for the loss in real income. Thus Gorbachev told the nineteenth Party Conference in 1988 that "any change in retail prices must on no account cause a drop in the people's standard of living"; while even as late as December 1987 his chief economic adviser A. Aganbegyan was confidently asserting that "the first thing perestroika will bring will be an improvement in living standards."[122]

Thus firms were instructed to adhere to the targets previously assigned to them for the thirteenth Five-Year Plan. Ministries were to use a new system of production orders *(goszakazy)* to ensure that production did not slack off. This was supposed to ensure that planners were still able to secure the allocation of vital resources (e.g., for the defense sector) even once the decentralized economic mechanism was in place, However, as it turned out goszakazy expanded to fill the space available, and as of mid-1988 90 percent of industrial output was being allocated through goszakazy.[123]

Even in factories which introduced cost accounting early on, and which have been hailed as success stories, reports indicate that they find themselves hemmed in by arbitrary planning decisions. Investment allocations are cut without warning; supplies are rationed; and profits are clawed back through higher targets for the next year.[124] One commentator reported that "Many managers think there are no normatives that cannot be 'broken from above.' "[125] Firms operating on incentive experiments in 1987 turned in only a 2.5 percent productivity rise as against a 4.1 percent rise in other plants.[126] This paradoxical result is probably due to harsher rules being applied to the successful, experimental firms in each sector, rather than to poor performance by these innovators. Either way, it is hardly a very good advertisement for the new economic mechanism!

This leads us on to our second factor: the design flaws which seem to run through the very core of the perestroika program. The fact that price reform is supposed to go ahead without hurting consumers, and the fact that firms are supposed to restructure production while still meeting plan targets, suggest that the Gorbachev leadership was not implementing economic reform in conformity with a well thought-out plan, but were simply stumbling from one measure to another.

The leadership had drawn certain general principles from the economic debates of the previous decade—val is bad and khozraschet is good; directive planning is bad and normative planning is good; prices should play a larger role; and so forth. However, the leadership shied away from confronting hard choices. Leading economic adviser L. Abalkin argued in June 1988 that economists are unable to get their views through to the leadership because the apparatus presents the top leaders with policy proposals containing only one variant.[127] L. Lopatnikov explained shortly thereafter that three different teams had started to work on the 1979 reforms, but Gosplan fused their three plans together when drawing up the final proposal.[128] In practice, the only way in which the reform debate produced a consensus on what needed to be done was by means of fudging the difference between contradictory proposals, and maintaining a discreet silence over sensitive issues. Just as in the debates of the late Brezhnev era, tough decisions over the need for unemployment, redundancy and bankruptcy have been finessed. They may be referred to in an elliptical fashion by "daring" reform commentators, but have not found a place in the perestroika program.[129] Crucial issues such as the need to develop a functioning capital market are only now emerging—three years after the reforms got under way.[130] It is hard to come away from the various measures, actual and proposed, that make up the perestroika "program" with a convincing, coherent picture of what the postreform economy will look like.

The one theme which has given intellectual coherence to Gorbachev's economic program (inasmuch as it has any at all) is that of attacks on the ministries. From the beginning there has been a strong trend to blame the bureaucrats for the ills of the Soviet economy. As we showed in Section F, many eminent economists were indeed of the opinion that the branch structure of central planning was a key flaw in the Soviet economic system. However, since 1985 the debate has become politicized in a crude manner, with populist diatribes against the "guilty men" in the ministries. One of the most salient pieces of rhetoric of the perestroika era has been the picture of "eighteen million bureaucrats" strangling the Soviet economy.

By 1988 it had become clear that economic reform was stalled. Rather than raise the question of gaps and contradictions in the reform program itself, Gorbachev responded by attributing the failures to the trusty shibboleth of "bureaucratic resistance." By June 1988 14 percent of ministry officials had been fired, and according to reports at the end of the year as many as one in three had been dismissed.[131] However, it hardly makes sense to continue holding the ministries responsible for allocating supplies, meeting plan targets, restructuring industry and supervising the introduction of economic reform, while *cutting* the number of officials.[132] The result will not be less planning, just worse planning.

The image of eighteen million bureaucrats is, in any case, inaccurate. *Argumenty i fakty* provided its readers with a breakdown of the eighteen million, as follows (excluding the Ministry of Defense):[133]

Total Administrative Apparatus	17,700,000
of which	
in enterprises	15,800,000
in ministries	975,000
in trusts	164,000
in social organizations	347,000
in soviets	317,000

Thus it turns out that ministry officials per se are but a fraction of the eighteen million. Two additional qualifications can be made. These are figures for *all* staff, and include for example 4.2 million doormen and messengers. Second, two-thirds of the ministry personnel work in regional subunits, rather than in republic level headquarters. Given the size of the economy being administered, 400,000 national officials does not seem out of line by Western standards.

H. CONCLUSIONS

Thus we are painting a rather gloomy picture. While the Gorbachev leadership has gleaned from the reform debate of the late Brezhnev era a fairly clear picture of the ills facing the Soviet economy, they seem nowhere near coming up with a coherent reform package which will provide a solution.

The problems multiply still further if one starts to bring into the picture the political dimension to the problem. In order to defeat opposition to his reforms from party conservatives, Gorbachev had to turn to more and more radical political measures—glasnost', democratization, and constitutional reform. These political reforms magnified the opportunities for the population to express their discontent with economic privation, and made it more difficult for tough economic decisions over price reform, layoffs and the spread of cooperatives to be forced through. On top of this one has factors such as the revival of national unrest, all of which serve to distract the attention of the leadership from the thorny problem of economic reform.

Gorbachev and his advisers probably regard themselves above all as pragmatists. They boldly reject the dogmas of the Brezhnev period, and seek workable solutions to individual problems. However, as T. Remington has argued, "The pragmatist in an ideocratic polity ends up by becoming a utopian."[134]

NOTES

The author wishes to thank Anders Aslund and the discussants at the September 1987 APSA panel, Blair Ruble, and Paul Goble, for their comments on this paper.
1. For cogent examples of these approaches, see A. Nove, *The Economics of Feasible Socialism* (London: Allen and Unwin, 1983), and P. Hauslohner, "Gorbachev's Social Contract," *Soviet Economy* 3, no. 1 (1987): 54–89.
2. For an analysis of the career movements of Soviet scholars in the economics field in recent years, see A. Aslund, "Gorbachev's Economic Advisors," *Soviet Economy* 3, no. 3 (1987): 246–69.
3. The phrase comes from a speech by M. Suslov, "A High Calling and Responsibility," *Kommunist*, no. 16 (1981): 4–11, 9.

4. See reviews of these debates by V. Kuz'menko, "Social Knowledge," *Kommunist*, no. 11 (1984): 111–17, and by H. Dahm, "The Role of Economics in Soviet Political Ideology," *Economics and Politics in the USSR*, ed. H. Hohmann et al. (Boulder, Colo.: Westview Press, 1986): chap. 2.

5. Iu. Kachalovskii, "Indicators and their functions," *Ekonomika i organizatsiia promyshlennogo proizvodstva* [hereafter *EKO*], no. 2 (1985): 75–88.

6. In *Ekonomicheskaia gazeta*, no. 26 (1986): 3–8, 7.

7. D. Valovoi, "Indicators for socialist economic management," *Kommunist*, no. 15 (1984): 50–61, 51.

8. Letter from a reader in *Partiinaia zhizn'*, no. 11 (1981): 63.

9. Iu. Ivanov, "The efficiency of socialist industry," *Kommunist*, no. 14 (1983): 39–49, 43.

10. *Pravda*, Oct. 24, 1983, 2.

11. A. Voss, "Party organizations and perfecting the economic mechanism," *Partiinaia zhizn'*, no. 10 (1981): 30–37, 35.

12. *Voprosy ekonomiki*, no. 11 (1986): 23–32.

13. G. Popov, "On perfecting the central management of the economy," *Voprosy ekonomiki*, no. 5 (1985): 82–92, 92.

14. W. Brus, *The Economics and Politics of Socialism* (London: Routledge & Kegan Paul, 1973).

15. K. Ryavec, *The Implementation of Soviet Economic Reforms* (New York: Praeger, 1975).

16. *Voprosy istorii KPSS*, no. 10 (1981): 57.

17. On this theme, see Iu. Iarkin, "The system of economic stimulation," *Kommunist*, no. 4 (1977): 48–59; and A. M. Rumiantsev, *Sotsial'nye i ekonomicheskie problemy sovremennosti* (Contemporary social and economic problems) (Moscow: Nauka, 1977).

18. V. Medvedev, "Leninist principles of managing the economy," *Kommunist*, no. 5 (1980): 20–31, 25; V. Garbuzov, "Soviet finances as a factor in raising industrial efficiency," *Kommunist*, no. 16 (1979): 16–28, 18.

19. N. Fedorenko, "Instruments for optimizing plan decisions," *Kommunist*, no. 16 (1978): 31–42; see also L. Kantorovich et al., "The wider use of optimization methods in the economy," *Kommunist*, no. 9 (1986): 44–54.

20. I. Syroezhin, "A new way of managing the economy," *Kommunist*, no. 14 (1980): 35–44.

21. S. Starostin and G. Emdin, letter in *Kommunist*, no. 13 (1981) 115–21, 120.

22. A. G. Aganbegian, *Upravlenie sotsialisticheskimi predpriiatiiami* (Managing socialist enterprises) (Moscow: Ekonomika, 1979); reviewed by P. Bunich in *Kommunist*, no. 16 (1981): 114–16.

23. Starostin and Emdin, letter, 120.
24. For articles defending NNO as a useful indicator alongside other value and physical indicators, see Iu. Iakovets, "On measures and stimuli for improving industrial efficiency," *Kommunist*, no. 6 (1979): 74–85; and one by Gosplan economist I. Shilin, "The economic mechanism," *Kommunist*, no. 14 (1980): 23–34. For a general analysis, see P. Hanson, "Success indicators revisited: The July 1979 decree on planning and management," *Soviet Studies* 35, no. 1 (1983): 1–13.
25. O. Latsis, "A fresh look," *Kommunist*, no. 13 (1986): 32–41.
26. V. M. Smekhov, "The logic of planning," *EKO*, no. 10 (1984): 90–104.
27. T. Zaslavskaia, "Economics through the prism of sociology," *EKO*, no. 7 (1985) 3–22, 12.
28. See, for example, N. F. Fedorenko, "Planning and management: What should they be?" *EKO*, no. 12 (1984): 3–20.
29. A. Matlin, "The law of value and planned price formation," *Voprosy ekonomiki*, no. 11 (1985): 76–87.
30. Iu. Ivanov, "The efficiency of socialist industry," *Kommunist*, no. 14 (1983): 39–49, 44. (This article carried the disclaimer that it was published as a "discussion piece.")
31. Iu. Borozdin, "Planned price formation in the new system of economic management," *Kommunist*, no. 16 (1986): 26–37.
32. For example, the article by P. Bunich, "Self financing," *Kommunist*, no. 14 (1986): 30–41.
33. D. Palterovich, "The economics of the instruments of labor," *Kommunist*, no. 10 (1984): 53–64, 61.
34. *Ekonomicheskaia gazeta*, no. 51 (1984): 11–14, 13, special section on functional cost accounting.
35. *Ekonomicheskaia gazeta*, no. 27 (1986): 15.
36. For an example of handwringing over the excessive number of success criteria, see the article by E. Kapustin in *Ekonomicheskaia gazeta*, no. 4 (1980): 11.
37. Point made by G. Popov in "The development of branch management in industry," *Kommunist*, no. 18 (1982): 48–59, 58.
38. The phrase is a subheading in *Ekonomicheskaia gazeta*, no. 11 (1981): 4, for example; and the title of a book *Ekonomnaia ekonomika* (The economical economy) (Moscow: Pravda, 1982).
39. O. Latsis in letter, *Kommunist*, no. 9 (1985): 119.
40. A. Matlin, "On the problem of developing the theory and practice of price formation," *Kommunist*, no. 5 (1984): 36–47, 43.
41. I. Goverman, "Association cost-accounting in action," *Kommunist*, no. 3 (1978): 57–68, 67; V. Senchagov, "Perfecting the economic mechanism in conditions of the intensification of industry," *Voprosy ekonomiki*, no. 9 (1985): 25–36, 32.

42. V. P. Moskalenko, "Cost accounting incentives for high final results," *EKO*, no. 3 (1986): 99–118.
43. *Ekonomicheskaia gazeta*, no. 24 (1986): 7.
44. A. Abalkin concedes it is still a formality in his article "Main directions of CPSU economic policy," *Kommunist*, no. 5 (1986): 22–32, 31.
45. For example, V. Senchagov cites the alleged successes of Bulgaria, East Germany and Czechoslovakia in his 1985 article ("Perfecting the Economic Mechanism," 32).
46. Bunich, "Self Financing," 37.
47. V. Kulikov, "Commodity-money relations and the concept of acceleration," *Kommunist*, no. 12 (1986): 11–22, 19.
48. The most well known is the leaked "Novosibirsk report," reprinted in *Survey* 28, no. 1 (1984): 88–108. Recent articles by T. Zaslavskaia include "Economic behavior and economic development," *EKO*, no. 3 (1980): 15–33; "Economics through the prism of sociology," *EKO*, no. 7 (1985): 3–22; and "The creative activities of the masses: Social reserves for growth," *EKO*, no. 3 (1986): 3–25.
49. T. Zaslavskaia, "The human factor of economic development and social justice," *Kommunist*, no. 13 (1986): 61–73. Her analysis is not unique, of course: compare, for example, the article by S. Shatalin, "Social development and economic growth," *Kommunist*, no. 14 (1986): 59–70.
50. L. Gol'din, "Stimuli for innovation," *Kommunist*, no. 16 (1983): 47–58, 53, 50.
51. E. Iasin, "Public property, economic stimuli and cost accounting," *EKO*, no. 12 (1984): 77–95.
52. V. Mar'ianovskii, "Cooperative forms of economic management in socialism," *Voprosy ekonomiki*, no. 7 (1985): 47–57. For example, only 6 percent of Soviet housing is cooperative, compared to 30 to 65 percent in Eastern European countries (51).
53. *Izvestiia*, April 30, 1987, 6.
54. Mar'ianovskii, "Cooperative Forms," 52–53.
55. *Pravda*, July 6, 1985, 1.
56. For example, in *Ekonomicheskaia gazeta*, no. 50 (1980): 18, *obkom* secretaries from Penza and Kaluga wrote in replying to criticism that they had unfairly restricted private plot activity, and pledging to promote their utilization in the future. The CC CPSU decree approving private plots was discussed in *Ekonomicheskaia gazeta*, no. 25 (1981): 10.
57. "In the name of socialist justice: Three interviews about the struggle with unearned incomes," *Kommunist*, no. 15 (1986): 85–96, 92, A. M. Voropaev speaking.
58. *Ekonomicheskaia gazeta*, no. 23 (1986): 4–5.
59. *Izvestiia*, April 24, 1987, 3; April 25, 1987, 2; April 30, 1987, 6.

60. A. Aslund, *Private Enterprise in Eastern Europe* (New York: St. Martin's Press, 1984).

61. In Poland in 1986 the private sector (excluding agriculture) accounted for 4 percent of national income but 65 percent of consumer services —E. Bugaev, "A realistic evaluation of what has been achieved: An optimistic look into the future," *Kommunist*, no. 14 (1986): 93–105, 99.

62. As G. Schroeder puts it in her article title: "Gorbachev—'Radically' Implementing Brezhnev's Reforms," *Soviet Economy* 2, no. 4 (1986): 289–301.

63. P. Ignatovskii, "On a political approach to the economy," *Kommunist*, no. 12 (1983): 60–72, 63, 66.

64. N. Glushkov, "Planned price formation," *Kommunist*, no. 3 (1985): 38–48, 41.

65. A. Buzgalin, "Centralism in the planned economy: Limits and methods," *Planovoe khoziastvo*, no. 9 (1985): 70–77, 71.

66. V. Cherkovets in *Voprosy ekonomiki*, no. 11 ((986): 13–22, 21, 15.

67. O. Leonova and A. Kolganov, review of V. Kolesnikov, *Spravedlivost' sotsializma* (The justice of socialism) (Moscow: Sovetskaia rossiia, 1986), *Kommunist*, no. 14 (1986): 126.

68. V. Kozlov, "The human factor in economic development: Lessons of the 1930s," *Kommunist*, no. 2 (1985): 55–64.

69. *Kommunist*, no. 17 (1986) for letters on this subject (61–68) and a report of the Leningrad meeting (123–27).

70. L. Abalkin, "Theoretical questions of the economic mechanism," *Kommunist*, no. 14 (1983): 28–38. Ignatovskii was the editor of *Planovoe khoziaistvo* at the time, and Abalkin head of the political economy faculty at the CC CPSU's Academy of Social Sciences.

71. Ibid., 33.

72. Review article by E. Bugaev entitled "A strange position," *Kommunist*, no. 14 (1984): 119–26, 123, 124.

73. V. Trukhanovskii, letter in *Kommunist*, no. 17 (1984): 127.

74. G. Popov, "On improving central economic leadership," *Voprosy ekonomiki*, no. 5 (1985): 82–92, 82, 88.

75. P. Bunich, "Centralized management and the independence of production collectives," *Voprosy ekonomiki*, no. 9 (1985): 48–58, 52.

76. Ibid., 52. See also the article by O. Latsis, "F. E. Dzerzhinskii and the formation of a planned economy," *Kommunist*, no. 13 (1983): 112–20.

77. Speech by Iu. Andropov, "Always on duty," *Kommunist*, no. 13 (1983): 4–8, 5.

78. K. Chernenko speech to electors, *Ekonomicheskaia gazeta*, no. 11 (1984): 3–6.

79. For an overview of the 1986 debates, see A. Nove, " 'Radical Reform,' Problems and Prospects," *Soviet Studies* 39, no. 3 (1987): 452–68.

80. A. Aganbegian, "The general course of economic policy," *EKO*, no. 11, (1985): 3–31; idem, *The Economic Challenge of Perestroika* (Bloomington: Indiana University Press, 1988).

81. L. Abalkin, "The interaction of productive forces and relations of production," *Voprosy ekonomiki*, no. 6 (1985): 111–22, 14.

82. L. Abalkin, review article in *Kommunist*, no. 11 (1986): 124–28, 124.

83. G. Popov, "The development of branch administration of industry," *Kommunist*, no. 18 (1982): 48–59; and B. P. Kurashvili, "State management of the economy: perspectives for development," *Sovetskoe gosudarstvo i pravo*, no. 6 (1982): 38–48. For a discussion of this issue see R. Amann, 'The Political and Social Implications of Economic Reform in the Soviet Union," in *Economics and Politics in the USSR*, ed. H. Hohmann et al. (Boulder, Colo.: Westview Press, 1986), chap. 7.

84. *Pravda*, Dec. 19, 1980, 3.

85. D. Gvishiani, "Decisive reserves of management," *Kommunist*, no. 4 (1984): 37–47, 42.

86. K. Beliak, "Branch administration of industry," *Kommunist*, no. 8 (1983): 94–99, especially pp. 94, 95.

87. V. Iskonnikov and S. Krylov, "On the combination of branch and territorial principles of management," *Kommunist*, no. 4 (1984): 48–58, 49.

88. Ibid., 50.

89. A. Klautsen, "Product quality," *Kommunist*, no. 16 (1986): 38–49.

90. Ibid., 43.

91. Ibid., 45.

92. E. Kolosova, "Five questions to a director," *EKO*, no. 12 (1984): 72–75.

93. L. Vedernikov, "A strict, practical test" *Kommunist*, no. 8 (1986): 40–49, 45.

94. Yu. Solov'ev, "Intensification: Restructuring in progress, the search for new approaches," *Kommunist*, no. 11 (1986): 3–12, 9.

95. G. Popov, in a comment at a roundtable at the Novolipetsk steel plant - "At the basic unit of renewal," *Kommunist*, no. 12 (1986): 23–40, 30.

96. L. Zlomanov and V. Lyubovnyi, "The soviets and territorial reserves for acceleration," *Kommunist*, no. 8 (1986): 18–27.

97. M. Malakhov, letter to *Kommunist*, no. 13 (1986): 57.

98. A. Orlov and D. Rubval'ter, "Restructuring the production of consumer goods," *Voprosy ekonomiki*, no. 1 (1986): 44–54, 49–52.

99. On these developments, see "Roundtable on reform," *Soviet Economy* 3, no. 1 (1987): 40–53, 41.

100. For a critique of the alcohol campaign as a throwback to Brezhnev's 1972 alcohol campaign, see M. Miroshnichenko, "Vo chto obkhoditsya—trezvost," *Ogonek*, no. 39 (1988): 20–23. On *gospriemka*, which began on an experimental basis in late 1985, see V. F. Opryshko,

"Gosudarstvennaya priemka produktsii," *Sovetskoe gosudarstvo i pravo,* no. 6 (1988): 69–77; and A. Tenson, "State Acceptance Commissions," *Radio Liberty Research,* no. 114, March 24, 1987.

101. For an interesting summary of the phases of perestroika, see B. V. Rakitskii and G. Ya. Rakitskaia, "Razmyshlenniya o perestroike kak sotsial'noi revolyutsii," *EKO,* no. 5 (1988): 3–28.
102. A. Aganbegian, *The Economic Challenge of Perestoika* (Bloomington: Indiana University Press, 1988).
103. In a speech on June 25, 1987, in M. S. Gorbachev: *Izbrannye rechi i stat'i,* vol. 5 (Moscow: Politizdat, 1988), 159.
104. B. Keller, "Adviser's Soviet Deficit Figure is Triple Kremlin's," *New York Times,* January 26, 1989 A3. Finance Minister B. Gostev gave a lower figure (7.3 percent of the budget) in October 1988 (*Pravda,* October 28, 1988, 4), but the Abalkin estimate has not been disputed.
105. *Argumenty i fakty* [hereafter AIF], no. 37 (1988): 6. For Gorbachev on leasing, see for example his speeches of August 5, 1987 and August 15, 1988 (op. cit., 254, and *Pravda,* August 15, 1988).
106. N. Shmelev, "Novye trevogi," *Novyi mir,* no. 4 (1988): 160–75, 162.
107. *Moscow News,* no. 38, September 4, 1988, 10.
108. *AIF,* no. 20 (1988): 4, on popular opposition. An example of bureaucratic opposition would be the complete absence of cooperatives in four Ukrainian provinces—*Kommunist Ukrainy,* no. 7 (1988): 49.
109. *AIF,* no. 3 (1989): 2.
110. N. Shvelev, "Novye trevogi."
111. *New York Times,* March 30, 1989, D9. In 1988 the deficit stood at $2.6 billion. Their total Western indebtedness rose from $21.8 billion in 1984 to $38.2 billion in 1986—although no one is suggesting that they are a poor risk. (C. Gall, "Burden of Empire," *Wall Street Journal,* December 7, 1987.)
112. L. Abalkin, for example, regards the import of consumer goods as an unsatisfactory, one-shot solution—"For a program of economic development," *Moscow News,* no. 6 (1989): 12.
113. *SSSR v tsifrakh v 1987 g.,* (Moscow: Finansy i statistika, 1988).
114. *Moscow News,* no. 27 (1988): 5.
115. P. Hanson, "Restructuring of the Restructuring," *RLR,* no. 58, February 9, 1988; A Gurevich, "Joint Ventures with the West," *RLR,* no. 263, July 5, 1987, *AIF,* no. 28, (1988): 8.
116. Issued June 30, 1987. See the collection of decrees *O korennoi perestroike upravleniya ekonomikoi* (Moscow: Politizdat, 1988); and texts such as *Khozraschet, samookupaemost', samofinansirovanie* (Moscow: Politizdat, 1988); G. A. Egiazaryan, ed. *Radikal'naya reforma khozyaistvennogo upravleniya* (Moscow: Ekonomika, 1988); and D. Valovoi, *Ekonomika v chelovecheskom izmerenii* (Moscow: Politiz-

dat, 1988). Also useful are the commentaries by P. Hanson in *RLR* e.g., "The enterprise law and the reform process," *RLR*, no. 269, July 14, 1987.

117. B. Kurashvili, "A time of political decisions," *Moscow News*, no. 23, (1988): 13. He even goes so far as to talk of a situation of "dual power" between the political and administrative apparatuses.
118. P. Bunich, "How to overcome the deceleration of acceleration," *Moscow News* no. 14, (1988): 8.
119. D. Valovoi, "Piramida," *Pravda*, September 19, 1988, 2.
120. L. Sherbakova, "Anketa direktorov," *EKO*, no. 3 (1988): 59–75.
121. M. Bornstein, "Soviet Price Policy," *Soviet Economy* 3, no. 2 (1987): 96–114, 116.
122. Gorbachev cited in *Moscow News*, no. 28, (1988): 9; Aganbegyan in *RLR*, no. 486, December 2, 1987, 4.
123. From a speech by Yu. D. Masliukov, head of Gosplan, in *Pravda*, October 28, 1988, 2. Only a handful of powerful firms have been able to throw off ministry attempts to impose goszakay (e.g., Uralmash). V. Gurevich, "Laws versus state orders," *Moscow News*, no. 33 (1988): 8; *Pravda*, August 28, 1988, 2. A Council of Ministers meeting in May 1988 rejected any radical dismantling of the system of central planning, choosing instead just to try to reduce the proportion of industrial output governed by *goszakazy* (*Pravda*, May 31, 1988).
124. A. Ianski, "Supplies: An old whip hitting harder," *Moscow News*, no. 36 (1988): 10; A. Iyanski, "VAZ: Postoyannoe obnovlenie i khozraschet," *EKO*, no. 5 (1988): 54–60; "Uroki Belorusskogo eksperimenta," *EKO*, no. 5 (1988): 29–38.
125. N. A. Vasil'eva, 'Direktory—o samofinansirovanii', *EKO*, no. 7 (1988): 84–91.
126. N. I. Alekseev, "Radikal'naya perestroika khozyaistvennogo mekhanizma," *Sotsiologicheskie issledovaniya*, no. 3 (1988): 7–16, 8.
127. L. Abalkin, "Chto poseesh', to i pozhnesh'," (As ye sow shall ye reap), *AIF*, no. 26 (1988): 1–2.
128. L. Lopatnikov, "The power of choice," *Moscow News*, no. 29 (1988): 8. The three teams were from TsEMI (Central Mathematical Economics Institute), the Council of Ministers and the State Committee on Science and Technology.
129. For example, a first deputy chairman of Gosplan specifically ruled out bankruptcy as an instrument of economic restructuring at a press conference reported in *AIF*, no. 18 (1988): 2. For an example of writers who conjure up a picture of 20 million unemployed, see V. Kostakov and V. Rutgaizer, *Sovetskaya kul'tura*, January 8, 1987.
130. For example, Bunich "How to Overcome," refers to the discussion of changes in the credit system as "the no-reform reform."
131. *AIF*, no. 38 (1988): 7; *Pravda*, September 27, 1987, 2. End-of-year

reports come from interviews with journalists at *Pravda* and *AIF* conducted by the author in December 1988.

132. Thus for example the Minister of the Oil Refining and Chemical Industry argued that "It is urgently necessary to define the status and position of the branch ministries. The demands on them are increasing while their rights are being limited." (N. Lemaev, "Chistaya produktsiya," *Pravda*, September 22, 1988, 2.)

133. *AIF*, no. 38 (1988): 7.

134. T. F. Remington, *The Truth of Authority*, (Pittsburgh: University of Pittsburgh Press, 1988), 83.

4

EFFECTS OF FISCAL REFORM ON INTERPROVINCIAL VARIATIONS IN MEDICAL SERVICES IN CHINA, 1979–1984

James Tong

1. REDUCTION OF REGIONAL INEQUALITY IN HEALTH SERVICES

Since the founding of the People's Republic in 1949, improvements in the level of China's public health services have been considerable. The infant mortality rate dropped from around 200 per thousand in 1949 to less than 35 per thousand in 1981, while the overall death rate declined from 20 percent to 7.1 percent in the same period. Life expectancy reached 66.4 for males and 69.4 for females in 1981.[1] These improvements can be attributed to government efforts to expand public health services, which resulted in a sixfold increase in the number of medical professionals from 505,000 in 1949 to 3.33 million in 1984,[2] and multiplied hospital beds more than twenty-eight times, from 85,000 to 2.41 million in the same period.[3]

More remarkable is the consistent narrowing of regional differences in public health services. Before 1949, medical facilities were substantially unequal across provinces. In 1949, poverty-stricken Guangxi province had only six hospital beds per hundred thousand population, while industrialized Shanghai had forty beds for the same population.[4] Shanghai residents, then, had six to seven times the hospital beds per capita available in Guangxi. If we take similar figures for 1934, to reduce the confounding effects of the anti-Japanese War and the Civil War, regional variations in medical facilities were even more marked. In that year, Guizhou had only 1.5 hospital beds per hundred thousand, Guangxi had 8, while Shanghai had 105.[5] A Shanghai resident, then, enjoyed an advantage 22 times that of a Guangxi resident and 70 times that of a Guizhou resident in hospital bed availability in 1934.

These regional differences were dramatically reduced after 1949. In 1980, Shanghai had 427 hospital beds per hundred thousand, Guizhou had 148, while Guangxi had 136.[6] The highest to lowest ratio in per capita hospital bed availability has thus been reduced to less than 1 to 3 among the 29 provinces.

The reduction of regional disparities in social services was no doubt mandated by Maoist ideology, which was committed to the elimination of structural inequalities, notably those between the city and country, worker and peasant, and mental and physical labor. In his treatise "On the Ten Major Relationships" (1956), Mao deplored the "irrational situation" where 70 percent of China's industries were located in the coastal regions and only 30 percent in the interior, and he pledged to even out the skewed distribution.[7]

However, the commitment to regional equality faces an increasing challenge in the post-Mao era. The pragmatist program making economic production the party's dominant goal implies that the task of maintaining equality may be reduced to second place. Reforms to give local authoritiees greater autonomy in planning and fiscal management would presumably diminish central control of local services. Movement toward a market economy would accentuate the natural advantages of the industrialized coastal regions destined to become the immediate beneficiaries of deregulated prices and decontrolled commerce. Post-Mao reforms then, do not appear to bode well for regional equality in social services.

The Present Study

This chapter examines the impact of post-Mao fiscal reforms on regional inequality. It traces the interprovincial distribution of hospital beds and medical personnel from 1979 to 1984, to determine whether decentralization has begun to reverse the long trend toward equal medical services. As will be explained below, the structural ambiguity of the fiscal system from 1985 on precludes its inclusion in the analysis. Unless otherwise specified, data for hospital beds and medical personnel are taken from annual volumes of the *Zhongguo Tongji Nianjian* [China statistical yearbook],[8] while budgetary data are collected from budget reports published by most provinces. They generally refer to final account figures officially adopted by a plenary session of the Provincial People's Congress rather than the readjusted budget or preliminary figures.

Assessing the degree of equality is a complex task. Studies on regional equality in social services in Communist systems disagree not only on the magnitude of spatial disparities,[9] and their direction of temporal change,[10] but also the effects of socioeconomic development levels,[11] and the degree of government redistributive effort.[12] As Bahry and Nechemias suggested, these disagreements may result from alternative operational definitions of equality, data selection methods, statistical procedures, and interpretations.[13] The present chapter offers a different analytical perspective. Following the lead of Bahry and Nechemias, who argued that studies focusing on regional differences or short-term temporal changes may not capture movement toward equality, we will first compare service levels before and after the establishment of the Communist regime in China.[14] Reasoning that the problem should be examined from both ends of the policy process, we will analyze both service levels as well as redistributive mechanisms, in particular, the role of central planning and fiscal controls in reducing regional inequality. We will explore how the centralized and need-based planning and fiscal systems reduced interprovincial variations in medical service delivery in China after 1949. We will then consider the question whether post-Mao reforms in the planning and fiscal systems have led to increasing interprovincial variations in public health services.[15]

Before we turn to the research task at hand, let us first note several source constraints. First, although several general reference works on the public health, planning, and the budgetary systems have recently been published, two important sets of data are unavailable or incomplete. Most official documents on the planning and budgetary process and compilations on economic laws and regulations are still unavailable.[16] Provincial budgetary data and planning targets for Culture, Education, Science, and Health (CESH) are available only for seventeen provinces in 1981 and 1982, ten in 1979 and eleven in 1980. Further, even where data are available, expenditure on public health is still subsumed under the larger expenditure category of CESH.[17] Unlike the practice in the mid-1950s, national and provincial budgets published in recent years do not disaggregate this larger item into subcategories, and data on public health spending exist only in fragments. Direct measurement of the relationship between public health funding and policy outputs is thus problematic.

Second, since 1977, there have been complex changes in central-provincial budgetary relations, public health funding, and the economic management system.[18] For instance, from 1979 on, the central government has expanded its support for provincial hospitals to cover not only staff wages, but also to provide a 200-yuan subsidy per bed for equipment purchases and building repair.[19] In addition, changes external to the economic management system also affected the public health budget. A 68.6 percent increase in the fifteen-to-nineteen age cohort relative to those in the twenty-to-twenty-four bracket in 1982,[20] must have affected age-specific health care programs like birth planning, pediatrics, and maternity. It would thus be difficult to sort out the interactions in these changes and draw inferences concerning their effects on public health services.

Third, until recently, data on public health services, mainly hospital beds and medical professionals, have been available only on the provincial level. And these data have been incomplete: annual provincial data on mortality, morbidity, life expectancy, and infant mortality rates for the 1979–84 period are unavailable. Such a high level of aggregation and lack of data on the outcome of medical services no doubt raise serious inferential as well as statistical problems. It is hoped that the recent publication of the annual *Urban Statistical Yearbook*, which lists more than 500 tables of basic statistics of 295 public places in China, including those on public health, will prompt further studies that will enrich and supplement the present analysis.[21] With these caveats in mind, the results of this preliminary investigation should be regarded as tentative.

2. REDUCING REGIONAL INEQUALITY: THE MAOIST SYSTEM

The centralized planning and fiscal control system established by the Communist regime after 1949 was well geared to reduce regional inequality in social services. Through the planning system, goals for local public health services were set by the State Planning Commission and the Ministry of Public Health, which prescribed targets for and levels of local services. Through the fiscal management system, these goals in the local Public Health Plan were translated into expenditure items in the local budget. These two systems then, institutionalized central control over local services, thereby reducing regional disparities across provinces. An elaboration of these instruments of central control follows.

Planning Controls

In China's centralized system, local needs in various functional areas are not determined by the size of local revenue but are set by the national and local economic and social development plans.[22] These plans set targets for, and place restrictions on local programs.[23] To illustrate, the Public Health Plan at various levels of government stipulates the targets for the number of (1) hospital beds; (2) medical professionals; (3) doctors in the rural areas; (4) people treated for major types of morbidity and rates of the latter; and (5) people receiving vaccination. These targets are known as basic figures (*jiben shuzi*). Objective-need criteria form the basis of these planned targets. The planned target of hospital beds, for instance, is based on (a) population density and the distribution pattern; (b) existing level of medical facilities; (c) morbidity rates; and (d) hospitalization and bed turnover rates. More beds are allocated to localities with higher levels of population density, local or occupational diseases, and hospitalization rates; and lower levels of medical facilities and bed turnover rates. A similar functional, need-based criterion controls the number of medical professionals and doctors in rural areas, as well as the planned targets for major morbidity rates, number of patients, and people receiving vaccination.[24]

Controls on Staff Size and Expenditure

Once the basic figures for the local Public Health Plan are set, staffing levels will then be determined. Targets for staff are also incorporated in the socioeconomic plans and are known as prescriptions on staff size *(ding yuan)*. In public health, a rather uniform standard is prescribed by the Ministry of Public Health for basic units nationwide. For instance, the overall staff size in a general hospital[25] in the central, provincial, or county level is determined by the number of beds, with a bed-to-personnel ratio set between 1:1.3 to 1.7.[26] In addition, there are also precise rules governing the distribution of different types and ranks of personnel within the hospital staff.[27]

A related set of control figures *(ding e)* converts the basic figures to major items of expenditure. Generally set by the finance ministry and finance departments at various levels,[28] some of these control figures prescribe an average or minimum rate of utilization of facility (e.g., an occupancy rate of 330 days per year for a hospital bed), or equipment (20 years of usage per machine).[29] Some prescriptions are expressed in monetary terms *(kebi ding e)*, e.g., a monthly stipend of 19.5 yuan per medical student.[30] To control for regional cost differeentials, they are also expressed in physical unit *(shiwu-ding e,.* e.g., the number of square meters of linen per hospital bed). Others include single item prescriptions *(danxiang ding e)* which specify the amount of each expenditure item (e.g., total expenditure on hospital linen), and the aggregate prescription *(zonghe ding e)* which stipulates the total amount for all items of the same category (e.g., total expenditure on hospital material acquisitions).

In addition, unit spending norms *(kaizhi biaojun)*, set by both the central and local governments, place limits on items of expenditure. Salary for all administrative cadres, for instance, are classified into thirty grades. Cadres of the same grade receive the same salary, with cost of living adjustments for each of the eight salary regions.[31] To take special needs into account, there are adjustments and compensations for different regions and professions. For instance, epidemiologists engaged in research on lethal contagious diseases and carcinogenic substances receive a monthly health subsidy of 15 yuan.[32] There are similar nationwide unit-spending norms govern-

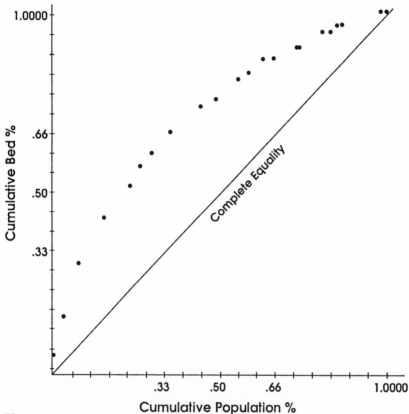

Fig. 4.1
Equality of Distribution of Hospital Beds in 1934.

ing the expenditure of each functional classification (mu) for (a) worker welfare; (b) medical student stipends; (c) business expenditure; (d) operating expenditure; and (e) miscellaneous items in the public health budget.[33]

Through these objective criteria to determine local need, the central government has reduced interregional variations in health care and maintained regional equality. To show the impact of these planning and fiscal control mechanisms graphically, Figs. 4.1 to 4.3 show the degree of equality of distribution of hospital beds in 1934, 1947, and 1980, based on data from official yearbooks.[34] These three figures align all provinces in descending order of per capita avail-

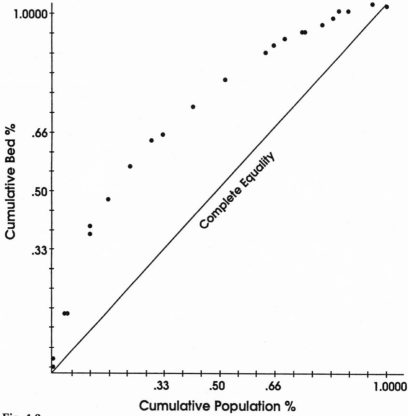

Fig. 4.2
Equality of Distribution of Hospital Beds in 1947.

ability of hospital beds, and then plot the cumulative hospital-bed-to-population ratios. If the per capita availability of hospital beds is completely equal across the provinces, the scatterplot would then approximate a straight, diagonal line. Conversely, the greater the curve, the more unequal would be the interprovincial distribution. As shown in these figures, interprovincial variation in per capita hospital bed availability was substantially greater in 1934 and 1947 than in 1980. In 1980, around 50 percent of the population shared 61 percent of the hospital beds. In 1934 and 1947, however, 50 percent of the population shared 75 percent of the hospital beds, while the remaining 25 percent of the beds were shared by the other half of the population.

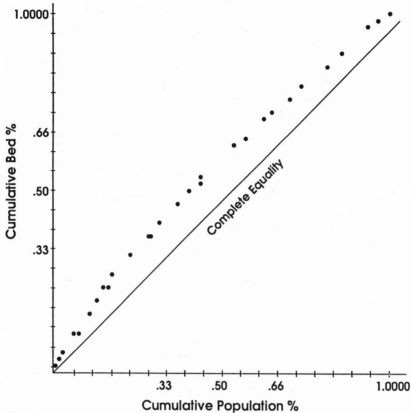

Fig. 4.3
Equality of Distribution of Hospital Beds in 1980.

3. INTERPROVINCIAL EQUALITY IN THE POST-MAO PERIOD

Decentralization in the post-Mao period has diminished central control of local administration. To summarize what has been detailed elsewhere,[35] post-Mao reforms conferred greater planning and budgetary authority on provincial authorities in four major areas. First, most provinces were to gain greater budgetary authority. Local expenditures would no longer be planned by central ministries, nor would the latter issue mandatory fiscal targets. In other words, the local public health budget would be worked out by local financial and public health authorities, based on the advisory but not mandatory targets issued by the central Financial and Public Health Ministries.[36] Second, as an incentive to increase revenue collection, most provinces were allowed to retain a share of revenue collected above the revenue-target. Third, the central government also dropped the practice of adjusting revenue sharing rates annually, a measure designed to minimize provincial revenue in excess of centrally prescribed expenditure targets. As a result, provinces which realized a favorable balance by collecting more revenue or saving on expenditures need not fear that their revenue sharing rates would be reduced in the subsequent year. Fourth, instead of having only one uniform system of central-provincial fiscal relations, five different budgetary arrangements between the central government and the provinces were introduced. These five systems vary in their degree of budgetary autonomy. These include: (a) the system in Guangdong and Fujian provinces; (b) the system in Jiangsu province; (c) the "majority province" system extant in fifteen provinces;[37] (d) the system operated in eight ethnic minority provinces in the southwest and northwest;[38] and (e) the "metropolitan system" in Beijing, Tianjin, and Shanghai. The coexistence of these five systems lasted from 1980 through 1982, when the experiment was terminated and all provinces, except Guangdong and Fujian, returned to a unitary fiscal arrangement with the central government in 1983. While a new fiscal regime was proclaimed in September 1984, to take effect in the following year, it was never implemented nationwide. The structural ambiguity of the fiscal management system since that time thus prevents us from extending our analysis after 1984.[39]

The five arrangements listed above are ordered according to decreasing levels of provincial budgetary autonomy. On the most autonomous end, the southern coastal provinces of Guangdong and Fujian remit a lump sum to the central government, the amount of which was fixed for five years. Other than this fixed amount, the provinces could retain almost all other locally collected revenue, and arrange the structure of their own spending. On the least autonomous end, the three metropoles Beijing, Tianjin, and Shanghai had to negotiate a revenue sharing rate with the central government which was to be adjusted every year. In between, Jiangsu, the eight ethnic minority provinces and fifteen majority provinces also had to negotiate revenue sharing rates with the central government. Unlike the three metropoles, however, their rates were fixed for five years.

These reforms in the planning and budgetary systems, then, conferred substantial autonomy to the provincial governments, and introduced greater differentiation in the expenditure structure among the twenty-nine provincial units. Given these new budgetary powers, and greater differences in the budgetary authority among the provinces, it stands to reason that the new planning and budgetary system would lead to greater interprovincial variations in public health services. To determine whether this indeed was the case, we have collected provincial data on (a) hospital beds; (b) medical professionals; and (c) revenues and expenditures from 1979 to 1984, and performed three sets of analyses.[40] First, on the national level, we have computed indexes of interprovincial variations in these medical service outputs, to examine whether such variations did indeed become wider. Second, we have analyzed the per capita rates of these service outputs for each of the five budgetary systems, to see whether there were significant changes in levels of health care among the five systems in this period. Third, we have correlated changes in revenue and expenditure in each budgetary system, with changes in the level of medical services, to find out whether increases in budgetary outlays were related to those in policy outputs.

Changes in National Distribution of Output Levels

Our first task is to compare the national distribution of health care outputs from 1979 to 1984, using the province as the level of aggregation. To show the overall direction and magnitude of change, we have computed Gini coefficients, which measure the size of the deviation of the observed distribution from a completely equal distribution, where, for example, 10 percent and 50 percent of the population share exactly 10 percent and 50 percent of hospital beds respectively.[41] The smaller Gini coefficients in 1984 over the 1979 figures in Table 4.1 suggest that the overall distribution in these medical services at the provincial level has not become more unequal; indeed, it has become more equal.

As an alternative measure of interprovincial variations in medical services, Table 4.2 presents maximum-to-minimum ratios of per

Table 4.1
Gini Coefficients for Distribution of per Capita Hospital Beds and Medical
Professionals of 29 Provinces in China, 1979–1984

	Year					
	1979	1980	1981	1982	1983	1984
Hospital Beds	.150	.148	.150	.146	.148	.152
Medical Profess.	.228	.230	.227	.224	.212	.241

Source: Computed from Zhongguo Tongji Nianjian, 1984, 1985, 1986, 1987.

capita hospital beds and medical professionals among the twenty-
nine provinces from 1979 to 1984. In 1979, for instance, the national
average was 2.22 hospital beds per thousand population. With 4.22
beds per thousand, Shanghai had the highest (maximum) per capita
bed availability, and that was 3.22 times Guangxi's figure of 1.31
beds per thousand population, the lowest (minimum) among the
twenty-nine provincial units. As shown in Table 4.2, the maximum
to minimum ratios among the twenty-nine provinces actually decreased, from 3.22 to 3.15 for hospital beds, and 4.62 to 4.06 for
medical professionals, during the years 1979 to 1984.

Inter-System Differences, 1979–82

The foregoing analyses only reflect overall changes. To see whether
there is any significant difference in the level of medical services

Table 4.2
Maximum/Minimum Ratios of Health Care Services per Thousand
Population Among 29 Provinces in China, 1979–84

	Year					
	1979	1980	1981	1982	1983	1984
Hospital Beds	3.22	3.15	3.16	3.13	3.16	3.15
Medical Profess.	4.62	4.49	4.41	4.27	4.09	4.06

Source: See Table 4.1.

Table 4.3
Hospital Beds per Thousand Population in 5 Fiscal Systems in China,
1979–84

Year	Metro. System	Minor. System	Major. System	Jiangsu	Guangdong Fujian	Grand Mean
1979	3.24	2.20	2.10	1.93	1.84	2.22
1980	3.32	2.23	2.13	1.95	1.81	2.25
1981	3.41	2.29	2.13	2.00	1.83	2.28
1982	3.46	2.26	2.14	1.97	1.84	2.29
1983	3.57	2.39	2.18	1.99	1.84	2.35
1984	3.73	2.41	2.22	2.03	1.86	2.40

among the five budgetary systems, Tables 4.3 and 4.4 present the
per capita rates for, and changes in, hospital beds and medical
professionals from 1979 to 1984. As the data reveal, there was no
trend toward greater variations among the five budgetary systems.
All the five systems register a steady increase in the level of per
capita hospital beds and medical professionals after 1978.[42] There is
no change in the rank order of the five systems in either measure
throughout the six years, with the metropolitan system taking the
lead, followed by the minority, majority, Jiangsu, and Guangdong-
Fujian in per capita beds, and the same order for medical professionals, except that the ranks of the last two systems are reversed. In
addition, the percentage increase in the 1984 over 1979 levels in
both hospital beds and medical professionals, as shown in Table
4.5, is not significantly different among the five systems at the 0.05
level of confidence.

Table 4.4
Medical Professionals per Thousand Population in 5 Fiscal Systems in
China, 1979–84

Year	Metro. System	Minor. System	Major. System	Guangdong Fujian	Jiangsu	Grand Mean
1979	7.45	3.06	2.76	2.53	2.47	3.30
1980	7.80	3.17	2.90	2.61	2.53	3.45
1981	8.13	3.45	3.10	2.70	2.70	3.67
1982	8.24	3.46	3.18	2.82	2.77	3.74
1983	8.41	3.57	3.26	2.89	2.80	3.84
1984	8.42	3.56	3.13	2.94	2.87	3.78

Table 4.5
Percentage Increase of per Capita Hospital Beds and Medical
Professionals, 1980–84

Output	Metro. System	Minor. System	Major. System	Jiangsu	Guangdong Fujian	Grand Mean
Hospital Beds	11.60	6.43	5.27	3.35	2.52	5.33
Medical Profess.	7.30	11.31	15.22	12.20	11.38	11.92

Correlation of Changes in Budget and Social Outputs

To see whether the increase in revenue and expenditure is related
to increase in the level of medical services, Table 4.6 correlates (1)
changes of the 1984 final provincial or municipal revenue (FR) over
1980, and (2) changes of the 1984 final provincial or municipal
expenditure (FE) over 1980, with changes in per capita hospital beds
and medical personnel in the same period.[43] Neither of the two sets
of correlation coefficients turns out to be significant at the 0.05 level
of confidence. Thus it appears that changes in the level of provincial
revenue and expenditure are not significantly related to changes in
the level of medical services from 1979 to 1984.

CONCLUSION

In the foregoing pages, we have attempted to show the redistributive
efforts of the Maoist regime in establishing regional equality in
medical services. Compared to the Nationalist regime before 1949,

Table 4.6
Correlation of Changes in Revenue and
Expenditure with Changes in per Capita Medical
Services, 1980–84

Fiscal Measure	Hospital Beds	Medical Professional
84FR/80FR	.3136	.2261
84FE/80FE	.1974	−0.0252

interprovincial inequality in medical services was drastically reduced under Mao. We have attributed these developments to planning and budgetary processes whereby physical and fiscal targets
that were need-based, centrally prescribed, and computed on per
capita ratios were instrumental in establishing regional equality.

In view of post-Mao reforms that granted provinces greater budgetary authority to arrange local spending, a share of budgetary
surpluses, and stable revenue-sharing rates fixed for several years,
we considered the question whether these reforms diminished the
capacity of the central government to maintain regional equality in
social services. Examining the degree of interprovincial variations
in the wake of these reforms, and correlating the level and changes
in medical services with provincial budgetary autonomy, we found
no consistent trend towards widening interprovincial disparities.
Indeed, the Gini coefficients suggest that interprovincial inequality
has narrowed, not widened, in recent years.

This surprising finding may be the result of regime commitment
to provide basic social needs, the existence of objective professional
criteria to determine such need in these areas, and an incremental
budgetary process that favors relatively even increases among these
spending categories.[44] It may also be due to the lag between budget
input and service output, where the results of both hospital construction and medical personnel training would show up only years
after the post-Mao reforms were initiated, and where we lack existing data. While these factors may have kept the provision of health
care at relatively equal levels across provinces, certain recent developments suggest that interprovincial disparities may widen. First,
the new strategy, adopted in early 1988, of developing an export-
oriented economy along the entire east coast of China would accel-
erate the growth of the coastal provinces,[45] and further enlarge the
existing gap in economic productivity and income between the industrial coast and rural interior.[46] Such a prospect has already dismayed deputies from the rural interior to the seventh National People's Congress convened in March, 1988.[47] Second, acceding to the
demands of the more affluent provinces and municipalities, the
central government has allowed the latter to retain a larger share of
locally-collected revenue to be used on local programs. Thus
Shanghai's share of local revenue was doubled from 12.1 percent in

1984 to 24 percent in 1985, while Tianjin's corresponding share was increased from 46 percent to 58 percent.[48] This trend of rich provinces demanding increasing shares of retained revenue will likely continue as more democratic elections would choose delegates to provincial congresses who are more responsive to local interests. Further structural reforms in central-provincial fiscal relations can thus be expected as the regime attempts to juggle the conflicting interests of the central government, the rich as well as the poor provinces.

NOTES

1. *Zhongguo Shehui Tongji Ziliao* (Social statistical data of China) (Beijing: Zhongguo Tongji Chubanshe, 1985), 25, 28, 223.
2. *Zhongguo Tongji Nianjian, 1985* (Statistical yearbook of China, 1985) (Beijing: Zhongguo Tongji Chubanshe, 1985), 610. Medical professionals include Western-style medical doctors *(xiyixi)*, physicians *(xiyishi)*, Chinese medicine doctors *(zhongyi)*, and nurses.
3. Ibid., 609. Hospital beds include those in hospitals in the county level or above, sanatoria, and other public health institutions.
4. *Zhonghua Nianjian, 1949* (China yearbook, 1949) (Nanjing: Zhonghua Nianjian Press, 1949).
5. *Neizheng Nianjian, 1935* (Civil affairs yearbook, 1935) (Shanghai: Commercial Press, 1936), G-273, 274.
6. These figures are taken from *Zhongguo Tongji Nianjian, 1981* and *Zhongguo Baike Nianjian, 1981* (Encyclopaedia yearbook of China) (Beijing: Zhongguo Da Baike Quanshu Chubanshe, 1981).
7. Mao Tse-tung, *Selected Works of Mao Tse-tung* (Peking: Foreign Language Press, 1977), vol. v, 286–87.
8. *Zhongguo Tongji Nianjian* (China statistical yearbook) (Beijing: Zhongguo Tongji Chubanshe), 1980–1986.
9. Schroeder found sizeable differences in urban housing and health care among Soviet republics, while Echols found social welfare among republics to be relatively equal; see Gertrude E. Schroeder, "Regional Living Standards," in *Economics of Soviet Regions*, ed. I. S. Koropeckyj and Gertrude E. Schroeder (New York: Praeger, 1981), 136–44; John Echols, "Politics, Budgets, and Regional Equality in Communist and Capitalist Systems," *Comparative Political Studies* 8, no. 3 (October 1975): 271–73.
10. Schroeder and Bielasiak found social welfare expenditure had become more equal over time but Zwick reported persistent regional inequalities in welfare spending; see Gertrude E. Schroeder, "Regional Differ-

ences in Incomes and Levels of Living in the USSR," in *The Soviet Economy in Regional Perspective*, ed. V. N. Bandera and Z. L. Melnyk (New York: Praeger, 1973), 183–86; Jack Bielasiak, "Policy Choices and Regional Equality Among the Soviet Republics," *American Political Science Review* 74, no. 2 (June 1980): 399; Peter Zwick, "Ethnoregional Socioeconomic Fragmentation and Soviet Budgetary Policy," *Soviet Studies* 31, no. 3 (July 1979): 395.

11. Clark found Communist nations failed to eradicate differences due to economic development, while Lampton found that government policy, and not only economic development, was also important in explaining the level of educational and health services; see Cal Clark, "Regional Inequality in Communist Nations: A Comparative Appraisal," in *Communism and the Politics of Inequalities*, ed. Daniel Nelsen (Lexington, Mass.: Lexington Books, 1983), 97; David M. Lampton, "The Roots of Interprovincial Inequalities in Education and Health Services in China," *American Political Science Review* 73, no. 2 (1979): 459.

12. Lardy found that fiscal decentralization in China had not undermined Beijing's redistributive effort in education and health spending but Donnithorne argued the opposite; Nicholas Lardy, "Centralization and Decentralization in China's Fiscal Management," *China Quarterly*, no. 61 (March 1975): 38–39; idem, "Centralization and Decentralization in China's Fiscal Management, Reply," *China Quarterly*, no. 66 (1976): 340–54; Audrey Donnithorne, "Comment," *China Quarterly*, no. 66 (June 1976): 328–40.

13. Donna Bahry and Carol Nechemias, "Half Full or Half Empty? The Debate Over Soviet Regional Equality," *Slavic Review* 40, no. 3 (Sept. 1981): 366–83.

14. Bahry and Nechemias, "Half Full," 38; Donna Bahry and Carol Nechemias, "Regional Development in the Soviet Union: The Debate over Inequality" (Paper presented at the Annual Meeting of the Southwestern Social Science Association, Fort Worth, Texas, March 1979).

15. For a debate on this question in an earlier period, see Lardy, "Centralization," and "Centralization, Reply"; Donnithorne, "Comment."

16. In the 1950s, there was no lack of basic official documents on the economic management system. These include the *Zhongyang Caizheng Fagui Huibian* (Collection of financial laws and regulations of the central government), which was published every year as an annual volume from 1955–59 by the Finance Publishing House in Beijing. Before 1955, the Financial and Economic Commission of the Government Administrative Council also published similar annual compilations under the *Zhongyang Caijing Zhengce Faling Huibian* (Collection of laws and regulations on financial and economic policies of the central government) in 1950, 1951, and 1952. Other supplementary series and single volumes include the *Shinian lai Caizheng Ziliao Huibian* (Collection

of materials on finance during the last ten years), published in 1959 by Finance Publishing House in Beijing; and *Xianxing Caizheng Fagui Huibian* (A collection of current laws and regulations) published by Beijing's Xinchao Shudian in 1951; as well as the *Zhongyang Shuiwu Faling Huiji* (Compendium of tax laws of the central government) published by the Main Tax Bureau of Beijing's Finance Publishing House in 1952.

17. The CESH budget, or the Wenjiao Weisheng Shiyefei includes three public health expenditure items: (1) health, consisting of budget outlays for medical institutions; (2) public medical care, consisting of medical care expenses for personnel under the medical care program; and (3) birth planning programs. In addition, it also includes expenditures of science, education, culture, publications, communications, sports, museums, earthquakes, and marine sciences. See *Guojia Yusuan* (The state budget) (Beijing: Zhongguo Caizheng Jingji Chubanshe, 1982), 138–39.

18. See Michel Oksenberg and James Tong, "The Evolution of Central-Provincial Fiscal Relations in China, 1950–1983: The Formal System" (unpublished, February, 1987).

19. See *Caizheng Yanjiu Ziliao* (Materials on financial studies), no. 17 (March 1, 1982): 5. For the three basic types of funding arrangements in public health institutions, see James Tong, "The Budgetary System and Expenditure on Health and Education in China" (unpublished, March 1984).

20. In the 1982 Population Census Ten Percent Sample, there are 7.431 million people in the twenty to twenty-four age bracket but 12.531 million in the fifteen to nineteen age cohort; see *Yijiubaer Nian Renkou Pucha Baifen Zhishi Chouxiang Ziliao* (Ten percent sample of the 1982 population census) (Beijing: Zhongguo Tongji Chubanshe, 1983), 264.

21. *Zhongguo Chengshi Tongji Nianjian, 1985* (Urban statistical yearbook of China, 1985) (Beijing: Zhongguo Tongji Xinxi Zixun Fuwu Zhongxin, 1985).

22. According to the Draft Regulations on Planning Work, issued by the State Planning Commission on March 28, 1963, Culture, Education, Science, and Health, together with more than thirty other categories, are included in the national economic plan; see *Jingji Jianshe de Falu Wenti* (Legal questions in economic construction) (Beijing: Zhongguo Shehui Kexue Chubanshe, 1982), 135–36; (hereafter *Falu Wenti*).

23. There are different kinds of plans, classified according to the temporal scope (long-term, middle-range, short-term); administrative level (national, local, basic unit); or functional systems (finance, personnel, CESH); see State Council, "Yiding Changqi Jihua de Tongji" (Notice on compiling long-term plans), (February 23, 1980); Central Committee, "Guojia Jihua Huiyuanhui Bianzhi Guomin Jingji Niandu Jihua Jianxing Banfa de Pishi" (State Planning Commission's statement of approval of

provisional methods on compiling the annual national economic plan), issued on August 5, 1953; cited in *Falu Wenti,* 136. In the Maoist period, these plans were made up of *mandatory targets (zhilingxing zhibiao)* which were proposed by the State Planning Commission, set by the State Council, ratified by the National People's Congress, and binding on local governments. The lower-level ministries and provinces could also issue mandatory targets supplementing but not contradicting the above set, and they had to be approved by the State Planning Commission and the State Council; see *Falu Wenti,* 139.

24. In addition to (a) population density, and (b) existing medical facilities; the number of medical professionals and rural doctors is also determined by (c) the number of medical institutions and hospital beds; and (d) the capacity of medical and nursing schools producing these personnel. The planned targets for *major morbidity rates, number of patients,* and *people receiving vaccination* is computed on the basis of (a) past occurrence and treatment rates; (b) level of medical facilities; and (c) magnitude of the epidemic outbreak; see Yang Qixian, Xiang Jingquan, and Ouyang Sheng, *Guomin Jingji Jihua Gailun* (a general discussion of the National economic plan) (Guiyang: Guizhou Renmin Chubanshe, 1982), 260–62.

25. The *Zonghe Yiyuan* is a multipurpose hospital, as opposed to more specialized hospitals like cancer or children's hospital.

26. General hospitals with under 300 beds have a bed-to-personnel ratio of 1:1.3 to 1.4; those with 300 to 400 beds have a ratio of 1:1.4 to 1.5; those with over 500 beds have a ratio of 1:1.6 to 1.7; see "Draft of Principles for Personnel Plan for General Hospitals" (December 2, 1978), in *Zhonghua Renmin Gongheguo Weisheng Fagui Huibian* (1978–1980) (Compendium of Public Health Statutes of the People's Republic of China, 1978–1980) (Beijing: Falu Chubanshe, 1982), 159 (hereafter *Weisheng Fagui Huibian*).

27. For instance, administrative cadres have to make up 8 to 10 percent, workers 18 to 22 percent, and professional staff make up the remainder. Among the latter, Western and Chinese medical doctors make up 25 percent; nurses 50 percent; pharmacists 8 percent; check-up personnel 4.6 percent; radiologists 4.4 percent; and 8 percent others, which include physiotherapists, anaesthiologists, dieticians, and so on. In the outpatient department, the number of doctors and nurses is determined by the work load, estimated on the basis of five cases per hour per doctor on average, depending on specialty; two nurses to a doctor; and one additional nurse on call for every eight nurses; see *Weisheng Fagui Huibian,* 162. For similar prescriptions restricting the size of staff of county Sanitation and Epidemic Prevention clinics, see James Tong, "Central Controls of Local Finance in China, 1949–1984" (unpublished, 1985).

28. *Xingzheng Shiye Caiwu* (Beijing: Zhongguo Caizheng Jingji Chubanshe, 1981), 112–13, 117–18.
29. *Guojia Yusuan* (Beijing: Zhongguo Caizheng Jingji Chubanshe, 1980), 148; *Xingzheng Shiye Caiwu,* 112, 116; *Weisheng Fagui Huibian,* 162.
30. Ministry of Education, Ministry of Finance, "Notice on the Book Allowance of Graduate Students" (Dec. 26, 1978), in *Caizheng Guizhang Xuanbian* (Selections of financial statutes) (Beijing: Zhongguo Caizheng Jingji Chubanshe, 1979), 353–54.
31. Since October 1979, the eleven salary regions have been reduced to eight. Cadres of the twentieth grade in Beijing receive a salary of 70 yuan, those in Shanghai 74, while their counterparts in Guangzhou 77.5; see *Xingzheng Shiye Caiwu,* 67.
32. Medical personnel in contact with radioactive substances; pathologists, custodians of cadavers, or those working in morgues receive a monthly subsidy of 10 to 12 yuan; see Ministry of Public Health, "Provisional Methods on Medical and Public Health Subsidies" (Dec. 30, 1979) and Ministry of Public Health, Ministry of Finance, Chief State Labor Bureau, "Notice on Implementing Public Health Subsidies for Epidemic Prevention Personnel" (October 31, 1979), both in *Weisheng Fagui Huibian 1978–1980,* 683–85. State employees in Shandong medical establishments receive a 12 yuan yearly heating subsidy, while those in colder Harbin get 30 yuan; see *Xingzheng Guizhang Xuanbian,* 69–70. Due to dietary restrictions, Muslim medical personnel who do not eat subsidized meals in canteens run by their own working units receive a special food allowance.
33. For a list of expenditure *mu* with unit spending norms in the CESH budget, see *Xingzheng Shiye Caiwu,* 119–20. Under "supplementary salary" for instance, are more than ten subclassifications like allowances for food staple, heating, travel, and health insurance.
34. These figures are taken from *Zhonghua Nianjian, 1948, Neizheng Nianjian, 1935,* G-273, 274; and *Zhongguo Tongji Nianjian, 1980.*
35. See Oksenberg and Tong, "Evolution of Central-Provisional Fiscal Relations."
36. Beginning in 1982, and on an experimental basis, these plans are mainly made up of three sets of targets—mandatory, directive, and forecast targets. *Mandatory targets (zhilingxing zhibiao)* are prescribed by the highest level of the central government. *Directive targets (zhidaoxing zhibiao)* are issued by the Planning Commissions and functional departments of various levels. While not binding, they are more than for reference only. If basic units depart from these targets, they have to inform the agencies that issue these targets. In contrast, *forecast targets (yucexing zhibiao),* used mainly in long-term plans, or items in annual plans that have greater elasticity in demand or supply, are for reference only. In the Public Health Plan, per capita hospital beds, medical doc-

tors, total work force and wage bill in units under state management are mandatory targets. Natural population increase rate is a directive target. See *Falu Wenti*, 140–43; Yang, Xiang and Ouyang, *Guomin*, 420–26.

37. These fifteen are Hebei, Shanxi, Liaoning, Jilin, Heilongjiang, Zhejiang, Anhui, Jiangxi, Shandong, Henan, Hubei, Hunan, Sichuan, Shaanxi, and Gansu. See *Yijiu Balingnian Caizheng Guizhang Zhidu Xuanbian* (Selections of 1980 financial statutes) (Beijing: Zhongguo Caizheng Jingji Chubanshe, 1982), 37.

38. These eight are Inner Mongolia, Xinjiang, Xizhang, Ningxia, Guangxi, Yunnan, Qinghai, and Guizhou; see *Guojian Yusuan* (1982), 53.

39. The main novelty in the new fiscal regime was the reclassification of various types of taxes as central and local government income. The reclassification effort was not completed in 1985 and 1986 due to delays in the reform to change enterprise ownership, which affected the recipient status of some taxes. Due to these complications, 1985 and 1986 were declared to be a period of transition between two fiscal regimes. For the new fiscal regime, see Xiang Jingquan and Guo Daimo, "Yijiu Bawu Nian Caizheng Guanli Tizhi Gaige" (Reforms in the fiscal management structure in 1985); *Yijiu Baliu Zhongguo Jingji Nianjian* (China statistical yearbook, 1986) (Beijing: Jingji Guanli Chubanshe, 1986), 4-11-13; State Council of the People's Republic of China, "Guanyu Shixing 'Huafen Shuizhong, Heding Shouzhi, Fenji Baogan' Caizheng Guanli Tizhi de Guiding" (Regulations on implementing the fiscal management structure of "dividing tax categories, determining revenues and expenditures, and contracting to each level") *Caizheng*, no. 5 (May 1985): 10–12.

40. The sources of these data on hospital beds and medical professionals are *Zhongguo Tongji Nianjian*, 1981–1984; *Zhongguo Baike Nianjian*, 1980–1984. Hospital beds include those from county hospitals and above. Medical professionals refer to doctors, nurses, and technical staff, and excludes nontechnical staff. Data on provincial revenue and expenditure are collected from published budgets and fiscal accounts from provincial newspapers.

41. The Gini Coefficient or concentration ratio measures the proportion of the total area under the diagonal that lies in the area between the diagonal and the Lorenz curve. Its computation formula is:

$$G = \left(\frac{1}{N^2} \sum_i \sum_j |x_i - x_j| \right) \Big/ \bar{x}$$

where X_i is the cumulative percentage distribution of the given variable (hospital beds); X_j the cumulative percentage distribution of the standardizing variable (population); and n is the number of class intervals (population deciles).

42. The exception is a drop in Guangdong, Fujian, and Jiangsu for per capita hospital beds in 1980.

43. For changes in fiscal accounts of 1984 over 1979, we have data from only four provinces, which is insufficient for statistical analysis. The present set of analysis includes budgetary data from seventeen provincial units—Beijing, Tianjin, Shanxi, Henan, Shandong, Shaanxi, Liaoning, Jiangsu, Zhejiang, Fujian, Sichuan, Hubei, Guangxi, Yunnan, Gansu, Qinghai, Ningxia, and Xinjiang.

44. For a description of the elaborate set of planning and budgetary controls regulating public health service outputs, see James Tong, "Interprovincial Variations in Health Care Services in the People's Republic of China, 1979–1982" (Paper delivered at the 1987 Annual Meeting of the Association of Asian Studies, Boston, April 10–12, 1987).

45. The new development strategy calls for opening up the coastal provinces for foreign trade on a massive scale. The Pearl and Yangzi River deltas, the southern Fujian triangle, and the Shandong and Liaodong peninsulas would be given greater autonomy to import raw materials, export goods, and retain foreign exchange earnings to build an export-oriented, labor and technology intensive economy. See Zhao Ziyang's speech in *Beijing Review*, February 8–14, 1988, 14–19; and Li Peng's "Report on the Work of Government to the Seventh National People's Congress," in *Beijing Review*, April 25–May 1, 1988: 35–37.

46. In the sixth Five-Year Plan (1981–1985), the difference between the ten provinces and municipalities in eastern China and the eleven provincial units in western China has widened considerably in size of urban population, value of industrial and agricultural output, per capita consumption and per capita rural income; see *Wen Hui Bao* (Hong Kong), November 13, 1987.

47. Han Baocheng, "Shanghai Takes on a New Look," April 25–May 1, 1988, 21.

48. Han Baocheng, "Importance Attached to Coastal Development," *Beijing Review*, February 29–March 6, 1988, 15; *China Urban Statistics, 1985* (London: Longmans, 1985), 680, 681, 688, 689; *China Urban Statistics, 1986* (London: Longmans, 1986), 472, 473, 476, 477.

5

THE CHINESE SPECIAL ECONOMIC ZONES, LABOR, AND WOMEN

Jean C. Robinson and Kristen Parris

The Chinese economic reforms represent the search for a new basis of political legitimacy for the Chinese Communist Party (CCP). Under the leadership of Deng Xiaoping, the party has recognized the need to meet long-suppressed popular demands for personal wealth, consumer goods, and increased individual autonomy as part of a new social contract. The reforms therefore address citizen interest while still securing party control. The reforms in theory attempt to change relations between producer and consumer, center and periphery, and state and society, thus making more efficient the structure of domination.

In this chapter, we will focus on the implications of the reforms for one constituent group in China—young women. The relationship between women and the reforms in general is sharpened in the specific context of women and employment in the Special Economic Zones (SEZs) of China. We understand the SEZs as microcosms of reform, as well as a Chinese model of export-oriented industrialization (EOI). By examining the employment of women in the SEZs, we uncover not only the ways in which women benefit from the reforms, but also the ways in which international and domestic pressures combine to disadvantage women. What we find here is that the requirements of the international market call for a search for comparative advantage. Because wages are protected in China, the regime has sought alternative ways to capitalize on whatever advantage they can isolate. The promotion of small light industry employing women funded by foreign investors has been one answer. In this context, international pressure combines with domestic pressures that stipulate strict sex roles, with the result that a new ideology on the appropriate division of labor has developed.

We will argue that the economic reforms have benefitted some women, but at the cost of reinforcing traditional roles for women and hindering economic success in the SEZs. Thus Chinese socialism produces contradictory effects: it uses women to serve the economic and political needs of the state while "protecting" women and thus limiting their opportunities.[1] It promotes economic reform to serve the political needs of the state while protecting workers and thus limiting national economic success. Our argument rests on a tripartite, implicitly comparative, analysis: the characteristics of the SEZs, in comparison to export-processing zones internationally and in the context of ideological demands on socialist modernization; the character and problems of labor in the zones, in comparison with the domestic Chinese economy, in the context of an ideological concern about exploitation by capital; and finally the character of women's labor participation in the zones, in comparison with employed women in the domestic Chinese economy and in other export processing zones, and in the context of ideological concerns about sexual equality.

MODERNIZATION, INDUSTRIALIZATION, AND SPECIAL ECONOMIC ZONES

In recent decades, there has been a resurgence of interest in less-developed countries in using exports to fund economic growth and to spur technological development. This reemergence of interest in export-oriented industrialization has coincided with the failure of import substitution strategies to secure economic growth in less developed countries. The interest in export-oriented growth has occurred simultaneously with the desire of foreign investors to develop bases in less-developed countries which offer lower labor costs than the developed nations.

Host nations pursue EOI in hopes that a highly-skilled labor force, technology transfers, stable employment patterns, and a multidimensional economy will result. Yet most countries which have engaged in export-oriented development have not realized these goals. The general trend has been that reliance on foreign-funded manufacturing has not raised the skills of workers nor the stability of employment for individual workers. What has stabilized has been the characteristics of the new EOI labor force: young, female, "unskilled" (an attribute to which we shall return).[2] Reliance on EOI has also resulted in the institutionalization of an old form of export commerce and manufacturing—the export processing zone—which has created a multidimensional but sharply divided economy.

Export processing zones (EPZs) are modern adaptations of the free trade zone systems which were widespread in the colonized world in the eighteenth and ninteenth centuries. However EPZs are unlike their predecessors in that they need not be sited near ports, nor do they necessarily confer special status on foreigners. They do provide a package of investment incentives that will encourage foreign and domestic entrepreneurs.[3] The export processing zones offer investors beneficial tax rates, a minimum of governmental intervention and a docile and inexpensive labor force. Host nations expect to receive capital for reinvestment, access to technology, job training, and new skills for workers, and military and development aid. Investors, for their part, expect special economic incentives, a tractable and exploitable workforce, and profit. The relation between foreign investor and host nation is theoretically one of exchange. In practice that exchange value is often unequal. As Lim points out, the heavy dependence on foreign capital, technology, skills and markets means that the profits from EPZs are mostly remitted overseas.[4]

The most common industries sited in EPZs are heavily concentrated in traditional labor-intensive production, especially textile and garments, but also include more technologically advanced manufacturing in electronic components, consumer goods, and even some capital-intensive products such as synthetic fibers, machines, and consumer durables. The work, regardless of the product, is repetitive, monotonous, and long, usually requiring few technical skills. Training and higher wages are dependent upon seniority but few workers benefit since the conditions and hazards of work mean that only a small number of workers accumulate seniority. For instance, in the Mazan zone of South Korea, "80 percent [of female employees] are between the ages of fourteen and twenty-four. Few are still employed . . . by the time they are thirty."[5] Work in the zones tends to be exhausting; again in South Korea, most workers receive one half-day off per week and work in three alternating shifts.[6] Job insecurity is exacerbated by the failure of companies to give new skills to workers. These skills will translate into demands for higher pay and since the only rationale for exporting production to the EPZs is economic advantage, it makes little sense from the investors' perspective to train workers for more technologically sophisticated jobs. Such action would only lead to an eventual move of the production to yet another zone in an area that boasts even cheaper labor. Indeed, recent history in Asia and Latin America testifies to the mobility of export-oriented production.[7] Now that workers in Hong Kong, Taiwan, and Korea are demanding higher pay, better benefits, and in some cases, unions and labor protection, companies have moved to new sites in Malaysia, the Philippines, Sri Lanka, and China.

EPZs are unusual in that they are characterized by almost universal employment of women. While researchers commonly note this fact in passing, little or no attention has been paid to the significance of women's employment except in feminist studies.[8] Yet, given the much lower proportion of females compared to males employed in the primary and secondary sectors in most economies, the predominance of females in the free trade zones suggests the emergence of a new relationship between gendered labor and industrialization.

This is a condition that is structured by the existing political economy of gender in most societies. Women are employed because they are cheaper than male workers and because it is assumed that women are less volatile and easier to control. Finally employers often assume that women are more productive (presumably because they are afraid of making trouble) and that they have greater manual dexterity, or as Elson and Pearson put it, "nimble fingers."[9] Interestingly, the dexterity of young women workers is not assumed to be a skill; it is something innate. This distinction enables employers, both local and foreign, to call their workers unskilled (and pay them less) despite the fact that many are highly skilled in the manual tasks like sewing, cutting, and weaving that are critical to work not only in the "traditional" garment industry, but also in the "high-tech" electronics industries.[10]

The predominance of women with EPZs is not serendipitous. It is functional to the purpose of the zones as sites for the production of profit. The employment of women ensures that labor will be inexpensive; it also fits well with cultural assumptions that women only need to engage in formal labor for a short time until they are married and work in their husbands' family enterprises. In societies undergoing the transition from primarily agricultural to industrial production, the mechanization of farming has led to a decreased need for labor in the countryside. Combined with a presumption that men should operate farming machinery, this leaves a significant group of young women to be employed elsewhere. The types of manufacturing pursued in most EPZs require skills that are quite similar to the domestic skills of these same young women. Here economy and culture feed off each other. EPZs intensify the already existing structure of gender. They also make that structure more contradictory because they expand the employment and earning opportunities for women and create a female-dominated work force. But these opportunities are based on and conditioned by women's acceptance of their subordinate position.

Special Economic Zones and Labor

With the initiation of its Open Door policies, China has itself become interested in export-oriented growth. Deng Xiaoping has gone so far as to say that he wants China to be a trade center more important than Japan by the end of the century.[11] Yet thus far, the Chinese economy remains dominated by an import substitution strategy. Furthermore, China faces a significant problem in its effort to develop an export orientation since it has neither the technology nor the financial resources to build upon its supply of cheap labor and raw materials. As a socialist country, China is at a special disadvantage because it cannot easily justify the exploitation of workers, especially in service to the interests of an international capitalist market.

Nevertheless, in December 1979, after seeking the advice of the United Nations Industrial Development Organization which had promulgated general regulations on the operation of free trade or export zones in 1969, the PRC designated four areas in the southern provinces of Guangdong and Fujian as Special Economic Zones.

Formal approval of Shenzhen and Zhuhai, both in Guangdong, was passed in August 1980. Shantou, also in Guangdong, and Xiamen in Fujian were approved in October 1980.

In setting up the SEZs Chinese officials went abroad to study the experience of other Asian EPZs. Indeed, the Chinese Zones were initially conceived of as Special *Export* Zones, but were later renamed as the understanding of their functions developed. Many of the concessions to foreign businesses in the SEZs look very much like those made by other Asian nations, including exemptions from certain customs duties, reduced taxes, and tax holidays.

One important difference between China's SEZs and export zones is that they are meant to be more comprehensive. The SEZs are administratively local governments as well as managing organs for special economic organizations.[12] Further, the SEZs were meant to develop not only export industries but also agriculture, commerce, tourism, and real estate. Another characteristic that sets China's zones apart is the fact that they were being built almost entirely from scratch. Foreign investors have been expected not only to engage in processing, packaging and manufacturing, but also in the building of infrastructure, in urban development, airports, harbors, and housing. The decision to locate zones in underdeveloped areas, in what were once parts of rural communes, was based in large part on the history of these areas and their geopolitical significance.

The SEZs have been defined as locales in which controls are "relaxed as compared with inland China for the purposes of promoting economic cooperation . . . with foreign businessmen, Overseas Chinese, as well as Hong Kong and Macau compatriots."[13] Not only are the major zones located on the coast but they are close to or bordering Hong Kong, Macau, and Taiwan. Shenzhen, at 328km², the largest of the SEZs, shares a border with the New Territories of Hong Kong. Zhuhai originally 6.8 square kilometers but not expanded to 15.16 square kilometers is adjacent to Macau. Shantou initially only 1.6 square kilometers but enlarged to include two separate areas totaling approximately 52 square kilometers, is just 200 miles from Hong Kong and Xiamen (Amoy) originally 2.5 square kilometers but now encompassing the whole 123.5 square kilometers city proper (Xiamen island) is located north of Shantou in

Fujian province across the strait from Taiwan. Key economic statistics for the four major zones are presented in Table 5.1.

Culturally, geographically, and politically, there exist intimate ties between China's southern and southeastern zones and the capitalist enclaves off-shore. A large number of overseas Chinese (*huaqiao*) have roots in the coastal areas; they speak the local dialect and have long-standing and well-developed connections to relatives and villages. This prior relation motivates them to invest in the PRC, a move strongly encouraged by the Beijing leadership. The need for space has also motivated Hong Kong and Macan investors. With exorbitant land costs and overcrowding on the islands, the Chinese zones seem almost natural sites of expansion. This is particularly true of Shenzhen, where there is a blurring of the boundary between Shenzhen proper and the Hong Kong New Territories. Finally, the CCP, from its earliest incarnation, has been guided by nationalism. It has consistently planned to reintegrate Hong Kong, Macan, and Taiwan back into the Chinese nation. Many reformers in Beijing hope that the successful operation of the SEZs will demonstrate the real possibility of incorporating these areas under Deng's principle of "one country, two systems." All of these factors operating over the past decade have made the economies of Hong Kong, Macan, and Guangdong increasingly interdependent.

The location of the SEZs on the coast, far from the industrial centers of the country, ensures not only easy access to Hong Kong, but greater potential for isolating the impact of foreign ideas. Of course, this also means that the potential for effective technology transfer may be limited. This characteristic has been countered now by the expansion of the special zone status to fourteen coastal cities and three delta areas. Some inland cities are also gaining certain privileges in dealing with foreign enterprises. The rapid expansion of the various zones has led one observer to suggest that the entire country seems to be "special."[14]

In December 1981, Xu Dixin, president of the Chinese Academy of Social Sciences (CASS), enumerated the SEZs' functions: (1) to act as bridges for introducing foreign capital, advanced technology and equipment and classrooms for training personnel; (2) to develop the national economy through competition; (3) to absorb foreign

Table 5.1

Key Economic Statistics for the Four SEZs, 1985 *

	Units	Total		Shenzhen	
		City & Counties	City Proper	City & Counties	City Proper
Population	10 Thous	873.11	161.48	43.52	19.14
numbers of workers & staff[1]	10 Thous	141.14	76.86	22.66	19.31
Gross industrial output value[2]	RMB 100 Million	96.96	62.25	27.58	23.56
Gross industrial output value[3]	RMB 100 Million	86.18	61.41	27.04	23.55
Light industry	RMB 100	65.47	45.86	22.15	19.37
Heavy industry	Million	20.71	15.55	4.89	4.18
Use of foreign capital: No. of agreements and contracts newly signed		701		322	
of which: Direct investment by foreign business		630		282	
Utilized foreign capital of which:	U.S. $10 Thous	52,671		32,925	
Direct investment by foreign business	U.S. $10 Thous	32,044		17,989	

[1] From *Statistical Yearbook of China—1986*
[2] Including industry at and below village level
[3] Excluding industry at and below village level
* *Statistical Yearbook of China—1986* (Beijing: State Statistical Bureau, 1986)

exchange and to transfer capital and technology to other regions; (4) to serve as "experimental units" in economic; and (5) to employ young people waiting for jobs.[15]

Since the beginning, however, the policy has experienced problems and controversy. In 1982 the SEZs were in crisis as a result of smuggling and black market activities. In 1984 they were being touted as highly successful reform models. A year later, conservative Hu Qiaomu was suggesting that they were little better than the

Zhuhai		Shantou		Xiamen	
City & Counties	City Proper	City & Counties	City Proper	City & Counties	City Proper
39.52	14.44	789.51	74.64	100.56	53.26
9.62	4.77	84.39	30.42	24.47	22.36
6.10	3.89	41.43	13.89	21.85	20.91
5.94	3.80	31.80	13.36	21.40	20.70
5.21	3.35	23.52	9.09	14.59	14.05
0.73	0.45	8.28	4.27	6.81	6.65
168		106		105	
137		106		105	
9,104		3,314		7,328	
5,263		1,464		7,328	

treaty port concessions imposed on China by the Western nations in the nineteenth century,[16] and in June of 1985, Deng, himself the primary proponent of the policy, was questioning the efficacy of the zones.[17] In 1986 the SEZs seem to have been reaffirmed and by the summer of 1987 Deng Xiaoping called the decision to establish the zones "a good one" and one that "has proved successful,"[18] although the economic success of the zones remains in doubt.

China's own past experience with treaty ports as well as the problem of dependence and worker exploitation in many EPZs has sometimes made the Chinese party leadership and other advocates of the EPZs defensive about the potential impact of foreign investment on China's independence and its development as a socialist country. Xu Dixin has addressed this issue by stating that the SEZs are "not based on 'unequal treaties', but on the basis of China's state sovereignty." They are special *economic* zones, not "special political zones." It is argued that the SEZs represent only a "minor change in state economic policy" and that they "are not in basic conflict with China's socialist economic system.[19] As Chan, Chen and Chin have argued, the SEZ policy has in fact evolved from a "minor change" in policy to an entirely new policy necessitating new ideological interpretations.[20]

China is in an anomalous position among countries with EPZs because it has a bureaucratically administered economy and a socialist ideology. The planned economy in China is unlike the domestic economies that surround EPZs of other nations. Centrally set wage and labor policies, and the highly bureaucratized nature of economic relations in China generally are all inimical to the requirements of EPZs for a mobile labor force with flexible wages. Thus China has encountered problems as it has attempted to implement the EPZ model. The extent to which the needs of the foreign investor should be accommodated and the effect that these concessions will, and should, be allowed to have on the domestic economy are part of an ongoing debate among the Chinese leadership at central and local levels.

The CCP has claimed to have eliminated exploitation of the workers as one of the achievements of the socialist revolution. Since the initiation of the SEZs and the economic reforms, exploitation has again become an issue as private entrepreneurs seek to make a profit.[21] The advocates of the SEZs have three options. They can ignore the contradiction between the theory of no exploitation and the emerging practice of labor utilization; they can formulate a new ideological interpretation of exploitation; or they can recognize current conditions as synonymous with or similar to the exploitation of labor by capital and attempt to protect the workers. The Chinese leaders advocating SEZs have pursued the latter two options by reformulating ideology to meet the new situation and by taking some steps to protect the workers (at least in comparison to workers in other EPZs).

Although still in the process of development and revision, the broad contours of the CCP's ideological reformulation have already taken shape. Admitting that, strictly speaking, the foreign enterprises constitute "a kind of capitalist economy," advocates of the zones have labeled it state capitalism and have cited Lenin as the starting point for this new interpretation. "Lenin clearly said, 'State capitalism is capitalism which we shall be able to restrict, the limits of which we shall be able to fix.' This provides us with a theoretical explanation of the nature of the enterprises financed in the special zones." [22] Since 1983, Deng Xiaoping and other reformers have attempted to extend this basic and temporary justification by introducing the idea of a "Socialism with Chinese Characteristics." [23] This is an effort to build a broad legitimation of the SEZs, the open door policies and the domestic reforms. More specifically, the advocates of the zones have conceded and sought to explain the existence of exploitation in the SEZs. "There is exploitation of surplus value in the form of profits earned by foreign investors . . . which is in contradiction with China's socialist system. However, in the long term, the exploitation of surplus value in the Special Zones is a 'buying-out' policy." [24] This is rationalized by analogy to the policy of buying out the "national bourgeoisie," a policy adopted in the 1950s. Under the current "buying out" policy, China cooperates with foreign and overseas Chinese investors in order to benefit China's modernization drive, and by implication all Chinese workers. [25]

The regime's recognition of the problem of exploitation is reflected in the debate over appropriate wage and labor policies. Part of this debate questions the nature of industrial development to be pursued in the zones. Some leaders have favored attempts to attract more capital-intensive projects in an effort to gain greater potential for technology transfer and skip the stage of reliance on labor-intensive industry. [26] China realistically has trouble attracting such industry because of a lack of skilled labor and managers. In addition such industry means fewer jobs for Chinese workers. [27] Other leaders have recognized the importance of China's comparative advantage in labor-intensive goods and light manufactures. Labor-intensive export industries may have less sophisticated technology that will not add significantly to the diversification of Chinese industry. But they require cheap and abundant labor—one of China's riches.[28] While China is interested in high technology, many are aware that transfers of technology are limited by objective conditions, including what China is willing and able to pay and what they are able to absorb and usefully integrate. Labor-intensive industries thus are the most important. For example, in Shenzhen, the textile industry, including processing and subcontracting, and the electronic assembly industry, both of which are highly labor-intensive, together accounted for approximately 70 percent of output value in 1986.[29]

Along with the debate over labor-intensive or capital-intensive industrial development have come arguments over whether wages should be higher or lower, relative to both domestic and other EPZ rates. If they are higher, it is more difficult to attract foreign investment since China doesn't seem to have any other comparative advantage to offer. Furthermore, high wages exacerbate domestic inequality. If wages are low, the exploitation problem is exacerbated. Although recently there has been a "smashing of the iron rice bowl" and a greater acceptance of income disparities, the party leadership remains concerned with the development of inequalities that arise from large income gaps.

The state has taken steps ostensibly to protect workers through wage and labor laws. A series of guidelines and regulations have been promulgated since 1980, when the first "Regulations on Special Economic Zones in Guangdong" were issued.[30] The original law was vague and primarily established that employees of foreign-run enterprises would work under a contract signed by the enterprise and individual workers. The contracts cover wages, welfare and insurance subsidies, and other conditions of employment, and allowed for the testing and dismissal of workers. In 1982, Guandong promulgated a set of revised regulations in an effort to fill in the details. As in the early regulations, the enterprise management has the right to test workers before employment and to dismiss them. In addition, all dismissals are now to be reported first to the SEZ municipal labor bureau. This has allowed the municipal government to exert pressure on companies. Though there have been some layoffs, dismissals remain rare occurrences. When they do occur, the new regulations specify that dismissed workers are entitled to a

Table 5.2
Average Monthly Wages in Shenzhen

1978	1979	1980	1982	1983	1984	1985*
47	66	87	96	113	175	197

(*Beijing Review*, no. 1 [January 1985]: 37).
*Chung-Tong Whu, "China's Special Economic Zones: Five Years After an Introduction," *Asian Journal of Public Administration* 7 (December 2, 1985), 127–43.

month's wages. We should note here that there are separate *national* regulations for joint-venture enterprises outside the Guangdong zones. The national regulations are similar to, although not identical to, the provincial regulations in the employment provisions.

From the first, no minimum wage was specified but officials insisted they be set at 50 percent of the current Hong Kong rate.[31] This established a high wage policy for the SEZs. The 1982 regulations state that "the terms of remuneration shall be negotiated" suggesting greater flexibility for the investor. Enterprises may incorporate any variety of wages and bonuses, including a basic wage, a floating wage tied to individual performance and enterprise profit (or loss), bonuses based on merit, an hourly rate or piece rate. Workers receive 70 percent of a total compensation package. Five percent is paid to the enterprise welfare fund and 25 percent "is for use as social labor insurance and various forms of subsidy the state provides for workers and staff." A 5 to 15 percent annual raise is specified "in accordance with proficiency of workers and staff." In spite of the apparent flexibility in the new regulations wages have remained high. Wages in Shenzhen were reported in 1984 to average about 45 percent of those in Hong Kong.

Average monthly wages cited in Table 5.2 are those wages paid directly to workers. The average wage for 1985 was twice the income of workers in Guangdong's state-owned enterprises outside the zone and 120 percent of the income of state sector employees in the nation.[32] (See Table 5.2.)

There has been a significant problem with inflation in Shenzhen, but generally wages seem to have kept pace, or out-paced inflation, especially in foreign-run enterprises. The estimated monthly cost of living increased to 53.8 yuan by 1983, up 60 percent from 1978.[33]

Table 5.3
Inflation in Retail Prices in Shenzhen

	1979	1980	1981	1982	1983	1984
% increase over previous year	+17.1	13.7	6.8	7.8	2.1	5.2
% increase over 1978	+17.1	33.1	42.0	43.3	46.3	53.9

(*Shenzhen Jingji Tequ Nianjian [Shenzhen Economic Yearbook]* [Hong Kong: Xianggang Jingji Dabao She, 1985], 552).

(See Table 5.3.) Thus, zone wages remain relatively high compared to domestic rates and low compared to Hong Kong. Productivity is also higher than the national average by 40 to 50 percent, but it is only 60 percent of the Hong Kong average.[34] Observers have argued that the low productivity and high wage undermines the comparative advantage the zones offer. Indeed, some entrepreneurs have turned to areas outside the zones, especially the Pearl River Delta zone surrounding Shenzhen, in order to pay lower wages and rectify the imbalance. In 1987, there were reports of wages at less than 150 yuan a month or about 1/10 of the comparable Hong Kong figure in the Pearl River Delta.[35] It should be noted that this wage is still higher than the average industrial wage nationally.

In addition to the protection of higher wages afforded the workers in the SEZs, the regulations specify that workers employed must be above the age of sixteen; that the SEZ enterprise is to operate on a six-day work week with an eight-hour day and overtime to be paid accordingly; and that the SEZ enterprise must abide by the Chinese government's regulations on women workers and give special consideration to "the protection of their health."

The Chinese government also requires welfare and labor insurance in zones. Such welfare and insurance benefits include maternity leave and transportation subsidies. Funds are also collected for a housing subsidy. The Fujian-Hitachi Joint Venture, for instance, provides a special welfare package including a subsidized lunch, mothers' nursing facilities as well as clothing and food for children, free spare-time education, a workers' club for recreation, and priority employment to the sons and daughters of current employees.[36]

A final source of potential protection comes from trade unions. Outside the zones, the umbrella organization of the All-Chinese Federation of Trade Unions (ACFTU) has served the state rather than autonomous worker interests. Whenever individual trade unions have tried to protect the workers against the state, they have been unsuccessful and subject to severe criticism. In the zones, the role of unions is equally ambivalent. Ninety-two percent of foreign enterprises in Shenzhen have unions: 78.3 percent in Zhuhai; 57.2 percent in Shantou and 63 percent in Xiamen.[37] At times, the aim of these unions seems to be to protect workers, and at other times, to protect the interests of the enterprise. Unions have been used to discipline and train workers who were "slack and indifferent in their work" at the Sino-Hong Kong printing and dyeing factory. Yet in a toy factory in Shekou which endangered workers' health by requiring four to six hours of overtime per day, the trade union intervened and negotiated that overtime should not exceed two hours a day, four times per week.[38] Both of these examples have been used by the state to demonstrate the good work of the trade unions; to us, this suggests the ambivalent attitude of the state toward the exploitation of workers in the zones.

WOMEN, ECONOMIC REFORM, AND THE SEZS

Women in general have become particularly important sources of support for the regime's open-door policies and domestic reforms.[39] The significance of women to the reforms goes beyond a mere material relationship. As in orthodox Marxism, so too in Chinese socialism, the status and condition of women is an ideological issue. Any material benefits accruing to women from the reforms provide a measure of legitimacy to socialist claims for sexual equality.

The government of the PRC has expressed concern about the economic and political inequality of women and occasionally tried to address the problems. The regime's solutions generally have been to focus on legal reforms and attitudinal changes. The Chinese Constitution elaborates a policy of equal pay for equal work, equal rights within and without marriage, and protection of the special needs and interests of women. Yet the focus of policy action, except for irregular periods during the Great Leap Forward and the Cultural

Revolution, has been on changing attitudes of both men and women so that they are valued equally.[40]

The concern over women's economic inequality has been expressed materially by giving women titles to land in the land reforms of the early 1950s, providing training for women in industrial and agricultural skills in the later decades, and encouraging women to seek scientific and technological knowledge in the 80s so that women too can contribute to and benefit from the economic reforms. In other words, government policy has sought to engage women in productive labor so that women can free themselves from the tyranny of "patriarchal" control and simultaneously contribute to the cause of building Chinese socialism.

Fifty-one million Chinese women are in the urban workforce, accounting for 82 percent of all urban women between the ages of sixteen and fifty-four.[41] Women find employment primarily in agriculture, the light industries, handicrafts, and the service sector.[42] These sectors pay the lowest wages. Because these jobs are often in collective or private enterprises,[43] rather than state-owned enterprises, they provide fewer benefits and lower status to employees. For women, this often results in continued dependence on husbands or fathers to gain access to the extra resources men have by virtue of employment in state-owned enterprises and heavy industrial factories. Women who do seek to obtain jobs in the traditionally higher-paying and higher-status state-owned factories frequently find that they must score higher than men on factory exams in order to obtain a job.[44] They may face further discrimination because they will be perceived as causing trouble and costing more money: state factories are obliged to provide maternity leave, prenatal and postnatal care, infant feeding breaks, nurseries, and alternative tasks for women when they are menstruating, pregnant, or breastfeeding. All of this acts as a disincentive for factory managers to hire women initially or to promote them once hired.[45] At the same time that these policies protect women in their roles as primary caregivers, and thus make it easier for them to have jobs outside the home, the policies do not attempt to alter the structure of the family or the roles of men and women in the family. In fact, the labor policies reinforce the societal norm that women's roles as mothers and homemakers is primary. This continues to disadvantage women—

because it limits both the jobs women are willing and able to take and the enterprises that are willing to hire them.

The economic reforms move away from the Stalinist model of development by giving new legitimacy to light industry, collective industry and private enterprise. In the process, they create new opportunities for women. But they do not address or resolve the fundamental contradictions that women face. The reforms both respond to and exacerbate China's long-term economic imbalance. By 1980 the leadership was confronting unprecedented budget deficits, shrinking revenues, rising inflation and a growing labor force as a result of the maturing baby-boom generation. These factors contributed to a new group known as "those waiting for work." Young women, because of cultural values and discrimination, tend more often to be unemployed. Statistics from 1986 show that 61.5 percent of youths waiting for jobs were women[46] although this probably understates actual joblessness. While waiting for jobs in the formal sector, unemployed youth have set up restaurants, nurseries, and small service shops;[47] others have found work in temporary collective factories. Although some of these private enterprise projects have netted young entrepreneurs handsome dividends, workers in such small enterprises have little job security and few formal benefits. Nevertheless, the potential for material gain, the greater work flexibility and autonomy from state intervention is appealing to many young men and women. But men continue to have more options, both in job and educational opportunities.[48]

This is not the official understanding of the effects of the economic reforms on women. Rather, the Chinese leadership sees the reform policies as an enhancement of women's liberation. Decollectivization of agriculture, for instance, has led to a diversification of the rural economy, providing new opportunities for women in sideline production and commerce and freeing other young women for work in new local industries. In both urban and rural areas, the reforms have led to increased opportunities of employment for women, such that their status and wealth have improved.[49] The strategies pursued by the state in terms of emphasizing production for export and light industry and handicraft production as part of the Open Door policies have created new income-earning options for women.

Similarly the increasing presence of modern technology is seen as a source of liberation for women. In production, technological innovations decrease the importance of physical strength and thus theoretically should open new occupations for women. In the home, technology can lead to a lessening of the burden of household chores, which in turn is expected to increase the amount of spare-time for women's education and training. The wider application of technology to domestic labor includes not only the production of consumer durables such as washing machines and refrigerators, but also prepared foods, better cleansers, and so on.[50] (We should note that, once basic modern utilities were introduced, technological applications to household labor in the West did not necessarily lead to diminished worktime in the home; instead standards of cleanliness, styles of food preparation, and clothing expectations became more complex and required more time.)[51]

The economic reforms are understood by the regime to be both advantageous and problematic for women's roles in the family. On the one hand, the greater income-generating possibilities for women increases their valorization within the family. It is argued that "feudal ideas and customs involving women's total material reliance on their husbands and the treatment of women as chattel who can be bought, sold and beaten at the pleasure of their husbands have been shaken to their roots." Thus *Renmin Ribao* enthuses that in one village in Guangdong, "about 10 men who used to beat their wives frequently treat them with the utmost respect due to the wives' great money-earning ability."[52]

On the other hand, the effect of the reforms is perceived as exacerbating, in some sense, the "double burden" of work and home. Women's federation officials have introduced a new twist, arguing that family size is decreasing, as young people set up independent housekeeping, and that "as family size is reduced, the total number of families increases. The larger the number of families, the more the housework,"[53] and women's housework burden is thus made heavier!

In addition, the government has recognized women's lower educational level and the absolutely greater number of illiterates who are women. They assume that educational opportunities for women will be improved as the reforms are institutionalized. But the immediate impact, as they recognize, is that some girls, especially in rural areas, are taken out of schools to participate in money-earning activities.[54]

At one level, the reforms are presented as beneficial to women as producers and consumers. At another level, official discussion of the reform's impact on women is that the new policies have enabled the feminization (nuxinghua) of Chinese women. Magazines now promote the use of cosmetics,[55] fashionable clothing, and hairstyles, and most significantly, "appropriate" behavior for women. Thus women are supposed to be hard-working, but at the same time, they "cannot do without some femininity."[56] The stereotypes of women as feminine carry over into the accepted understanding of the appropriate and therefore rational sexual division of labor. The argument is made that the reforms allow women to "participate in work more suited to their abilities, and physiological and psychological characteristics." This is presented as a thoroughly rational way of organizing production, one which will ensure greater productivity. In Dongguan City, in the Pearl River Delta open area, women who work in textiles, toys, embroidery, and other processing industries are praised for "their cleverness, deftness, patience and meticulousness —all female characteristics—enabling them to surpass men in production."[57]

Work in the Special Economic Zones offers an apparently exhilarating counterpoint to serving up Laoshan Cola on a hot city street or braiding straw into baskets in one's home village. SEZs are rumored to be the places where even women workers can get rich, where they can experience the heady freedom of living away from home in an almost Western environment, and where they have the easiest access to modern clothes, music, makeup, and leisure activities. The Women's Federation further argues that the zones give women a chance to show their talents and develop their skills.[58]

Statistics on the number of women employed in the zones are scattered and incomplete, suggesting that Chinese analysts share with most foreign researchers of EPZs a sex-blind approach. Yet the data we do have supports the view that the employment of women is central to the development and working of the zones. Light industries which rely predominantly on female labor outside the zones are the primary industries within the SEZs.[59] All SEZs have enterprises that focus on the types of production that are deemed to be women's work. Textiles, garment manufacturing, silk and pearl embroidery work, small electronics, leather goods, toys, and plastic have consistently been the industries in which women typically found employment in both the domestic market and zones. These are also the areas in which China has a potential comparative advantage in the international market. So too, in many factories of the Special Economic Zones, women comprise up to 80 and 90 percent of workers. There seems to be little variation across the zones in this respect. For instance, women comprise 80 percent of the workforce of Zhuhai's electronic, textile, garment, and food industries.[60] In Dongguan city in the Pearl River Economic Zone, 1,592 processing factories employ 82,000 women out of a total of 91,000 workers. For all processing industries in Dongguan City, women are 80 to 90 percent of the workforce.[61]

The predominance of women in the export factories, however, differs little from the numbers of women in EPZs internationally. Furthermore, as in other countries, women's work in the zones reinforces both traditional skills for women and the traditional division of labor. In spite of the assertion that Chinese women can "develop talents" through labor in the SEZs, there is little opportunity to gain new skills. Women are being urged to "continue learning on the job", but they remain structurally in a disadvantaged position to acquire new skills, because of their family responsibilities and their ghettoization in "women's work."

As we have shown, a distinguishing characteristic of the SEZs, compared to other export-processing zones, is their high wage policy. Women employed in the SEZs have the opportunity to earn more than women doing the same work outside the zones. China's reportage literature often focuses on life in the SEZs. One selection, "SEZ Spring," reports that girls and old ladies who once worked in the fields now earn 450 yuan per month working in assembly plants in Shenzhen.[62] In that year (1984) the average annual income for agricultural workers was 355 yuan. In the Pearl River Delta Zone where labor costs are lower, young women still earn a good income. "A 16- 17-year-old girl can earn more than 100 yuan per month, sometimes over 200 to 300 yuan per month, 1 or 2 months after beginning work in the factory."[63] Former peasant women from Guangxi and Fujian earn 250 yuan per month in a luggage factory owned and run by a Hong Kong businessman. Compare these wages to the average annual income of 397 for agriculture and 1,176 yuan in industry.[64]

The wages women earn have contradictory implications for their position in Chinese society. Higher wages and factory experience are often assumed to lead to more modern values and greater independence. Thus, increasing attention is directed to the ability of married women to earn more than their husbands and therefore effectively to counterbalance male dominance in the family.[65] A survey in Shenzhen suggests that the "social position, economic position, family and marriage position, and self-awareness [of women] after participation in labor, have all been raised." Still there is a recognition that discrimination *(zhongnan qingnu)* continues in recruitment and mobilization of workers, distribution of housing and other areas.[66] While comparisons of wages for men and women are not available for China and officials claim that women are paid equally for "equal work," there is some evidence that in the SEZs, at least, wages for women are lower than those of men regardless of the kind of work performed. In a Hong Kong-run toy factory in Shekou district in Shenzhen, for example, newly recruited men were paid a basic wage of 100 yuan while women were paid only 80 yuan a month.[67]

At the same time that SEZs are places for the inculcation of modern values, they are also a place where traditional discrimination continues and high wages reinforce traditional customs. The potential for earning more money is appealing to both single women and their families, for in this new age of socialist materialism, marriage customs seem to require dowries and bride price, although these are both actively opposed by the government. Especially for women whose families have little to offer male suitors (and their families), employment in a SEZ factory may mean the difference between finding a "good" husband and just settling for someone. The combination of high wages and availability of imported consumer goods is critical here. In other words, such employment fulfills the emerging needs of families in contemporary China while catering to the hopes of the young.[68]

In most EPZs, very young women are hired for short-term grueling labor. These are unprotected women with few other employ-ment options.[69] In China, the state has established legal restrictions on age of first employment as well as provisions protecting women's health and safety. Scattered data suggest that the average age of workers in SEZs and open cities is young; for instance, in Weihai textile mills, it is twenty-one; in the Fujian-Hitachi plant, the aver-age age of newly recruited workers is twenty.[70] The available evi-dence suggests that women's work in SEZs is short-term. Their contracts are for specific time periods, e.g., two to twelve years. Their household registration (hukou) remains in their home town and they are expected to return when the contract is fulfilled. Job insecurity, especially when compared to the domestic Chinese case, is a concern for many workers in the zones. While dismissals have been rare in the four original zones, it remains a threat. Further, it is apparently more common in the Delta zones. The potential for dis-missal, lay off, or unrenewed contracts makes working in the zones much more of a risk for workers in the zones then than in the domestic economy.[71] Still, Chinese women in the zones do not seem to suffer from the low wages, long hours, forced overtime, and job insecurity of many women in EPZ factories, where the most com-mon alternatives to such employment may be prostitution or porno-graphic modelling.[72] Interestingly, there is some evidence of in-creased prostitution since the Open Door, especially in Guangdong province (which has three SEZs and the Pearl River Economic Zone).[73] But SEZs have not existed long enough to know what will be the fate of women when they return to their native villages or simply when they cease work in the zones.

It seems clear that compared to the situation of women working in EPZs internationally, women in China's SEZs are in an advanta-geous position. We have observed the continuation of traditional sex roles within the zones; this is a replication of what occurs in the domestic economy. Women's work and family roles under the eco-nomic reforms represent continuity with the past, albeit with the legitimizing force of a new ideology of "femininity." Chinese women do not suffer the "super-exploitation" that is common throughout export processing zones. Indeed in other zones, it is these very conditions that are fundamental to the economic success of EOI strategy.

CONCLUSIONS

After the Revolution, the Chinese leadership continued to train and employ women in those sectors which were traditionally female—textiles, handicrafts, and other light industries. During the "radical" eras of the Great Leap Forward and the Cultural Revolution, although women continued to be employed predominantly in the traditional female areas, Party ideology promoted the slogan "anything that men can do, women can do as well" (*nanzi neng gande, funu yiyang nenggan*) thus suggesting that labor should not be sex-typed. Since the Cultural Revolution, and partially as a reaction to it, the current reforms return to the values of the immediate postrevolutionary era. They present continuity in the continued training and employment of women in women's work, and a reversion in ideology which reifies traditional sex roles by associating them with the efficiency of a rational division of labor. The SEZs reflect these trends.

Employment in the Special Economic Zones provides increased opportunity for women to earn money and gain independence, at the same time that it protects them from the extreme exploitation experienced by women in export processing zones elsewhere. This protection arises from the state's ideological sensitivity to the problem of worker exploitation by private, and especially foreign, enterprises. And it is reinforced by China's own historical experience with treaty ports. More particularly, it derives from a perceived need to protect *women* workers, when women are presumed to be a priori mothers and wives.

The Special Economic Zones do not though represent progress in terms of widening appropriate sex roles for women. Both in the context of labor and family, women's employment in the SEZs reinforces traditional sex role expectations. Women are assumed to be patient, passive, dexterous, and imbued with psychological and physiological characteristics that make them productive workers only in certain traditionally female industries.

Although the Women's Federation promotes the idea that women's employment in the zones will help them develop their personal talents, they also argue, in the Chinese socialist tradition, that such labor contributes to socialist construction and modernization. The zones were established in an effort to spur more rapid economic growth through export-oriented development. In this regard, the relatively good treatment of women workers is dysfunctional.

China's high wage policy and efforts to protect SEZ workers have worked to undermine China's comparative advantage in labor-intensive goods. Combined with relatively high land-use fees, and a sometimes unwieldy bureaucracy, the high wages make China's SEZs an unattractive investment site for most foreign investors. In lamenting the failure of Shenzhen, one Chinese observer complains that "none of the special economic zones of all the kinds established in the world has adopted a high wage policy of this sort."[74]

Other open zones such as the port cities and delta zones offer lower wages and may have been established partly as a result of the problems—including wage inflation—of the four original SEZs. Most investors in the zones are from Hong Kong and Macau; they have been shopping in the Pearl River Delta economic zone for lower labor costs. Entrepreneurs from Hong Kong and Macau have special cultural and language ties to the PRC. Moreover the proximity and high cost of land on these tiny islands do make China attractive to them. But these labor and land costs have not yet attracted substantial investment from international business outside of Hong Kong and Macau. In light of the high wages in the zones, the U.S.-China Trade Association has encouraged Chinese officials to consider promoting import-substituting projects for foreign investment.[75] This would open up China's large and highly attractive domestic market to foreign business, a move China has been resisting. Thus high wages and labor protection have helped to undermine China's early attempt to develop an export-oriented growth strategy in the zones.

The experience of other export processing zones has shown that women are critical to their development. Therefore we looked at women in China's SEZs and found that while they do have a special role, their experience does not replicate that of other zones. We argue that three factors account for this. One is the PRC's ideological commitment to limiting the exploitation of workers by private capitalists, especially foreigners. The second is the perception that women need special protection. The third factor derives more from nationalist concerns than socialist concerns. The Chinese regime is unwilling to yield sovereignty to foreign investors, nourished by the memories of China's humiliation at the hands of "imperialists" during the treaty ports era in the nineteenth century. Special Economic Zones were set up to be China's windows onto the world. What they have become are windows into the politics of Chinese economic reforms.

NOTES

1. Recently, there have been several important studies of the relationship between Chinese women's status and the policies and actions of the socialist state. For rural life, see Kay Ann Johnson, *Women, the Family and the Peasant Revolution in China* (Chicago: University of Chicago Press, 1983); for urban life, see Martin King Whyte and William Parish, *Urban Life in Contemporary China* (Chicago: University of Chicago Press, 1984). For general analyses, see Margery Wolf, *Revolution Postponed: Women in Contemporary China* (Stanford: Stanford University Press, 1985); Judith Stacey, *Patriarchy and Socialist Revolution in China* (Berkeley: University of California Press, 1983); and for a different view, Phyllis Andors, *The Unfinished Liberation of Chinese Women 1949–1980* (Bloomington: Indiana University Press, 1983).
2. See F. Frobel, J. Heinricks and O. Kreye, *The New International Division of Labour* (Cambridge: Cambridge University Press, 1982); also Diane Elson and Ruth Pearson, "The Subordination of Women and the Internationalization of Factory Production," in *Of Marriage and Market: Women's Subordination in International Perspective,* ed. K. Young, C. Wolkowitz, and R. McCullagh (London: CSE, 1981); and June Nash and Maria Patricia Fernandez-Kelly, *Women, Men and the International Division of Labor* (Albany: SUNY Press, 1983).
3. Kwan-yiu Wong and David K. Y. Chu, *Modernization in China: The Case of the Shenzhen Special Economic Zone* (Oxford and Hong Kong: Oxford University Press, 1985).
4. Linda Lim, "Capitalism, Imperialism and Patriarchy," in *Women, Men;* also see Linda Lim, "Women Workers in Multinational Corporations: The Case of the Electronics Industry in Malaysia and Singapore," *Michigan Occasional Papers,* no. 9 (Ann Arbor: Women's Studies Program, University of Michigan, 1978).
5. INSTRAW (UN-International Research and Training Institute for the Advancement of Women), *Women and International Development Cooperation: Trade and Investment* (Dominican Republic: UN-INSTRAW, 1985), 36.
6. Noeleen Heyzer, *Working Women in Southeast Asia* (Milton Keynes: Open University Press, 1986), 107.

7. See Aline K. Wong and Yiu-Chung Ko, "Women's Work and Family Life: The Case of Electronic Workers in Singapore," *Women in International Development, Working Paper #64* (Lansing: Office of Women in Development, Michigan State University, 1984).

8. In addition to the research noted above, also see Kathryn Ward, "Women and Transnational Corporation Employment: A World System and Feminist Analysis," *Women in International Development, Working Paper #120* (Lansing: Office of Women in Development, Michigan State University, 1986); Wendy Chapkis and Cynthia Enloe, *Of Common Cloth* (Amsterdam: Transnational Institute, 1983) and Diane Elson and Ruth Pearson, "Nimble Fingers Make Cheap Workers: An Analysis of Women's Employment in Third World Export Manufacturing," *Feminist Review* 4 (Spring 1981): 87–107.

9. Elson and Pearson, "Nimble Fingers."

10. Heyzer, *Working Women*, 103.

11. Anthony Rowley, "Mercantile Might," *Far Eastern Economic Review*, February 28, 1985, 93.

12. Thomas Chan, E. K. Chen, and Steve Chin et al., "China's Special Economic Zones: Ideology, Policy, and Practice," in *China's Special Economic Zones: Policies, Problems and Prospects*, ed. Y. C. Jao and C. K. Leung (Hong Kong: Oxford University Press, 1986), 89.

13. Sun Ru, "The Conception and Prospective of the Special Economic Zones in Guangdong," *Chinese Economic Studies* 4 (1980): 70.

14. Xu Jiwen, "The Transformation of China's Open Door Strategy," *Jiushi Niandai* 6 (1985): 51.

15. Xu Dixin, "China's Special Economic Zones," *Beijing Review* [hereafter BR] December 14, 1981, 15–16.

16. Hu Qiaomu, *Mingbao* (June 1985): 5.

17. Xu Xing, "The Reverberations of Shenzhen," *Zhengming* (August 1985): 22.

18. "Deng Calls for Speed-up in Reform," *BR*, August 24, 1987, 15.

19. Xu Dixin, "China's Special Economic Zones," 14. Many articles remind their readers that the zones are economic, not political in nature; see "A Preliminary Analysis of Special Characteristics of My Country's Special Economic Zones," *Shehui Yanjiu* 6 (1985): 39–42.

20. See Chan et al., "China's Special Economic Zones: Ideology," 87.

21. On this issue as in others, the SEZs have led the way in the reforms. Exploitation, which first became an issue with foreign capitalists in the SEZs, has now become an issue in the larger economy as the private sector is tolerated and allowed to grow.

22. Xu Dixin, "Salient Feature: State Capitalism," *BR*, January 23, 1984, 31.

23. Chan, Chen, and Chin, "China's Special Economic Zones: Ideology," 96.

24. Xu Dixin, "State Capitalism," 31.

25. The Chinese leadership accepts the Maoist formulation that individual interests—in this case, worker interests—are subsumed in the collective interest. See Andrew Nathan, *Chinese Democracy* (Berkeley: University of California Press, 1985) for a discussion of the collective interest, as developed by Mao and his nineteenth-century precursor, Liang Qichao.

26. George Fittings, "Export Processing Zones in Taiwan and the People's Republic of China," *Asian Survey* (August 1982): 735.

27. Whether or not one purpose of the SEZs is to provide jobs appears to be subject to debate. In 1981 Xu Dixin's statement on the zones included employment as one of the five purposes. Others have also noted employment as an important function of the SEZs, see fn 16. However, in 1984, Zhao Ziyang maintained that the SEZs "are not being developed for the purpose of providing jobs." *Xinhua,* January 20, 1984, FBIS, February 1, 1984, 13.

28. Xue Muqiao, "Present Conditions and Reform in China's Economic Readjustment," *Economic Reporter* (July 1981): 2.

29. *China Trade Report* [hereafter CTR] (March 1987): 7.

30. 1980 and 1982 regulations are translated in "New Regulations for Guangdong SEZs" *China Business Review* [hereafter CBR] (September–October 1980): 54–56, and Michael Moser, "Guangdong's SEZs," CBR (March–April 1982): 40–46. Information on wage and labor regulations is drawn from the latter unless noted.

31. Lei Qiang and Wang Jun, "Preliminary Analysis of Microlevel Effectiveness and Macro-level Control of Shenzhen Special Zone's Wage Distribution," *Xueshu Yanjiu* 1 (1985): 6.

32. Ibid., 8.

33. Li Kehua, "Looking at the Direction of My Country's Wage Reforms from the Perspective of the New Wage System of Shenzhen SEZ," *Xueshu Yanjiu* 6 (1984): 14.

34. Lei and Wang, "Preliminary Analysis," 6., and CTR (May 1987): 6.

35. CTR (May 1987): 1, 6.

36. You Tingyan, "On Labor and Personnel Management in Joint Ventures" PRC (March 1985): 9 (Paper presented to the conference on "The Role of Foreign Investment in National Development," Hangzhou).

37. *China Report: Economic Affairs* [hereafter CEA] 26 May 1987, 11.

38. CEA, 26 May 1987, 11.

39. See Elizabeth Perry and Christine Wong, eds., *The Political Economy of Reform in Post Mao China* (Cambridge: Harvard University Press, 1985), for a broad-ranging discussion of the reforms.

40. See "More Women Aware of Legal Rights," *Xinhua* (February 18, 1985): 17–18 (trans. in JPRS-CPS-85-024 [March 13, 1985]: 17–18); "Regulations Concerning Protection of the Legitimate Rights and Interests of the Women and Children of Tianjin Municipality," *Tianjin Ribao*

(October 26, 1984): 3 (trans. in JPRS-CPS-85-012, [February 5, 1985], 96–99); and Hao Lihui and Liu Jie, "Local Laws and Regulations Concerning Protecting the Legitimate Rights and Interests of Women and Children," *Faxue* (November 10, 1984), (trans. in JPRS-CPS-85-018 [February 27, 1985]: 22–27).

41. "From the Chinese Press," *BR*, October 12, 1987, 26.
42. According to the State Statistical Bureau, in 1984, when women made up 36.4 percent of the workers and staff they accounted for over 58 percent of both state textile and garment industries and over 50 percent of state catering and service industries. In the same year women accounted for 55.4 percent of total collective industrial workers (no further breakdown is available), 61.7 percent of collective catering and 59.7 percent of collective services. In 1982, women accounted for 76.5 percent of total workers in textile, knitting, and dyeing industries. See John Scherer, ed., *China Facts and Figures Annual, 1986* (Gulf Breeze, Fla.: Academic International Press, 1986), 84.
43. According to Renmin Ribao [hereafter *RMRB*] (overseas edition) 8 June, 1987. Women accounted for 32.8 percent of the total workers in state enterprises, 46.9 percent in collectives 47.3 percent in "others" (presumably private and joint ventures).
44. For example, see Zhang Xiping," "Cultivation of New Women, "Qingnian Yanjiu, trans. in Stanley Rosen, ed., "Chinese Women," *Chinese Sociology and Anthropology*, 48; Luo Qing, "Reform has provided Women with Vast Opportunities to Use Their Talent," *RMRB*, March 8 1986, 4. (trans. in JPRS: CPS-86-037 [May 6, 1986]: 10–20). Also see "Womens' Appeals and Aspirations," *RMRB*, April 12, 1985, 4 (trans. in JPRS: CPS-85-047 [May 18, 1985]: 75–76); and State Statistical Bureau, "High Employment Rate Among Urban Women," *BR*, October 12, 1987.
45. For instance, see "Unfair Hiring Practices in Ningxia," *China Daily*, November 8, 1985.
46. "From the Chinese Press," *BR*, October 12, 1987, 26. The ILO put total unemployment at 1.8 percent in 1985, but this figure relies on official reports which are low. In 1984 when urban unemployment was officially reported to be 2.3 percent, Tom Engle argued that 9 percent was a more reasonable figure, and even that would not account for redundant workers who make up to one-third of the total urban workforce. See "Reforming the Labor System," *CBR* (March–April 1985): 40. Also see Deng Zemin, "Pay Attention to Solving the Employment Problems of Young Women," *Anhui Ribao*, August 9, 1985, 2 (trans. in JPRS-CEA 86-014 [February 7, 1986]: 114); and Zhuang Jianguo, "Survey and Analysis of Employment Problem Among Young Women in Shanghai Waiting for Employment," *Laodong Kexue Yanjiu Ziliao*, trans. in Rosen, "Chinese Women," 105–11.

47. See "Home Helpers Lighten Housework for Busy Women," *Xinhua*, March 5, 1986 (trans. in *JPRS-CEA-86-033* [March 28, 1986]: 87), and All-China Women's Federation, "Chinese Women Courageously Shoulder the 'Double-Responsibility,' " *RMRB* (March 9, 1986), 4 (trans. in *JPRS-CPS-86-037* [May 6, 1986]).

48. Zhuang "Survey and Analysis"; Kristen Parris, interviews in PRC, 1986; Zhang "Cultivation of New Women"; and *China News Analysis*, #1334 (May 1, 1986).

49. Luo Qing, "Reform has Provided," 15. Also N.A., "The Reform Calls for and Trains a Generation of New Women," *Zhongguo Funu*, 4 (April 1985): 4–6.

50. See *Xinhua*, May 21, 1986 (trans. in *JPRS-CAG-86-023* [June 12, 1986]: 87); Luo Qiong, "Women and Reform," *Hongqi* (March 1, 1985), 17, (trans. in *JPRS-CRF-85-010* (June 5, 1985) 32–38); "Women's Appeals and Aspirations," 75. Also see Jean C. Robinson, "Of Women and Washing Machines: Employment, Housework and the Reproduction of Motherhood in Socialist China," *China Quarterly* 101 (March 1985): 32–57, and Tao Shefung, "My Bias Toward the 'Equality of the Sexes,' " *Zhongguo Funu* (ZGFN), 8 (August 1985): 8–9, 25.

51. See Ruth Schwartz Cowan, *More Work for Mother: The Ironies of Household Technology from the Open Hearth to the Microwave* (New York: Basic Books, 1983).

52. "The Open-Door Policy and Reform Have Infused the Womens' Movement with New Life," *RMRB* (February 26, 1986), 4, (trans. in *JPRS-CPS-86-037* (May 6, 1986) 32.)

53. All-China Women's Federation, "Chinese Women," 4.

54. See Beverley Hooper, *Youth in China* (Victoria: Penguin Books Australia, 1985), 100–101; "Women in China Make Headway to Equality," *China Daily*, March 6, 1982, 5; Also see Fei Xiaotong, "The Wenzhou Way," *Xinhua Wenzhai* 8 (1986): 59–61.

55. For lessons on applying make-up, see *Zhongguo Funu*, 6 (June 1985). Also see Ren Ke, "Why I Studied Make-up in School," *Women of China*, 1 (January 1986): 28–30.

56. Wei Shu, "Proper Image of Chinese Women in Our Time Defined," *Fujian Qingnian* (September 1, 1985), 30–31 (trans. in *JPRS-CPS-86-023* [March 5, 1986]: 72); Hooper, *Youth in China*, 102; 106–9. Also see "The Pluralist Trends of Contemporary Feminine Life," *ZGFN* 2 (February 1985): 16–27.

57. "The Open-Door Policy and Reform: Women in the Workforce," *Women of China* 3 (March 1986): 13. Also see Elson and Pearson, "Nimble Fingers"; and Wang Shu-hui, "The Need to Recognize a Rational Sexual Division of Labor," *Shehui* 6 (1986): 28–29.

58. Xiao Huan, "People in Shenzhen," *Women of China* 10 (October 1985):

10; Wu Ting, "Shantou under open Policy," *Women of China* 12 (December 1985): 5.

59. Luo Qing, "Reform Has Provided," Also see State Statistical Book, *Statistical Yearbook of China, 1986* (Beijing: State Statistical Bureau, 1987).

60. See "Shenzhen—An Economic Zone in China," *Women of China* 10 (October 1985): 8; "Zhuhai Transformed," *Women of China* 11 (October 1985): 6; "The Open Door Policy and Reform."

61. "The Open Door Policy and Reform" Population figures show that since the establishment of the SEZs, the male population has increased in Shenzhen and the male/female sex ratio has increased from 87.90 to 107.31. Shenzhen and the surrounding counties have long been an area that lost its young men over the borders to Hong Kong. The SEZ may now be offering opportunities to young men that work to stem and even reverse the flow. This is especially true because in these early years much of the domestic and foreign investment went to construction and development of infrastructure and real estate—typically male dominated occupations. This suggests there are increased opportunities for both women and men available in Shenzhen now, relative both to Shenzhen prior to the establishment of the zone and to opportunities currently available in the domestic Chinese economy. Shenzhen appears to offer better opportunities than do other EPZs for both men and women.

62. Wei Xiu and Li Zhengjie, "SEZ Spring," in *Laizi Tequ de Baogao* (Report from the SEZs), (Beijing: Zhongguo Wenlian Chuban Gongsi, 1984), 39. Authorities apparently saw the lure of Shenzhen as so great that they built a high fence with checkpoints around the zone and require a special internal passport for domestic Chinese tourists to the city. (But not for foreigners.)

63. "The Open Door Policy and Reform."

64. *China Trade Report,* May 1987.

65. Luo Qing, "Reform Has Provided."

66. Liu Wen, "Looking at the Change in China's Traditional Values from the Perspective of Shenzhen," *Weiding Gao* 21 (1985): 4. Also see "The Open Door Policy and Reform"; Lu Zhou, "On the Road to Becoming Decision Makers," *Women of China* 3 (March 1986): 18. Also "Rural Reform Gives Women a Bigger Say," *China Daily,* January 7, 1986, and "Economic Reforms Helping Raise Women's Status," *Xinhua,* December 8, 1984 (trans. in *JPRS-CEA-85-012* [February 3, 1985]: 1).

67. Wei and Li, "SEZ Spring," 46. This wage differential was reported without comment.

68. On November 4, 1986, *RMRB* reported that in Shanghai, the cost of weddings had doubled from 4,000 yuan in 1983 to 8,000 yuan in 1986. Many youth are said to be unable to afford such costs. Although we

have no direct evidence from zones that address this issue, data from all parts of China demonstrate that possession of consumer goods, access to housing, personal wealth along with good looks are the most important criteria that young people list for future spouses. See Qi Huizhi, "Do Women Hold Up 'Half the Sky'?" *BR* 29, no. 9 (March 3, 1986): 3; Hooper, *Youth in China*, 198–202; Wei Shu, "Proper Image," 73; Luzhongguo, "Romance and Marriage Among Tangshan Youths," in Stanley Rosen, ed., "Chinese Women II," *Chinese Sociology and Anthropology* (forthcoming).

69. INSTRAW; Elson and Pearson, "Subordination of Women"; Ward, "Women and Transnational"; Heyzer, *Working Women*.

70. Xiao Huan, "A New Director," *Women of China* 6 (June 1986); You Tingyan, "On Labor."

71. The Delta zones are known for firing more workers than others zones. One employer in the Pearl River Delta claims to fire 20 percent of those he hires. *CTR*, May 1982, For comments on job insecurity see Tan Jian Guang, "Changing Ideas Among Guangdong Youth Experiencing the Open Door Policy," *Shehui Kexue* 4 (1985): 28; and Chung-Fong Wu and David F. Ip, "Forsaking the Iron Rice Bowl: Employment and Wages in China's Special Economic Zones," *Asian Journal of Public Administration* 7 (December 1985): 234–35.

72. See, for instance, ILO, *Rural Development and Women in Asia* (Geneva: ILO, 1981); "Tourism and Prostitution," *ISIS* 13 (November 1979); ES-CAP, *Social Development Newsletter* (July 1983); Sawon Hong, "Urban Migrant Women in the Republic of Korea," *Korean Women—View From the Inner Room*, ed. L. Kendall and M. Peterson, (New Haven: East Rock Press, 1983).

73. *China Daily* 22 June 1987, 3, reports that new laws against prostitution have been enacted to deal with the problem; also see Sun Li, "A Preliminary Discussion of Female Criminality," *Jilin Daxue Shehui Kexue Xuebao* 1 (1985): 7; Wu Ting, "Shantou."

74. Zhang Gang, "Shenzhen: Abortive Reform Project" *China Spring Digest* (July/August 1987): 6 (trans. from *Zhongguo Zhi Qun*, [May 1982]: 9–15).

75. Roger W. Sullivan, "The Investment Climate," *CBR* (January–February 1987): 9.

6

ECONOMIC REWARD AND INEQUALITY IN THE 1986 PROGRAM OF THE COMMUNIST PARTY OF THE SOVIET UNION

Alfred B. Evans, Jr.

Soviet political leaders and social scientists view the world through the prism of Marxism-Leninism—the system of thought derived from Lenin's adaptation of Marxism to Russian conditions and the Russian revolutionary tradition. However, that ideology is not a fixed, unvarying source of policy guidance, but rather a framework for perception and analysis which is constantly being reshaped in response to changing conditions. To an unusual degree, Soviet leaders and their scholarly advisors feel compelled to present their views of Soviet society and the outside world in a systematic fashion, preserving the claim to a capacity for "scientific" decision-making based on the interpretation of laws of social development. We do not have to accept the pretext of scientific rigor in the formulation of policy by the Soviet regime in order to enjoy the opportunity to delineate changes in the outlook of successive leaderships which are expressed in programmatic documents adopted at different times. The last two programs of the Communist Party of the Soviet Union offer valuable insights into the objectives and perceptions of top Soviet leaders of two different periods, and in particular shed considerable light on those leaders' preferences for the distribution of economic benefits among members of Soviet society.

In 1986, the Twenty-Seventh Congress of the Communist Party of the Soviet Union approved a new party program, officially labeled a new version of the Third Party Program, which effectively replaced the program that had been adopted by the Twenty-Second Congress of the CPSU in 1961. While the 1961 Party Program was inspired by

Khrushchev's values and hopes, the 1986 version bore the imprint of Gorbachev's goals and aspirations (though since Khrushchev had headed the Soviet Communist Party for almost eight years before the adoption of the 1961 Program, and Gorbachev had been general secretary of the CPSU for less than one year before the final version of the 1986 program was accepted, it is not surprising that the expression of the top leader's thinking is much less complete in the latter document). There are important similarities between the two documents, both of which promise the enhancement of the Communist party's leadership of Soviet society and the achievement of a higher standard of living for the Soviet people. However, there are also a number of striking differences between the latest two programs adopted by the party, a quarter of a century apart. This essay will deal with differences between the two most recent programs of the CPSU with respect to their views on economic reward and inequality in Soviet society. The analysis which follows will draw on the speeches of the highest party leaders and the published works of Soviet scholars as well as the text of each of those two programs to explore the ideas expressed in those official documents. This chapter is designed to compare the dominant tendency of thought among Soviet scholars of the Khrushchev period with the predominant point of view of the current period, so as to illuminate the analysis favored by the most influential elements of the political leadership at each time. Therefore, little attention will be devoted to different positions held by various social theorists in each period. That approach is not meant to create the impression of monolithic unanimity within the Soviet scholarly community, either in the early 1960s or in the late 1980s, since it can be shown that debates over issues of economic reward were waged in each period. The purpose of this analysis is to identify shifts in the outlook of Soviet leaders, which reflect long-term changes in the relationship between regime and society.

It will be concluded that Khrushchev's program pushed much more strongly for the equalization of economic reward than does Gorbachev's program. While a major question of the late 1950s and early 1960s was how to decrease economic inequality, the issues of the late 1980s are primarily those of the extent and means by which inequality should be increased. However, the question raised by the new party program and the writings of some Soviet scholars is not simply the degree of economic differentiation in Soviet society, but the proper basis of such differentiation. Reform-minded Soviet social scientists criticize the measures of equalization encouraged by Khrushchev not only for being excessive in some respects, but also for being generally superficial and creating a facade of illusory equality, behind which flourished growing, spontaneous means of unofficial and frequently illegal access to material benefits, associated with a hidden but tenacious system of economic inequality. The reformers repudiate the current system of reward in Soviet society as containing large elements of irrationality and inequity. However, the drive to reform the distribution of public and private goods in the Soviet economy is fraught with political peril, since it threatens arrangements defended by many Soviet citizens as part of the fundamental "social contract" between the regime and the people.[1] The current campaign to implement the principles of "social justice" is really an effort to replace one conception of just distribution with another, which has great potential to polarize major groups in the society. As the Gorbachev leadership has more sharply sensed the rumblings of discontent from those who feel protected by existing guarantees, it has become more cautious and hesitant in approaching the resolution of some of the tasks most essential for successful economic restructuring.

The central thesis of the program adopted by the Twenty-Second Party Congress was that Soviet society had entered the stage of "full-scale construction of communist society" (*razvernutoe stroitel'stvo kommunisticheskogo obshchestva*). The 1961 program mapped a plan for the transition to a fully communist society, envisioned by Marx as the "higher phase of communist society," within two decades. It was promised that the Soviet Union would outstrip the U.S.A. in per capita production during the 1960s, and would finish building the material and technical base of communism during the 1970s. Soviet society would enter the historical phase of communism during the early 1980s, as the Soviet people reaped the benefits of unprecedented material abundance. In accordance with Khrushchev's pronouncements, the 1961 Party Program characterized the stage of full-scale construction of communism as a period of transition from socialism to communism in the USSR, entailing a transformation of the system of material reward and drastically reducing economic inequality in Soviet society. The "socialist principle" of reward according to labor would gradually be replaced by the "communist principle" of distribution according to need.[2] Nevertheless, Khrushchev insisted that linking economic reward to the laboring contributions of Soviet citizens would still be necessary during the transition period in order to stimulate the growth in production required for the realization of Communist abundance. Yet while the 1961 program conceded that for the next twenty years payment according to work would remain the main means of satisfying the needs of the Soviet population, it predicted that by the end of the 1970s Soviet society would come "right up to" the application of the principle of distribution according to need.[3] During the subsequent period, after Soviet society had entered the phase of communism, the principle of distribution of material benefits according to need would be fully put into practice, eliminating the inequality in economic status caused by differences in training, skills, and productivity among Soviet citizens.

Khrushchev identified reward according to labor primarily with wage payments, and affirmed that wages would be the principal source of the real incomes of the Soviet people until the completion of the transition to communism. However, he called for a progressive decrease in inequality in wages throughout the transition period. The Seven-Year Plan adopted by the Twenty-First Party Congress in 1959 predicted a more rapid increase in the wages of workers of lower and average levels of pay than in the wages of those with higher pay, leading to a reduction in differentiation between the highest and the lowest wages, and between the highest and the average.[4] Soviet scholars of the Khrushchev period argued that with continued economic growth the level of education and skills of the working class would rise, while mechanization and automation would gradually eliminate heavy and unskilled manual labor.[5] The 1961 Party Program predicted that "diminishing differences in labor skills and productivity will be accompanied by a steady reduction of disparities in the level of pay."[6] At the Twenty-Second Party Congress, Khrushchev promised that the category of low-paid workers would cease to exist by 1970.[7] In addition, Boris Sukharevskii reported in 1961 that restrictions were being applied with the objective of lowering the maximum incomes in Soviet society to the level necessary for satisfying "reasonable demands."[8] Decreases in differentiation in wages were seen as the principal means of reducing inequality in incomes.

The other major means of equalizing economic well-being in the Soviet Union was to be the expansion of social funds of consumption *(obshchestvennye fondy potrebleniia)*. In his main address to the Twenty-First Party Congress in 1959, Khrushchev attributed a heightened ideological significance to those funds, proclaiming that "we have a truly communist way of raising the well-being of the working people. . . . Satisfaction of the individual requirements of each person must proceed . . . not only through raising wages, but also through social funds, the role and significance of which will increase more and more."[9] The theme that social funds were a transitional form, approximating Communist distribution, was elaborated extensively in subsequent years. At the Twenty-Second Party Congress, in introducing the new party program, Khrushchev claimed that "distribution among the members of society through these funds is not contingent upon the quantity and quality of their labor—that is to say, it is free of charge."[10] A number of Soviet scholars asserted that since the provision of benefits through public funds did not depend directly on the laboring contributions of beneficiaries, the enlargement of those funds would progressively realize distribution according to need.[11]

Soviet ideology of the early 1960s foresaw a qualitative enhancement of the role of collective means of the satisfaction of needs. The 1961 Party Program indicated that during the next twenty years social funds would grow more rapidly than wage payments.[12] While per capita real income in Soviet society was to increase by more than three-and-one-half times from 1961 to 1980, social consumption funds were to grow by more than ten times during the same period.[13] Khrushchev pledged that by the beginning of the 1980s those funds would account for "about half" of the total income of the Soviet people.[14] In the course of the transition to communism, the range of benefits financed by public funds would widen. By 1980, social funds would provide not only education and medical treatment, but also housing in state-owned apartments, utilities, public intra-urban transportation (streetcars, buses, trolleybuses, and subways), lunches at places of work, child care, boarding schools, and some everyday services, all free of charge to their users. Subsequently, during the complete realization of the features of full communism, the satisfaction of needs from social funds would become the predominant, and finally the sole form of distribution of goods and services.[15] Even within the last decades of socialism, the expansion of social funds would contribute to the reduction of inequality by moderating the impact of wage differences and raising the standard of living of families with large numbers of children.[16]

During the transition from socialism to communism the importance of private economic activity and personal property would diminish. The only type of legal economic activity outside the socialist sector which was recognized as significant by Soviet thought of the Khrushchev years was farming on private plots, always referred to by Soviet sources as "personal subsidiary agriculture," and said to be withering away. With the further development of production on collective farms and state farms, private plots would gradually cease to be necessary either to help fill society's need for food or to supplement the earnings of farmers, so that private agriculture would "exhaust itself economically" and farmers would "voluntarily relinquish it."[17] With the approach of Communist society, the sphere of personal ownership of consumer goods would also contract. While there was controversy about the ultimate fate of personal property, it was expected that during the transition period many objects of consumption would be transferred from personal to social ownership.[18] In full communism each person would draw necessary articles from social stocks and would have some degree of disposal over those articles for personal use, but objects of personal consumption could not be mortgaged, bequeathed, or set aside for future use. Therefore one Soviet scholar concluded that "in those conditions personal property will die off."[19] In Communist society the distinction between one's own possessions and those of society would cease to be of concern to the vast majority of citizens.

In the Communist social community the interests of all individuals and groups would be fused with the interests of a single enormous *kollektiv*. Despite the great emphasis on the reduction of economic inequality in Khrushchev's program, one author of the Khrushchev period noted that "for communists, equality is not an end in itself."[20] The elimination of differences in economic well-being was necessary for the removal of the barriers separating one person from another and dividing society into a welter of conflicting interests. The liquidation of economic inequality would allow the expression of a fundamental harmony of social interests. Khrushchev argued that the new historical phase would be characterized by "*communist* equality, signifying an identical relationship to the means of production, complete equality in distribution, and harmony between the individual and society based on the organic combination of personal and public interests."[21] In similar fashion, his party program asserted that "harmonious relations will be established between the individual and society on the basis of unity of public and personal interests."[22] The objective of economic equalization was an integral component of Khrushchev's vision of the consolidation of a solidary nationwide social consensus.

The reduction of economic inequality was encouraged not only by Khrushchev's ideological preconceptions and goals but also by conditions in the Soviet economy at the time of his ascendancy. Stalin's denunciation of egalitarianism or wage-leveling (*uravnilovka*) in 1931 had been followed by increases in differences between higher and lower wages.[23] In the early years of Soviet industrialization, skilled workers and technicians were in very short supply, while unskilled laborers, often fresh from the countryside, were abundant. A more differentiated structure of wage rates was intended to encourage the stabilization of labor in industrial enterprises and the acquisition of education and productive skills by workers. As Nove puts it, "the supply-and-demand situation pointed strongly in the direction of widening differentials, e. g., between a skilled man with factory experience and the newly arrived villager."[24] As a result of Stalin's policies, the disparity between the income of higher paid workers and that of lower paid workers grew during the first few Five-Year Plans and the Second World War.[25]

A policy of openly reducing income inequality was introduced in the middle of the 1950s with substantial increases in minimum wage payments, restrictions on the highest salaries, and sharp increases in pensions. Yanowitch described the effect of the rapid decline in the dispersion of wages in the USSR during the late 1950s as an "income revolution" narrowing the gap between higher paid and lower paid personnel.[26] He contended that the moderation of income differentials under Khrushchev was a rational response to changes in economic conditions. "The principal reasons for the policy of reducing income inequality are rooted in 'objective factors,' that is, in the changing relative scarcities of skilled and unskilled labor."[27] The educational and skill levels of new entrants into the labor force had risen greatly since the early 1930s. Skilled labor was much more plentiful, and unskilled labor less predominant than during the first Five-Year Plans, while many jobs still demanded unskilled manual labor. In relation to the needs of the Soviet economy in which huge amounts of work were still not highly mechanized or not mechanized at all, unskilled and semi-skilled labor were becoming scarcer. Economic rationality and ideological transformationism both pointed in the direction of an assault on the economic inequality inherited from the Stalin years.

The agenda of Soviet politics in the 1980s is quite different, however. Since the election of Mikhail Gorbachev to the post of general secretary of the CPSU in March 1985 the main catch phrase in Soviet scholars' discussions of economic reward has been "social justice" *(sotsial'naia spravedlivost')*. Gorbachev repeatedly called for fuller realization of social justice in his speeches prior to the Twenty-Seventh Congress of the Soviet Communist Party,[28] as well as in his report to the Congress, in which he even said that "the strict implementation of the principle of social justice is an important condition for the unity of the people, *the political stability of society*, and the dynamism of its development."[29] The program adopted by the Twenty-Seventh Party Congress classified the "ever fuller implementation in all spheres of social relations of the principle of social justice" as one of the basic tasks of social policy.[30] The term "social justice" was not new to Soviet ideology in 1986, and in fact had been the focus of considerable attention since the Brezhnev period. However, under Gorbachev the term was assigned a more central emphasis, and was given a new content. The full meaning of social justice was only hinted at by Gorbachev's speeches, which associated the demands of social justice with the struggle against parasitic attitudes and unearned income, and with the need to follow more closely the principle of reward according to labor. The new party program, by providing no direct definition of social justice, left the way open for a vigorous and at times acrimonious debate on the subject.

Gorbachev and the new program did suggest a guideline for discussion with their insistence that the basic principle of justice to be applied in Soviet society during the present stage is that of socialism and not of communism. The assertion in the new program that in the current period of "accelerated social and economic development" Soviet society must deal with the task of "ensuring a qualitatively new level of people's well-being, with the consistent implementation of the socialist principle of distribution according to labor"[31] contrasts sharply with the prediction by the previous program that Soviet society would be on the verge of introducing distribution according to need by the end of the stage of full-scale construction of communism. Distribution according to need is mentioned by the new program only in connection with the Communist society which is the ostensible goal of the remote future. The postponement of full communism is understandable in view of recent intimations by some Soviet scholars that the present prospect is for increases in inequality in the distribution of material benefits. In *Pravda* in June 1985 D. Valovoi declared that Marx had "resolutely opposed egalitarianism in the first phase of communist society" and that "the egalitarian principle of distribution is alien to socialism."[32] M. N. Rutkevich, who previously had been an advocate of the reduction of differences in reward, apparently adapted to change in the attitudes of the political leadership by asserting in the fall of 1986 that a general law of socialism was the use of social inequality as a means of advancing toward fuller equality.[33] Complete equality has been postponed to the ultimate Communist future, while greater inequality is slated for the foreseeable future.

A variety of recent Soviet sources have emphasized that one of the most prevalent and pernicious deviations from the principles of social justice is wage leveling. The argument that leveling was a growing problem was implied in a number of Gorbachev's speeches during his first year in power, including his report to the Twenty-Seventh Party Congress, which complained that paying good workers and negligent workers the same amount of money is a distortion of the socialist principle of reward, and therefore of the essence of social justice.[34] In April 1986 Gorbachev openly charged that the errors which the Soviet leadership of a few years before had permitted had included "negative processes, taking place in the sphere of distribution," which were manifested in "leveling tendencies in the pay of labor, which did not correspond to the demands of the basic principle of socialism."[35] The new party program had promised the pursuit of a policy which would serve as a reliable barrier to wage leveling.[36] N. Rimashevskaia complained in October 1986 that differences in wages were still excessively small, as the result of a leveling tendency dating from the 1960s, featuring the increase of minimum and average wages "at a disproportionate rate."[37] B. Rakitskii agreed in *Pravda* in January 1987 that elements of wage leveling, which had grown stronger in recent years, had undermined the incentive function of wages. He expressed the hope that a resolution just approved by the Central Committee of the CPSU, the Council of Ministers, and the All-Union Central Trade Union Council would eliminate the influence of leveling from pay scales.[38]

Unlike the 1961 Party Program, the new program holds out no promise of the gradual replacement of wages as the main determinant of the material welfare of Soviet citizens. On the contrary, the new program makes it clear that wages will remain the principal source of income throughout the historical phase of socialism, and that improvements in wages will form the basis for raising living standards.[39] In addition, in has become increasingly apparent that Gorbachev's insistence on more closely tying wage payments to the quantity and quality of labor spells a widening of differentials in wage rates.[40] Since Gorbachev's rise to the office of general secretary of the CPSU, some Soviet economists have more openly described the existing differences in pay between unskilled and skilled workers, and between workers and engineers, as inadequate.[41] Stanislav Shatalin's advocacy in September 1986 of the creation of a more flexible and effective system of material incentives for workers without limits on the scale of differentiation in wages was echoed by *Kommunist*, the theoretical and political journal of the Central Committee, in February 1987.[42] Becoming increasingly open in advocating wage differentiation, in June 1987 Gorbachev insisted that wages should depend on each worker's personal contribution to the results of production and should "not be restricted by any sort of limit."[43] However, *Kommunist*, in a summary of letters received in response to its publication of articles on social justice, revealed that many members of Soviet society still harbored decidedly egalitarian sentiments. The journal quoted one letter writer as saying that "the sooner scholars find (under the supervision of a worker) the path to introduction in life of the measure of 'pay no higher than a worker's pay,' the sooner we shall feel the activation of the human factor, deliverance from unfavorable tendencies, and the decisive acceleration of our society's socio-economic development."[44] It would be hard to imagine a train of thought more at variance with the dominant point-of-view among current Soviet leaders.

In accordance with the present leadership's emphasis on preserving wage payments as the main source of income for Soviet working people, no major expansion in the role of social funds of consumption is projected. While Gorbachev and the new party program endorse the growth of spending from social funds, the 1961 program's pledges that public funds would grow more rapidly than wages and that social funds would furnish half of the real income of Soviet people within twenty years are notably absent from the new program.[45] In addition, the assumption that such funds are acquiring qualitatively new functions, which was the point of departure for the discussions of the early 1960s, has been quietly abandoned. Gorbachev set the tone for recent discourse on public consumption funds by remarking at the Twenty-Seventy Party Congress that "these are by no means philanthropic funds,"[46] implying that such resources should not become the primary means of support for ablebodied citizens, and that the benefits yielded by social funds are not gratuitous.

The current leadership is perhaps the first ever in the USSR to seek a precise delineation of the proper functions of social consumption funds. At the Twenty-Seventh Party Congress, Gorbachev attempted to enumerate the social purposes which those funds should serve, declaring that "they play an important role in ensuring equal access to education and culture for all members of society, in equalizing conditions for raising children, and in making life easier for those who for one reason or another need one-time or permanent assistance. They are also a means of encouraging skilled, conscientious labor."[47] The functions assigned to social funds by Gorbachev and Soviet economists sympathetic to his perspective include: (1)

providing benefits such as education and health care, which, it is thought, should be made available to all regardless of their ability to pay; (2) reducing inequalities in opportunity for young people from families of different means and in varying locales; (3) assisting in the support of children, the elderly, and others who are not fully capable of providing for themselves or have earned a comfortable retirement; and (4) supplementing wages in stimulating the productivity of labor. Gorbachev's position does not hint at broadening the functions of social funds, or at the acceptance of a redistributive function for such resources. The new party program, while acknowledging purposes of social funds of the sort mentioned by Gorbachev, also referred to the functions of "lessening differences in the material position of citizens, families, and social groups that are objectively inevitable under socialism," and "radically improving the well-being of low-income groups in the population."[48] Unlike Gorbachev's speech to the party Congress, the program did suggest a redistributive function for social funds.

However, some Soviet economists have openly argued against using social funds to mitigate inequality resulting from differences in wages, contending that such a policy detracts from rewards to material self-interest.[49] Their advocacy of greater payments and services from public funds for the "better workers" seems consistent with Gorbachev's view that social funds are "also a means of encouraging skilled, conscientious labor."[50] *Kommunist,* in reviewing the discussion of social justice in its pages in late 1986, even went so far as to reject a statement in favor of redistribution through social funds which was strongly reminiscent of language in the new party program. "Social funds of consumption initially were seen basically as a means of smoothing out the economic inequality in the sphere of consumption that is inevitable even in socialism. However, with the growth of the standard of living of the population, that is beginning to cease to be their leading function."[51] What is at issue in the Soviet Union today is not how much the redistributive function of social funds will be expanded, but whether it will be contracted, and whether the function is a proper one at all in a relatively mature socialist society. The approach of the current leadership does not rule out increases in spending from social consumption funds for some purposes. In *Kommunist* in September 1986 Shatalin strongly urged the raising of pensions and assistance to families with children to more adequate levels.[52] But while support for non-able-bodied members of the population may actually be enhanced, neither Gorbachev nor the new party program suggest the assumption by social funds of the task of gradually replacing wages as the main source of income for working citizens, or in other words, the use of public consumption funds to realize distribution according to need.

In sharp contrast to the 1961 Party Program, the new program of the CPSU does not promise the widening of the range of services offered free of direct charges to users and paid for by social funds. In fact, recent debate has focused on the question of introducing more payment by their recipients for services which are now offered without fees or at subsidized prices. In the article in *Kommunist* which stimulated debate on the contemporary meaning of social justice, Tat'iana Zaslavskaia, one of the most prominent supporters of economic reform, argued that the provision of services for free reduces the material incentive for efficient labor by artificially limiting the range of benefits which may be acquired with money that has been earned, and contributes to the scarcity of many types of services by encouraging their wasteful use.[53] Mikhail Rutkevich, though hardly an advocate of reform under previous leaders, by 1986 contended that increasing the number of polyclinics charging for medical care, introducing payment for intracity telephone conversations from private phones, and requiring dues for membership in clubs using cultural institutions and sporting facilities "will put in order the use of social funds and will aid the observation of the principle of social justice."[54] Such proposals have been the target of vocal opposition from some other Soviet scholars, and from other Soviet citizens. In an article which appeared in *Kommunist* a few weeks after its publication of Zaslavskaia's essay, A. Bim and A. Shokhin stressed that even if greater payment for services did lead to an increase in their availability, the result would be the growth of inequality in the satisfaction of some demands of primary social importance, since access to services would be eased only for those with more ability to pay for them.[55] In its summary of the debate provoked by Zaslavskaia's suggestions, *Kommunist* reported receiving some letters containing outspoken criticism of the idea of extending the requirement of pay for services. One letter writer insisted that the provision of free education and medical service is "one of the most important achievements and advantages of socialism. And to renounce that is unjustifiable."[56] Zaslavskaia's critics implied that the assurance that some essential services will be provided free of direct charges is part of an unwritten but deeply cherished "social contract" between the Soviet regime and the Soviet people, and that breaching that contract would be a violation of mutual trust. Resistance to change in the subsidization of services is strong, but it is striking that the thrust of proposals for change now is in the opposite direction from that of the Khrushchev period, when the sphere of free services was expected to widen rapidly.

One of the benefits most heavily subsidized in the USSR is housing in apartments built by the state. Differentiation in rent is restrained by payments so low as to cover only a fraction of the actual cost of housing. Both Gorbachev and the new party program have endorsed the construction of more housing with cooperative or individual financing as a means of ameliorating the country's still serious shortage of housing space.[57] In addition, some Soviet social scientists have advocated instituting fuller payment for apartments by their occupants, so that rents would fully reflect the quantity of housing space and qualitative criteria concerning construction, amenities, and location.[58] In *Kommunist* in September 1986, adding fuel to the debate ignited by Zaslavskaia, Shatalin took the position that while the Soviet state should ensure the provision of a basic level of housing space, beyond that socially guaranteed minimum, housing ought to be "a commodity which should be fully paid for."[59] Though the subsequent article by Bim and Shokhin expressed sympathy for that suggestion,[60] *Kommunist* evidently received a number of letters protesting the notion of greater payment for housing.[61] Despite the likelihood of considerable opposition, both the new party program and Gorbachev's report to the Twenty-Seventh Party Congress had shown a tendency to favor increases in rents. The program cautiously hinted at such an attitude by saying that "the practice of attracting the means of the population for improving housing and living conditions, cultural and recreational facilities, and tourism and other activities will be broadened."[62] Gorbachev went farther by arguing that "proposals that justified changes be made in the system of payments for housing, closely linking it to the size and quality of all occupied living space, deserve attention."[63] While the 1961 program promised the elimination of rent payments within twenty years, Soviet sources today are discussing the wisdom of sharp increases in the scale and differentiation of rents.

Perhaps the most controversial proposal related to the distribution of economic benefits which has been unveiled recently is that of raising the prices of some food products. Meat and milk products are among the commodities whose prices are most highly subsidized by the Soviet state, with the retail price of those products often less than half the cost of their production. Proposals for making the prices of meat and milk reflect production costs have come into the open since Gorbachev's promotion to the post of general secretary of the CPSU.[64] Zaslavskaia's article in *Kommunist* in September 1986 charged that the gap between social costs and retail prices for many food products make possible "a covert distribution of incomes according to criteria, lying not in the sphere of labor, but in the structure of personal consumption."[65] Shatalin asserted that raising prices on meat products "would substantially improve the situation in the consumer market, and would create a more well-founded demand for various types of commodities and normal economic conditions for producers."[66] That is, higher prices would restrain demand for meat products, and also heighten incentives for expanding the production of those products. However, the suggestions by Zaslavskaia and Shatalin for more realistic prices for meat and milk were the subject of the most vehement criticism reported by *Kommunist*. A relatively calm response was that of S. Gushchin, who was of the opinion that selling meat and milk products at prices that would cover costs would lower the standard of living of Soviet workers.[67] The journal noted that the majority of letters addressing that topic were filed with indignation, based on the assumption voiced by V. Shevchenko that "the stability of retail prices on goods of first necessity is our great achievement."[68] Again, the accusation was that a proposal for change had threatened the terms of the social contract. Perhaps the highest Soviet leaders saw the potential for explosive conflict over the question of increases in meat and milk prices, for that issue was avoided both by Gorbachev's major address to the 1986 Party Congress and by the new party program. The program did say in general terms that the formation of prices should be improved so that prices would "more accurately reflect the level of socially necessary outlays, as well as the quality of products and services,"[69] but did not specifically apply that enjoinder to food prices.

Gorbachev was more forthcoming in encouraging the development of small-scale private enterprise to help to fill gaps in the availability of services for the population. He promised that "the state will facilitate the development of various forms of satisfying public demand and providing services." By adding that "proposals for bringing order into individual labor activity must be considered carefully,"[70] he seemed to imply that private activity supplying badly needed services should be legalized and openly regulated rather than being wiped out, or being allowed to continue with a partly illegal status while exerting a corrupting influence. In late 1986 the Central Committee and the Council of Ministers passed a resolution intended to permit the open expansion of small-scale private enterprises, largely in the service sector, with more precise and realistic legal guidelines.[71] Soon afterwards, O. Latsis furnished a theoretical justification for the new decree, reasoning that the need for "individual labor activity" actually increases with the movement of socialism to higher levels of development.[72] His point was that in the more industrialized socialist countries, the growth of the number of manufactured consumer goods and the enhancement of money incomes create greater demand for services to consumers, which may often be offered more efficiently by small-scale private enterprises than by larger socialized units. He concluded that individual labor activity "may be preserved for a long time" in the economy of each socialist country.[73]

One of the clearest contrasts between Soviet ideology of the early 1960s and that of the current time pertains to their treatment of the subject of private plots in agriculture. While theorists of the Khrushchev period foresaw the withering away of private farming with the further development of socialist agriculture, contemporary analysis emphasizes the value of private plots in helping to solve the problem of shortages of food in the USSR. The new party program concedes that the "subsidiary farms of enterprises and individual plots of citizens," as well as other units of agricultural activity, "will be used to augment food resources." The 1986 program also flatly predicts that the collective farm market, in which the produce from private plots may be sold for a profit, "will retain its importance."[74] Official Soviet thought foresees a long-term future for the largest element of private enterprise in the Soviet economy.

The inevitable consequence of an expanded role for small-scale private enterprise will be the growth in incomes from private economic activity. However, that prospect is not looked on with unequivocal enthusiasm by most Soviet sources, despite the current willingness to allow greater differentiation in wages in the socialist sector. Zaslavskaia complains that excessive differences in reward for labor from private activity in comparison with the remuneration of work in socialized production may lead to the formation of a social stratum with a disproportionately large share of society's wealth.[75] There seems to be broad agreement on that point among many with differing opinions on other issues. Popular dissatisfaction was articulated in a letter to *Kommunist* by A. Riabov, who said that "it is difficult to agree that the average pay of labor in the individual sector should be significantly higher than the pay of labor in social production," and in another letter by I. Karpova, who charged that "the people occupied in individual labor activity have super-high earnings."[76] Zaslavskaia regards that part of the income derived from private enterprise that is not due to greater effort or skill on the part of the producers but that is caused by taking advantage of market conditions as unearned.[77] There is evidence of considerable resentment toward the richest returns from the sale of private plot output in collective farm markets. Both Zaslavskaia and Rutkevich, who may be considered opponents on most issues, view profit attributable to superior climatic or soil conditions or favorable geographical locations as essentially unearned, and support the introduction of differential rent payments on land used in private economic activity.[78] A suspicion of profit gained, not through personal diligence but through an exploitation of supply and demand in an unregulated market, reflects not only the influence of Marxist preconceptions, but also the widespread daily observation of the relatively enviable standard of living of some Soviet private entrepreneurs.

Even those willing to allow greater differentiation in wages seem to share a feeling that inequality in income should not be unlimited. As Vadim Z. Rogovin puts it, "From the Leninist conception of distributive policy flows the demand that differentiation in the incomes and personal property of various groups of the population have definite limits and should not create any unlimited advantages in consumption and accumulation."[79] He argues for the limitation of "super-incomes" such as those created by some authors' royalties, permitted by loopholes in existing laws, and reports that Lenin "considered that to earn excessively much in socialist society is not only shameful but impermissible."[80] Many Soviet scholars who favor freer competition for economic reward advocate the use of taxation to moderate extreme differences in incomes. Rogovin calls for improvements in tax policy in order to eliminate "excessively high incomes" which are the basis of "the socially unjustifiable and unjust differentiation of different groups of the population."[81] Shatalin and Grebennikov favor raising the minimum of earnings subject to personal income taxation, and applying a more steeply progressive tax to incomes above that point.[82] Of course, the result of those changes would be to exempt more low-income people from taxation and to take a larger share of higher incomes. Rogovin sees more progressive tax rates as a means of reducing the disparity in affluence between industrious wage-earners and the more successful private entrepreneurs, and hopes that the personal income tax will limit incomes to a specified maximum.[83] The party program is largely silent on the issues raised by such proposals, but its pledge that the reduction of personal income taxes will continue does not hold out much encouragement for those who wish to use taxes to limit income differentials.[84] Caution was also counseled by Gorbachev's admonition to the Twenty-Seventh Congress, quoted earlier, that "in curbing unearned income we must not allow a shadow to fall on those who receive additional earnings through honest labor."[85]

Gorbachev did give encouragement to proponents of a stiffer inheritance tax by saying that "we should also think about proposals for the improvement of tax policy, including a progressive inheritance tax."[86] Some scholars complain that families with very high incomes are able to transfer to their children holdings of personal wealth which are significant sources of unearned income, and support a parasitical way of life.[87] Rogovin favors a progressive inheritance tax as a means of moderating the passing on of exceptional accumulations of money and possessions. "In light of the steady growth in the extent of private property, it is time that we returned to an economically meaningful tax on inheritance . . . in cases in which the amount of the inheritance substantially exceeds the means of livelihood of most of the population."[88] However, concern over the inheritance of large estates does not mean hostility for private property as such. While Soviet ideologists of the Khrushchev period foresaw the dwindling of the sphere of personal property and debated the question of the survival of such property in full Communism, the new program promises that the Communist party "will take the necessary measures . . . to safeguard the constitutional right of citizens to personal property."[89] Acceptance of a long-term future for private property in the Soviet Union is also implied by the words of Gorbachev and the party program encouraging more extensive construction of individual and cooperative housing.[90] It should also be noted that while the 1961 program of the CPSU pledged that every Soviet family would live in a separate apartment within twenty years, the 1986 program says that "virtually every Soviet family will have separate housing—an apartment or an individual house—by the year 2000."[91] The language of the new party program clearly suggests greater tolerance for privately owned housing and single-family structures.[92] Though current demands for a progressive inheritance tax reflect a distaste toward unusually large concentrations of personal wealth, Soviet ideology today regards the principle of private ownership of personal property as legitimate.

Perhaps the most controversial source of inequality in material well-being in the Soviet Union under Gorbachev is the institutionalized privileges of party officials and other members of the Soviet elite. High-ranking party and state functionaries have the exclusive use of special stores, chauffeur-driven automobiles, larger and better-furnished apartments, special medical facilities, country cottages, and certain resort facilities. In Soviet society, access to channels for the institutionalized distribution of privilege is a crucial determinant of a higher standard of living.[93] The very existence of such privileges was scarcely hinted at by most Soviet publications before Gorbachev came to power, and the appropriateness of such privileges was never debated openly. That issue broke into the open shortly before the Twenty-Seventh Party Congress, when *Pravda* quoted extensively from a letter from N. Nikolayev of Kazan which said that "one cannot close one's eyes to the fact that party, Soviet, trade union, economic, and even Young Communist League officials sometimes objectively deepen social inequality, taking advantage of all sorts of special refreshment bars, special stores, special hospitals, etc." Nikolayev argued that such privileges violated the demands of social justice and should be abolished. "An official has higher earnings in monetary terms. But in other respects, there should be no privileges."[94] That theme was taken up again during the party Congress in a speech by Boris El'tsin, who had become head of the Moscow party organization since Gorbachev had come to power. El'tsin reported that workers talking about questions of social justice had questioned special benefits for leaders, and proposed that "where benefits for leaders at all levels are not justified, they should be abolished."[95] However, in another speech to the Twenty-Seventh Party Congress, Egor Ligachev, the second-ranking official in the party secretariat, implicitly repudiating such criticism, rebuked *Pravda* for unspecified errors.[96] Discussion of that issue has continued to simmer since the last party congress, with popular criticism of leaders' privileges voiced in letters to the press, and with a further exchange on the subject between El'tsin and Ligachev during the Nineteenth Conference of the CPSU in July 1988.[97] The status of institutionally controlled privileges in current Soviet ideology is uncertain.

While current Soviet leaders may be uncertain as to how to deal with some questions raised by the discussion of social justice, they have allowed the more open expression of the thought of scholars who advocate change in the pattern of economic reward in the USSR. Those scholars not only agree with the new party program's conclusion that wages will remain the principal source of income for Soviet workers during the foreseeable future, but also repudiate the influence of past policies of wage leveling and call for increases in wage differentiation. Far from favoring the rapid expansion of social consumption funds, those scholars have welcomed attempts at a more restrictive definition of the role of such funds, and have suggested the expansion of the payment of fees for services to the population. They even proposed charging higher rent for apartments and raising the prices of some food products. Widening the gap in wages between higher and lower paid laborers and heightening the influence of income on access to goods and services would on the whole encourage greater inequality in living standards among members of Soviet society. However, the advocates of change are not unequivocally in favor of an increase in the degree of economic differentiation in the Soviet Union, since their proposals would limit or decrease some sources of inequality. Contemporary reformers seek a revision of the basis of economic differentiation in the USSR which would detract from the influence of particularistic connections and enhance emphasis on achievement-related criteria.

In a highly simplified perspective, it might be said that there are three ways in which members of Soviet society may acquire desired material benefits. The first way is through paying money for goods and services in a legal market, either public or private. The second is by receiving benefits from the state or other public organizations, with the benefits subsidized by social consumption funds or enterprise or collective farm funds. The third is by resorting to semilegal or illegal means, including *blat* (personal connections, influence, and tradeoffs), purchases in the "second economy," or outright bribery. The changes currently proposed by reform-minded Soviet scholars would heighten the importance of the first channel of access to benefits, while reducing the significance of the other channels. A Soviet family's ability to acquire goods and services would be more dependent on its ability to pay for them, which would in turn depend to a greater degree than at present on its members' legal earnings. The result would be a shift in the basis of economic differentiation, to the advantage of those with greater skills and higher incomes, and to the disadvantage of those whose connections are relatively good or whose benefits from public sources are relatively generous in comparison with their money incomes.

If the egalitarianism of the Khrushchev years was to a considerable degree a reaction against trends of the Stalin period, the views on social justice expressed by many Soviet scholars under Gorbachev must be understood as a reflection of dissatisfaction with tendencies in Soviet society in the Khrushchev and Brezhnev years. It is quite likely that the material expectations of Soviet citizens have been rising steadily during the post-Stalin decades, in response to Soviet leaders' repeated promises of improvements in the population's standard of living, and as a result of rising levels of education and wages. Expectations appear to have risen especially rapidly among those of the younger generations with more education, who were raised during a long period of peace and economic growth, spared the personal memory of extreme hardships and deprivations, and constantly told that higher levels of education and skills would be rewarded economically, while becoming more aware of living standards generally shared by economically developed countries.[98] Interviews of former citizens of the USSR by the Soviet Interview Project strongly indicate that younger and more educated people tend to be those most dissatisfied with living conditions in the Soviet Union.[99]

The dissatisfaction among younger, better educated, and more skilled Soviet citizens may have been stimulated in part by the reaction to wage reforms instituted under Khrushchev. It is clear that the differences between higher and lower wage earners in the USSR decreased from the middle of the 1950s to the later 1960s.[100] There is disagreement among Western scholars over trends in the differentiation of wages in the Soviet economy from the late 60s to the early 1980s, but it seems likely that no major change in wage inequality took place during those years.[101] The net result of policies under Khrushchev and Brezhnev was that differentials in payments between highly educated specialists and manual workers were quite low, and in many instances perhaps economically inadequate.[102] It may also be concluded, on the basis of an abundance of testimony from Soviet sources, that differences in reward between the more diligent and productive workers and the less diligent and productive were generally low, and often nonexistent.

Though wage differentiation was reduced or restrained under Khrushchev and Brezhnev, during the past few decades increases in money incomes in the USSR have far outpaced the expansion of the supply of goods and services on which people can spend their earnings. One consequence of that combination of trends had been the chronic scarcity of many goods, including some food products and a number of manufactured articles of daily use. Another consequence has been increasing reliance by Soviet citizens on nonmarket or illegal means of acquiring goods. There seems to be general agreement that since the 1970s, the use of *blat* has become more essential, the second economy has grown dramatically, and corruption in regime-sponsored institutions has spread substantially.[103] It is implicit that at the same time any niches of right or privilege in claiming scarce benefits subsidized by the state or other organizations became even more precious than before.

The trends of the preceding periods have produced pressure for revisions in the system of economic rewards in the Soviet system under Gorbachev. The existing structure of reward is being attacked for two reasons. In the first place, the differentiation of wages in the economy is seen by some as not being great enough to stimulate efforts by Soviet citizens to get more education, develop higher skills, and work harder, and therefore as being a hindrance to the acceleration of economic development and technological innovation tirelessly advocated by Gorbachev. That argument, associated with discussions of the need to enhance the contribution of the "human factor" to Soviet economic growth, is a criticism from the viewpoint of technical rationality or efficiency. The second reason that the existing structure of distribution of economic benefits is being subjected to vehement criticism is that that structure is inimical to the values and interests of what may be very roughly referred to as the "new Soviet middle class." The most skilled blue-collar workers and the highly educated professionals who have reached maturity since the Great Patriotic War believe that they are not adequately rewarded at the pay window, that long lines and empty shelves are inexcusable, and that others are getting the best of the system by dubious means. In demanding a merit-based standard of social justice, they decry the failure of existing mechanisms of distribution to measure up to the standard of reward based on achievement. Younger, more educated, and more skilled members of the labor force make up the main constituency for reform in the Soviet Union today.

Yet the issues raised by the advocates of reform in distributive relations are enormously divisive. While relations inhibit the achievement of the aspirations of some groups, they provide economic security for other groups. Those who are relatively well off under existing arrangements include less skilled workers, less diligent laborers, officials with generous privileges, individuals with exceptionally high earnings, and those with particularly enviable personal connections. That is a motley coalition indeed, but the largest force threatened by change consists of older, less educated, and less skilled manual workers. The outpouring of indignant letters to *Kommunist* in opposition to suggestions for reform in the system of reward reveals that many feel that the proposed changes would be an unconscionable violation of the unwritten but crucial social contract between the regime and the Soviet people. The greater candor in the identification of problems and greater frankness in the discussion of suggestions for change which have been promoted by Gorbachev's campaign for increasing glasnost' have made it possible for opposed points of view to emerge more openly and conflicting social forces to coalesce with more self-consciousness than might have been imagined a few years ago. The danger is that proposals for reform in economic reward will polarize large segments of Soviet society.[104] While there are growing, articulate, and restless social forces pressing demands for change, there is also a large, determined, and entrenched grouping of popular interests whose opposition to change must be taken seriously by political leaders.[105] That popular "conservatism" is indicated by the fact that efforts to expand small-scale private enterprise not only have encountered formidable bureaucratic interference but also have aroused considerable indignation over the prospect of exceptional earnings for successful entrepreneurs.[106]

There have been some indications that Mikhail Gorbachev is proceeding carefully with changes that would arouse the most resistance from segments of the Soviet population. In chatting with constituents in his electoral district in Moscow in June 1987 he seemed to classify "attainable housing" among the social guarantees of socialism, separate from the "measure of consumption," which, he said, should depend on each person's labor.[107] Later in the same month, in a speech to a Central Committee meeting on economic reform, though he called for a "radical reform of the formation of prices," he did not specifically mention plans for raising the prices of food products, nor did he speak of the prospect of increasing apartment rents. He did endorse a series of more moderate changes, such as the rapid growth of paid services, the shifting of more resources to individual and cooperative housing construction, and the attraction of more support from the population in payment for the development of facilities for tourism and recreation.[108] In the June 1987 Central Committee Plenum the Soviet leadership seemed committed to the further pursuit of a course of compromise measures, including also the introduction of food products of supposedly enhanced quality for higher prices in state-owned shops, and the expansion of cooperative food stores in urban areas, which may increasingly offer food products, especially meats, that are of better quality but are more expensive than those found in the state shops.[109] It may safely be said that even a leader as confident and impatient as Mikhail Gorbachev is cautious in attempting a revision of the social contract between the Soviet regime and the people over whom it governs.[110]

It is understandable that the raising of food prices and apartment rents is a particularly sensitive issue, since meat prices have remained stable in the USSR since the early 1960s, bread prices have been fixed at the same level since the late 1920s. In Murmansk in October 1987 Gorbachev admitted that the discussion of pricing policy had "aroused a certain uneasiness among the working people and the entire population of the country," and responded in a defensive tone, denying repeatedly that economic reform was designed to lower the living standard of the Soviet people.[111] While addressing the Central Committee in June 1988 he admitted that "the unsettled state" of the problem of price reform was "very greatly complicating the implementation of economic reform," and reported that a "serious study of the question of retail prices" was underway.[112] However, in Kiev in February 1989, acknowledging popular opposition to price increases, Gorbachev announced that talk of such changes would be dropped "for two or three years."[113] The drive for a major revision in retail food prices seemed to be stalled by early 1989.

The Soviet system does not provide many citizens with opportunities for the attainment of living standards close to those of most industrialized nations, but it has succeeded in guaranteeing a high degree of economic security for virtually all members of society. Soviet scholars who have become more prominent under Gorbachev have rejected the contention that secure though mediocre living conditions and the claim of firm social solidarity provide an excuse for refraining from competition with capitalist countries in technological innovation and material affluence.[114] Thus the dominant trend in current thought contrasts sharply with that of the last years of Brezhnev's leadership, and of the short span of Chernenko's interregnum. The period beginning in March 1985 is proving to be a period of reform in Soviet politics and economics, as was the period of the late 1950s and early 1960s. It is not difficult to identify a number of personal linkages and ideological affinities between the two periods. However, a comparison of the party programs of 1961 and 1986 and an examination of detailed expositions of the themes in those two documents reveals that while the reforms sponsored by Khrushchev were intended to create a more egalitarian distribution of economic rewards, contemporary advocates of reform would on balance offer Soviet citizens greater individual opportunity and less economic security.[115] The meritocratic conception of social justice advanced by reformist Soviet scholars under Gorbachev is arousing sharp conflicts of opinion, which reveal that the most formidable obstacle to economic restructuring may be posed not by entrenched bureaucrats, as Gorbachev has often suggested, but by large groups within the Soviet population. Often the most stubborn conflict may even be waged within the mind of the individual citizen, who complains of many inequities in the established arrangements, but at the same time cherishes the protection afforded by those same arrangements. The paradox of Gorbachev's program is that it is premised on the necessity of unleashing the energy and enthusiasm of people who for reasons of personal self-interest may have ambiguous and often inconsistent feelings about reform.

NOTES

1. The implications of changes in social policy for the shared expectations of Soviet leaders and citizens are explored by Peter Hauslohner, "Gorbachev's Social Contract," *Soviet Economy* 3, no. 1, 54–89.
2. Nikita S. Khrushchev, "On the Program of the Communist Party of the Soviet Union," *Current Sovet Policies* 4, ed. Charlotte Saikowski and Leo Gruliow (New York: Columbia University Press, 1962), 98.
3. "The Program of the Communist Party of the Soviet Union," *Current Soviet Policies* 4, 15.
4. "Control Figures for Development of the USSR National Economy in

1959–1965," *Current Soviet Policies* 3, ed. Leo Gruliow (New York: Columbia University Press, 1960), 21.

5. E. L. Manevich, "Raspredelenie po trudu i printsip material'noi zainteresovannosti v period perekhoda ot sotsializma k kommunizmu" (Distribution according to labor and the principle of material incentive in the period of transition from socialism to communism), *Voprosy filosofii*, no. 2, (1963): 20; Boris Sukharevskii, "Stroitel'stvo kommunizma i blagosostoianie naroda" (The construction of communism and the people's well-being), *Kommunist*, no. 14 (1961): 23. In retrospect, it may be noted that Manevich endorsed Khrushchev's wages policy reluctantly, while Sukharevskii did so enthusiastically, and that nuances of difference could accordingly be found in their published works of the early 1960s. The point here is not that Manevich was fully expressing his personal position, but rather that his writings, like others of the period, had to be adapted to the dominant viewpoint of the political leadership.

6. "The Program of the Communist Party," 21.

7. Khrushchev, "On the Program," 111.

8. Boris Sukharevskii, "Zarabotnaia plata i obshchestvennye fondy potrebleniia" (Wages and social funds of consumption), *Voprosy ekonomiki*, no. 8 (1961): 39.

9. Nikita S. Khrushchev, "On Control Figures for Development of the USSR National Economy in 1959–1965," *Current Soviet Policies* 3, 51–52.

10. Khrushchev, "On the Program," 98.

11. N. Kozel'skii, "K voprosu ob obshchestvennom fonde potrebleniia" (On the question of the social fund of consumption), *Voprosy ekonomiki*, no. 7 (1963): 72; Iu. N. Kozyrev, "O raspredelenii fonda obshchestvennogo potrebleniia v period razvernutogo stroitel'stva kommunizma" (On the distribution of the social fund of consumption in the period of full-scale construction of communism), *Voprosy filosofii*, no. 10 (1960): 34; Sukharevskii, "Zarabotnaia plata i obshchestvennye fondy potrebleniia," 43.

12. "The Program of the Communist Party," 21.

13. N. Buzliakov, "O razvitii obshchestvennykh fondov potrebleniia" (On the development of social funds of consumption), *Voprosy ekonomiki*, no. 4 (1962): 38.

14. Khrushchev, "On the Program," 98.

15. "Program of the Communist Party," 22–23.

16. L. M. Gatovskii, "Ob ekonomicheskikh osnovakh perekhoda k kommunizmu" (On the economic foundations of the transition to communism), in *Ot sotsializma k kommunizmu* (From socialism to communism), ed. P. N. Fedoseev et al. (Moscow: Izdatel'stvo Akademii Nauk SSSR, 1962), 61; V. Komarov, "O razvitii obshchestvennykh fondov

potrebleniia v period razvernutogo stroitel'stva kommunizma" (On the development of social funds of consumption in the period of full-scale construction of communism), *Voprosy ekonomiki*, no. 1 (1961): 38.

17. P. Golubkov, "Voprosy razvitiia kolkhozov na puti k kommunizmu" (Questions of the development of collective farms on the path to communism), *Voprosy ekonomiki*, no. 11 (1961): 68.

18. Gatovskii, "Ob ekonomicheskikh osnovakh perekhoda," 51. The debate among Soviet scholars in the early 1960s concerning the future of personal property in communism is outlined by Jerome M. Gilison, *The Soviet Image of Utopia* (Baltimore: Johns Hopkins University Press, 1975), 129–31.

19. E. Manevich, "Ekonomicheskoe stimulirovanie truda i formy perekhoda k kommunisticheskomu raspredeleniiu" (The economic stimulation of labor and the forms of transition to communist distribution), *Voprosy ekonomiki*, no. 5 (1961): 85.

20. P. Mstislavskii, "Kommunizm i ravenstvo" (Communism and equality), *Kommunist*, no. 15 (1961): 29.

21. Khrushchev, "On the Program," 101.

22. "Program of the Communist Party," 15.

23. Alec Nove, *An Economic History of the USSR* (Harmondsworth, England: Penguin Books, 1982), 209; Nove, *The Soviet Economic System*, 2d ed. (London: George Allen and Unwin, 1980), 212.

24. Ibid.

25. Murray Yanowitch, "The Soviet Income Revolution," *Slavic Review* 22, no. 4 (December 1963): 685–86. Michael Ellman, *Collectivisation, Convergence and Capitalism* (London: Academic Press, 1984), 121–22, generally concurs with Yanowitch's conclusions, but presents figures suggesting that inequality in earnings in the USSR may have peaked around 1946. Decreases in inequality in wages apparently began during the later part of the Stalin period. I am grateful to Professor Peter Hauslohner for bringing the trend of the late 1940s and early 1950s to my attention.

26. Yanowitch "The Soviet Income Revolution," 684, 686–92.

27. Ibid., 696.

28. Mikhail S. Gorbachev, *Zhivoe tvorchestvo naroda* [The lively creative activity of the people] (Moscow: Politizdat, 1984), 31–32; Gorbachev, "O sozyve ocherednogo XXVII s"ezda KPSS i zadachakh, sviazannykh s ego podgotovkoi i provedeniem" (On the convocation of the coming Twenty-Seventy Congress of the CPSU and the tasks connected with its preparation and execution), *Kommunist*, no. 7 (1985): 9.

29. Mikhail S. Gorbachev, "Politicheskii doklad Tsentral'nogo Komiteta KPSS XXVII s"ezdu Kommunisticheskoi partii Sovetskogo Soiuza"

(The political report of the Central Committee of the CPSU to the Twenty-Seventh Congress of the Communist Party of the Soviet Union), *XXVII s"ezd Kommunisticheskoi partii Sovetskogo Soiuza, 25 fevr.–6 marta 1986 g.: Stenograficheskii otchet* [The Twenty-Seventh Congress of the Communist Party of the Soviet Union, Feb. 25–March 6, 1986: Stenographic record], vol. 1 (Moscow: Politizdat, 1986), 66. Emphasis added.

30. "Programma Kommunisticheskoi partii Sovetskogo Soiuza" (The Program of the Communist Party of the Soviet Union), *XXVII s"ezd* 1: 584.

31. Ibid., 574.

32. D. Valovoi, "Sotsialisticheskaia ekonomika i ee kritiki" (The socialist economy and its critics), *Pravda*, June 7, 1985.

33. M. N. Rutkevich, "Sotsialisticheskaia spravedlivost' " (Socialist justice), *Sotsiologicheskie issledovaniia*, no. 3 (1986): 16.

34. Gorbachev, "Politicheskii doklad," 68.

35. Mikhail S. Gorbachev, *Bystree perestraivat'sia, deistvovat' po-novomu* [Reforming more rapidly, acting in a new way] (Moscow: Politizdat, 1986), 5.

36. "Programma Kommunisticheskoi partii," 580–81.

37. N. Rimashevskaia, "Income Distribution and Justice," *The Current Digest of the Soviet Press* 38, no. 45 (December 10, 1986): 6 (reprinted from *Ekonomicheskaia gazeta*, no. 40 [1986]: 6–7).

38. B. Rakitskii, 'Ekonomicheskaia effektivnost' i sotsial'naia spravedlivost' " (Economic efficiency and social justice) *Pravda*, January 9, 1987. The antileveling thrust of the recent discussion of wage policy is noted by Walter D. Connor, "Social Policy under Gorbachev," *Problems of Communism* 35, no. 4 (July–August 1986): 42.

39. "Programma Kommunisticheskoi partii," 586.

40. Gorbachev, "Politicheskii doklad," 68. That conclusion is also supported by the analysis of Janet Chapman, "Income Distribution and Social Justice in the USSR" (Paper presented at the Annual Convention of the American Association for the Advancement of Slavic Studies, Boston, November 1987), 14–18.

41. E. L. Manevich, "The Economic Mechanism and the Use of Labor Resources," *Problems of Economics* 29, no. 5 (September 1986): 52 (reprinted from *Ekonomika i organizatsiia promyshlennogo proizvodstva*, no. 12 [1985]: 21–37); L. Rzhanitsyna, "Intensifying the Stimulation of the Effectiveness of Labor," *Problems of Economics* 29, no. 1 (May 1986): 59–60 (reprinted from *Voprosy ekonomiki*, no. 6 [1985]: 82–89).

42. S. Shatalin, "Sotsial'noe razvitie i ekonomicheskii rost" (Social development and economic growth), *Kommunist*, no. 14 (1986): 62; "O chelovecheskom faktore i sotsial'noi spravedlivosti: nekotorye itogi

diskussii" (On the human factor and social justice: some results of the discussion), Khrushchev *Kommunist*, no. 3 (1987): 104.

43. M. S. Gorbachev, "O zadachakh partii po korennoi perestroike upravleniia ekonomikoi" (On the party's tasks in the radical restructuring of economic management), *Pravda*, June 26, 1987.
44. "O chelovecheskom faktore," 114.
45. Gorbachev, "Politicheskii doklad," 68; "Programma Kommunisticheskoi partii," 586.
46. Gorbachev, "Politicheskii doklad," 68.
47. Gorbachev, ibid.
48. "Programma Kommunisticheskoi partii," 586.
49. E. M. Agababian, ed., *Sotsial'no-ekonomicheskaia effektivnost' narodnogo potrebleniia v razvitom sotsialisticheskom obshchestve* (The social-economic efficiency of the people's consumption in developed socialist society) (Moscow: Nauka, 1985), 92–93; V. Z. Rogovin, "Social Justice and Improving Distribution Relations," *Soviet Law and Government* 25, no. 1 (Summer 1986): 12 (reprinted from *Politicheskoe samoobrazovanie*, no. 6 (1985)).
50. Gorbachev, "Politicheskii doklad," 68.
51. "O chelovecheskom faktore," 107.
52. Shatalin, "Sotsial'noe razvitie," 69–70.
53. T. I. Zaslavskaia, "Chelovecheskii faktor razvitiia ekonomiki i sotsial'naia spravedlivost' " (The human factor in the development of the economy and social justice), *Kommunist*, no. 13 (1986): 72–73.
54. Rutkevich, "Sotsialisticheskaia spravedlivost'," 19.
55. A. Bim and A. Shokhin, "Sistema raspredeleniia: na putiakh perestroiki" (The system of distribution: on the paths of restructuring), *Kommunist*, no. 15 (1986): 71.
56. "O chelovecheskom faktore," 106. That writer also mentioned subsidized housing as an important achievement.
57. Gorbachev, "Politicheskii doklad," 70; "Programma Kommunisticheskoi partii," 587.
58. V. Z. Rogovin, "Sotsial'naia spravedlivost' i sotsialisticheskoe raspredelenie zhiznennykh blag" (Social justice and socialist distribution of vital benefits), *Voprosy filosofii*, no. 9 (1986): 10.
59. Shatalin, "Sotsial'noe razvitie," 68.
60. Bim and Shokhin, "Sistema raspredeleniia," 73.
61. "O chelovecheskom faktore," 106.
62. "Programma Kommunisticheskoi partii," 587.
63. Gorbachev, "Politicheskii doklad," 70.
64. M. Sokolova, "O putiakh realizatsii sotsial'nykh garantii" (On the ways of realizing social guarantees), *Kommunist*, no. 17 (1986): 53.
65. Zaslavskaia, "Chelovecheskii faktor," 71.
66. Shatalin, "Sotsial'noe razvitie," 67. Nikolai Shmeliov, "Avansy i dolgi"

(Advances and debts), *Novyi mir*, no. 6 (1987): 151–52, suggests increasing the prices on all food products.
67. "O chelovecheskom faktore," 107.
68. Ibid., 108. See also "Mneniia i predlozheniia" (Opinions and suggestions), *Kommunist*, no. 17 (1986): 64.
69. "Programma Kommunisticheskoi partii," 583.
70. Gorbachev, "Politicheskii doklad," 21.
71. "New Law Sanctions Individual Enterprise," *The Current Digest of the Soviet Press* (hereafter *CDSP*) 38, no. 46 (December 17, 1986): 1–8. The compromises built into that law showed that official support for private economic activity was still quite tentative. Elizabeth Teague, "Mikhail Gorbachev and 'The Lessons of Poland'," in *Solidarity and the Soviet Worker* (forthcoming). Partly because of remaining restrictions, the actual expansion of private enterprise under the new law has generally been viewed as disappointing.
72. O. Latsis, "Indivual'nyi trud v sovremennoi sotsialisticheskoi ekonomike" (Individual labor in a contemporary socialist economy), *Kommunist*, no. 1 (1987): 78.
73. Ibid., 81.
74. "Programma Kommunisticheskoi partii," 578–79, 586.
75. Zaslavskaia, "Chelovecheskii faktor," 67.
76. "Mneniia i predlozheniia," 64, 66.
77. T. I. Zaslavskaia, "Tvorcheskaia aktivnost' mass: sotsial'nye rezervy rosta" (The creative activity of the masses: social reserves of growth), *Ekonomika i organizatsiia promyshlennogo proizvodstva*, no. 3 (1986): 21.
78. T. I. Zaslavskaia, "The Human Factor and Social Justice," *CDSP* 38, no. 5 (March 5, 1986): 3 (reprinted from *Sovetskaia kul'tura*, Jan. 23, 1986); Rutkevich, "Sotsialisticheskaia spravedlivost'," 20. See also Rogovin, "Sotsial'naia spravedlivost'," 20.
79. Rogovin, "Sotsial'naia spravedlivost," 20.
80. Ibid., 15.
81. Ibid.
82. S. Shatalin and V. Grebennikov, "Personal Income, Taxes, and Social Justice," *CDSP* 38, no. 44 (December 3, 1986): 11 (reprinted from *Ekonomicheskaia gazeta*, no. 42 [October 1986]: 2, 4).
83. Rogovin, "Social Justice and Improving Distribution Relations," 16. Zaslavakaia also favors a progressive tax on personal incomes.
84. "Programma Kommunisticheskoi partii," 586.
85. Gorbachev, "Politicheskii doklad," 69.
86. Ibid.
87. Rogovin, "Sotsial'naia spravedlivost," 20.
88. Rogovin, "Social Justice and Improving Distribution Relations," 17.
89. "Programma Kommunisticheskoi partii," 580.

90. Ibid., 587; Gorbachev, "Politicheskii doklad," 70.
91. "Programma Kommunisticheskoi partii," 587.
92. Carol Nechemias, "Recent Changes in Soviet Rural Housing Policy" (Paper presented at the Conference on Soviet Agriculture in Gorbachev's First Five-Year Plan, at the Kennan Institute for Advanced Russian Studies, Washington, D. C., April 3–4, 1986), 18.
93. Hedrick Smith, *The Russians* (New York: Times Books, 1983), 29–56; Mervyn Mathews, *Privilege in the Soviet Union* (London: George Allen and Unwin, 1978), 36–55.
94. T. Samolis, "Cleansing: A Frank Discussion," *CDSP* 38, no. 6 (March 12, 1986): 2 (reprinted from *Pravda*, Feb. 13, 1986), 2.
95. B. N. El'tsin, "Rech' tovarishcha Yel'tsina B. N." (Speech by Comrade B. N. El'tsin), *XXVII s"ezd*, vol. 1, 143. Those remarks were characteristic of the boldness that may have played a role in bringing about El'tsin's later removal from the post of head of the Moscow Party organization.
96. E. K. Ligachev, "Rech' tovarishcha Ligacheva Ye. K." (Speech by Comrade E. K. Ligachev), *XXVII S"ezd*, vol. 1, 236.
97. Amy Corning, "Attitudes Toward Privileges in the Soviet Union," Radio Liberty Research Report, July 14, 1988; "Conference Speakers Debate Reforms," *CDSP* 40, no. 35 (September 28, 1988; reprinted from *Pravda*, July 2, 1988), 8, 12. In *Voprosy filosofii* in September 1986 Rogovin repeated the assertion that special privileges arouse popular dissatisfaction: "several advantages, which now are factually utilized by some workers, especially workers of the apparatus of administration, violate socialist principles of distribution and therefore evoke social discontent and tension." Rogovin, "Sotsial'naia spravedlivost'," 8. The Soviet press has also printed some letters contending that reports of the privileges of Communist party officials, in particular, have been exaggerated; S. Karnaukhov, "About Privileges and Openness," *CDSP* 40, no. 31 (August 31, 1988): 19 (reprinted from *Pravda*, August 1, 1988).
98. John Bushnell, "The 'New Soviet Man' Turns Pessimist," in *The Soviet Union Since Stalin*, ed. Stephen Cohen, Alexander Rabinowitch, and Robert Sharlet (Bloomington: Indiana University Press, 1980), 179–99.
99. See the summary of the findings of the Soviet Interview Project by James R. Millar and Peter Donhowe, "Life, Work, and Politics in Soviet Cities," *Problems of Communism*, 36, no. 1 (January–February 1987): 46, 51–52. Among detailed reports on the SIP, see especially James R. Millar and Elizabeth Clayton, "Quality of Life: Subjective Measures of Relative Satisfaction," in *Politics, Work, and Daily Life in the USSR*, ed. James R. Millar (Cambridge: Cambridge University Press, 1987), 33, 37; and Donna Bahry, "Politics, Genera-

194   *Alfred B. Evans, Jr.*

tions and Change in the USSR," in *Politics, Work and Daily Life*, 91–94.

100. Murray Yanowitch, *Social and Economic Inequality in the Soviet Union: Six Studies* (White Plains, N.Y.: M. E. Sharpe, 1977), 24–25; Alastair McAuley, *Economic Welfare in the Soviet Union: Poverty, Living Standards, and Inequality* (Madison: University of Wisconsin Press, 1979), 222–41; Gertrude Schroeder, "Consumption," in *The Soviet Economy Toward the Year 2000*, ed. Abram Bergson and Herbert S. Levine (London: George Allen and Unwin, 1983), 344.

101. Ibid.; Jerry Hough, "Issues and Personalities," *Problems of Communism* 31, no. 5 (September–October 1982): 25–26. The effects of wage reforms from the 1950s to the 1970s in reducing wage differentials are detailed by Janet G. Chapman, "Recent Trends in the Soviet Industrial Wage Structure," *Industrial Labor in the USSR*, ed. Arcadius Kahan and Blair A. Ruble (New York: Pergamon Press, 1979), 151–83. Chapman, "Income Distribution and Social Justice," 3–4, shows inequality in the earnings of Soviet workers in 1985 as higher than in 1968, but still substantially lower than in 1956.

102. The decline in the difference in wages between engineering-technical workers and manual workers from 1965 to 1980 is detailed by Hough, ibid., and by Yanowitch, *Social and Economic Inequality in the Soviet Union*, 30–31. In some cases, manual workers are actually paid more than engineers. Shmeliov, "Avansy i dolgi," 155. As a result, there are frequent instances of people educated to be engineers or other specialists who elect to take jobs as blue-collar workers.

103. Gail Warshofsky Lapidus, "Social Trends," in *After Brezhnev: Sources of Soviet Conduct in the 1980s*, ed. Robert F. Byrnes (Bloomington: Indiana University Press, 1983), 238, 242; William Zimmerman, "Mobilized Participation and the Nature of the Soviet Dictatorship," in *Politics, Work, and Daily Life*, 349–50. The thesis that the Soviet regime under Brezhnev tolerated a substantial growth of illegal economic activity, as well as legal and semilegal private enterprise, is presented by James R. Millar, "The Little Deal: Brezhnev's Contribution to Acquisitive Socialism," *Slavic Review* 44, no. 4: 697–98.

104. The possibility of such polarization is emphasized by Tat'iana Zaslavskaia, "Ekonomika skvoz' prizmu sotsiologii" (The economy through the prism of sociology), *Ekonomika i organizatsiia promyshlennogo proizvodstva*, no. 7, 1985, 21–22. The polarization of opinions on proposals for expanding paid medical services, raising apartment rents, and raising food prices is demonstrated by P. Aven, "Mekhanizm raspredeleniia i sotsial'naia spravedlivost' " (The mechanism of distribution and social justice), *Kommunist*, no. 15 (1987): 112–22.

105. Archie Brown, "Soviet Political Developments and Prospects," *World Policy Journal* 4, no. 1 (Winter 1986–1987): 65, notes that opposition

to reform in the USSR may come not only from bureaucrats but also from workers.

106. "Individual Labor," *CDSP* 39, no. 36 (October 7, 1987): 1–4 (reprinted from *Izvestiia*, September 9, 1987); E. Maksimovsky, "Socialism Gives a License to the Cooperative," *CDSP* 39, no. 41 (November 11, 1987): 5 (reprinted from *Sovetskaia Rossiia*, July 24, 1987); Irina Kruglianskaia, "Other People's Money," *CDSP* 39, no. 51 (January 20, 1988): 9–10 (reprinted from *Izvestiia*, December 12, 1988).

107. "Vstrecha na izbiratel'nom uchastke" (Meeting in electoral district), *Pravda*, June 22, 1987, 1.

108. Gorbachev, "O zadachakh partii po korennoi perestroike upravleniia ekonomikoi." Gorbachev's words were imitated by the resolution passed by the Central Committee. "Osnovnye polozheniia korennoi perestroiki upravleniia ekonomikoi" (Basic propositions on the radical restructuring of economic management), *Pravda*, June 27, 1987, 1–3.

109. Increasing reliance on cooperative stores in urban areas was noted by Elizabeth Teague, "A Greater Role for the Cooperative Sector," *Radio Liberty Research Report*, August 22, 1986, 2. Chapman, "Income Distribution and Social Justice," 28, also points out that Soviet state farms and collective farms have been given the right to sell a larger proportion of their produce in the collective farm markets, where prices tend to be much higher than in state food stores. There are also signs of encouragement for the development of cooperative cafes in Soviet cities. Elrad Parkhomovsky, "The Law of Small Numbers," *CDSP* 39, no. 18 (June 3, 1987): 9, 19 (reprinted from *Izvestiia*, May 1, 1987).

110. Elizabeth Teague, "Gorbachev's First Two Years in Power," *Radio Liberty Research Report*, March 9, 1987, 4; idem, "Mikhail Gorbachev and 'The Lessons of Poland'."

111. M. S. Gorbachev, "Speech by Comrade M. S. Gorbachev," *CDSP* 39, no. 40 (November 4, 1987): 4 (reprinted from *Pravda*, October 2, 1987).

112. M. S. Gorbachev, "O khode realizatsii reshenii XXVII s"ezda KPSS i zadachakh po uglubleniiu perestroiki" (On the course of implementation of the decisions of the Twenty-seventh Congress of the CPSU and the tasks of deepening restructuring), *Kommunist*, no. 10 (1988): 13–14.

113. "Gorbachev Vows to Freeze Prices, Boost Food Output," *Los Angeles Times*, February 23, 1989.

114. That point of view, decisively repudiated by Gorbachev and recent Soviet scholarly writings, is described by Alfred Evans, Jr., "The Decline of Developed Socialism? Some Trends in Recent Soviet Ideology," *Soviet Studies* 38, no. 1 (January 1986): 1–23.

115. It should be noted that while recent proposals would encourage the growth of differences in economic well-being among individuals of different levels of skill and productivity, they would not necessarily

entail any decrease in emphasis on reducing inequality between urban and rural dwellers, and between industrial and agricultural workers. The effects of changes in policy on economic differences among regions and nationalities in the Soviet Union are still another question, which deserves separate attention. Any discussion of policy affecting the distribution of economic benefits should recognize that there are many distinct dimensions of inequality in human societies.

7

GORBACHEV'S REFORMS: THE IMPLICATIONS OF RESTRUCTURING FOR WORKERS' EMPLOYMENT SECURITY

Linda J. Cook

I. INTRODUCTION

The provision of full, secure, and stable employment is one of the long-standing achievements of Soviet socialism. In the past several decades, the system has effectively protected Soviet workers against the displacement, unemployment, and downward mobility which have affected industrial working classes in most other developed nations. Gorbachev's program of economic revitalization now calls for a restructuring of the labor force which would significantly reduce job stability and security for at least some groups of workers. The reformers have set forth plans for large-scale reductions in the use of manual labor, massive transfers of workers from production to service sectors, and dramatic increases in the efficiency and productivity of labor throughout the economy. The prominent reform advocate Tat'iana Zaslavskaia has written of the anticipated effects:

Reductions will release [millions] of largely unskilled workers and those least productive or "valued" by labor collectives . . . redistribution of manpower among sectors, enterprises, professions, and job groups . . . will be accompanied by great difficulties, mobility, and "psychological restructuring" of groups of workers historically noted for high stability . . . and [there will be] disproportions and difficulties in finding jobs for some population groups.[1]

The reformers' challenge to job security raises a number of important questions about the representation and institutionalization of workers' interests in the Soviet system. We may usefully begin by

197

considering *why* Soviet workers have been assured stable employment, and how this guarantee has been protected, defended, and
institutionalized within the economic and political system. Three
conceptually distinct (though not mutually exclusive) explanations
can be proposed: (1) coincidence with separate elite interests; (2)
selective representation of workers' interests; (3) the "social contract" between regime and society.

1. It can be argued that Soviet workers have had job security
because the economic and planning mechanisms motivate industrial managers to retain and hoard labor, i.e., that workers' interest
in stable employment has been protected primarily because it has
coincided with a distinct interest or goal of a powerful elite group.
Such a view sees workers' security as highly contingent, as a spin-
off of the priorities (or dysfunctions) of the industrial management
system, and by implication as politically vulnerable if that coincidence is weakened or ended.

2. It has been argued that workers' job security is effectively
protected by a set of political institutions (mainly trade unions but
also to some extent the relevant state committees, courts, local youth
boards, and so forth) which have been vested with the role of representing workers' interests and overseeing enforcement of formal
legislative guarantees of employment rights. Analysts differ in their
assessments of the political independence and effectiveness of such
institutions, but most would agree that they have played some role
in defending workers' claims to job security.[2]

3. It has also been argued that workers' employment security
constitutes a central condition of an implicit social contract between
the post-Stalinist regime and Soviet society.[3] The social contract
argument assumes that the political leadership has purposefully
traded guarantees of welfare and security for political quiescence
and a degree of mass legitimacy. It implies that the regime is constrained by societal expectations or demands which must be either
accommodated or repressed.

In this chapter I will first look at each of these three factors,
managerial interests, representation of workers' interests, and elite
commitment to a social contract, and argue that they have func-
tioned as mutually-reinforcing bases for protection of workers' security in recent decades. I will then look at the reform process to

determine how it is addressing each of these three factors. What kinds of ideological constraints and institutional resistances do they pose to the Gorbachev leadership's program of labor force restructuring? How do the reformers propose to change managerial incentives, reorganize responsibilities for employment, and redefine the state's social welfare role?

Management's Incentives to Retain and Hoard Labor

The conditions of the Soviet economy and production process create inflated demand and competition for labor throughout much of the industrial sector. The pressures and incentives which push managements to overman their enterprises are generally well-known. First, the central imperative faced by the Soviet manager is to fulfill a material production plan within an established time frame. He must do so under conditions of uneven and uncertain supply of inputs, which in turn produces unevenness in the enterprise's production cycle, and in a full-employment, labor-short economy which makes available neither reserves nor temporary and flexible labor resources. He must respond to periodic demands on his labor force from state and local authorities to carry out tasks which are completely extraneous to his enterprise's production assignment. And he faces comparatively weak pressures to use labor efficiently or to minimize its costs. Given this combination of incentives, the typical behavior of managers is to try to keep on hand a work force large enough to meet demand at the peak of the production cycle. Such overmanning in turn exacerbates shortages of and competition for labor, inducing management to keep the workers it has, since it generally can't count on replacing them.[4]

The managerial propensity to overman is reinforced by the method of establishing the size of the enterprise's labor force and wage bill. Both are determined by negotiations between the enterprise and its ministry, with the total wage bill largely dependent on the number and classifications of workers. It is in the interest of enterprise management to maximize (within reason) the size of its labor force in order to maximize claims from the center. One goal of all attempts at economic reform, including the present, has been to revise the criteria for defining the wage bill, to link them to productivity rather than the size of the work force, to create a system which will allow managers to eliminate superfluous workers while retaining (and redistributing) their wages, and ultimately to make wages dependent on enterprise earnings. The success of such reforms would not only make employment less secure, but would produce variation in wage rates according to enterprise earnings, in place of the relative uniformity of wage scales throughout industry under the present system.

Finally, the Soviets' reliance on an "extensive" pattern of economic development, i.e., development based mainly on increases in productive capacity and labor inputs rather than productivity and efficiency, have maintained a growing demand for labor which has exceeded the growth in supply. The result, from the 1970s, has been high levels of job vacancies in many sectors, an inability to staff newly constructed enterprises, severe labor shortages in some regions, and efforts to pull more marginal labor resources (i.e., pensioners, students) into the work force.[5] The exhaustion of increments to the labor force in the most industrially-developed regions of the country is one of the central factors pushing the regime in the direction of reform.

Both managerial incentives to inflate labor forces and (partly as a result) high "market" demand for labor have created structural supports for workers' job security, quite apart from elite political commitments or legislative guarantees. Peter Hauslohner's study of managers' behavior during the 1965 economic reform offers an apt illustration. The reform gave managers greater control over staffing levels, with the intent that they would reduce labor forces and improve the efficiency of labor utilization. Hauslohner concludes that managements generally used this control to expand staffs instead. They did so in spite of the fact that the political elite had explicitly acknowledged a willingness to tolerate some displacement of workers, and in the apparent absence of any increase in trade union or legal challenges to dismissals.[6] The 1965 reform thus provides evidence that the independent motivations and calculations of Soviet managers have in and of themselves contributed powerfully to protecting jobs, and suggests that managers will continue to respond to the long-established incentives for hoarding labor until and unless those incentives are changed fundamentally.

Institutional and Legislative Guarantees of Employment Security

Soviet labor codes and legislation have in recent decades established strong legal underpinnings for workers' employment rights. Regulations with regard to hiring, transfers, dismissals, and layoffs provide substantial de jure guarantees for individual workers. The strengthening and reinforcement of workers' legal claims to job security has led Blair Ruble to conclude from a review of labor legislation that, "Over the past two decades the focus (of legislation) has moved . . . from the right to work . . . toward guaranteeing the right to continue at one's current job."[7] Gorbachev's reforms call for an abrupt reversal of direction in this area.

Under present Soviet labor codes, management's right to terminate a worker's contract without cause (i.e., except in cases of disciplinary violations) is subject to several restrictions. First, management can lay off a worker only if it is reducing the total number of workers or job slots (or changing the mix of occupations and specialties) at the enterprise overall; any vacant positions must be filled by within-enterprise transfers before currently employed workers can be dismissed. Secondly, management is required to offer a worker dismissed from his job because of staff reductions or reorganization any other available job within the enterprise which suits his specialty, qualifications, experience, health, and so on. Third, management must gain the approval of the factory trade union committee for the dismissal by certifying that it has fulfilled both of these conditions, and that the worker could not be transferred within the factory or that he refused the job offered.[8] The law does not prohibit worker layoffs, but the thrust of legislation has been to limit managerial control and flexibility in staffing and personnel decisions, to place obstacles in the way of dismissing any worker who does not egregiously violate labor discipline, and to give workers the stable expectation of remaining at a single enterprise.

In addition, Soviet employment and dismissal policies impose on enterprises a number of restrictions which serve social and welfare goals extraneous to production. In cases of layoffs, the enterprise may preferentially retain its most qualified and productive workers; then it must observe seniority rules and veterans' preferences. Preference goes next to employees whose families include two or more dependents or those with only a single breadwinner, and so forth. Moreover, certain categories of workers, including youth and some women, are protected against dismissals except in cases when the enterprise itself is liquidated, and then only with mandatory job placement, and all enterprises are required to hold a quota of openings for work and training of youth.[9] Welfare organizations outside the factory may intervene on behalf of these workers in cases of violations. The imposition of such regulations, which often protect less productive and more vulnerable workers, further restrict management's control over the selection and composition of its labor force and have already begun to come into conflict with the productivity pressures of the current reforms.

How effectively are such job protections enforced in Soviet industry? Both trade unions and courts have responsibilities for monitoring managerial compliance with labor legislation and ruling on workers' grievances and challenges to dismissals. Workers who claim they have been dismissed in violation of any of the above provisions may appeal the decision, first to the factory trade union committee, then through higher levels of the trade union bureaucracy or in civil court. Available evidence indicates that in most cases both unions and courts have strongly defended procedural guarantees. Rates of reinstatement of workers who challenged dismissal in the courts have been consistently high—50 to 60 percent for the years 1960 to 1980 for the USSR as a whole—and decisions and guidelines from the higher courts during the Brezhnev period have generally extended workers' rights.[10] At the same time, the facts of these very cases, along with the results of separate investigations and evaluations, indicate that violations are not uncommon and that previous central reforming initiatives directed toward streamlining labor forces have produced some large-scale illegal dismissals. Moreover, workers clearly can be dismissed for political nonconformity, either of regime norms or of informal factory norms, and other political considerations and influences may intrude on trade union and court decisions.[11] The overall picture that emerges is one of general if imperfect managerial compliance with legislative protections and reasonably effective oversight and enforcement.

However, a more critical consideration of the legislation and institutional oversight procedures currently in place suggests that they will provide little formal protection for workers' jobs in the face of the large-scale labor force reorganization and sectoral reductions planned by the reformers. Managers do have the right, according to the labor code, to reduce and reorganize their labor force, change its skill mix, and retain the most skilled and productive workers in preference to others. Layoffs of substantial numbers of workers concentrated in a small range of skill levels or categories (i.e., low-skilled manual workers, as envisioned) would render largely irrelevant the procedural guarantees and preferences which have been elaborated and reinforced in recent decades. The requisite total labor force reductions would be real enough, and it would certainly prove impossible to transfer many of these similarly and poorly qualified workers simultaneously within factories that were automating and drastically reducing their reliance on manual labor. Trade unions would have no formal or legal basis to block such layoffs, as long as managements had conformed to the administrative requirement of certifying the above conditions. Indeed, while Soviet labor legislation would presumably block the paring down of a factory's labor force by dismissal of individual incompetent or unproductive workers, it would seem to make de jure allowances for large-scale layoffs even without weakening or revision.

Perhaps the most important effect of these limited formal obligations, for our purposes, is that they have evolved into broad informal expectations in Soviet society that managements are responsible for the subsequent job placement of dismissed workers.[12] The combination, over a long period, of extensive protections against individual dismissal, rarity of large-scale layoffs, and the common practice of transferring redundant workers within factories, has produced an assumption among workers generally that the informal rules of the game protect them against unemployment, displacement, and the responsibility and insecurity of negotiating in the labor market. This expectation acts as an informal but apparently powerful constraint on managerial behavior, making managers unwilling (because of the administrative burden, diffuse social pressures, or both) to dismiss workers who will prove difficult or impossible to transfer.[13] It is probably significant in this regard that careful study of the Shchekino experiment, touted as a model for the streamlining and efficient use of labor, concluded that more than two-thirds of those workers "released" were ultimately moved to other jobs at the same enterprise.[14] The current reformers repeatedly point to such expectations as a block to necessary labor force cuts, and their program includes an explicit restructuring and reassignment of responsibilities for employment.

Social Contract

The assurance of full and secure employment has long been an integral part of the Soviet regime's formula for legitimacy, central both to elite claims that the system is just and to popular attitudes of acceptance. Many scholars argue that the social stability and mass legitimacy of the Soviet (and other state socialist) systems are based on an implicit social contract between regime and society. According to the standard analysis, in the post-Stalin period, when the political leadership ended its reliance on terror and (for the most part) coercion to enforce political order, it sought popular acceptance of its political monopoly in exchange for assurances of welfare, security, relative equality, and improving living standards.[15] The social contract argument assumes that the regime has provided such guarantees as an anticipatory response to societal demands that might otherwise become politicized. Post-Stalin leaderships may also have succeeded, as various authors have claimed, in limiting such demands, manipulating expectations, and segmenting groups with shared interests.[16] But through the past several decades, Soviet political leaders have acted to keep all segments of Soviet society tied into a highly dependent relationship to a comprehensive and paternalistic welfare state.

During the post-Stalin and especially the Brezhnev period, these three factors—managerial interests, legislation and practice relating to job stability, and elite commitment to a social contract, served as mutually reinforcing supports for workers' employment security. The following section will examine the intended, and some actual, effects of Gorbachev's reforms on workers' job stability. It will then consider how the reformers' program is confronting the multiple defenses and protections of workers' job rights which have been institutionalized within the Soviet system.

II. THE REFORM PROGRAM AND THE THREAT TO EMPLOYMENT SECURITY

Gorbachev's reform program calls for a major and rapid transition in the structure of production and employment in the Soviet economy, a shift toward a postindustrial system characterized by high levels of automation and a much-expanded service sector. This reform is being imposed on a labor force which has undergone very gradual structural changes in recent decades, and as a result retains a high proportion of workers in material and manual production. The share of Soviet workers employed in material production stood at 76.2 percent in 1970 and declined by 1.7 percent in the Ninth Five-Year Plan, 1.3 percent in the Tenth, and 0.7 percent in the Eleventh, to 72.5 percent in 1985, showing a low and declining rate of shift from production to nonproduction spheres over these years.[17]

Changes in the structure of employment within sectors of material production have likewise proceeded slowly, with the result that some one-third of industrial workers, one-half of construction workers, (and two-thirds of agricultural workers) remain engaged in manual, usually low-skilled, often physically arduous labor.[18] In a 1987 total Soviet labor force of approximately 131 million, 50 million were classified as manual.[19] A combination of lack of incentives for technical innovation in the planning mechanism, direction of investment to new construction rather than retooling of obsolete plants, and insufficient investment in the machine-building sector which is critical to technical modernization throughout industry, largely explain the continuing heavy reliance on manual labor.

Gorbachev's reform program calls for dramatic cuts in the levels of manual labor throughout Soviet industry and construction. The Comprehensive Program for the Social and Economic Development of the USSR to the Year 2000, approved by the Twenty-seventh Party Congress, establishes a goal of reductions in the use of manual labor to 15 to 20 percent from the current level of one-third, i.e., a decrease of as much as 50 percent in industry over the next fifteen years, and Ryzhkov has confirmed a target of more than 50 percent reductions, projecting the release of more than 20 million from their present employment as manual workers.[20] The 1986–90 Five-Year Plan stipulates that the number of manual production workers be decreased by more than 5 million by 1990, i.e., more than 10 percent of the total, while the volume of work performed manually in construction is to be reduced by 25 percent.[21] Reductions are to be concentrated in several industrial sectors, including coal, timber, food, railroads, and machine-building as well as construction, and within industrial sectors, especially among those engaged in auxiliary functions such as lifting-transport, loading-unloading, and warehouse work.[22] The Central Statistical Administration's report on fulfillment of the state plan for 1986 indicates that more than 1 million manual workers were in fact "released for other work."[23]

The Gorbachev leadership insists that restructuring will pose no threat to full employment or workers' job security. It makes credible claims that large numbers of released workers can be reabsorbed into the existing economy, at least during the early stages of the reform. The general secretary himself has emphasized the possibilities for transfer of labor to manpower-short production sectors, pointing out that industry alone had 700,000 vacancies (in June 1986) with a predominant system of one-shift equipment use, and that a planned increase in the shift coefficient would produce some 4 million vacancies.[24] But it must be recognized that even such transfers within the industrial sector, carried out on any substantial scale, would entail unprecedented (even if temporary) displacement and dislocation for large numbers of workers, undermining the accustomed stability of their working lives. Reallocation of the labor force will also face regional and linguistic barriers in the multiethnic Soviet state.

Moreover, in the somewhat longer term the reform is to mean much more than transfers of workers within industry. It is intended that technological modernization and productivity increases will produce deep cuts not only in use of manual labor but in levels of employment in the material production sector overall, with a corresponding shift of labor into the service sector. The reformist economist Abalkin has projected that 15 to 20 million surplus workers in agriculture and manufacturing will be moved into the service sector by the end of the century, 3 million during the 1986–90 Five-Year

Plan.[25] The more radical Kostakov argues that much "excess" labor should move out of the state sector into the recently-legalized cooperative sector, and that some relatively marginal labor resources should be removed from the productive economy entirely. He makes the critical point that a "mathematical equivalence" between numbers of workers released and numbers demanded in different sectors means little because, "as a rule, the professional structures of those 'freed' and those for whom there is demand do not correspond."[26] Indeed, one might question how many of the low-skilled manual workers who are the prime target of labor force cuts could move into the service sector (defined as culture, education, health care, and leisure), except in the most menial capacities. Nor does it seem likely that many will muster the initiative, resources, and entrepreneurial skills to enter the cooperative sector. Again Zaslavskaya frankly confronts the likely effects, admitting that the process of reform

does not exclude a worsening of the situation in finding jobs for honest and conscientious people, insufficiently well-educated and not ready for retraining. [Some] will need material and social assistance including . . . expanding family and cooperative forms of work, creating facilities for early retirement, etc. It is difficult to imagine at the present time the entire set of social problems related to the acceleration of scientific and technical progress.[27]

I argued in the first part of this chapter that job stability for Soviet workers has been assured by a system of incentives which motivates managements to hoard labor and imposes on them informal obligations for transfer of redundant workers, a set of institutional and legal obstacles to dismissal, and an elite commitment to full and secure employment. How is the reform process confronting each of these established supports for employment security? Reform policies have in fact been designed to restructure managerial incentives for utilization of labor, reorganize responsibilities for employment, and redefine both workers' social and legal protections and the state's welfare functions. In the following section, I will discuss in turn the reform policies directed toward each of these goals.

Restructuring Managerial Incentives

In the early stages of the current reform, the Gorbachev leadership relied on a number of campaigns, experiments, and reorganizations to create pressures for streamlining and reductions throughout all sectors of the industrial labor force. The campaign for "certification" of work places, initiated in 1983 under Yuri Andropov, was designed to bring administrative pressures to bear from above by requiring that industrial managers check all work stations, i.e., workers and equipment, eliminate those which were obsolete or unproductive, and report on results. The extension during the same period of the brigade system, which gave work collectives both the power and economic incentive to shed members judged to be superfluous or inefficient, was intended to create corresponding pressures from below. The center also pressed for broader application of the Shchekino method, a plan for releasing workers by combining operations, expanding service zones, and increasing the volume of work performed by individuals.

The campaigns for certification of workplaces and establishment of economic accountability brigades produced some limited effects, but overall results were disappointing. The 1986 plan fulfillment report concluded on job certification and streamlining that, "in many industries work was developing slowly and producing no tangible results," and on brigades, that "the proportion of the most progressive forms, operating on an economic accounting system and contract basis, continues to be low."[28] These poor results give evidence of continuing, predictable managerial resistance against administrative pressures for labor force reductions, resistance which helped push the Gorbachev leadership toward the broad restructuring of planning and incentive systems codified in the Law on State Enterprises.

The Law on State Enterprises,[29] approved by the June 1987 CPSU Central Committee Plenum, replaces administrative pressures with economic levers for the efficient use of labor. The law will, if fully implemented, place most enterprises on a self-financing and competitive basis and force consistently unprofitable production units into bankruptcy. It is to be implemented for enterprises in all sectors of material production during 1988–89. The law is designed to give managements and labor collectives greater control over wage levels and disparities, to make wage bills dependent on enterprise profits rather than central allocations, and to make profits in turn increasingly dependent on private contracts between enterprises and the purchasers of their products and services rather than on state contracts.[30] These measures are intended to create a combination of pressures and incentives which will motivate managers to reduce the size and increase the efficiency of their labor forces. Full implementation of the Law on the Enterprise would produce an unpredictable scale and pattern of redundancies throughout the Soviet economy, and the mass elimination of jobs through liquidation of insolvent enterprises.

Reorganizing Responsibilities for Employment

Gorbachev's reform also includes a number of measures which remove from factory managements both formal and informal obligations for the future employment of those released in labor force reductions. First, responsibility for transfer and placement of dismissed workers is being shifted from the employing enterprise to state labor bureaus. Secondly, the leadership has begun to restructure labor's social and legal protections in directions which will both unfetter management's control over staffing and ease the transition of workers into new jobs or out of the labor force. Thirdly, democratization and self-management policies are supposed to institutionalize workers' involvement in hiring, firing, (and wage distribution) decisions, placing on workers themselves some of the onus for dismissals and displacement.

Prominent reformers have for some time insisted that managements must be relieved of responsibility for placement of released workers, and that this responsibility should revert to the state; in Kostakov's terms, managers should answer only for the effectiveness of labor, and the state for full employment.[31] Virtually all major reform advocates have called for a policy of comprehensive state planning of labor allocation,[32] and as it began implementation of the Law on State Enterprises in January 1988 the party adopted such a policy. A major Central Committee resolution, "On Ensuring Efficient Employment of the Population, Improving the Job Placing

System, and Strenghthening Social Guarantees for the Working People,"[33] set forth plans for a national system of employment centers and bureaus which are to provide vocational guidance, retraining, and job placement to workers released in the course of labor force reductions or plant closings. The statewide system of job placement bureaus is intended "to resolve the tasks of predicting, planning, and regulating the population's employment . . . and organizing the systematic, prompt redistribution of manpower resources in the national economy,"[34]

The resolution stresses that Soviet citizens have the right to work. It retains the provision that workers released from a particular enterprise or institution have priority in assignment to any suitable vacant position within that enterprise/institution or in any facility under its jurisdiction. The resolution itself, along with commentary by officials from the State Committee for Labor and Social Questions and the Council of Ministers Bureau for Social Development, indicates an expectation that many "excess" workers will be re-absorbed through introduction of additional shifts at their enterprise, or transferred to work in plant modernization, construction, services, or subsidiary production under its auspices.[35] Job placement bureaus are to work in cooperation with enterprises, labor organs of local soviets, trade union organs, and ministries, to "make provision in good time and on a planned basis for subsequent placing in jobs [of released workers]." And at one point the resolution hedges, leaving open the possibility for direct interference in dismissals by local political authorities: "In exceptional cases, with a view to better organized placing for released workers, local soviet *ispolkoms* may, with the consent of the labor collectives, defer schedules for releasing workers from enterprises, organizations, and institutions."[36]

But in spite of the clause on "exceptional cases," and some continuing ambiguity on the responsibility of managements to their released workers, the resolution on employment clearly envisions and provides for large-scale labor force dismissal and displacement throughout the Soviet economy in the coming years. It stipulates that labor contracts may be broken, "in connection with the implementation of measures to cut the number of workers or establishment." It instructs governmental, political, and social organizations to encourage, assist, and organize movement of released workers to labor deficit areas, including Siberia and the Far East. It provides for the organized transfer of labor resources from the generally well-paid production sector to the more poorly-remunerated service sector, directing local Soviet ispolkoms to, "carry out systematic, purposeful redistribution of released workers to enterprises and organizations in the sphere of services to the population, ensuring the accelerated development of that sphere."[37] It calls on the population to accept that the existing employment structure "inevitably leads to stagnation," that large-scale transfers of labor between sectors and regions are necessary to economic revitalization, and that the state is taking all possible measures to plan and manage transfers and to cushion their inevitably painful effects on workers.[38] Finally, workers themselves are to participate in decisions on labor force reductions; according to *Pravda*: "Questions connected with release, retraining, and placement . . . are to be resolved on a democratic basis, . . . with the direct and active participation of the labor collective."[39]

Establishment of a network of state employment agencies to coordinate retraining and placement of released workers will certainly ease the transition of many who have been accustomed to stable employment. Workers who lose jobs also have the right to seek new employment independently (although employing organizations are required to inform employment centers about job vacancies and all workers released or hired.) But overall, both the likely end of over-demand for labor and the beginning of a direct state role in its allocation will mean a deterioration in the effective rights and bargaining position of Soviet workers. Since the 1950s workers have enjoyed not only job stability but the right to quit jobs and seek new ones at their own initiative, a right which has afforded real leverage to skilled workers in labor-short production sectors and which was preserved throughout the Brezhnev period, even in the face of perceived excessive labor turnover and severe regional labor shortages.[40] Workers who were deemed "excess labor" could generally rely on their enterprise managements for new placements. The small number of state employment bureaus in operation during this period were used mainly by workers with few skills or opportunities. By contrast, it seems likely that in the near future many workers will find themselves released from jobs into a labor-surplus economy, dependent for direction, retraining and placement on state agencies with a generalized mission of rational labor allocation. These circumstances will provide for expanded state control over allocation of the labor force.

The reformers have also begun a revamping of labor's social and legal protections which replaces some of the security and guarantees of the present system with measures to ease the transition of workers to new jobs or out of the labor force. As the chief of the Ministry of Light Industry's Legal Department stated in a discussion of job cuts (referring critically to employment guarantees for women with young children), "Labor legislation laid down in the period of the economy's extensive development is not designed to cope with the massive reductions in staff going on practically simultaneously and practically everywhere."[41] The Resolution on Employment introduces or extends material and social assistance for released workers, including maintenance of the worker's average wage for a period of up to three months after dismissal and during retraining (in effect, unemployment compensation); maintenance of a continuous term of service, with attendant benefits and payments, for the same period; and maintenance after transfer of benefits accrued at a former place of work.[42] Proposals have been made for the extension of a system of early retirement on partial pension, to cushion the impact of reductions on older and less-productive workers.[43] And reformers such as Kostakov have proposed increases in social benefits, including pensions, student stipends, and mothers' benefits, as well as extension of the cooperative sector, in order to ease marginal labor sources out of the state sector.[44]

Redefining the State's Welfare Function

Finally, the reformers are seeking to "re-negotiate the social contract"[45] through a broad ideological assault on the comprehensive welfare state and a simultaneous restructuring of the state's welfare function. The most prominent of Gorbachev's academic specialists, including Zaslavskaia, Aganbegian, and Kostakov, represent the Soviet system as a hypertrophied welfare state which has become dysfunctional economically, socially, and morally. They argue that excessive social guarantees have undermined productivity by providing benefits with no relationship to work performance. A too-egalitarian system of wages and income has at the same time failed either to reward and encourage talent and education or to recognize individuals' unequal contributions to the economy.[46] These arguments repudiate the Soviet welfare state as presently constituted, and provide the ideological basis for transition to a system which is less paternalistic and more meritocratic, which guarantees society less while seeking to liberate its potential to produce and prosper. The reformers' critiques have been accompanied by an effort to redefine and constrict the state's welfare function. The leadership has begun to move from a comprehensive welfare state which subsidizes and guarantees living standards for the entire population, to a more limited one which provides specific benefit packages to disadvantaged groups and individuals. Such change can be seen clearly in the area of employment policy, where temporary wage compensation and placement services are beginning to replace broad guarantees of stability and security.

III. THE IMPACT OF RESTRUCTURING ON EMPLOYMENT SECURITY

Restructuring of Soviet industry has proceeded slowly in the months since reformers introduced of the Law on the State Enterprise in June 1987. Despite the formal transfer of much of industry to self-financing, most enterprises continue to function under de facto ministerial tutelage, and the bulk of production remains geared to the fulfillment of state orders rather than private contracts. Technical re-equipping of enterprises and efficiency improvements have been very limited. Ministries continue to subsidize unprofitable enterprises through redistribution of revenues from the profit-making.[47] Consequently, the "economic levers" for efficient use of labor as yet function poorly, and pressures and incentives for managers to release workers remain weaker than anticipated. Nevertheless, new conditions of economic management are being introduced gradually, and Soviet sources reported the release of substantial numbers of workers as well as the insolvency of numerous enterprises during 1988. The following section of the paper will examine the impact of these developments on employment security.

According to the USSR State Committee for Statistics (Goskomstat), from January through September 1988, state enterprises and organizations in production sectors released 1 million persons, "as a result of the transition to intensive methods of economic management and new conditions of labor remuneration."[48] Approximately one-third of those released retired on pension, while the remainder reportedly found new jobs in the state sector or moved to individual or cooperative activity. For the eighteen months ending in June 1988 the All-Union Central Council of Trade Unions (AUCCTU) reports that 1.5 million workers and employees were released and found work or were sent for retraining and upgrading of qualifications.[49] In assessing the significance of these numbers, we must keep in mind that some of those reported as released remain at their original place of employment. There is evidence that, as in past Soviet reforms, many workers counted in layoff statistics are simply being reabsorbed into other sectors of their own enterprise or reemployed through the introduction of additional shifts. For example, the job placement bureau in the region of Kabardino-Balkaria anticipated layoffs of 14,000 to 15,000 people, but assumed that many would remain at their enterprise in new jobs and planned a doubling of the number of workers on second and third shifts in industry within several months.[50] Indeed, reform policies seem to intend and encourage such reabsorption.[51] Many other released workers have been able to find new jobs or upgrade skills and make a comfortable transition within the local economy. However, Soviet sources also recount numerous cases in which dismissed workers moved to inferior jobs, lost benefits or retired onto pensions earlier than planned, or failed to find local opportunities for reemployment and faced relocation or a period of literal unemployment.[52] The chief of the Moscow City Job Placement Bureau, in response to a question about clients who could not find appropriate vacancies in the city, replied that his service listed jobs in other cities and republics and that "people are going."[53] The listing he cited, from an Earth Physics Institute seeking an experienced construction engineer for a seismological expedition in Tajikistan, suggests the particular difficulties that may confront highly specialized professionals who must seek new jobs. In some cases, dismissals dump onto local labor markets large numbers of workers with similar skills and backgrounds, complicating their reabsorption into local enterprises. In the Belorussian city of Novopolotsk, for example,

the "Polimir" Production Association . . . cut over 400 worker posts and 114 engineering and technical posts. Other industrial pillars of the city are also preparing for . . . staff cuts. . . . In addition, all enterprises in the city are closely allied, and therefore the manpower which is not needed at "Polimir" will scarcely be needed at [other] plants. Not unemployment, of course, but a clear reserve of manpower.[54]

A substantial number of Soviet enterprises have also been declared bankrupt in recent months, under the self-financing provisions of the Law on the State Enterprise, but here, too, the implications for dislocation of their labor forces remain unclear. In the fall of 1988, for example, the USSR Industrial and Engineering Bank declared fifty factories, plants, and organizations insolvent, the Bank for Housing and Social Construction declared seventeen enterprises bankrupt, and the largest pig iron foundry in Transcaucasus and a garment factory in Odessa were denied access to credit and financing and pressed to liquidate their assets.[55] However, at least for cases on which information is available, the enterprises were not fully disbanded. In some instances, part of their production facilities were taken over or leased by profitable enterprises which continued to employ part of their labor forces, in others shops were turned over to production cooperatives or managements worked out arrangements for temporary financing. For example, the massive Tsentrolit foundry in Georgia, which employed thousands of metallurgists, auctioned part of its production capacity to an auto plant and intended further leasing to cooperatives. The trade union and city council promised interim support for workers who chose to remain during "plant diversion," and anticipated that others would easily find new jobs, but substantial displacement of workers seems inevitable.[56] In the case of the much smaller Odessa garment factory, which employed women workers in a region dominated by mining, some production sections were absorbed into a nearby factory and some seamstresses found higher-paying jobs, but others were left unemployed and continued to seek work.[57]

While it is very difficult, on the basis of available evidence, to estimate the extent of layoffs and displacement up to this point, there are indications that the effects have fallen disproportionately on some sectors of the labor force. A number of sources point to the relatively greater vulnerability of women to dismissal. The chief of the Moscow Job Placement Bureau, in a March 1988 interview, admitted that job cuts in the city seemed to affect women more than men.[58] The chair of the Soviet Women's Committee, Z. P. Pukhova, speaking at the Nineteenth Party Conference, argued that, "women are the first to be dismissed . . . in staff reductions," and that the reform's pressures for more efficient labor organization, "have jeopardized the most vulnerable part of the labor collective—women with children."[59] The AUCCTU, in a resolution on released workers, claimed that women, young workers, and those nearing pensionable age have been particularly vulnerable to dismissal. The resolution also made it clear that vocational training was often not available to released workers, and that few or ineffective steps were taken to find work for many of them. Moreover, dismissals were commonly carried out in violation of legislative guarantees and mandated procedures. Again, the AUCCTU resolution pointed to "numerous violations of the labor rights of workers" in the course of staff cuts, dismissals without trade union consent, without warnings of release, or payment of redundancy allowances.[60]

Finally, reports indicate that labor force reductions have led to increases in complaints and appeals about violations of labor legislation, disputes over workers' rights to employment and procedures for dismissal, and pressures on trade unions to protect their members' jobs. In late 1987 the industrial press reported a growing number of lawsuits seeking reinstatement, and characterized the atmosphere in labor dispute commissions as increasingly strained.[61] Pukhova, in her conference address, spoke of "tens of thousands" of appeals to the women's committee on employment rights.[62] Finally, the trade unions are responding to the new pressures by promoting the education of members in labor rights and promising workers more extensive access to legal counseling, in order to help insure strict compliance with labor legislation in dismissals. The unions plan to establish legal advice offices in all large labor collectives, "to explain legislative acts regulating the order of dismissal of workers and employment."[63] While the unions cannot prevent dismissals, they can, and seem determined to, use strict enforcement of existing labor legislation as a means to impede and complicate staff reductions, protect the rights of some of their members, and shore up their own organizational legitimacy as defenders of workers' rights.

CONCLUSION: POLITICAL IMPLICATIONS OF THE THREAT TO EMPLOYMENT SECURITY

What are the potential political ramifications of Gorbachev's employment policies? The limited evidence available at this point suggests that Soviet workers are absorbing costs which they have not had to in the past, and expressing their dissatisfaction. Labor force reductions are indeed creating grievances, both individual and collective, and workers are seeking redress from the constituted authorities. Labor dispute commissions are seeing more challenges to dismissals, workers are protesting layoffs in letters to newspapers and officials, and trade unions have objected strongly to violations of procedural guarantees. There have been no reports of overt worker resistance to layoffs or protest outside official channels, and the reactions of workers to the policies are most commonly characterized as passive and apprehensive.

In the longer term, the reform promises to create stronger productivity pressures and insecurity of jobs and income for all Soviet workers. But it presents a greater threat to older, less-skilled workers in some industrial branches, and promises compensating benefits for some of the younger, higher-skilled, and better-educated. Such a concentrated threat could, on the one hand, increase the potential for collective response by producing pockets of discontent among groups of workers who suffer simultaneous dismissals and find few local opportunities for reemployment. On the other hand, such discontents would tend to be concentrated among poorly educated, low-skilled groups of manual workers, with relatively weak capacities for organization and long socialization in the authoritarian Soviet political culture. If the costs of labor force restructuring, i.e., dislocation, downward mobility, and unemployment, fall mainly on older manual production workers, the effects of the reform will be cruel but probably not destabilizing. If, on the other hand, mass dismissals produce long-term dislocation and hardship for broader strata of the labor force, undercutting stability and security without increasing prosperity, the regime may face serious, politicized discontents.

There is also the prospect in the Soviet Union today of the emergence of a new "politics of labor." The present political reforms open up unprecedented possibilities for the representation and institutionalization of workers' interests, both in the industrial sphere and in the polity. Provisions for enterprise self-management, which extend broad formal rights to workers' collectives to elect managers and participate in production and allocational decisions, have recently been introduced. Workers may be able to use self-management rights either to resist the effects of restructuring on their security or to respond creatively to their new dilemmas, for example, by trying to reorganize poorly managed or insolvent enterprises into self-managed production collectives. The revitalization of the soviets also opens up the political process to new forms of representation of group interests, and we might watch for the emergence in both local and national soviets of spokesmen and alliances articulating the concerns of some groups of workers affected by the reform, seeking resources to prevent bankruptcy of enterprises which employ their constituents, and defending workers' claims in the system in competition with those of other social groups.

Finally, there is evidence of doubt and perhaps of division within the political elite over current employment policies, both on normative grounds and on grounds of potential political effects. Burlatsky has commented, in a discussion on the Law on the State Enterprise, "Guaranteed work and social security are the chief gains of the new socialist system; no one in our country will agree to renounce these gains which were achieved at a higher price," At the same time, a sector chief of the Institute of Economics and World Socialist Systems has spoken of "fear of social upheavals, of negative consequences in the social sphere. . . . Suddenly we'll earn less, the enterprise will collapse, someone will be out of a job."[64]

Perhaps more significantly, Politburo hardliner Ligachev has made the employment issue a theme of his speeches. In a recent meeting with the *aktiv* of the Gorky Province party organization, for example, Ligachev remarked:

Any notions alleging that in our socialist society the economy can develop without orienting itself to the politically expressed interests of the working people, that it can develop exclusively according to the laws of the market, are just unfounded. . . . The capitalist market, after all, is not just a market for goods and capital . . . [but] a manpower market, with its merciless laws and chronic unemployment. . . . Should we really reproduce all this in our own country?[65]

NOTES

1. T. Zaslavskaia, "The human factor in economic development and social justice," *Kommunist*, no. 13, (September, 1986): 70.
2. Victor Zaslavsky, for example, stresses the partial, selective, and manipulative nature of such interest representation; see *The Neo-Stalinist State: Class, Ethnicity, and Consensus in Soviet Society* (New York: M. E. Sharpe, 1982); Jerry Hough has, in various works, presented such institutions as more genuinely representing and defending workers' interests; see, for example, Hough, "Policy-Making and the Worker," in *Industrial Labor in the U.S.S.R.*, ed. Arcadius Kahan and Blair A. Ruble (New York: Pergamon Press, 1979), 367–98, esp. 375–76, 387.
3. See, for example, Walter D. Connor, "Workers and Power," in *Blue-Collar Workers in Eastern Europe*, ed. Jan Triska and Charles Gati (London: George Allen and Unwin, 1981), 157–72; Peter Hauslohner, "Gorbachev's Social Contract," in *Soviet Economy* 3, no. 1 (1987): 54–89.
4. See V. Kostakov, "Employment—Deficit or excess? (discussion and commentary)," *Kommunist*, no. 2, (January, 1987): 78–89, for a discussion of overmanning and its tenacious causes in the Soviet economy, as well as Zaslavsky, *The Neo-Stalinist State*, 47.
5. On the use of marginal labor resources see Kostakov, "Employment," 82; on the inability to man newly built factories see Gorbachev, "On the five-year plan of economic and social development of the USSR for 1986–90 and the tasks of party organizations for its realization," in *Kommunist*, no. 10, (1986): 9–12.
6. See Peter Austin Hauslohner, "Managing the Soviet Labor Market: Politics and Policymaking under Brezhnev" (Ph.D. diss., University of Michigan, 1984), 224–32.
7. Blair Ruble, "Full Employment Legislation in the USSR," in *Comparative Labor Law* 2, no. 3 (Fall 1977): 177.
8. See the discussion, by a consultant of USSR Gossnab's legal department, on laws governing worker layoff procedures, in "Procedure for discharging workers when enterprises and organizations lay off workers or eliminate job slots," *Materialno-Tekhnicheskoe Snabzhenie*, no. 1 (January 1986): 75–79.

9. *Labor Legislation in the USSR* (Moscow: Novosti Press Agency, 1972), 10–19, 43–53.

10. Blair Ruble, *Soviet Trade Unions: Their Development in the 1970s*, (London: Cambridge University Press, 1981), esp. 64–89; Nick Lampert, "Job Security and the Law in the USSR," in *Labour and Employment in the USSR*, ed. David Lane (New York: New York University Press), 256–77.

11. On large-scale illegal layoffs during the initial Shchekino experiments see Karl Ryavec, *Implementation of Soviet Economic Reforms: Political, Organizational, and Social Processes* (New York: Praeger Publishers, 1975), 194; on the effects of extraneous political considerations on court reconsiderations of dismissals, see Lampert, "Job Security."

12. On informal expectations about management's responsibilities for dismissed workers see, for example, L. Degtyar and G. Iaremenko, "The social effectiveness of economic decisions," *Kommunist*, no. 18 (December, 1986): 89–99; Kostakov, "Employment."

13. A similar argument that informal understandings and expectations play a greater that formal rules in structuring worker-management relations and behavior is found in Lampert, "Job Security."

14. See Peter Rutland, "The Shchekino Method and the Struggle to Raise Labour Productivity in Soviet Industry," in *Soviet Studies* 36, no. 3 (July 1984): 349.

15. See Connor, "Workers and Power"; Hauslohner, "Gorbachev's Social Contract."

16. For arguments that the Soviet elite preserves stability by segmenting groups and limiting expectations see (respectively) Zaslavsky, *Neo-Stalinist State*; Seweryn Bialer, *Stalin's Successors: Stability, Leadership, and Change in the Soviet Union* (New York: Cambridge University Press, 1980)

17. M. N. Sidorov, "Structural Shifts in the National Economy Examined," in *Izvestiia Adakemii Nauk SSSR, Seriia Ekonomicheskaia*, no. 2 (March–April, 1986) (translated in Joint Publications Research Service: USSR: Economic Affairs [hereafter *JPRS*], July 24, 1986, 1–19); (statistics partially calculated).

18. Figures are from the stenographic report of the Eighteenth Congress of the All-Union Central Council of Trade Unions, held in February 1987.

19. Total of manual workers is from S. Ivanov, "Reduction of manual labor," in *Ekonomicheskaia gazeta* [hereafter *EG*], no. 5 (January 1986): 7; and total for labor force (worker, white-collar and kolkhozniks) is from "Economic bases of social justice," in *EG*, no. 4 (January 1987): 16.

20. "On the state plan for economic and social development of the USSR for 1986–1990 (Report of N. I. Ryzhkov)" in *Pravda*, June 19, 1986, 1–2.

21. Gorbachev, "On the five-year plan,"; "Builders in the beginning of the five-year plan," in *Ekonomika stroitel'stva*, no. 1 (January 1986): 3–11, (translated in *JPRS*, May 30, 1986, 19).

22. V. Mart'ianov and V. Tambovtsev, "Complete plan for reduction in use of manual labor (course of working out and directions of development)," in *Sotsialisticheskii trud*, no. 10 (October 1985): 12–17.

23. *Pravda*, January 19, 1987, 1–2.

24. Gorbachev, "On the five-year plan."

25. "Abalkin: Economy to Shift to Service Industries," reported from Kyodo, Tokyo, July 11, 1987 (in *Foreign Broadcast Information Service: Soviet Union* [hereafter *FBIS: SU*], July 17, 1987), S1.

26. Kostakov, "Employment," 86.

27. Zaslavskaia, "The human factor," 70–71.

28. "Report from the USSR central statistical administration on fulfillment of the state plan for economic and social development of the USSR for 1986," *Pravda*, January 18, 1987, 1–2.

29. "USSR law on the state enterprise," *Pravda*, July 1, 1987 1. 4; the law was passed in June 1987, and its implementation began in January 1988.

30. See the interview with Abalkin on the reform and the Law on Enterprises, by *Der Spiegel*, July 6, 1987 (in *FBIS: SU*, July 10, 1987), S 5.

31. Kostakov, "Employment."

32. See, for example, Kostakov, "Employment"; Zaslavskaia, "The human factor."

33. The resolution was passed by the Central Committee, Council of Ministers, and AUCCTU: "On ensuring efficient employment of the population, improving the job placement system, and strengthening social guarantees for the working people," *Sotsialisticheskaia industriia* (hereafter *SI*), January 19, 1988, 1–2.

34. "On ensuring efficient employment," 2.

35. See the commentary by Viktor Buynovskiy, deputy chairman of the USSR State Committee for Labour and Social Issues, from *TASS* (in English), January 20, 1988, in *FBIS: SU*, January 21, 1988, 49; and the interview with I. Prostiakov, deputy chairman of the USSR Council of Ministers for Social Development, in "Subject to Reduction . . . ," *Pravda*, January 21, 1988, 2.

36. "On ensuring efficient employment," 1.

37. "On ensuring efficient employment," 1–2.

38. See "Subject to reduction;" and "Prokhorov on 'Job Placement' Resolution," *TASS* (in English), in *FBIS: SU*, January 22, 1988, 46.

39. Quoted in *FBIS: SU*, January 20, 1988, 45; for another discussion of self-management which stresses the importance of workers' involvement in hiring and firing decisions, see *Literaturnaia gazeta*, December 2, 1987, 11.

40. See Peter A. Hauslohner, "Managing the Soviet Labor Market, especially chaps. 6–8; Zaslavsky, in *Neo-Stalinist State*, points to the significance of workers' rights to personal mobility within the labor sphere for the maintenance of political stability. He argues that the possibility of quitting provides a safety valve for discontent and directs it into individual (versus potential collective) acts.

41. "Our jobs are being cut," in *SI*, December 5, 1987, 2.

42. "On ensuring efficient employment," 2.

43. "Our jobs are being cut," 2.

44. Kostakov, "Employment," 86.

45. Hauslohner, "Gorbachev's Social Contract."

46. See the extended discussion of social justice and the Soviet welfare state in *Kommunist*, beginning with the Zaslavskaia article, "The human factor in economic development and social justice," in no. 13 (September, 1986): 61–73, and continuing in subsequent issues with a series of reply and discussion articles, especially one by A. Bim and A. Shokin, "The system of distribution: On the path of perestroika," in the October 1986, issue no. 15, pp. 64–73, and one by Kostakov, "Employment," on full employment in the January 1987 issue, no 2, pp. 78–89.

47. For an authoritative assessment stressing the slow pace of restructuring, see Gorbachev's address to the Nineteenth Party Conference in *Pravda*, June 28, 1988, esp. 2.

48. See USSR State Committee for Statistics Report, "Stepping up work. On the USSR's socioeconomic development in the first nine months of 1988" in *Pravda*, October 25, 1988, 3.

49. See the AUCCTU resolution, "On the work of trade union organizations in ensuring effective employment of the population . . . ," in *Trud*, July 6, 1988, 1.

50. See the article, "Employment Problems in Kabardino-Balkaria," from *Sovetskaia Rossiia* (trans. in *FBIS: SU*, April 5, 1988).

51. See the discussion in ibid., 18.

52. For reports of dismissals and their consequences for workers, see, for example: "Roundtable on restructuring," *Literaturnaia gazeta*, June 3, 1987, 10 (translated in *FBIS: SU*, June 3, 1987, S3), which discusses a letter of protest from 400 women left unemployed by layoffs in the Belorussian Railroad settlements; L. Telen' "There is such a service," in *SI*, December 29, 1987, 1; "Our jobs are being cut"; "Who should resolve the dispute?" *Trud*, December 16, 1987, 4; "Job Rationalization Problems Viewed," translated in *FBIS: SU*, January 22, 1988, 247.

53. See, Interview with V. Sukhov, "Work seeks a worker," in *Trud*, March 3, 1988, 2.

54. Telen', "There is such a service," 1.

55. On these bankruptcies, see *Trud*, Sept. 16, 1988, 2; Viktor Veprik, "Odessa Garment Factory Declared Bankrupt," *TASS*, November 18,

1988, reported in *FBIS:SU,* December, 1, 1988, 100; Aleksandr Sharshunov, "Georgian Pig Iron Foundry Files for Bankruptcy," *TASS,* October 16, 1988, reported in *FBIS: SU,* October 18, 1988, 78.

56. Sharshunov, "Georgian Pig Iron Foundry."
57. Veprik, "Odessa Garment Factory."
58. "Work seeks a worker."
59. See "Speech by Comrade Z. P. Pukhova, chair of Soviet Women's Committee," *Pravda,* July 2, 1988, 11.
60. AUCCTU, "On the work of trade union organizations."
61. On increases in labor disputes over dismissals and redundancies see, for example, *Trud,* December 16, 1987, 4; Telen', "There is such a service," 1.
62. "Speech by Pukhova," *Pravda,* July 2, 1988.
63. See, "AUCCTU Leader on Workers' Legal Protection," *TASS,* August 24, 1988, reported in *FBIS: SU,* August 25, 1988, 39.
64. "Roundtable on Restructuring," *Literaturnaia gazeta,* trans. in *FBIS: SU,* June 24, 1987, S 3–4.
65. See the text of Ligachev's remarks in "Ligachev Gives Hard-line views on Policy," *Current Digest of the Soviet Press,* August 31, 1988, 5.

8

THE POLITICAL IMPLICATIONS OF NEW TECHNOLOGY FOR THE SOVIET UNION

Joel C. Moses

INTRODUCTION: POLITICAL IMPLICATIONS OF THE MICROELECTRONICS REVOLUTION

More is at stake in the Soviet Union from the Gorbachev reforms since 1985 than merely the successful transformation of the Soviet system into Oleg Bogomolov's "new model of socialism." Even if the Gorbachev reforms share common features with those now evolving in several other ruling Communist nations, the universal model for future success has never been just a Hungary or China for reform advocates in the Soviet Union. It is the United States and Japan. If any common thread links all Soviet economic and political reforms since 1985, it has been the intent to restructure the Soviet economy by instituting technological changes exactly modeled after the technological achievements in these advanced Western capitalist nations over the past two decades. The real universal model for Soviet reformers is not just a new socialism. It is the "microelectronics revolution," as Western social scientists have commonly termed the cumulative economic-technological achievements in these advanced nations. The undeniable Soviet lag behind these nations in the microelectronics revolution has stirred Soviet reform efforts. The irony is that Soviet emulation of Western achievements has emerged at the same time as major concerns about the political implications of the microelectronics revolution for their own futures have arisen in the same advanced Western nations.

Western Context

Few in the West would now deny that the microelectronics revolution over the past two decades represents a fundamental turning point for Western industrial civilization in the last quarter of the twentieth century. The new industrial revolution of robotics, computers, numerically programmed machine-tools, bioengineering, and even completely automated factories challenges the normal functioning of Western institutions, core political values, and the very quality of life for nations incorporating these new technologies on a massive scale. The implications of the microelectronics revolution are already contributing to a new political realignment of groups and issues in many Western nations. In this new political realignment, the traditional division between liberals and conservatives is becoming meaningless in attempting to fathom the lines of cleavage in differences of values and perspectives emerging as the new politics in many Western nations. In this new political alignment, opponents and advocates of the microelectronics revolution and its implications defy conventional classification. Opponents and advocates straddle shifting ideological groupings better labelled "pessimists" and "optimists" relative to the debates unfolding in their countries.[1]

For the pessimists in the West, this new industrial era of the microelectronics revolution is bringing with it uncontrollably negative social and political consequences. Pessimists have been particularly alarmed by what they foresee as the inevitable effects of this new industrial era on reducing employment opportunities and intensifying group conflict and political instability in highly industrialized capitalist nations.

For pessimists, the new microelectronics era in the West is very likely to cause a major and permanent technological displacement from the labor force of millions of industrial workers, now normally employable as skilled workers in traditional manufacturing occupations. These millions of industrial workers displaced by industrial microelectronics are destined to become a permanent unemployable underclass. As robotics reduce the labor-intensiveness of Western industry, they will also make redundant many skilled vocations of welders, painters, assemblers, machine-tool operators, warehouse workers, and even designers. Their former jobs will now be carried out by peopleless robots and computer-integrated warehousing, shipping, and even design technologies. Pessimists worry that, in stark contrast to past technological breakthroughs, those displaced in this new emerging microelectronics era are much less likely to find alternative job opportunities. The reason is the unprecedented and total scale of innovations being introduced across-the-board throughout all sectors of Western economies. Therefore, unlike blacksmiths in a horse-and-buggy economy at the turn of the century who were able to find eventual employment in the newly created automobile industry which displaced them, the very nature of the microelectronics revolution eliminates the demand for workers in even newly created sectors of the economy. With peopleless word processors simultaneously eliminating many clerical jobs and automated machines replacing many bank tellers, the new technology is unlikely to generate any equivalent compensatory demand in new jobs for those displaced from the manufacturing sector.

Furthermore, the automated technology in manufacturing and assembly can be easily operated by even semiskilled workers, and the very high cost of industrial robotics and computer electronics for many Western corporations has justified even more their attempts to find equivalent savings through a reduction of their labor costs. Thus, job opportunities for unemployed industrial workers in the West are also threatened by a related trend of cost-conscious Western corporations retooling an increasing amount of their production facilities to microelectronics. The same corporations have relocated and will continue to shift even more of their manufacturing-assembly operations with the new technology overseas to the newly industrialized but labor-cheap, non-unionized, and labor-surplus countries like South Korea or Singapore.

At the same time that the new technology threatens to eliminate a sizeable core of the traditional industrial working class in the West, the new era for pessimists will also by typified by new political tensions. These tensions will arise from the more rigid class polarization between haves and have-nots and will itself result from the very nature of the new industrial revolution. The haves will be the highly paid and privileged stratum of computer engineers and other technical specialists overseeing ever new generations of microelectronic technology. The have-nots are becoming the permanent army of underclass and unemployable former industrial workers and those semiskilled and low-paid auxiliary personnel, whose numbers have increased as the irreversible consequence of substituting microelectronics for human labor in industry.

The perceived and real opportunities for social mobility into a loosely defined middle class are also becoming much fewer for a large segment of have-nots in Western capitalist nations. For pessimists, those opportunities of upward mobility contributed to the overall political stability of Western nations over past decades. In contrast, pessimists already see downward social mobility for the children of the former middle class as the emerging long-term trend in nations like the United States. Graduating from universities with general educations unsuited to the rapidly changing technology of Western economies and the fluctuating demands of the job market, they will become dismayed and disillusioned in finding a wide gap between their aspirations and formal academic credentials and their reduced real life opportunities for any meaningful jobs and incomes. Thus, the political lines of conflict will increasingly form along the polarized class divisions resulting from substituting microelectronics technology for human labor on a massive scale in Western economies. Political turmoil and extremism are likely in the future scenario for many Western capitalist nations during future decades, and it is a scenario dictated by the very unprecedented scale of technological change in Western economies over the past two decades.

For optimists, the future emerging from the microelectronics revolution for Western economies and nations seems quite different.[2] For one reason, they envisage more jobs actually being created as a net result, even with the inevitable phasing out of unproductive labor-intensive and manual skilled jobs. Drawing from past experiences of technological breakthroughs since the nineteenth century, they anticipate that the new microelectronics era in a free market will generate unforeseeable ripple effects in new kinds of employment and sectors to maintain and produce the software and technology ancillary to the new revolution. Education and research will assume even greater importance in the microelectronics era and will easily absorb those displaced or now unable to find jobs with the reduced demand for workers and employees in manufacturing and assembly. Many new small private entrepreneurs and small businesses specializing in high technology will stimulate job creation in a wide range of new and highly paid professions.

Greater rather than less political harmony is also in the likely scenario for optimists of the new microelectronics era. The new technology promises to enhance the quality of both leisure-time and job satisfaction for many adult workers. At a minimum, the new technology will reduce the amount of time now expended in industry for mind-numbing physical labor and monotonous routines—all of which will now be performed by peopleless technology. Furthermore, the very number of hours available for nonwork leisure-time and personal growth through such activities as continuous adult education should all increase. With machines substituting for human labor and working round-the-clock, the number of hours now required for humans to be at work in shifts will significantly decline.

For optimists, the new technology has even greater promise for improving and even democratizing labor-management relations within the workplace.[3] Because the new technology almost requires a greater degree of initiative and creative independence on the part of workers in industry to operate efficiently, the dehumanizing regimentation and standardized tasks associated with Taylorism and the now increasingly obsolete "hard" assembly-line production methods will be eventually eliminated. With this greater degree of initiative and creative independence resulting from the very nature of microelectronics, Western workers should feel even less alienated at work and gain a higher sense of personal job satisfaction, self-worth, and self-esteem from their labor efforts. The norm required of the new technology will be workers collaborating in autonomous group-based teams without any rigid supervision on robotics and computers. Workers will complete all phases of manufacturing on finished goods from start to finish.

As a consequence, many Western optimists see a direct association between the microelectronics revolution and economic democracy instituted to an increasing extent in Western capitalist firms over the past two decades. In essence, workers because of microelectronics will achieve an unprecedented degree of real participation in management and shopfloor decisions and a real influence over the terms and conditions of their employment. On the societal level, the new technology for optimists promises greater social prosperity for all, with the unprecedented scales of productivity and efficiency emanating from the new era of microelectronics. In turn, greater prosperity should mean a reduction of social class divisions and conflict and increased political stability in Western capitalist nations. An expanded range of opportunities for personal and financial growth and for real social mobility will be held out to even more in the West.

Whatever the probable trends identified by Western analysts of this new microelectronics era, all by consensus anticipate that the implications of the new era will extend well beyond narrow economic effects on productivity and output. This third industrial revolution will constitute a new stage in the evolution of Western industrialized economies in all facets. It is likely to usher in profound and uncertain changes for Western nations in where we work, how we work and interrelate in the workplace, how we interact as social classes and groups in society, and how we politically organize and define our interests in the public arena.

Soviet Context

If the new industrial era of microelectronics has alarmed some and buoyed others in Western capitalist nations, somewhat parallel terms of debate have structured the emerging discussion and projected consequences of the microelectronics revolution in the Soviet Union over recent years and even prior to the ascendancy of Gorbachev in 1985. On the one hand, Soviet analysts contend that the microelectronics revolution represents a universal qualitative change in "productive forces" alike for all highly industrialized nations. As a qualitative change in the base of productive forces, the "objective" consequences from this new stage of industrial development will be the same for both capitalist and socialist systems. By necessity, it will force inevitable "dialectical contradictions" altering all facets of "production relations" in the workplace, society, and politics of highly industrialized nations.

On the other hand, Soviet analysts hasten to add that the real technological promise of the new era and successful resolution of its "dialectical contradictions" can only be realized under the public ownership of the means of production inherent to Soviet socialism. To support their claims, they usually cite trends which on the surface do suggest an impressive technological expansion of the Soviet economy over recent years since 1980. Thus, one Academy of Sciences official concluded that between 1981 and 1984 the production of microprocessors in Soviet industry had increased by nearly 400 percent and the production of microcomputers had nearly doubled.[4] A research associate in the Institute of Economics also emphasized that during the first half of 1984 alone 6.8 thousand industrial robots (in Soviet terminology, "programmed automatic manipulators") had been manufactured in the USSR with 2.5 thousand of them actually phased into industrial production.[5] At the time Gorbachev was elected General Secretary in 1985, published Soviet statistics found rapid and impressive technological advances over the past decade since 1975. Over the decade, the annual production of numerically programmed machine-tools increased by 150 percent and the annual production of industrial robots increased no less than by a factor of fourteen thousand.[6]

At the same time, even before greater candor in discussing major economic-social problems became the norm in 1985–88 under Gorbachev, many Soviet analysts were already warning of major problems. On a real technical level, the Soviet Union was falling significantly behind the West in the production of highly sophisticated microelectronics and, even more significantly, their successful and effective incorporation into actual production. An article published the very same month that Gorbachev was elected general secretary in *Kommunist*, the central theoretical journal of the party's Central Committee, outlined the major problem areas.[7] As the authors found, many Soviet computers manufactured by Soviet industry actually break down soon after they are shipped to Soviet enterprises, and standard operating procedure for the twenty different Soviet ministries manufacturing quite different prototypes of robots is not to supply fully packaged servicing personnel and parts. Indeed, the authors hinted that Soviet computer industry may deliberately build in defects—forcing Soviet enterprises which purchase robots into a dependency on the industry and thus guaranteeing the twenty competing and superfluous ministries high profits in follow-up repairs and servicing.[8]

A very typical situation for a senior research associate of the Institute of Economics was the robot complex installed at the Zil Automotive Plant to paint the front and rear of engine chassis.[9] Although costing hundreds of thousands of rubles, the robot complex was eventually supposed to save the plant over the long term by eliminating labor costs for workers normally employed to complete the painting of chassis by hand on the assembly line. The problem is the built-in defects of the robot complex. Workers are still required at high hourly wages to paint over the numerous individual parts of the engine chassis missed by the robot complex, because of its mechanical imperfections and improper software program.

For the Soviet analysts in *Kommunist* by 1985, the lack of any coordination and the waste of technical resources among superfluous Soviet ministries more concerned with meeting quotas for selling robots than making sure they ever work are both only symptomatic of more systemic failures. For them, the lag of Soviet industry and society in creating the very conditions to compete in civilian and military production of microelectronics with the West is irrefutable. For one reason, the vast majority of Soviet industrial robots are still first-generation, able to perform only the simplest and most basic kinds of manipulations on the assembly line.[10] Therefore, highly misleading is any aggregate comparisons of the Soviet Union with Western capitalist nations on the number of industrial robots manufactured and installed into actual production over the past decade. Industrial robots counted in Western statistics include only those second- and third-generation units capable of recognizing and adjusting to external objects with sensors and some programmed degree of independence.

For the Soviet analysts in *Kommunist*, a major factor accounting for Soviet technological backwardness in microelectronics is the overall deficiencies in the quality of Soviet education.[11] There is a critical shortage of any computers in high schools on which to instruct students, and those provided for teaching by industry are so obsolete that students acquire little practical knowledge of modern computers and computer science.[12] There is even a more critical shortage of instructors trained in computers and computer sciences, with few technical institutes in the USSR even granting degrees in computer sciences. Finally, Soviet managers in industry as a rule personify the national "computer illiteracy" with little formal training or practical experience in using computers, even if the computers and robots they were provided with did not constantly break down or fail to operate correctly because of defective software.

These technical-educational deficiencies have been only the least controversial aspects of discussion and public openness over the microelectronics revolution raised in the Soviet Union over recent years. At the same time Gorbachev was elected general secretary, the very same Soviet analysts broadened their indictment against the systemic roots of the Soviet lag in the microelectronics revolution. They now contend that the social and political consequences and requirements of incorporating the new technology in "production relations" are universal for all highly industrialized nations. Although Marxist-Leninist ideology traditionally rejected any presumed technocratic convergence in the effects of microelectronics for Soviet socialism and Western capitalism, these Soviet analysts have restructured the debate within the Soviet Union since 1985 exactly parallel to the terms and issues of public policy debate over the microelectronics revolution in Western nations. In the context of assessing issues and problems associated with the Soviet lag in the microelectronics revolution, the very most politically sensitive and controversial domestic reforms in the Soviet Union have appeared in print and been actively supported.

The two most sensitive and controversial issues and reforms have been the democratization of workplace relations in Soviet industry and unemployment. Some Soviet analysts contend that the very nature of the Soviet production process must fundamentally change because of computers and robotics to allow a much greater degree of real autonomy, independence, and participation in management and shopfloor decisions to workers. Thus, they have used the otherwise highly technical disputes about microelectronics to advance "democratic principles" in Soviet industry and indict "hard" assembly-line procedures and regimented control of workers under Soviet management. Those procedures and control originated during the first Five-Year Plans of Stalin in the 1930s and still remain the

prevailing industrial work culture throughout much of Soviet industry in the 1980s despite their inherent incompatibility with microelectronics technology.

The issue of unemployment in the Soviet economy has also been
legitimated in the debate because of perceived requirements in the
nature of the new industrial era. Soviet analysts now anticipate that
a significant technological displacement of many Soviet manual
industrial workers must become the normal and desirable consequence of the microelectronics revolution. They urge a much higher
priority be assigned to massive job-training, vocational reeducation,
and job-placement programs to deal with displaced Soviet workers
and a more fluid labor market as the inevitable social and economic
consequences of incorporating microelectronics effectively over the
next two decades. Aware that unemployment would violate orthodox Soviet doctrine about the socialist state's requirement to guarantee
jobs for all Soviet adults since the 1930s, they began in 1986–87 to
float revisions of Soviet labor doctrine and redefine the meaning of
that requirement in light of the new industrial era. Under the changed
circumstances of the microelectronics revolution, the doctrinal revision would be "effective employment" rather than full employment. The socialist state would satisfy its moral obligation in spirit
by guaranteeing a sufficient number of workplaces rather than actual
jobs for all Soviet adults. Soviet analysts envisage a close logical
relationship between the issues of workplace democratization and
unemployment. Real worker participation in management and shopfloor decisions will become even more necessary, because the most
politically volatile problems to be decided will be those reducing
and perhaps even closing down unprofitable enterprises and letting
go of redundant workers with the new labor-saving technology and
automation.

Those who have raised these issues of workplace democratization
and unemployment share with other reformers in the Soviet Union
the commitment to decentralize the Soviet economy and institute
democratic political reforms consistent with the transformation of
the Soviet Union into a new model of socialism. They depart from
other Soviet reformers in their rationales for those needed reforms
and the universal model to which they link them. It is the microelectronics revolution and the advanced Western nations of the United

States and Japan. In essence, they are challenging some of the most neo-Stalinist assumptions and authoritarian institutions underlying Soviet reality. For these Soviet analysts, those assumptions and institutions formed in an earlier era of simple machinery, Taylorism, and mass assembly-line procedures must change. They must be adapted to the quite different requirements of high-precision technology, specialized small-serial production, and fully automated production lines as the universal attributes of the microelectronics revolution. These Soviet analysts have manipulated a quite real and justifiable fear among Soviet leaders that their country is falling irreversibly behind the West in the microelectronics revolution to rationalize far-reaching economic and political reforms.

WORKPLACE DEMOCRATIC REFORMS

A reformist position on economic-political issues linked to microelectronics antedated Gorbachev's election in 1985 and emerged during the reassessment of labor problems in the early 1980s under Brezhnev.[13] Among Soviet reform advocates in the early 1980s, the general problems of declining Soviet labor productivity were directly linked to the technological changes in industry evolving in both capitalist and socialist nations. An increasing number of articles in Soviet specialized journals openly refuted neo-Stalinist assumptions about Soviet workers. Those neo-Stalinist assumptions since the 1930s have equated higher productivity and labor discipline with stringent controls and regimentation of workers on the job. In contrast, Soviet reform advocates supported changes in Soviet labor policy to allow a freer movement of workers and structural reforms to democratize the Soviet workplace. They urged these changes as the universal requirements of microelectronics technology and automation to bring the Soviet economy up to the level of Western advanced nations.[14]

Since 1982, these are the Soviet reform advocates who cited more objectively the views of Western liberal economists on the workplace reforms and reorganization of industrial relations required to incorporate computers, robotics, and numerically programmed machine-tools effectively into modern Western industry. Like the Western liberal economists, the Soviet reform advocates reasoned that the new era of high technology and fully automated factories cannot operate without parallel reforms in industrial relations to deconcentrate authority between management and workers in the workplace. As much as Taylorism emerged from and proved compatible with simple mass-assembly line production in the 1920s, the new technology and automation of the twenty-first century requires a quite different administrative arrangement to organize, pay and motivate workers. With major psychological adjustments for management and workers alike, the new administrative arrangement requires an expanded autonomy and greater real initiative for workers, an easing of detailed administrative controls over worker activities, and more joint worker-supervisor production teams completing all phases of production from start-to-finish on whole units. No longer can there be a rigid division of labor and spheres of authority separating workers, technicians, and supervisors in industry. Highly skilled worker-technicians must be authorized to carry out many diverse tasks on their own, and they must be given independent responsibility for resetting computers and robots on their own initiative. These are the universal administrative reforms in industrial relations alone compatible with the effective incorporation of microelectronics technology and automation foreseen by Soviet reform advocates. These are the changes in organizing, paying, and motivating workers dictated by the new industrial era and exactly identical in their form and content for capitalist and socialist systems alike.

For Soviet reform advocates, any nostalgic attempt to resurrect the kind of punitive discipline and regimentation of Soviet workers identified with the origins of Taylorism and Soviet industry of the 1930s is flawed. The nostalgia fails to appreciate how outmoded and even counterproductive to economic growth that kind of discipline and regimentation have become for Soviet industry with microelectronics in the 1990s. No longer can tasks be standardized and predicted and tied to piece-rate wage tariffs to motivate and control Soviet workers in industry. Inherent to the very nature of microelectronics is that tasks for workers cannot be broken down and simplified for repetition beforehand. With workers resetting machine-tools and robots to manufacture small-series units, the production cycle requires the continuous independent initiative, judgment, personal responsibility, and flexible adaptation of workers and supervisors to constantly changing and unforeseeable circumstances on the shop-floor.

For Soviet reform advocates, the microelectronics revolution has totally redefined the nature of labor problems and solutions in the USSR. The only real issues of labor policy under these changed circumstances must become workplace democracy, a highly mobile workforce, and a future computerized Soviet enterprise run by highly skilled and conscientious workers. As much as 1979 and 1983 party-state resolutions on labor policy presumed that the problems of declining labor productivity and morale derived from too high a tolerance of job turnover and lack of administrative controls over workers on the job, the real labor issues for Soviet reform advocates with microelectronics are too much job stability for workers and too much management rigidity in the workplace. By necessity of the microelectronics revolution, Soviet workers must be given greater choice, independence on the job, and personal responsibility. Like their counterparts in Western advanced nations over the past two decades, Soviet workers must become motivated to learn new voca-tions and alter their careers with the unprecedented scale of techni-cal innovations and new vocations appearing each decade in this new industrial era. A lifelong pattern of continuous reeducation in vocational institutes and the acceptance of occupational mobility must become ingrained in Soviet workers as the absolute necessities to effect real economic expansion. No longer should Soviet workers remain passive to management or assured of their jobs in the same enterprises for their entire adult work-lives.

Industrial Work Brigades

For Soviet reform advocates in the 1980s, the reform model in Soviet industrial relations to realize the degree of real independence among Soviet workers required in the technological era became the highly publicized work brigades of a "new type." These new type industrial work brigades figure prominently in all central policy directives on the Soviet economy or labor issues since 1979, and all Soviet industrial workers were supposed to be reorganized into these semi-autonomous contractual workgroups as the single most important reform of Soviet industrial relations throughout the decade of the 1980s.[15]

In their ideal form, the new work brigades are supposed to be independent economic and political decision-making units within Soviet industrial enterprises. The new brigades have the authority to contract with enterprise management over their group unit assignments and distribute material benefits among their members. As a model of more democratic industrial relations, the new brigades decide the specific work assignments of their members, the admission and release of their members (subject to the formal approval of enterprise executives and consistent with Soviet labor laws), the skill-grade promotions awarded their fellow members, and the "work contribution indices" assigned members as the numerical weight for their share of the collective brigade wages and bonuses. As an outlet for political participation by workers in the production process, the new brigades are also supposed to make all their decisions at open meetings of the brigade collective or through their elected "brigade councils." The new brigades were even supposed to be invested with the authority of electing their own brigade leader, rather than having the position appointed by management in Soviet enterprises. Model Soviet enterprises were cited even prior to 1985, where brigade leaders were actually elected in secret balloting by the brigade membership as a rule.[16] Even under somewhat restrictive regulations for brigades adopted in 1983, the brigade membership was still authorized to give its majority "consent" to any individual appointed brigade leader by management with an implied veto by the membership for any appointment considered unacceptable.[17] On the enterprise level, a Soviet form of worker coparticipation in management decision-making was instituted even prior to 1985. A council of brigade leaders was established to represent the interests of all brigades in an enterprise now projected as the major shopfloor production subunits for Soviet industry.

Western skeptics would have good reason to doubt that the democratic ideals associated with the new work brigades could ever be fully realized in the Soviet context. Even the most ardent Soviet advocates of the reform have constantly bemoaned major failures in the manner that new brigades have been implemented.[18] In many instances, the new brigades exist only on paper, as Soviet managers throughout the 1980s hastened to meet formal quotas to establish the new brigades issued by their ministerial superiors. Thus, the "new" brigades tend to resemble the "old" brigades. Both workers and management continue to interact and think by traditional patterns of narrow task delegation and hierarchical subordination akin to Taylorism and the authoritarian Soviet work culture. In a similar departure of theory from reality, the new democratic outlets for worker participation like enterprisewide brigade councils are often convened by management without even the nominal presence of any worker representatives and with the enterprise director serving as chair.

Although new brigades are supposed to be paid as a collective contractual group by the total number of finished units, the chronic delays of shipping supplies to Soviet enterprises idle Soviet work brigades for long periods. Brigades lack any real legal authority to force their own enterprise management into meeting its contractual obligations and supplying them with parts and materials to operate as self-sufficient production units. Economic uncertainty has also contributed to widespread resistance to the new brigades by skilled workers and foremen. Skilled workers fear a significant loss in their high piece-rate earnings and bonuses, if their monthly wages became dependent on the final economic results of collective brigades and a collective division of the brigade wage fund. Foremen rightfully fear a decline in their status if not outright elimination of their position, if truly self-administered work brigades were invested complete authority over work assignments and wages now the prerogative of Soviet foremen.

Despite these failures, the model implicit to the new work brigades for Soviet reform advocates is very clear. The model is the very similar reforms in industrial relations typical of advanced Western nations like the United States, Sweden, West Germany, and Japan over recent decades. Very revealing is that Soviet articles on group-based teams in Western firms explain their appearance with exactly the same rationales offered by Soviet reform advocates of new work brigades.[19] Like quality-of-work-life teams in automotive plants of General Motors or start-to-finish workteams in Swedish Volvo plants, the new Soviet work brigades are supposed to provide an outlet for worker independence, self-responsibility, and participation in enterprise decision-making. Like semi-autonomous teams in these Western firms, the new Soviet work brigades are supposed to reduce the number of workers inefficiently employed on repetitive tasks through traditional assembly-line production, distribute at least the bonus segment of wages among workers by their proportionate contribution to the finished units, and encourage workers to acquire new skills substitutable for those of redundant workers released to enlarge the shares from the wage pool. The common reason forcing the change from "hard" authoritarian procedures to "soft" participatory team procedures in both Western firms and Soviet enterprises is the same in these Soviet articles—the very nature of new technology and automation.

Workplace Democratization

The new work brigade was not an isolated reform in industrial relations advocated in the Soviet Union over the past decade. Even before Gorbachev's election as general secretary and the elevation of "democratization" as a national priority, the brigade reform was touted as only the first step on the shopfloor level to institute even more comprehensive forms of "worker self-management" at the enterprise level. Worker self-management on an enterprise-wide level would correspond to the principles set down in the new work brigades since 1979. All Soviet workers in an enterprise would have a decisive influence over the election and removal of enterprise management and a participatory role in shaping enterprise decisions through their representatives on newly instituted labor collective councils.

Workplace democratization as both a political imperative and ultimate solution to economic decline in the USSR has been more clearly associated with reform-oriented institutes in the Soviet Union like the Institute of State and Law in the Academy of Sciences. Over the past decade, articles in the monthly journal of the institute have consistently blamed problems of poor worker productivity and morale in the Soviet Union on the antidemocratic work environment in which many Soviet workers cannot influence either the policies or leadership of their own production units.[20] As a consequence, uninvolved and psychologically apathetic workers in the Soviet economy lack any postive inducement to work hard or identify with the economic performance of their units. They exhibit all the subsequent reactions to the disincentives from their antidemocratic work environment in their frequent job changing, tardiness, absenteeism, alcoholism, stealing, low labor productivity, and general indifference to their jobs and production units. The predominant assumption in the articles has been that the Soviet economy wastes or underutilizes vast labor potentials because of the politically antidemocratic conditions in the Soviet workplace.

In turn, Soviet managers, unaccountable to their own workers, lack any positive incentives to administer their production units efficiently. Their willingness to tolerate dishonesty and corruption has become the equivalent managerial negative reaction arising from the same antidemocratic work environment. At a higher level, the waste of economic potential, inefficiencies, and corruption within Soviet production units derive from those same pathologies endemic to a rigidly centralized national economy under ministries.

For reform advocates in the Institute of State and Law, the only effective long-term solution has always been posed as economic-political democratization at both levels.[21] Labor-management relations within Soviet production units must become democratized through laws and procedures instituting real worker self-management. Through elections of their own management and participation in labor collective councils, workers would have a real influence over the key decisions of wages, working conditions, and the individuals administering them. Economic relations between ministries and production units must be simultaneously democratized, by decentralizing authority and responsibility to the level of production units and by instituting full-scale market reforms. With the elimination of central controls over production and pricing decisions, Soviet managers and production units would be placed under conditions in which they would have real incentives to encourage worker participation in order to ensure the quality and profitability of their operations in a competitive market for goods. With the decentralization of the economy, workers would be placed under conditions in which they, too, would be induced to participate—to ensure their own jobs and high earnings and to influence the choice of enterprise managers best qualified to run the production units efficiently and profitably. Democratic accountability of management through worker self-management would also eliminate the source of official cheating and corruption in granting bonuses, housing, and other perquisites within production units. On the national level, market principles in self-regulating the economy would unleash the productive potentials and eliminate the shortages which contribute in great part to widespread national corruption in the Soviet Union.

UNEMPLOYMENT

If the democratization of industrial relations would constitute a radical departure in Soviet politics, reform-minded Soviet analysts have challenged an even more basic Soviet tenet by their equal contention that the microelectronics revolution will likely create widespread technological displacement of many Soviet industrial workers in the next two decades. Evidence that unemployment and the technological displacement of Soviet workers have emerged as real prospects can be gleaned on three levels in the Soviet policy literature over recent years.

The first level includes an increasing number of revealing articles which have begun more openly to address problems in releasing and retraining many hundreds of thousands of older manual industrial workers in the Soviet economy. The discussion has particularly focused on fading Soviet industrial branches like machine-building and metals, already being transformed by the installation of numerically programmed machine-tools and robots. The second level includes a general emerging consensus over labor policy in the USSR over the past decade which, if it has not encouraged some unemployment, at least has seriously revised the meaning of full employment under socialist doctrine. The third level since Gorbachev's election in 1985 includes an unquestionably greater candor and frankness in airing politically sensitive issues like unemployment. As a marked shift, there has been both a greater willingness to discuss pending unemployment in the Soviet context and to accept the phenomenon as an inevitability with microelectronics. Surveying the consequences of the microelectronics revolution in their own country and under Western capitalism, Soviet analysts have begun, albeit guardedly, to assess the displacement of workers less as the "subjective" failure and inhumanity of capitalism than as the "objective" universal outcome of the microelectronics era for all highly industrialized nations. Redefined in their analyses, the successful displacement of workers has become the major precondition for any long-term positive economic results in expanding output and productivity during this new industrial era for capitalist and socialist systems alike.

Soviet Rustbelt

On the first level, Soviet analysts of the microelectronics revolution have been increasingly concerned over recent years with Soviet industrial workers in the forty- to forty-nine-year-old age group employed in older industrial branches. Many Soviet workers in this age group have high-paid manual jobs which provide large bonuses in addition to their take-home pay. These workers are also the very ones most likely to be let go by enterprises implementing state policies to eliminate unproductive manual jobs and to install new automated robots and computer technology. In terms which echo the policy concern in the United States over unemployed steelworkers and machine-tool operators in Pittsburgh and Gary, Soviet analysts worry about the willingness or ability of these highly paid workers at this age to accept the relocation, change in jobs, and retraining attendant with technical advances in Soviet branches like machine-building and metals.[22] Initial surveys of the forty- to forty-nine-year-old manual workers displaced by technology from their former jobs in the 1980s have found many losing benefits accrued over a long period in their previous jobs and others experiencing a decline in take-home pay in their new jobs after retraining. Many, too, have suffered major health problems contracted from chemicals or unfamiliar new machinery in their new jobs. As a consequence, many in the same age group still working in high-paid manual jobs have expressed reluctance to leave their jobs and retrain with the phasing out of their workplaces through technology and automation. Their reluctance has persisted despite Soviet policy requiring their former enterprises to pay for their retraining and to find them new jobs.

Thus, economic-labor policies intended to facilitate the introduction of microelectronics in Soviet industry have been redefined. Questions are now being openly asked how microelectronics is likely to affect workers such as those in the vulnerable forty- to forty-nine-year-old group and how their pending loss of pay and work status can be fully reconciled with long-standing official endorsement of full employment for all Soviet citizens as a tenet of Soviet socialism. Some Soviet analysts have proposed a deliberate slow-down in eliminating those manual jobs in which workers of this age group still predominate in branches like machine-building. The jobs should be retained until the older workers themselves reach retirement age or decide to leave the enterprises on their own.[23]

Other Soviet analysts—especially those affiliated with reform-minded institutes like the Institute of the World Economy and International Relations and the Institute of the International Workers' Movement—have consistently assumed a more "optimistic" outlook not unlike that held by optimists in Western nations on the impact of microelectronics.[24] Soviet analysts at these two institutes presume that the economic changes and workplace reforms in leading nations like the United States and Japan will have the equivalent positive consequences of absorbing displaced workers in the Soviet context. Like the United States and Japan, the Soviet Union should experience a significant growth in the educational and service sectors, and the increasing number of jobs in both sectors should easily employ workers displaced from fading manufacturing branches. In addition, the Soviet optimists project an increasing availability of part-time jobs for Soviet workers to share any reduced absolute number of workplaces through microelectronics. The precedent for them is the significant expansion of part-time employment in both the United States and Japan. They also anticipate a reduction in the number of job-seekers in the labor market of the Soviet Union at any one time as a universal consequence of the microelectronics revolution. They reason that the microelectronics revolution will force Soviet workers like their counterparts in the United States and Japan to undergo constant retraining and reeducation to qualify for new vocations throughout their adult work-lives. As a consequence, more workers will be enrolled in any one year full-time in vocational-technical institutes, and the fewer number of workplaces will exactly match a declining absolute number of job-seekers in the market.

Key to their optimistic appraisal is the overall conclusion that the institutions and policies of even state-monopoly capitalism in a United States or Japan are successfully coping with the displacement of workers through microelectronics. This perspective has been particularly evident in articles on the microelectronics revolution and unemployment in Western capitalism published by reform-oriented institutes like the Institute for the Economics and Organization of Industrial Production and the Institute of the International Workers' Movement: Canadian coal-mines reducing employment by 42 percent from 1972 through 1981 because of new technology and automation; industrial robots in Western firms replacing two to three people on average and returning their initial costs in two to two-and-a-half years through labor savings; Japanese machine-building industry producing with twelve workers on numerically programmed machine-tools in three days the equivalent of 215 former workers on standard machine-tools over three months; and 10 to 20 percent of all assembly-line jobs in Japan and the United States automated by 1990 with labor savings more than the combined capital expenditures for retooling.[25]

Although the obligatory criticisms of joblessness and exploitative state-monopoly capitalism bracket the introductions and conclusions of these Soviet articles, they are more than overshadowed by the general thrust of the articles and the balanced interpretation of the unemployment phenomenon in the West. The technological displacement of Western workers is seen more as an "obstacle" to the successful incorporation of microelectronics than as an insuperable "dialectical contradiction." The restructuring of economies and transformation of jobs are interpreted more as a necessary short-term realignment of productive forces returning capitalism to a high state of output, not as a critical new revolutionary stage leading to the imminent collapse of capitalism.

Very revealing is that the articles almost as a rule tend to give equal weight to both the optimistic and the pessimistic scenarios for unemployment in the West, as those scenarios have been drawn by Western economists.[26] The articles presume unemployment from microelectronics is a potentially controllable phenomenon even under Western capitalism and summarize numerous efforts in the West to retrain and reassign displaced workers. The emphasis on reform efforts dealing successfully with unemployment in the West is probably intentional. It is intended to reassure Soviet political leaders, otherwise inclined to be pessimistic about any massive displacement of the Soviet workforce through microelectronics. The irony is that by the late 1980s Soviet advocates of the microelectronics revolution for the USSR were arriving at the same optimistic scenario as the least radical and non-Marxist analysts in Western capitalist nations.

Prominent officials on the USSR State Planning Committee have been among those most clearly aligned with the optimistic perspective about unemployment and the microelectronics revolution in the Soviet Union. For three economists on the committee, the release and reassignment of many Soviet manual workers in industry have become absolutely essential, if the Soviet economy even hopes to reach the level of technical expansion and labor productivity required for any growth the rest of the century.[27] The dilemma for them is reconciling these economic priorities with the short-term interests of older Soviet workers likely to lose their jobs with new technology and automation. Because many displaced workers will confront real problems in finding jobs and wages equivalent to those eliminated, the economists foresaw job-placement bureaus in the USSR receiving major funding to help the displaced workers. The bureaus should almost be converted into local unemployment agencies, responsible for the retraining and reassignment of displaced workers and providing financial support (unemployment insurance) during the interim of their temporary unemployment.

Writing in the party's Central Committee journal in early 1987, a senior official of the State Planning Committee was even more precise.[28] He calculated that at least 10 of the 130 million jobs in the Soviet economy could be efficiently eliminated. He singled out the old industrial regions of European Russia in particular with their labor-intensive branches like food-processing as a priority area for future workforce reductions and even the closing down of some inefficient plants.[29] For the senior official, compensatory economic growth and employment opportunities in European Russia would come from the expansion of capital-intensive microelectronics branches staffed by the highly skilled and educated European workforce.

Policy Consensus

On a second level, a willingness to consider eliminating the jobs of the many underemployed and unproductive manual workers in Soviet industry did not emerge unexpectedly. The potential has underlied decisions and actions adopted over the past decade in the USSR since the late 1970s to resolve openly recognized problems of declining rates of labor productivity and morale. Since 1979, soviet policy directives have consistently instructed all Soviet ministries to meet annual quotas in the number of manual jobs eliminated in their enterprises. Personnel ceilings were supposed to be set and enforced by local levels of government in the Soviet Union relative to their estimates of local labor resources available for all enterprises in their jurisdiction. [30] In essence, the general policy consensus in the Soviet Union over the past decade has formally required Soviet industry not just to stabilize but actually cut back total employment. Redundant and underemployed workers were supposed to be released and less labor-intensive and more highly productive technology and automation substituted for them. The released workers were supposed to be retrained and reassigned to other enterprises within the same jurisdiction experiencing labor shortages or to other provinces and republics singled out for national priority investment and economic expansion.

The explicit rationale was to intensify labor discipline and increase productivity. Soviet analysts and decision-makers since 1979 have contended that the excess number of work positions force many soviet industrial managers into competing for workers. Forced to compete for workers and retain many above actual production needs because of inefficiencies in the centralized economy, Soviet managers inflate labor shortages nationally and encourage high annual labor turnover among skilled workers in the artificially tight labor market. The labor deficit results not from any absolute shortage of workers or decline in fertility, but from the inefficient use of workers in unproductive make-work jobs and worktime losses. With the ease of finding jobs for skilled workers, the excess number of positions also contribute to the allegedly lax moral climate, in which hard-core violators among Soviet workers have become emboldened to defy labor regulations during the past decade.

In this context, Soviet analysts and decision-makers promoted experiments in certain Soviet locales to establish a ceiling or certified number of workplaces allowed all Soviet enterprises—in essence, "full-time equivalency positions" in Western management parlance for all Soviet enterprises.[31] With a ceiling on their workplaces, Soviet enterprises were supposed to phase out unused machinery, eliminate redundant workers, employ the remaining on multiple-machine or expanded work-areas, increase wages for the fewer number of employed workers, and reduce their artificially high demand for workers. By eliminating workplaces, the reform was intended to reinstill labor discipline, by forcing Soviet workers to compete for a fewer number of jobs.

Individually, the measures and reforms over recent years to eliminate unproductive jobs do not signify a radically new departure in Soviet labor policy. The very same rationale of hiring fewer workers and paying them more by eliminating unnecessary jobs in enterprises prompted adoption of the much heralded but little implemented Shchekino chemical combine reform in 1967.[32] By the mid-1980s, the change was that all labor reforms were supposed to embody these principles as the only feasible alternative with labor deficits, poor workers motivation, and declining rates of labor productivity stifling any economic growth. Since 1979, Soviet labor policy has been relatively consistent in assuming that fewer Soviet manual jobs should be retained in the future and that any increased labor productivity would come from technological retooling of workplaces.

Numerically programmed machine-tools illustrate the projected trade-offs of this retooling. Each numerically programmed machine-tool costs 53 thousand rubles—more than six times the average cost for each of the 200,000 standard and manually reset machine-tools in Soviet industry now scheduled to be replaced during the 1990s.[33] To return their high initial costs, the new machine-tools will require the equivalent displacement of many tens of thousands of currently employed machine-tool operators on standard machines in Soviet industry.

Deliberately understated until 1985 was the probable fate for so many displaced machine-tool operators and other industrial jobs. An indirect indication of the political sensitivity surrounding the problem was the reaction to an article in *Pravda* in 1980 by Gavriil Popov, the iconoclastic economics professor at Moscow State University. Popov generated a storm of denunciatory letters-to-the-editor and official rebuke at the time for proposing that Soviet enterprises should no longer be held legally responsible for retraining and finding new jobs for their workers dismissed through automation. Popov further suggested that the displaced workers be given a kind of unemployment insurance by the state which, along with various workfare jobs as street-repairers and gardeners, would sustain them until they were able to find new jobs on their own. [34]

The Gorbachev Factor

Popov's open airing of unemployment as an option seemed the rare exception in 1980 under the more orthodox and politically cautious approach to labor problems associated with the Brezhnev leadership through November of 1982. Yet, on a third level, with Gorbachev's election as general secretary in March of 1985, a distinct shift in tone to greater frankness and candor became quickly evident in official policy discussions of many economic-labor problems and solutions. Gorbachev's commitment to intensify Soviet economic growth with new technology even inspired Vladimir Kostakov, deputy director of the Scientific Research Institute for Economics in the State Planning Committee, to raise the prospects of unemployment in the Soviet economy on the very eve of the Twenty-seventh Party Congress through a two-part article and interview in the national Soviet publication *Sovetskaia kul'tura.* [35]

For Kostakov, many Soviet people released from their former jobs because of technology and automation will have to accustom themselves to looking for jobs and adjust psychologically to a microelectronics era in which finding employment will become more their own concern than a provision of the Soviet government. Responding to anguished letters from Soviet readers concerned that microelectronics in the USSR would produce the same problem of technological unemployment in Western capitalism, Kostakov refuted any parallels between the situation in the Soviet Union and the West. Displaced workers would be retrained and employed in expanding nonproductive sectors like education and healthcare. Others would be given new jobs in Soviet industry through reforms intended to eliminate the underemployment of skilled manpower in most branches. Yet Kostakov emphasized that his frank airing of unemployment as an inevitable short-term reality confronting many Soviet workers in the future represented a significant political change from the Brezhnev era: "Just ten years ago, talk about the implementation of these profound transformations would have been considered daydreaming and idle, irritating hare-brained scheming . . ."[36]

If the articles in *Sovetskaia kul'tura* were intended to prepare a Soviet public for acceptance of a significant policy shift toward unemployment, the very same Vladimir Kostakov may also have been attempting to convince leading party and state officials with an article rationalizing unemployment written for the party Central Committee journal *Kommunist* in early 1987.[37] Indicting a wide range of practices and policies for perpetuating artificial labor shortages and for wasting labor resources in the Soviet economy, Kostakov saw their elimination not just in granting autonomy to enterprises but in rethinking the issue of employment for Soviet workers:

The necessity of removing social barriers to the growth of labor productivity dictates a new approach in providing for full employment. . . . In our view, it would be more correct to understand full employment as such a situation when the demand of the population for workplaces is being provided for. . . . The effect can be great here, inasmuch as there exists an overemployment for some categories of the population—youth, women, and particularly women with small infants, and pensioners. . . . A successful resolution of the problems of employment requires a serious restructuring of psychology on the part of each one. Now it's considered natural that, if a workplace becomes unnecessary, the person here should be given another job and a better one at that in the same enterprise. The Constitutional statute, guaranteeing each the right of choosing a job relative to their personal inclinations, should be inalterable. But, making a choice, each should to a greater degree be considered both from their own peculiarities and from societal necessity.[38]

Kostakov was very candid in underscoring the range of problems like plant closings and unemployed workers in the Soviet Union which will inevitably result from this new approach:

In the capitalist world, the word "dismissal" is practically identical with unemployment. It is apparent for what reason we are trying not to use this term. . . . But the urgency of this problem sharply grows immediately after an enterprise transfers over to complete economic-accountability and self-financing. A logical consequence of this transfer should be the liquidation of those enterprises which cannot conduct themselves without a loss. . . . It is also clear that the decision about the liquidation of a consistently unprofitable enterprise will not be automatic nor a quick-fix. It should be adopted after careful and comprehensive review of the problem. Nonetheless, it's obvious that such decisions will be met in practice. Under these problems, one arises: what should be the fate of the work collective of a given enterprise, recalling the necessity of observing the principles of a socialist society? The problems are not few. They include the fact that the occupational structure of those "let go" and those for whom there is a demand, as a rule, don't coincide: there are possible incompatibilities by territory and by time—they have let go a workforce somewhere now, but the need for personnel is in another locale sometime later on. These are all complex problems. [39]

Not insensitive to the human costs of his envisioned changes, Kostakov optimistically outlined a number of priorities to effect his policy of "rational full employment" with a minimal negative impact on displaced workers. [40] While relieved of any responsibility to find new jobs for their displaced workers, Soviet enterprises would still bear some indirect financial obligation by contributing to a central state social security program. Administered by local state labor departments, the program would financially support displaced workers during the interim of their retraining and placement in new jobs. Kostakov also foresaw the service sector absorbing a sizeable contingent of the displaced workers. To prevent any loss of wages and self-esteem, he urged much higher wages and prestige for jobs in the service sector as a major national priority. The current over-employment of youth, women, and pensioners would be humanely resolved for Kostakov by increasing stipends for students to remain in university day divisions full-time, by increasing the size and length of maternity leaves for women to stay out of the labor pool, and by raising pensions to relieve older Soviet citizens of having to work in order to supplement their meager state retirement benefits. All three workgroups would also be encouraged to accept part-time jobs, and part-time workdays and workweeks would be interpreted in the future as consistent with the moral obligation of the socialist state to provide jobs for all of its citizens.

Despite the optimistic forecast by Kostakov that unemployment poses no real threat in the USSR and that the many displaced Soviet workers will quickly find new jobs, the situation may not seem as orderly and predictable for the top Soviet leadership. A political future in which many Soviet workers may be without a job and income for lengthy periods cannot be reassuring. Indeed, General Secretary Gorbachev cited the universality of technological displacement as one of the emerging "world problems" before a forum of Western and Communist intellectuals in 1986:

I was in England in 1984 and visited a large automobile concern. I found it in a situation when, fundamentally restructuring production, they had incorporated new technology and the production of new automobile models. I very highly assessed the technology and the automobile models, but I openly asked for an answer as to what had happened to those people who had been working prior to the modernization? It turns out that almost half of them were deprived of a job. Here is the problem which deserves to be fundamentally engaged, so that as a result of technological breakthroughs and bursts the human personality should not become devalued. [41]

An indirect measure of leadership concern can be gauged by the kinds of articles and themes prevalent since 1985, particularly in such bellwether outlets for official discourse as the party Central Committee journal *Kommunist*. In 1986, *Kommunist* became an even more relevant barometer of changes in leadership attitudes toward microelectronics and employment with the appointment of Ivan Frolov as its new editor-in-chief. As both a former sector head in the Institute of Philosophy and editor of its monthly journal *Problems of Philosophy*, Frolov had held the position of chair of the Council on the Philosophical and Social Problems of Science and Technology in the USSR Academy of Sciences prior to assuming the editorship of *Kommunist*. Described as among the "most controversial of reform-minded Soviet philosophers" and identified with Gorbachev's political network from Moscow State University in the 1950s, Frolov in the prior council role had already made his views quite clear through a lengthy article in *Pravda* on the human costs and consequences of the microelectronics revolution on a global scale. [42] He concluded the article by citing explicit parallels in the technological changes and societal challenges evolving in the Soviet Union to those of unemployment and inequality from the microelectronics revolution in Western capitalist systems. For Frolov, there was an urgency for Soviet scientists to raise and discuss the "real social problems" emerging in the USSR from microelectronics "without sensationalism and utopianism."

During Frolov's tenure as editor-in-chief of *Kommunist* and before his reassignment to the personal staff of Gorbachev in 1987, the microelectronics revolution and unemployment figure prominently in many key articles of the journal throughout the latter half of 1986 and the first few months of 1987. The tone was set in an article by V. V. Kulikov, deputy director of the Institute of Economics in the USSR Academy of Sciences.[43] Advocating expanded commodity-monetary market relations, private economic activities, and self-responsibility and greater independence for workers and managers, Kulikov saw a very logical progression from his general reform proposals to the issue of employment. Kulikov proposed absolving enterprises of any obligation to find jobs for their displaced workers and supported creation of a special state service to retrain and reassign the workers. He also raised the possibility of the Soviet State Bank declaring badly failing Soviet industrial enterprises "insolvent." Insolvency by declaration of the bank would not force the closing of these enterprises, but would transfer temporary control of their operations from their ministries to a special interdepartmental commission.

The clearest indication of Frolov's impact on *Kommunist* and its new approach to issues like employment came with the publication of a major article by Tat'iana Zaslavskaia, author of the 1983 secret Novosibirsk memorandum and perhaps one of the most outspoken advocates of full-scale economic and political reforms under Gorbachev.[44] Zaslavskaia ranged widely in her article from the lessons of Chernobyl' and the necessity for worker self-management to the fairness of curtailing state food subsidies. Yet all issues raised in her article focused on the common theme of returning Soviet economic and social practices to the mean of something termed "social justice." The major obstacle for Zaslavskaia preventing "social justice" is the current soviet labor policy which discourages worker initiative, overemploys workers in make-work jobs, and guarantees Soviet workers employment without any effort on their part and without any motivation for them to work. She cited sociological surveys that barely a third of Soviet workers actually put out a full effort in their jobs and that, if Soviet managers had the independent authority to regulate the size of their own workforce and the wages paid their own workers, they would let go on average 15 to 20 percent of them.[45] On the issue of technological displacement from microelectronics, Zaslavskaia foresaw an increasing use of part-time workers and flexible work schedules in the Soviet Union over the next two decades to minimize the need for outright layoffs of workers.[46]

Responding to Zaslavskaia's article, Stanislav Shatalin went beyond even her logic and proposals. A ranking official in the newly organized Institute for Economics and Prognoses of Scientific and Technical Progress, Shatalin linked the very threat of unemployment for Soviet workers to other changes all intended as a new "incentive mechanism" to stimulate labor productivity and technological expansion.[47] For Shatalin, the "rational employment" of the Soviet population and the real "principles of socialism" have nothing in common with the "principles of welfarism, automatically guaranteeing a workplace for each"; and "a person should struggle every day from an economic standpoint to retain for himself a suitable workplace."[48] Those displaced by structural-technological changes in the Soviet economy and the elimination of their jobs should be retrained and placed in new vocations by an all-Union employment service, financed in part by fees assessed to enterprises and associations.

Zaslavskaya's article continued to focus a number of additional articles in response and letters-to-the-editor in *Kommunist* throughout 1987.[49] The numerous letters-to-the-editor generally endorsed the far-reaching changes advocated by her and Shatalin. Some even proposed relisting the category "employment" as a conditional state in Soviet economic statistics and educating the Soviet population that their own "effective" employment in the future should not automatically be equated with "full" employment in its past meaning.[50] Nor did readers of *Kommunist* have to search very far for precedents of unemployment and unemployment insurance for workers in contemporary Communist countries. As two Soviet economists concluded from a review of recent labor policy changes in several *Comecon* countries, Hungary, Czechoslovakia, Bulgaria, and the German Democratic Republic to various degrees since 1980 have instituted reforms absolving their state enterprises of finding jobs for displaced workers.[51] All have set up various kinds of state employment organs to oversee the retraining of workers and to provide material support for them until they are placed in new jobs. Not discounting the experience of these *Comecon* countries, the Soviet economists also did not underestimate the political uncertainties. As they cautioned, a great deal of "ideological and educational work in restructuring the social conscience" of affected workers must be undertaken in order to convince them of the necessity to change workplaces and even entire occupations. [52]

Vladimir Kostakov in the State Planning Committee has emerged as the most visible national advocate of unemployment in the Soviet future through his articles and interviews in newspapers like *Izvestiya* to change public conscience. [53] With the infusion of new technology and automation, he projects that 16 million manual jobs may be eliminated in the Soviet economy during the 1990s. To balance a fewer number of workplaces with job-seekers, an increasing number of Soviet workers will have to accustom themselves to sharing part-time jobs in the state industrial sector or in service-trade cooperatives. Within the overall Soviet labor force, Soviet women will be especially vulnerable to Kostakov's projected layoffs and part-time employment over the next decade.

The problem is that the Soviet leadership no longer may be able to assume passiveness among Soviet working women to their pending unemployment out of economic necessity. The political activeness that has been encouraged by the Gorbachev leadership and surged spontaneously among all segments of Soviet society since 1985 may also be stirring Soviet working women and organizations representing their interests like the Committee of Soviet Women. Indicative of the problem for the Soviet leadership was a stormy plenary meeting of the Committee of Soviet Women in the fall of 1988. Reporting on the session, an *Izvestiya* journalist attributed the incensed feeling of Committee delegates in the audience to mounting fears among Soviet working women about the future course of Soviet policies. At least 15 million of the 16 million manual jobs slated for likely elimination in the 1990s are currently held by women. [54]

CONCLUSION

The prospects still seem highly uncertain for successful implementation of Gorbachev's wide-ranging economic reforms, but at least a certain patterned consistency underlies those policy decisions enacted in 1988–89. They would tolerate unemployment as an economic necessity and grant Soviet workers greater freedom in the workplace.

One example is the national pay reform which was enacted in 1987 for gradual implementation over the current Five-Year Plan by 1991. Under the terms of the pay reform, all Soviet enterprises will have almost complete autonomy to set the size of their workforces and the wages paid their own workers. The reform is premised on Soviet enterprises reducing the number of their workplaces to those actually needed for economic efficiency with new technology and automation. The reform allows Soviet enterprises to retain a much higher percentage of their earned profits for self-financing and retooling of their own operations and for wage supplements to their productive workers.

In a series of interviews, officials from the State Committee for Labor and Social Questions have attempted to defuse concerns over unemployment from the new pay reform. In one such interview, the vice-chairman of the state committee admitted that many jobs are likely to be eliminated by the pay reform, but he promised that no one whose position is abolished would be left without some kind of job.[55] Allegedly, certain "special measures" will provide released personnel with new jobs or vocational retraining, during which time they will continue to receive state support equivalent to their former monthly wages. The head of the wages department of the state committee was also guardedly optimistic.[56] In "extreme cases" workers displaced from their enterprises by the pay reform and unable to find new jobs in the very same enterprises will be transferred to different enterprises by local job-placement bureaus. Citing the precedent of the Belorussian Railroad, which has successfully eliminated a number of positions over recent years, he also anticipated that many of those whose jobs would be abolished over the next five years will already probably be very close to retirement. For Leonid Kostin, the first vice-chair of the state committee, any unemployment from the pay reform should be minimal because of demographic changes.[57] Only 5.6 million new workers entered the Soviet labor force throughout the decade of the 1980s, and displaced workers in the next five years should therefore have little difficulty in finding new jobs compared to a previous decade like the 1970s, when the Soviet labor force grew by 22 million. Kostin estimated that as a result of the new pay reform only three of 75 million workers employed in material production in the Soviet Union would actually lose their jobs.

In a related action, the USSR Supreme Soviet enacted a law effective May 1, 1987, legalizing a wide range of "individual labor activities" and small family-type private businesses in artisan crafts and services. Within a year of the law's passage, there were a reported 19.5 thousand cooperatives in the Soviet Union employing about 250,000 workers.[58] On the one hand, opportunities for cooperatives in the Soviet Union remain limited because of ambiguities and restrictions in the 1987 law. Restrictions limit the number of people who can be hired by cooperatives; the law delegates authority to local Soviets in granting permits for cooperatives with ultimate discretion to interpret the law's vague references on legal activities; and the law fails to guarantee artisans and service personnel the right to buy needed materials and tools from wholesale outlets still under state control.[59] On the other hand, prominent Soviet labor economists like Kostakov, leading officials on the State Labor Committee like Kostin, and skeptical Western observers like Sergei Voronitsyn at Radio Liberty in Munich do agree on a clear residual intent of the law on cooperatives.[60] By allowing individual enterprises and the creation of many part-time service jobs, the law provides an additional future safety valve to absorb some of the projected 16 million Soviet workers displaced from the state sector over the next decade. Its very passage as much seems motivated by an anticipation of such pending unemployment by the Soviet leadership as by their desire to improve the quality of consumer goods and services.

Finally, by enactment of the 1987 Soviet Law on the State Enterprise, workers throughout the Soviet Union under its provisions of self-management now have the right to elect and remove their own administrative superiors by secret balloting and competitive elections. Only their choice for enterprise manager must be "confirmed" by their related state ministries. The law also authorized the establishment of labor collective councils elected by workers in all production units to represent their interests in enterprise-wide decision-making. Principles once advocated only by reformists in institutes like State and Law in the early 1980s, worker self-management has been consistently championed by Gorbachev himself in numerous speeches and even Central Committee plenary sessions.[61] For Gorbachev, these workplace reforms have almost become a litmus test in his ability both to intensify economic production and democratize many facets of Soviet society and politics.

Widespread skepticism by workers, strong opposition by enterprise managers, and ambiguities in the 1987 law have so far limited its effectiveness.[62] By requiring ministries to "confirm" those elected enterprise managers by workers, the law essentially invalidates any democratic authority of the labor collectives themselves. Without legal mechanisms or arbitration procedures, the law almost invites either worker skepticism or political stalemate between the ministries and labor collectives over individuals elected manager by the collectives but then rejected as unacceptable by the ministries. Nevertheless, the impetus for worker self-management in the Soviet Union seems irreversible over the next decade. At a minimum, worker self-management provides a political safety valve for economic reforms calculated to lay off 16 million workers in the 1990s. As advocates of worker self-management contend, any workforce reductions must be included among those key decisions which cannot be legally authorized in the future by an elected management without at least the indirect participation of all affected workers through their empowered labor councils.[63]

Whether reforms like these can ever be effectively implemented in the Soviet Union, the USSR under Gorbachev is very likely to experience the same conflict between pessimists and optimists contributing to a realignment of politics in contemporary advanced Western nations like the United States. Yet the USSR remains an authoritarian system which has traditionally denied workers much self-determination or democratic control in the workplace. It also remains a system which over several decades has guaranteed jobs for all Soviet workers. Thus, the implications of the microelectron-

258   *Joel C. Moses*

ics revolution will likely generate even greater political conflict than in the West—once the issues, contending positions, and painful tradeoffs focus over the next few years in the Soviet Union.

NOTES

1. For an excellent and balanced overview of the major issues and alternatives by "pessimists" and "optimists" of the microelectronics revolution in the West, see the review essay by Roger Draper, "The Golden Arm," *New York Review of Books* 22, no. 16 (October 24, 1985): 46–52.
2. Ibid.
3. See, for example, Charles Sabel, *Work and Politics: The Division of Labor in Industry* (New York: Cambridge University Press, 1982); Rosabeth Moss Kanter, *The Change Masters* (New York: Simon and Schuster, 1983); and Michael J. Piore and Charles Sabel, *The Second Industrial Divide: Possibilities for Prosperity* (New York: Basic Books, 1984).
4. I. Frolov, "Questions of Theory: High-Level Interface—On Certain Social Problems in the New Stage of Development of the Scientific-Technical Revolution," *Pravda*, November 23, 1984, 2–3.
5. S. Kheinman, "The Scientific-Technical Revolution and the Intensification of Production," *Voprosy ekonomiki*, no. 7 (July 1985): 26–37, esp. 33.
6. *Narodnoe khoziaistvo SSR v 1984 godu: statisticheskii ezhegodnik* (Moscow: Finansy i statistika, 1985), 179.
7. B. Vinokurov and K. Zuev, "The Real Problems of Developing Computer Technology," *Kommunist*, no. 5 (March 1985): 18–29.
8. Ibid., 23.
9. V. Palterovich, "The Conditions for the Effectiveness of Flexible Automation," *Voprosy ekonomiki*, no. 11 (November 1984): 23–33, esp. 32.
10. On the prevalence of first-generation robots in the Soviet Union, see Chaim Groys, "Robots in Soviet Industry," *Radio Liberty Research Bulletin* [hereafter RLRB], 258/84, July 3, 1984. For an overview of Soviet industrial robots and robotization from an economic perspective, see Herve Gicquiau,· "Robotique et Robotisation de L'Industrie Sovietique," *NATO-Economics Directorate*, April 17–19, 1985.
11. Vinokurov and Zuev, "Real Problems," 24–27.
12. On widespread deficiencies in computers and computer education in Soviet schools, see "Tomorrow's Technology into the Hands of Tomorrow's Leaders," *Ekonomika i organizatsiia promyshlennogo proizvodstva* [hereafter EKO], no. 11 (November 1984): 82–105. Attempts to increase the production of even personal computers for instruction have failed because of bureaucratic opposition from four Soviet ministries still producing incompatible hardware and software programs: B.

Naumov, "Personal Computers in the Starting Blocks," *Izvestiya*, July 11, 1986, 2 (trans. in *The Current Digest of the Soviet Press* (hereafter *CDSP*) 38, no. 28 [August 13, 1986]: 10–11).

13. See Joel C. Moses, "Consensus and Conflict in Soviet Labor Policy—The Reformist Alternative," *Soviet Union/Union Sovietique* 13, no. 3 (Fall 1986): 301–47.

14. See, for example, Yu. Iakovets, "The Scientific-Technical Revolution and the Training of Personnel," *Sotsialisticheskii trud* [hereafter *ST*], no. 1 (January 1984): 8–16; B. Mil'ner, "A Complex Approach to the Organization of Management is Necessary," *ST*, no. 11 (November 1984): 7–17; G. Popov, "Under the Conditions of Scientific-Tehcnical Progress," *ST*, no. 11 (November 1984): 18–28; Iu. Shiriaev and V. Voropaev, "Technical Progress in the Current World Economy and Some Problems of Labor," *ST*, no. 12 (December 1984): 67–78; V. Vasil'ev, "Flexible Production Systems," *Planovoe khoziaistvo*, no. 12 (December 1984): 19–30; E. D. Vil'khovchenko, "Taylorism — Yesterday and Today," *Rabochii klass i sovremennyi mir* [hereafter *RKiSM*], no. 5 (November–December 1984): 72–78; Palterovich, "Conditions for the Effectiveness," and Frolov, "Questions of Theory."

15. On the reform and the political obstacles to its implementation, see Darrell Slider, "The Brigade System in Soviet Industry: An Effort to Restructure the Labour Force," *Soviet Studies* 39, no. 3 (July 1987): 388–405.

16. See, for example, A. Oleinik, "Depending on the Initiative of the Labor Collective," *Partiinaia zhizn'*, no. 5 (March 1986): 36–39, esp. 36.

17. An implied veto is the interpretation of Article 18 in the 1983 Law on Labor Collectives by a leading Soviet specialist on labor law: R. V. Livshits, "The Law on Labor Collectives and the Problems of Its Realization," *Sovetskoe gosudarstvo i pravo* [hereafter *SGiP*], no. 2 (March 1986): 27–35, esp. 33.

18. Slider, "Brigade System." For Soviet perspectives of problems in implementing the brigade reform as intended, see, for example, V. Evlikov, "Workers' Participation in the Management of Production," *ST*, no. 1 (January 1981): 104–10; L. N. Kogan and A. V. Merenkov, "Start-to-finish Brigades: Opinions, Evaluations and the Experience of Installation," *Sotsiologicheskie issledovaniia* [hereafter *SI*], no. 1 (January–March 1983): 86–92; Ye. P. Batalin et al., "The Development and Improvement of Collective Forms of Labor at the Current Stage," *ST*, no. 6 (June 1984): 7–22; M. E. Ille and V. V. Sinov, "On the Development of Self-Management in Brigades," *SI*, no. 3 (July–September 1984): 59–64; P. M. Baltaksa, "Let's Orient Ourself to the Brigade," *EKO*, no. 5 (May 1984): 63–78; and Nina Maksimova, "Brigades at the Cross-roads: Notes about Economics and Morality," *EKO*, no. 8 (August 1985): 152–99.

19. See, for example, I. I. Dakhno and M. N. Kapralova, "The 'Volvo' Experiment (from Swedish Experience)," *EKO*, no. 4 (April 1980): 172–84; B. I. Mil'ner, "Managing Production in Japan: A Multiplicity of Forms and Methods," *EKO*, no. 7 (July 1984): 162–78; and O. I. Kosenko, *Demokratiia i upravlenie proizvodstvom* (Moscow: Politizdat, 1985), 112–32.

20. See, for example, Yu. P. Orlovskii, "The Place and Role of the Labor Collective in the System of Labor Relations," *SGiP*, no. 4 (April 1979): 64–72; *idem*, "Strengthening Work Discipline as a Means of Realizing the Economic and Social Policy of the Party," *SGiP*, no. 1 (January 1980): 8–18; I. V. Gudimov, "Labor Activeness, Discipline, and Work Incentives," *SGiP*, no. 3 (March 1980): 53–59; V. N. Kudriavtsev and B. M. Lazarev, "Discipline and a Sense of Responsibility," *SGiP*, no. 6 (June 1981): 67–76; G. I. Liakh, "The Participation of Toilers in the Management of Production," *SGiP*, no. 8 (August 1982): 34–41; E. L. Belilovskii, "Protectionism and Legal Means of Combatting It," *SGiP*, no. 8 (August 1982): 25–33; A. M. Kurennoi, "The Participation of Labor Collectives in the Management of Enterprises," *SGiP*, no. 3 (March 1984): 83–88; M. V. Tsik, "Socialist Democracy and Self-Management," *SGiP*, no. 4 (April 1985): 3–11; A. M. Kurennoi, "Production Democracy and Labor Law," *SGiP*, no. 7 (July 1986): 53–60; Livshits, "The Law on Labor Collectives."

21. On the Institute of State and Law and the issue of worker self-management, see Joel C. Moses, "Worker Self-Management and the Reformist Alternative in Soviet Labour Policy, 1979–1985," *Soviet Studies* 39, no. 2 (April 1987): 205–8.

22. See, for example, L. Danilov and V. Karev, "Technical Progress and the Releasing of Workers," *ST*, no. 5 (May 1983): 100–104; N. Tokaev, "To Consider More Completely Social Aspects in the Mechanization of Labor," *ST*, no. 1 (January 1984): 38–42; and M. Baskakova, "Some Problems in the Utilization of the Labor of Women Workers in Machine-Building," *ST*, no. 4 (April 1986): 69–71.

23. Danilov and Karev, "Technical Progress."

24. See the two-part roundtable discussion by analysts from the two institutes on the prospects of unemployment and social problems from "optimistic" and "pessimistic" scenarios of the microelectronics revolution: "The Scientific-Technical Revolution and the Problems of the Unemployed in Developed Capitalist Countries," *RKiSM*, no. 2 (March–April 1986): 76–88, and no. 3 (May–June 1986): 99–111.

25. "The Scientific-Technical Revolution and the Problems of the Unemployed,"; V. L. Luk'ianov, "A New Stage of Automation," *EKO*, no. 7 (July 1985): 172–84; N. D. Gauzner, "The Current Stage of the Scientific-Technological Revolution and the Working Class (Economic Role, Employment and Working Conditions)," *RKiSM*, no. 3 (May–June 1985):

34–47; V. S. Azhaeva, "Microelectronics and Employment: The Canadian Experience," *RKiSM*, no. 4 (April 1985): 119–24; and F. Burlatskii, "International Life: The Technological Revolution and the Ethics of Robots," *Literaturnaia gazeta*, October 31, 1984, 14 (trans. in *CDSP* 37, no. 9 [March 29, 1985]: 12–14).

26. See, in particular, "The Scientific-Technical Revolution and the Problems of the Unemployed," and Azhaeva, "Microelectronics and Employment."

27. I. Maslova et al., "The Influence of Technical Progress on the Releasing and Reassignment of Regular Workers," *Planovoe khoziaistvo*, no. 8 (August 1985): 42–48.

28. Vladimir Kostakov, "Employment: A Deficit or Surpluses?" *Kommunist*, no. 2 (January 1987): 78–89.

29. Ibid., 82, 87.

30. R. Tikidzhiev, "The Problems of Balancing the Reproduction of Fixed Capital and Labor Resources," *Planovoe khoziaistvo*, no. 12 (December 1981): 44–53; N. Rogovskii, "Technical Progress—The Foundation of Raising Labor Productivity," *Planovoe khoziaistvo*, no. 7 (July 1982): 27–34; and I. Malmygin, "The Capacity of an Enterprise and a Workplace," *Planovoe khoziaistvo*, no. 3 (March 1984): 40–47.

31. Iu. Konishchev, "The Person in a Workplace," *Kommunist*, no. 8 (August 1984): 41–52; and "On the Broad Implementation of the Certification of Workplaces, Their Rationalization, and On Measures for the Improvement of Rate-setting of Work," *ST*, no. 2 (February 1986): 3–16.

32. Peter Rutland, "The Shchekino Method and the Struggle to Raise Labor Productivity," *Soviet Studies* 36, no. 3 (July 1984): 345–65.

33. G. Kulagin, "The Real and Alleged Deficit (On Some Problems of Using Labor Resources under the Conditions of Scientific-Technical Progress)," *ST*, no. 1 (January 1985): 82–91, at 87.

34. G. Kh. Popov, "How the Shchekino Method is Developing," *Pravda*, December 27, 1980, 3. The article remained the butt of sarcastic criticism two years after its publication: A. M. Dobrusin, "Personnel Work —The Directive to Reduce, The Directive to Hire: Many Problems Are Hidden Behind Them," *EKO*, no. 8 (August 1982): 123–33, esp. 128–33.

35. Vladimir Kostakov, "One Person Must Work Like Seven," *Sovetskaia kul'tura*, January 4 and February 3, 1986 (trans. in *CDSP* 38, no. 3 [February 19, 1986]: 1–4).

36. Ibid., February 3, 1986.

37. Kostakov, "Employment."

38. Ibid., 86–87.

39. Ibid., 85–86.

40. Ibid., 87–89.

41. M. S. Gorbachev, "The Time Demands New Thinking," *Kommunist*, no. 16 (November 1986): 3–14, at 6–7.
42. Frolov, "Questions of Theory." On the characterization of Frolov and his identification with Gorbachev's Moscow State political network, see Jerry F. Hough, "Gorbachev Consolidating Power," *Problems of Communism* 36, no. 4 (July–August 1987): 31.
43. Kulikov, "Commodity-Monetary Relations in the Conception of Acceleration," *Kommunist*, no. 12 (August 1986): 11–22, at 18–19.
44. T. Zaslavskaia, "The Human Factor in the Development of Economics and Social Justice," *Kommunist*, no. 13 (September 1986): 61–72.
45. Ibid., 63–64.
46. Ibid., 70.
47. S. Shatalin, "Social Development and Economic Growth," *Kommunist*, no. 14 (September 1986): 59–70.
48. Ibid., 63.
49. See, for example, "Opinions and Suggestions—From Letters-Responses to the Article 'The Human Factor in the Development of Economics and Social Justice,'" *Kommunist*, no. 17 (December 1986): 62–68; "Problems and Arguments: From the Respones to the Article of Academician T. I. Zaslavskaia," *Kommunist*, no. 1 (January 1987): 62–73; "About the Human Factor and Social Justice; Some Results of the Debate," *Kommunist*, no. 3 (February 1987): 97–108; Kostakov, "Employment"; and idem, "The Author Responds to the Readers—Full Employment: How Do We Understand It?" *Kommunist*, no. 14 (September 1987): 16–25.
50. "Opinions and Suggestions," 62–63.
51. L. Degtiar' and G. Yaremenko, "The Social Effectiveness of Economic Decisions," *Kommunist*, no. 18 (December 1986): 89–99, esp. 89–91.
52. Ibid., 91.
53. See, for example, Vladimir Kostakov, "General Employment and the Labor Market," *Izvestiia*, January 11, 1989, 3.
54. "Among Us Women: While the Men Talk—Report by Feuilleton Writer Marina Lebedeva from the Plenary Session of the Soviet Women's Committee," *Izvestiia*, October 23, 1988, 6 (trans. in *CDSP*, 40, no. 43 [November 23, 1988]: 23–24).
55. B. V. Gavrilov, "Earned Pay—The Reform of the Pay System Begins," *Izvestiia*, September 26, 1986, 2 (trans. in *CDSP* 38, no. 39 [October 29, 1986]: 1–4, esp. 4).
56. "Improve the Economic Mechanism: To Each According to His Work," *Trud*, August 30, 1986, 2 (trans. in *CDSP* 38, no. 39 [October 29, 1986]: 4).
57. L. Kostin, "Economic Departments in the Economic Reform: Restructuring and Wages," *Izvestiia*, September 11, 1987, 2 (trans. in *CDSP* 39, no. 37 [October 14, 1987]: 9, 24).

58. "The USSR State Committee of Statistics Reports," *SI*, no. 4 (July–August 1988): 153.
59. Sergei Voronitsyn, "Prospects for New Law on Individual Labor," *RLRB*, 1/87, December 19, 1986.
60. Kostakov, "The Author Responds to the Readers," 20–21; Kostin, "Economic Departments in the Economic Reform"; and Voronitsyn, "Prospects."
61. See, for example, M. S. Gorbachev, "Restructuring is an Urgent Matter That Affects Everyone and Everything," *Pravda*, August 2, 1986, 1–2; and idem, "On Restructuring and Cadre Policy of the Party, Plenum of the Central Committee, CPSU, January 27, 1987," *Kommunist*, no. 3 (February 1987): 5–48, esp. 18–29.
62. V. N. Narkoriakov, "Who's the Boss in the Plant?" *Kommunist*, no. 6 (April 1988): 18–27; "(Roundtable-Conference Proceedings) Electability of Leaders in Enterprises, Establishments and Organizations," *SGiP*, no. 1 (January 1988): 51–69, and no. 2 (February 1988), 39–50; and Zh.T. Toshchenko et al., "Economic Consciousness: Orientations and Prejudices," *SI*, no. 3 (May–June 1988): 16–23.
63. See, for example, B. P. Kurashvili, "The Basic Link of the Economic System (Towards a Conception of the Law on the Socialist Enterprise)," *SGiP*, no. 12 (December 1986): 12–21, esp. 18, 20; and Gravilov, "Earned Pay."

9

THE IMPACT OF REFORM ON THE ATTITUDES AND BEHAVIOR OF CHINESE YOUTH: SOME EVIDENCE FROM SURVEY RESEARCH

Stanley Rosen

China's reform process—initiated at the Third Plenum of the Eleventh Central Committee in December 1978—has undeniably altered the country's economic landscape over the past nine years. Among the *new* "socialist newborn things" are private enterprises hiring tens, even hundreds of workers; stock and bond markets; and decollectivized agriculture. However, despite—or more accurately, because of—such major changes, China has entered a transitional period.

The economic reforms are far from completed, as the country searches for an appropriate mix between central planning and market mechanisms. Moreover, reform of the political and ideological systems has been far slower and more controversial. Reformers, after all, have no convenient indicators, such as per capita income or industrial growth rate, with which to document the success of political and ideological change for skeptical colleagues. The resolution adopted at the Sixth Plenum of the Twelfth Central Committee in September 1986 sought—not very successfully—to "coordinate" and interrelate reforms in the economic, political, and ideological realms. The October 1987 Thirteenth Party Congress—with its adoption of the concept of the "preliminary stage of socialism"— managed to move this coordination a step forward. Still, the current transitional stage is likely to be a lengthy one. The search for "socialism with Chinese characteristics" has been undertaken in the absence of blueprints; the Chinese term *mosuo* ("groping," "feeling one's way") has frequently been employed to describe the quest.

The contention that has characterized economic, political, and ideological reform in this transitional period has received a great deal of attention from Western academics. Relatively little, however, has been written about the effects of this incomplete reform process on Chinese society and values. Unprecedented social changes— often highly controversial—have been accompanying the reforms. In fact, one of the most encouraging aspects of the entire reform effort has been the work of Chinese social scientists who have moved quickly to investigate new social phenomena. No less than over politics, economics, and ideology, debate over the social effects of the new policies is common.

This paper focuses on the impact of China's reforms on one segment of Chinese society—youth. Much of the paper will examine—directly and indirectly—the changing values and behavior or youth as the country seeks to build "Chinese-style socialism," and the Chinese leadership's response to the challenge posed by the new "thinking generation." Under the inducements of a more open system, with increasing opportunities for wealth and mobility, new patterns of behavior have affected virtually every area of Chinese social life and created open conflict between divergent value systems. The underlying argument of this paper is that the reform process, with its broad emphasis on the expansion of the market, has created an environment which promotes greater permissiveness in society and provides the freedom to pursue materialistic goals. As the state's ability to control social change has declined, the options available to young people have multiplied. Increasingly, it appears that upward mobility may be achieved without a job in a state enterprise or a university education, or even party membership. Thus, while the party still retains a commitment to define social values for the mass population, they are no longer in a position to do so. Indeed, in a sense, the reform program of the party has become dependent on the unified support of an increasingly heterogeneous society. As I have argued elsewhere, the party is seeking to unify public opinion and harmonize interests, politically and ideologically, at a time when economic and social forces are pulling society *away* from the state.[1]

The areas that are documented—value change among college students, attitudes toward the party and military, job preferences and lifestyles of women, and schooling and the labor market—were selected because they are central issues of particular concern to Chinese social scientists and the political leaders. Highly visible changes in each of these areas have stimulated widespread debate. Authorities remain divided over three interrelated questions: (1) How much value change has occurred? (2) Should the changes revealed by survey research be seen, on balance, as positive or negative? and (3) What is the proper response in dealing with Chinese youth in the 1980s?

The discussion will introduce and draw heavily upon survey research, which has become increasingly important as an analytical tool for Chinese social scientists. The growth of such surveys, sometimes reflecting highly negative attitudes, and the increasing willingness of respondents to answer questions about their personal beliefs and motivations, is in itself a major change in the past decade. Publication of these survey results and of detailed statistical data has given us a much more complete picture of Chinese society than at any time since 1949.

Much of the analysis presented by Chinese social scientists is designed to provide support or justification for a given policy, a situation not unheard of elsewhere. Surveys can be seen as arguments in a political debate, with policy implications. Having discussed the policy uses of survey research elsewhere, this important issue will be addressed less fully here. It is helpful, however, to address briefly a fundamental methodological question: how reliable are Chinese surveys?[2]

While a healthy skepticism toward survey data is appropriate anywhere, Chinese scholars readily acknowledge special problems in their data, both at the data gathering and analysis stages. At the data gathering stage, there are at least three basic problems, reflecting not only deficiencies in social science methodology, but broader features of the country's past and its Communist present. First, there is little basis in Chinese traditional political culture to suggest that citizens will reveal their true feelings on a questionnaire, even if they are not required to give their names. In China's past and in

Taiwan as well, such data collection implies governmental attempts at social control and makes respondents cautious. Nothing in post-1949 China, marked as it is by radical political movements, has altered this picture.

A second problem, common in the Soviet Union and Eastern Europe, is that many surveys seem to be conducted in support of a political agenda or to affirm a predetermined conclusion. Surveys can be seen as arguments in a political debate. Third, the sensitive quality of much survey research, combined with the nature of Chinese society, makes it difficult for the researcher to choose an appropriate sample. Access to respondents is usually through their organizations, and within the organization they are commonly selected not by probability sampling but on the basis of personal relationships (*guanxi*).

Likewise, three other problems stand out, at the data analysis stage. First, reflecting the lack of sophistication in sampling procedures, results are often overgeneralized. Second, the distinction between descriptive and inferential statistics is sometimes blurred and not given proper attention. A third problem of data analysis stems from the necessity noted above to reach a "positive" conclusion. Many surveys aggregate the responses of individuals to specific questions into larger, all-encompassing categories. Derived arbitrarily by the researchers, these categories often combine a variety of disparate responses from open-ended questionnaires to make it appear that respondents support a particular government policy.

One should not ignore the seriousness of the problems cited above. Nevertheless, it would be a mistake to throw out the baby with the bath water. Chinese surveys can provide a great deal of information about Chinese society unavailable from other sources. Moreover, surveys clearly vary in their quality. Aware of certain pitfalls, one can judiciously select those which appear to be reasonably sound methodologically, as well as informative. There are also some obvious rules of thumb. For example, one almost always avoids surveys published in English for a foreign audience, or in Chinese for large circulation newspapers such as *Renmin ribao*. Publication in such forums is clearly intended for propaganda or indoctrination. Thus, the method of dissemination tends to be an important indicator of a survey's purpose. The survey's discussed below are drawn primarily from academic journals with a restricted circulation, aimed primarily at professional researchers.

VALUE CHANGE AMONG COLLEGE STUDENTS

Chinese social scientists have conducted hundreds, perhaps thousands, of surveys to determine the attitudes and opinions of Chinese youth. The surveys range from large-scale national samples of tens of thousands to local surveys encompassing no more than a single classroom.[3] The results reported in these surveys, particularly on questions of direct political import, tend to be rather mixed. Some surveys—for example, those done among high school students in the rural areas—often show moderate or strong support for the pursuit of Communist values, the Four Modernizations and party or youth league membership. Other surveys—most notably, those of college students—tend to paint a far more bleak picture regarding the political commitment of Chinese youth. The situation is complicated by various methodological problems associated with Chinese surveys. Although things appear to be improving in this regard, respondents still tend to be less than fully honest in filling in questionnaires. Some informants estimated a rate of unreliability as high as 30 to 50 percent, depending on the sensitivity of the questions. The authors of one study on the outlook towards life of young workers felt it necessary to state that the workers filled out the questionnaire honestly. As they put it, only a small number (at most 10 percent) had been warned by their parents not to be deceived, that this could be used to catch "Rightists."[4]

There is strong evidence, however, based in part on the surveys, but also on the behavior of Chinese youth, and on interviews done in China, that political commitments and unquestioning loyalty toward the Communist party have been replaced in the hierarchy of youth values in post-Mao China by independence of thought and judgment, respect for talent, and a patriotism separated from party leadership. Table 9.1, from a survey conducted in late 1982 on the values and ideals of college students in Shanghai, documents this change. While noting that respect for talent, patriotism, and creativity were admirable and in accord with the goals of the Four Modern-

Table 9.1
Attitudes of Youth on Proper Standards for a Good Youth in the 1980s

Responses	Percent
Has Talent and Dedication to Work	52.2%
Is Patriotic and Able to Preserve National Dignity	46.5%
Shows Independent Thought and Creativity in Work	27.5%
Has Communist Ideals	25.8%
Is Quietly Immersed in Hard Work and Observes Discipline	11%
Is United with the Masses and Finds It a Pleasure to Help People	10%
Puts the Public Interest over Private Interests	9%
Upholds Truth and Dares to Struggle Against Evildoers and Evil Deeds	6.7%

Source: Geng Xionglin and Zhu Yuejing, "Contemporary Youth Seeking After an 'Ideal Image' and Moral Emulation Education," *Shanghai gingshaonian yanjiu*, no. 3 (1984): 7.

Note: Since the total percentage is 188.7 percent, it appears that students may have filled in an open-ended questionnaire and that the researchers then compiled the answers and devised the various categories. Student responses might have fitted more than one category. This is not made clear in the article. The same conjecture can apply to Table 9.2.

izations, there was concern expressed that students, particularly in their early university years, lacked proper recognition regarding the importance of "Communist ideals." A follow-up study was done in March 1983 on 630 young students of the entering class of 1981 from more than 10 Shanghai universities. The results are presented in Table 9.2. As the authors pointed out, the fact that 58.6 percent

Table 9.2
What Ideological Qualities Should University Students in the 1980s Possess?

Responses	Percent
Love the Country and Love the People	16.5%
Dare to Think and Be Good at Thinking	58.6%
Honest and Fair-Minded	35.9%
Listen to What the Party Says and Be a Revolutionary Successor	3%

Source: Geng and Zhu, "Contemporary Youth," 7.

chose "Dare to Think and Be Good at Thinking" while only 3 percent chose "Listen to What the Party Says and Be a Revolutionary Successor" as the standard for university students in the 1980s was a striking indication of the change in student values compared to the 1950s and 1960s. Other studies also found rather similar results that "the students were concerned with talent and ability rather than ideals; knowledge rather than politics; and independent thought rather than obedience." The authors warned that this trend among freshmen and sophomores "should not be ignored."

More recent surveys—covering college students on both famous and more obscure campuses—have shown similar results; patriotic sentiments and intellectual values win out over socialist ones. Asked to choose their ideals, 61.7 percent of Qinghua University students sampled chose "the revitalization of China;" 40.1 percent chose "the progress of mankind;" 32.3 percent chose "Communism;" and 20.3 percent chose "individual and family happiness." Those who chose Communism were primarily party members and party activists. Similarly, when asked the main historical responsibility of contemporary Chinese college students, 80.6 percent chose "Studying hard, and surpassing advanced world standards"; 26.9 percent chose "Arouse the masses and inspire a nationalistic spirit"; and 31.3 percent chose "Be of one heart and mind with the party and promote reform."[5]

A survey conducted among students at the Shandong Maritime Institute showed a suspicion of cadres and political leaders generally. When asked who they most venerated, the forty names chosen ranged from Marx to Einstein, and included Hitler, Kissinger, Jesus, and Chiang Kai-shek. Over 70 percent of the students chose positive, noncontroversial figures. Zhou Enlai led all others with twenty-seven votes (23 percent of the students responding), while Mao Zedong and Napoleon each received ten votes. Interestingly, Deng Xiaoping got five votes, and four students chose themselves. The attitudes expressed toward approved political thought and the political cadres who control their lives—those who decide job allocations, screen applicants to the party, compile dossiers, and so forth—were particularly negative. When asked their deepest impression of current cadres, the largest number (41.9 percent) chose "contemptible, hateful, and detestible," followed by "none of the above"

Table 9.3
The Interest Expressed by University Students in Beijing in Participation
in Various Kinds of Activities

Activity	Interested	Not Interested	Rank
Sports	92.1%	6.5%	1
Social Practice and Investigation	90.1%	7.7%	2
Various Reports and Lectures	84.7%	13.2%	3
Work-Study Program	81.3%	16.4%	4
Art, Literature, and Entertainment	77.5%	10.2%	5
Work Done for the Public in Addition to One's Job (shehui gongzuo)	73.5%	23.5%	6
Public Activities (shehui huodong)	67.5%	29.7%	7
Voluntary Labor	63.0%	33.5%	8
Activities of the Party and Youth League	52.3%	44.4%	9
Political Study	35.0%	51.1%	10

Source: Wang Sunyu et al., "A Preliminary Exploration of Party Construction Work Among University Students," in Xin shigi daxuesheng sixiang zhengzhi jiaoyu yanjiu, ed. Beijing Municipal Party Committee Research Office (Research on Ideological and Political Education of University Students in the New Period) (Beijing: Beijing Normal University Press, 1988), 209.

(41 percent), and then "frightening" (10.2 percent). Only 2.5 percent chose "worthy of respect and approachable."[6] A survey among college students in Sichuan showed that many students who support the reform policies see a contradiction between the Third Plenum (December 1978) initiatives and Mao Zedong thought. Fewer than 50 percent of the humanities and social science students queried thought the "correct" reform policies "adhered to and carried forward Mao Zedong thought."[7]

Nor have students been as willing to engage in overtly political—or even collectivist—activities as they have in private activities, or those in which they can exercise independent judgment, relatively free from party and youth league discipline. Table 9.3 presents the results from a recent large-scale sample survey in Beijing.

Survey results such as those above have been cited by reformers engaged in youth work to argue that university students "who hold positive views of values such as 'striving for the realization of communism and the four modernizations' and 'making contributions for the country and society' . . . are in the minority." Rather, the students are "life-oriented," eager "to obtain (and not sacrifice) all that they are entitled to . . . in the course of making contributions to society." As one young reformer, Yang Dongping, notes, this transformation of youth attitudes from the "strongly political," when "one billion people (were) all great critics," to the more personal, is rather similar to developments in industrialized countries, and may simply be "a normal phenomenon of a society of peace and prosperity that is focused on economic construction." Under these conditions, Yang and others wonder, How can political socialization be carried out effectively?

In the course of answering, Yang provides a devastating critique of current political education in China, which may produce apparent compliance in external behavior, but has not touched the student's internalized value system. When even the external compliance breaks down—as perhaps occurred in the student demonstrations in 1985 and 1986—political education is inevitably "reduced to a case by case, fire-rescue type of preaching." What is needed, Yang argues, is to bring the students more directly into the political process, "to provide them with better political treatment than other members of society."[8]

Despite such appeals from reformers, more "conservative" party leaders have used similar surveys to argue that ideological education needs to be strengthened, that Chinese youth are subject to too little control. Thus, after the 1986 student demonstrations, Lei Feng, the "rust-free screw" concerned only with serving the people, was revived as a model; the State Education Commission announced regulations in April 1987 which reintroduced political standards for college and university enrollment; and commentaries in the press began to argue that training in skills was secondary to the primary educational task of fostering "correct political orientation."[9]

Caught in the middle of this debate are China's political work cadres, who face the unenviable task of promoting "spiritual civilization" and instilling a "Communist value system" into a youth culture that has become increasingly materialistic. Recent surveys have revealed the demoralization of political workers at Beijing's university and high school campuses. For example, a large-scale survey on politics and ideology was administered to students, teachers, and political workers at universities in Beijing from April 1986 to July 1987 (30,000 questionnaires were distributed). Among other findings, the survey showed that few political work cadres were willing to continue in such jobs over a long period of time, particularly at the best universities.[10] A similar attitude was prevalent among middle school political workers, where only a small number were below the age of thirty, and many were unhappy in their jobs.[11]

Interviews conducted at colleges and high schools in China support the conclusions from these surveys, and suggest that the measures offered by the conservatives will very likely be ineffective. For example, interviews with students at Guangzhou's best high school revealed at least two very different strategies among top students. One type of student planned to go to a local key university, like Zhongshan or South China Engineering, and major in a field like construction engineering or computer science, both of which are in high demand. Then, upon graduation, they would be able to make up to 300 yuan a month from rich suburban townships or rural enterprises. There was no need to try to get into the nation's top universities, such as Beijing or Qinghua University. Their second choice, quite often, was Shenzhen University, again because of financial considerations. Another group of top students was very committed to the reforms and modernization, and very independent in thinking. They wanted to attend one of the nation's best universities and play an important role in the reform process. In neither case was there any interest in politics courses as they were being taught, nor great respect for the youth league or the party.

A discernible impatience with the pace of reform also revealed itself in interviews with university students in Beijing. While graduate students and young teachers felt the reform process to be quite rapid, many younger students thought the opposite, that few meaningful changes had yet taken place. The surveys done by the Research Institute under the Economic Structural Reform Commission back this finding for university students more generally. A 1986 survey showed that university students and graduate students made the highest demands on the reform process, but gave a very low rating to the results of the reforms.

PARTY RECRUITMENT

China's leaders by the 1980s were sitting atop a party apparatus which had been steadily aging since 1949. Whereas party members twenty-five years old and under had made up 26.6 percent of all party members in 1950, by 1983 the equivalent figure was 3.36 percent. In Shanghai the change was even more stark, going from 41 percent just after 1949 to 2.25 percent in 1983.[12] The change in values among university students described in the previous section is congruent with party membership figures for university students in the 1980s, compared with the 1950s and 1960s. An internal report from the Ministry of Education in 1983 contrasted the situation with the eve of the Cultural Revolution by saying that things were so bad that:

In a few schools there is not a single student who has applied to join the party. Moreover, the schools' party and youth league committees have not placed this issue on the agenda. . . . At Beijing Normal University, where student party members made up 12.5 percent in the first half of 1966, the number is down to 2 percent. At Qinghua University the equivalent figures have gone from 13 percent to 1.9 percent. At other schools the numbers are lower. . . . At many colleges and universities the percentage of student party members is the lowest since the founding of the People's Republic of China . . . and in some schools with long histories there are fewer student party members now than the number of underground party members there in the pre-Liberation period.[13]

The Shanghai figures are more complete and show an even sharper drop, as Tables 9.4 and 9.5 reveal. By the end of 1983, the percentage of student party members at Shanghai's top universities ranged from 0.3 percent to 0.56 percent of the undergraduate student body.[14]

The impasse in recruitment work was reflective of a generation gap pitting contemporary youth, holding 1980s values, against conservative party members, still seeking the ideal youth of the 1950s. The problem came from two directions. On the one hand, in the course of modernization, the ideals of young people continue to evolve away from the traditional criteria—e.g., selflessness, disci-

Table 9.4
Party Membership at Three Shanghai Universities (the end of 1983)

	Fudan University	East China Normal University	Shanghai University of Science and Technology
Regular Course Students (benkesheng)	6,661	4,841	2,660
Party Members	37	17	8
Percentage	0.56%	0.35%	0.3%

Source: Li Yongjin, "Pay Attention to Recruiting Members Among University Students," *Ma'anshan gangtie xueyuan gaojiao yanjiu*, no. 2 (April 1985): 89.

Note: Among freshmen and sophomores, Fudan had 7 party members out of 3,497 students; East China Normal University had 1 party member out of 2,427 students; Shanghai University of Science and Technology had no party members in the lower years.

pline, obedience—associated with party membership. As a number of surveys show, professional or academic success is given top priority by young people, who calculate that early party membership may constrain the pursuit of more material goals. At the same time, they realize that they are more likely to become the objects of party courtship *after* they achieve academic or professional success.[15] There is in fact some evidence of this. One survey conducted by the Communist Youth League Committee of the Beijing Municipal Broadcasting and Television Industrial Company showed that

Table 9.5
Party Membership at Shanghai Universities, 1956–62

	1956	1957	1958	1959	1960	1961	1962
University Students	39,859	38,663	45,840	55,913	63,435	63,648	58,575
Party Members	3,302	3,263	4,457	3,450	3,632	3,872	2,811
Percentage	8.3%	8.4%	9.7%	6.2%	5.7%	6.1%	4.8%

Source: See Table 9.4.

Note: The percentage for 1957 was incorrectly recorded in the original as 9.7 percent and has been recalculated.

20 percent of their youth league organizations investigated reported that applicants to the party with a higher educational background were treated as activists and allowed to take part in the party's organizational activities. Those workers with little educational background who applied, however, were denied access to such activities.

At the same time that youth have been less than eager to join, local party leaders at the grassroots level have been reluctant to absorb the "new youth" into the party; some cadres have argued that they "would not rest assured if they should allow this crop of university students to take over from them." In effect, they have been looking for Lei Feng and finding the independent, critical individuals closer to those written about Liu Binyan in *The Second Kind of Loyalty*. Under these conditions, a large number of "veteran comrades" argue that, since the "university students of the 1980s are inferior to those of the 1950s," the "conditions are unripe" for recruiting any college students into the party.[16] Young workers have complained in surveys that the leadership disparages young people who "dare to think," since such independence is "unlikely to accomplish anything but likely to spoil everything.[17]

The dangers of a student body not under the control of the party have been brought home to the authorities numerous times in recent years. Let us take two opposing examples of the importance of party influence on student behavior. In 1980, when university students ran for positions as local people's representatives, a number of them campaigned on an anti-Marxist, anti-Mao Zedong thought platform, and received broad support and applause. The impact on freshman and sophomore students was particularly electric. Because there were no party members in most of the classes and grades, no rebuttal was offered to these candidates.

On the other hand, in the Department of Philosophy at Shandong University, the party has maintained a strong presence. From 1979 to 1981, the department had 268 students, of whom 175 (67.3 percent of those without party affiliation) applied to join the party. Twenty-five applicants were accepted; added to the eight prior party members, that made up 11.9 percent of the total students. When students from most of the departments at Shandong University went on strike and boycotted the cafeteria, students from the philosophy

Table 9.6

Question: Some of Your Friends Have Joined the Party, Others Are Striving to Do So. What Is Your Observation and Understanding of This?

Responses	*Percent*
They Believe in Communism and Want to Make a Contribution	4%
They Think the Party Is Good and Are Joining in Order to Be Further Educated	10%
In Reality They Want a "Party Card" Which They Can Use as Capital to Receive Future Benefits	59%
Other Responses	Omitted

Note: N = 2,063

Source: Zhao Yicheng, "Jiazhide chongtu" (Value Conflict), *Weidinggao*, no. 8, April 25, 1988, 19.

department reportedly refused to join in the "anarchism and liberalism."[18]

Facing an increase in independent student activity in the 1980s —ranging from small group salons to campus demonstrations—the party in universities began a major recruitment campaign in 1984 which has, at least in terms of numbers, already paid dividends. Nationally, party membership among Chinese undergraduates has improved to perhaps 3 to 4 percent of the student body on many campuses. In Beijing, by 1986 the figure had reached 5.5 percent. However, this is still well below the high tide of the mid-1950s. Moreover, there are wide variations from campus to campus. At certain key institutions—such as Beijing and Qinghua Universities —reportedly 20 to 25 percent of the students were being recruited into the party before graduation. At other colleges, the figures are rising much more slowly. More significantly, given the widespread recognition—and complaints—about the "impure" motives of those who join, party membership itself offers little indication of a person's value system. Indeed, Table 9.6, from a survey of students at eighteen Shanghai universities, suggests that those who join the party are perceived by their peers to do so for instrumental reasons.

While it is demonstrably true that at least some of the current attitudes and opinions of Chinese youth—for example, the skepticism regarding political commitments—can be traced to the political twists and turns of the 1960s and 1970s, additional survey data reveals a more direct impact of post-Mao economic reforms on social change. As examples of this, we turn next to surveys of a less overtly political nature, on military recruitment from the rural areas, on women workers, and on school dropouts.

MILITARY RECRUITMENT AND THE IDEOLOGY OF YOUNG SOLDIERS

The impact of economic reform has had a demonstrably negative effect on the ability of the People's Liberation Army to attract qualified recruits.[19] In part this is due to sharp cuts in military expenditures in recent years. From 1950 to 1980, on average each year the percentage of military spending in the state's total expenses was 17.2 percent. Since 1981, the percentage has decreased every year. By 1988, it had dropped to 7.49 percent. Thus, even with a substantial increase in pay for ordinary soldiers—a decade ago pocket money was fixed at between 6 and 12 yuan a month; now it is several dozen yuan—military allowances cannot compare to the earnings of enterprising youth in either city or countryside. Moreover, joining the military no longer confers a high social status. The Chinese press has frequently noted that youth have become indifferent to serving in the military, with stories on the low educational and moral quality of many recruits. One Renmin ribao report noted that a group of 150 new recent recruits in northern China turned out to be largely made up of criminals, including a murderer, an escaped prisoner, and the head of a criminal gang. Moreover, the report continued, "the deaf and sick have also joined the services" and "schizophrenics and epileptics are not uncommon." The recent extension of the conscription age limit for urban Chinese youth by one year to 21 is not likely to have a major impact.

In part of course the low quality of the recruits reflects the decline of recruitment standards. In some areas the quota can only be filled if no written test is given and the medical check-up is perfunctory. Moreover, the military itself has been forced to adjust to the prevailing economic winds. While bemoaning the influence the economic reforms have had on "commercializing the comradely relationship," the army is responsible for raising 30 percent of its food expenditure. Only 70 percent is provided by the state. The typical new recruit appears to reflect commercial over spiritual values. Thus, a recent Fudan University survey found that 33.3 percent of the armymen sampled maintained that "studying is useless," and many opted for "engaging in trade at the expense of studying."

Not surprisingly, many surveys on military recruitment explicitly take the new economic reforms as their starting point. Perhaps because of the difficulty of recruiting soldiers from wealthy rural areas, a seemingly disproportionate number of these surveys analyze the motivations, attitudes, and behavior of those who joined despite their economic success at home. Although presumably not representative of the majority of recruits, PLA officials have explicitly recognized the potential advantages of attracting these beneficiaries of the economic reforms.

Perhaps the most intriguing is a survey of 1,109 new recruits conducted in 1986 by members of the youth division of the General Political Department of the PLA.[20] In addition, panel discussions were held with seventy-three cadres at the regimental, battalion, company, and platoon levels. What is particularly interesting to the authors of the survey is a subsample of 628 soldiers (56.6 percent) who had been engaged in commodity production or trade before enlistment; 96 percent were from the rural areas. Since their income levels had ranged from 700 to over 7,000 yuan a year, we are not looking at poverty-stricken rural youth. Representing a potentially great change in the recruitment base of the PLA, the subsample is the focal point of the authors' analysis.

The findings are very revealing. First, we note that the military has begun to attract well-to-do peasants who hope to parlay military service into enhanced status or wealth. For example, about 38 percent of the subgroup of 628 hoped to increase their status (over 90 percent of them "had their eye on party membership"); over 40 percent wanted to learn a trade (over 80 percent of these wanted to learn truck driving, a lucrative occupation in the countryside).[21] Some of the recruits were particularly forthright, as the following passage shows:

A new recruit of a certain regiment had been in the transportation business at home. The village cadre extorted money from him and they were at odds with each other. His purpose in enlisting was to gain admission to the party so that he could stand up against the village cadre when he returned home after discharge. A soldier of rural origin was enlisted to a certain regiment in 1986. He had been driving a truck at home, but had been unable to obtain a driver's license despite his many efforts at finding connections and giving out gifts. He declared: "My purpose of enlisting is to get a driver's license." What is new is not that soldiers joined partly for personal desires but that they could now openly disclose their personal intentions.

Second, influenced by their business practices, these recruits placed a high value on building a *guanxi* (connections) network. Some would offer cigarettes to superiors in place of a salute. When the larger sample of 1,109 recruits was asked, "What kind of people do you admire most in society?" 28 percent responded: "Those who are able to cultivate relations." Of this 28 percent, the subsample of 628 made up 18 percent. As one soldier noted on the back of his questionnaire, "I admire heroes and models, and I admire even more those who are able to make money and cultivate relations, because they fare well wherever they go."

Third, given their specific purposes for joining the military, it was not uncommon for the new recruits to become disheartened if they felt they had "over-invested" in becoming a soldier, that the gains were not equal to the hardships. Among the 628 surveyed, 113 (17.9 percent) had developed an unfavorable impression of the army. The large majority of them had either not been assigned to tasks that would allow them to acquire the skills they desired (e.g., driving a truck), felt they had no chance to be admitted to the party, or could not get along with their leaders. The survey also showed that 53 percent had not been assigned tasks which utilized their talents and were unhappy with their jobs.

Fourth, despite the low level of education of the recruits, they had little desire to upgrade their basic educational level. When asked, "Do you want to learn a skill or study some culture," 99.3 percent of the 628 opted for learning a skill.

While recognizing certain obvious shortcomings, the authors of the survey argue that these economically independent recruits "are the biggest contingent of talent in the history of our army." But there is substantial opposition within the military from cadres who criticize the new-style rural recruits arriving from a more prosperous countryside as "slick, speculative operators," "the dregs of society," "profiteers," and imbued with a "merchant mentality."

Another survey, contained in a lengthy collection of essays analyzing conditions among young soldiers in the Nanjing military district, sheds additional light on the attitudes of new military recruits from the countryside.[22] In a study of 127 such recruits—supplemented by discussions with more than twenty cadres—several "disturbing" trends were noted. The level of dissatisfaction with military life was high; 54.3 percent surveyed wanted to return before the end of their three-year tour of duty. "Several years earlier," the equivalent figure had been 20 to 30 percent. Interest in learning a specialty or technical skill had increased but concern with politics decreased. Company level cadres reported that in the early 1980s more than 80 percent of the young soldiers wanted to join the party or receive certificates of merit. But survey results show that only 52.8 percent desired party membership and only 30 percent were seeking to obtain such moral awards as certificates of merit. The soldiers' families reinforced the recruits' lack of commitment; 41.7 percent of family heads wanted the recruits to return home as early as possible. Although the survey does not correlate opinion with income level, by providing detailed tables on the rising income levels, occupations, ownership of agricultural machinery, and so forth of the soldiers' families since the December 1978 plenum, it does make the more general point that the above changes in outlook were closely related to the flourishing economic conditions in the home areas of the recruits. Peasant youth no longer relied on the military just to leave the countryside.

SURVEYS ON WOMEN WORKERS

Economic reforms have also had a major impact on the attitudes and behavior of young women, particularly with regard to employment and lifestyle issues. With Chinese enterprises now responsible for their own profits and losses, putting productivity and economic efficiency at a premium, many factory directors have been reluctant to hire women. At the same time, there has been an effort eliminate "surplus employees," estimated to number as many as twenty million. In areas of increasing economic prosperity, many Chinese women have given up jobs to take care of family and household chores. An open debate has been raging in the Chinese press over the past several years regarding the relationship between the number of women in the work force and the successful realization of women's liberation.

The All-China Women's Federation and its local affiliates have been highly critical of attempts to ease women out of the labor force, although their arguments tend to appear mostly in journals and newspapers for women. General, large-circulation newspapers like *Renmin ribao* for the most part have published articles in support of a more "realistic" approach to women's liberation, noting that "many young women are exchanging ill-paid and unsatisfying menial and manual work for the challenges and satisfactions of taking care of their children."[23] Other reports cite "experts" who note that "the high proportion of China's female employment resulted from the intervention of governmental bodies and the neglect of working efficiency in the enterprises and institutions."[24]

As enterprises and units openly solicit male applicants only, the impact has been felt on the educational system at various levels. Interestingly, the problem is especially serious with regard to hiring policies of ministries and departments at the central level. Universities have complained often about the discrimination, but apparently to little avail. To take just one case, one-third (seventy) of the units contacting Shanghai's Fudan University to hire their graduates in 1984 stated explicitly that no women would be accepted. When necessary, hiring units would simply cut quota numbers to avoid taking in women.[25] A similar situation prevails for graduates of vocational schools. Anticipating the difficulties of placement for graduates, vocational and technical schools have simply closed various specializations to women and generally cut female enrollment.[26]

Subjectively, the improved economic situation has led to several changes in the outlook of young women regarding employment. They are no longer so eager to find a job. In a sample of sixty-three such youth interviewed in Shanghai—where around 65 percent of unemployed youth are female—75 percent came from families where the average per capita income was over 40 yuan. Sixty percent of them felt no pressure at home; 40 percent felt only slight pressures financially.

Moreover, unemployed young women have become more selective. Most of the sixty-three interviewees rejected jobs which involved hard work (e.g., textile worker) or unsanitary conditions; which involved occupational hazards (e.g., hospital work); which necessitated long distance commuting (e.g., suburban factory work). More favored were jobs with high pay, but light work (e.g., salesperson or bus conductor); 16 percent preferred technical or skilled jobs. The desire to become a factory worker has declined, while commercial or service jobs are now more attractive. Of the sixty-three women, 22 percent wanted factory jobs (a big drop from previous surveys) and 31.7 percent wanted service jobs. The latter figure rises to 40 percent if one includes those who wanted to set up private business operations.[27]

Studies of the changing labor market done in other cities show similar results. For example, many surveys have been done on young textile workers.[28] In Suzhou, there had been no problem recruiting textile workers before 1983. Beginning in 1984, textile companies have been notably unsuccessful in recruiting new workers, even after lowering their qualification requirements many times. Vocational schools have had to shut down classes because of a lack of applicants; graduates have been turning down assigned mill jobs to seek something on their own. First the mills went to suburban rural areas to recruit; when they still could not meet the hiring quota, they recruited contract labor from the countryside. However, given the improved rural economy, rural women have not been enthusiastic about becoming urban textile workers. For example, two Suzhou factories hired 250 contract workers from local counties in 1985. Within three months most had left, some without waiting to get back their deposits on signing the contracts. The transfer and absentee rates for existing workers showed an equally dismal picture.[29] More recent surveys confirm the continuation of these trends.

The impact of reform on lifestyle issues is equally striking, suggesting a clear decline in the ability of the state to dictate morality. A study done in Harbin, where 80 percent of the 14,800 young textile workers are apprentices or first or second-grade workers averaging under 38 yuan a month, revealed that most of the single women spent at least half their income on clothing, accessories, cosmetics, and hairstyling. Very few saved anything from their salaries. Many of the married women reported being unhappy; for example, of the 210 married women workers at the Harbin No. 2 Knitwear Mill, 50 percent admitted to unhappy marriages.[30]

More details on love and marriage patterns are provided in a survey of three plants in Wuxi. The comparison with the 1970s is striking:

In Wuxi, textile mills have traditionally had a rule that new worker apprentices may not engage in romantic activities during their apprentice periods, or their apprenticeship will be extended and they cannot become regular workers on schedule. Most members of the highest age group had entered the mills in the mid-1970s and had had no boyfriends during their apprentice period, or, if they had, were quiet about it. Now, however, most apprentices come in with boyfriends. At the No. 2 Silk Reeling Mill, this was true of 80 percent of the newcomers, who made no secret of the fact. The regulation was impossible to enforce.

Cohabitation and premarital pregnancy were almost unknown among the highest age-group when they came in during the mid or late 1970s. The few who had had problems of this type suffered much public censure and felt great shame. Now it is no longer a rare phenomenon among the lowest age-group. According to information provided by the offices concerned, 80 percent of current hospital abortion cases are of unmarried girls, 3 times the number before 1980. Cohabitation is even more common. Seventy-nine women workers between the ages of 18 and 22, or 9.4 percent of that age-group, are living with boyfriends without the benefit of marriage. This is a 70 percent increase as compared to the mid or late 1970s.[31]

Among the reasons given for this change are the influence of "unhealthy Western ideas such as 'sexual liberation,' " which the women are likely to accept uncritically; greater financial independence and less reliance on their families; and a low educational level. Given the difficulty of recruiting textile workers, entrants need only score minimally on a test to be accepted. Most are junior high school graduates or senior high school dropouts. There is no interest in furthering their education; rather, they "set high sights on material betterment and stimulation." As the researchers noted, "Many of the youngest group told us that, with so much time on their hands, what better way to spend it than playing around with the opposite sex? They called this 'living a more fulfilling life.' "

Other surveys—both in urban and rural areas—show similar

new trends on the question of sexual activity. Premarital abortions have greatly increased. In Beijing, the total number of abortions performed was 157,000 in 1980; 189,000 in 1981; 234,000 in 1982; 251,000 in 1983; and 246,000 in 1984. Premarital abortions made up 27.9 percent of the total number in 1981; a more recent sample survey of two hospitals showed a rate of 23.1 percent (although the rate in one of the two hospitals was over 40 percent), which would mean 57,000 such abortions in 1984. In Shanghai, premarital abortions totalled 39,000 in 1982; 50,000 in 1983; and 65,000 in 1984. In Dalian the proportion of premarital to total abortions was 22 percent.

Drawing on the above statistics, the authors of a survey on abortions among unmarried women in Beijing explained the phenomenon as follows:

Traditionally, Chinese women had a very conventional attitude toward sex. People cared about their reputations and women were expected to be "chaste." After the founding of the People's Republic, new concepts on sex were based upon socialist morality. Romance, marriage, sexual behavior, and birth became the unalterable legal sequence. Whosoever reversed this sequence was subject to prosecution by law and censure by public opinion. In the past few years, however, with the policy of opening to the world while invigorating the domestic economy, many ideological influences have infiltrated China from abroad, and new trends have appeared among a part of the Chinese youth, especially urban youth, on the question of sex. Apart from the few who were out to enjoy Western "sexual freedom," many other young people—90 percent or more in our survey—began to have sex before being lawfully wedded. This shows a breakthrough of the legal confines of socialist morality on this question. Sociologists should study this attitude change. In the past, due to "leftist" influences, few people made it a topic of research.[32]

EDUCATION, DROPOUTS, AND JOBS

Economic reform has created particularly serious problems for China's educational system. The expansion of market mechanisms now provides more options for students—and, to a lesser extent, teachers—at every educational level. The result has been an exodus out of the schools, which has not yet reached its peak. In part this simply represents a rational economic calculus by individuals. Teachers find themselves confronting double-digit inflation with an average annual salary of $360, one of the lowest of major vocations. College graduates and experienced instructors have spurned teaching for higher-paying work. Of the teachers who have remained in classrooms, 70 percent are unqualified.[33]

Nor does it necessarily pay, economically, for students to remain in school. An illiterate manual laborer earns more than a college graduate, and the gap has been widening. The response has been a steady increase in school dropouts, affecting primary school pupils and, more recently, graduate students as well. At one end of the system, there are 40 million children between the ages of six and fourteen who have dropped out of school. At the other end, in 1988, for the first time, there were too few applicants for the places available for post-graduate students, with 1989 enrollments expected to decline by 1,000 places. The number of graduate students who dropped out quadrupled in 1987. Indeed, in decrying the situation, *Renmin ribao* noted that if the salary and bonus structure is not altered, a dropout from junior middle school will, by 1995, be $4,000 richer than a student who goes on to college.[34]

The problem has been exacerbated by the "bifurcated" system established to guarantee that education serves economic development. Alongside a small "elite" sector to train the first-class scientists and engineers necessary to meet the ambitious targets of the Four Modernizations program, there also exists a large "mass" sector, expected to provide basic educational skills, with the possibility of additional vocational training, for the majority. In the past decade, the gap between the two sectors has become wider and wider, with less and less interchange possible.[35]

For students able to work their way up through the "key" schools in the elite sector, the reward is often entrance to a top university. For those who get tracked out of the elite sector somewhere on the educational ladder, the realization sets in early that none of the potential benefits of academic success—advanced graduate training, overseas study, allocation of a secure, desirable job on the frontiers of Chinese modernization—will be likely. This is particularly true of those streamed into "middling" or "slow" classes in high school. The desire to "invest" in one's education, therefore, is often directly proportional to one's place within this educational hierarchy. Many studies have documented the seriousness of the problem.

National and local surveys have been conducted to discover the reasons for the high dropout rate, which generally is highest among second and third year junior middle students. Their findings show the key factor to be the effects of economic reform. For example the vice-minister of education cited four major reasons for leaving school: (1) Since manual labor pays more than mental labor, many uneducated parents have concluded that studying is useless, that their children should quit school and earn money; (2) Businesses have been eagerly hiring children as cheap labor; (3) The cost of tuition, books, and other school expenses has become too big a burden for rural parents; (4) Many schools concentrate on preparing students for college and ignore those who cannot keep up. The backward students often lose self-esteem, start to cut classes, and eventually drop out.[36]

All of these reasons bear some relation to the economic reforms. For example, an important component of the elite-mass division in the educational sector is the reliance on the local areas to fund basic education; the central government is most directly concerned with the key universities. To raise the money necessary to support educational undertakings, particularly in the countryside, local governments have simply been passing the costs on to the population. Thus, each school pupil in the rural areas of Hubei province paid an average of 38.5 yuan ($10.40) in tuition in 1987, 85 percent more than the year before.[37]

Even poor study achievement can sometimes be traced to the differential economic rewards currently offered in Chinese society, as the following letter to a newspaper makes clear:

We are students from an ordinary middle school in Jiabei district. Last semester, two classmates who had poor study achievements and felt they could not catch up, dropped out of school. Now, one works as a contract worker in a barber shop and makes about 90 yuan a month. The other has set up a fruit stall and makes about 150 yuan a month. When this news reached us, the whole class became excited. A great many became disheartened about studying, asking, What's the use? Those who are uneducated can follow this model to make money, and make more than the intellectuals! The study atmosphere in the classroom has become worse and worse. As class cadres, seeing more and more students failing, we have become very worried, and have tried our best to persuade everyone. But we are at a loss as to what to say to them.[38]

The official response, of course, is to urge students to stay in school; however, the reasons given—e.g., to improve one's spiritual life or to give one a greater competitive advantage in the job market —often seem unconvincing. As one letter writer put it, "Even those who love to read books can't buy them on low salaries . . . teahouses where they play music tapes and other such (entertainment) places belong to the world of the private entrepreneur. Therefore, we can see that the happiness of the higher spiritual life is inseparable from money." [39] It is perhaps not surprising that three million children left school to join the work force in 1987, despite a law requiring Chinese to attend up to the ninth grade, or that the national dropout rate for middle school students increased 2.6 percent in 1988.[40]

CONCLUSION

In the course of pursuing economic development and "Chinese-style socialism," major changes are occuring in Chinese society. Given the nature of the quest, no one an yet say what form a modernized, "socialist" China is likely to take. Still, the transitional period has already provided enough hints to indicate the direction of social change, and the challenges now faced by some of China's most hallowed institutions. Our analysis has suggested a number of points.

First, the transitional society is one which presents many more alternatives for Chinese youth. In this more open society, "investment" options can be taken relatively quickly. For example, if one has not been able to enter a key junior or senior high, continuing one's schooling may be considered to be a poor investment, since the likelihood of entrance to a good university is remote. On the other hand, dropping out and finding a well-paying job, or helping one's family prosper, become attractive possibilities. The introduction of a nine-year compulsory education law in 1986 is an attempt to reduce or at least delay some of these options, but it is too early to predict the effectiveness of this measure.

Second, the "freedom" to invest has become possible in part

because of a clear decline in the state's ability to control social change. Efforts to stimulate the economy and regularize political and personal life have created an environment which supports a "privatization" of values. Moreover, the post-Mao ideological vacuum, which offers little policy justification beyond the development of the economy, has contributed to the use of money as a standard for success. The encouragement of private entrepreneurship, the daily floating population in virtually all Chinese cities, and increased opportunities for labor mobility, are all products of the economic reforms, while the large numbers of school leavers, increases in juvenile delinquency, premarital abortions, divorces, and so forth all reflect the decline in social control. As recent polls show, there is in fact an apparently widespread public perception that China's leaders lack the answers to the country's problems. Moreover, there is an equally widespread conviction that inequality of opportunity has made Chinese society unjust. These popular beliefs have impeded the party's efforts to integrate and control China's increasingly heterogeneous social forces.

Third, institutions which have long been established as the major conduits for social mobility and as measures for success—the party, the military, state enterprises, the schools—are being forced to adjust under the new socioeconomic conditions. For the party and military, there are questions of *who* to recruit, and *how* to socialize them. For example, peasant youth are becoming more economically independent and no longer look to the military as a possible escape route from a backward countryside. Rather, they often see military service as a necessary price to pay to protect their wealth (through party membership) or to expand their wealth (by learning a valuable skill). Should the military recruit these new rich peasants and seek to convert them into political "Reds," socializing them to support Communist values? Is it possible that the institutions themselves will be resocialized away from such values, following an influx of these new recruits?

Although it has not been featured in this paper, this same problem has been faced in recent years by the Communist Youth League (CYL). In an era which stresses economic development, the traditional values of the CYL have been called into question, and the league has become moribund in many areas, particularly in the countryside. Chinese authorities have sought to revive and reorient the organization, by tying its future to the success of the economic reforms and their beneficiaries. Thus, a report from the Central CYL Secretariat was unambiguous in noting that the primary task of rural league branches is to help youth get rich. CYL cadres from new wealthy peasant households, the report went on, made up only 10 percent of all league cadres in the countryside; the goal was to bring this figure up to 50 percent.[41] Some areas have carried the message too far, such as the regulation reported in parts of Hubei province which stipulated that only youth from households in which the average income per person was 300 yuan would be considered.[42] Of course, the party and military are not likely ever to reach this point; but they do face some of the same dilemmas of adjustment to an increasingly market-oriented society as the CYL.

Fourth, concern with politics has inevitably declined. Before the Cultural Revolution it was common for Chinese youth to adopt strategies which led them either to seek academic/professional success (the "expert" path) or to engage in political activism (the "Red" path).[43] During the Cultural Revolution, of course, concern with politics was necessary for all youth who sought upward mobility. Now, political interest *follows* success in other areas. New rich peasants will seek party membership or military entrance *after* economic success. Students who apply for party membership do so only *after* achievements in their academic and professional careers. The declining interest of young people in politics is not surprising. What is ironic, however, is the party's own contribution to this decline. While the media continues to emphasize the crucial importance of fostering a Communist value system, party recruitment in recent years has been concentrated heavily on the achievers, i.e., those with university degrees, professional positions, and so forth. With the party reaching out to the expert, those who are only "Red" have nowhere to go.

NOTES

1. See Stanley Rosen, "Public Opinion and Reform in the People's Republic of China," *Studies in Comparative Communism* (Summer–Fall 1989).

Impact of Reform on Chinese Youth 291

I have explored this theme in two other recent papers; thus, some of the data used here also appears in these other papers. See "The Impact of Reform Policies on Youth Attitudes," in *Social Consequences of Chinese Economic Reforms*, ed. Deborah Davis and Ezra F. Vogel (Cambridge: Harvard East Asian Publications, forthcoming) and "Value Change Among Post-Mao Youth: The Evidence from Survey Data," in Perry Link, Richard Madsen, and Paul Pickowicz, eds., *Popular Culture in Contemporary China* [Boulder, Colo.: Westview Press, forthcoming].

2. See Stanley Rosen and David S. K. Chu, *Survey Research in the People's Republic of China* (Washington, D.C.: United States Information Agency, 1987).

3. For some large-scale studies, see *1983 Zhongguo nongcun qingnian diaocha ziliao* (1983 Chinese Peasant Youth Investigation Materials) (Beijing: Shehui kexueyuan qingshaonian yanjiusuo, 1984) in which about 25,000 rural youth from nine provinces were surveyed, and *Shehui diaocha yu yanjiu*, no. 4 (1985): 32–42, in which 12,000 young workers from seven cities were surveyed.

4. *Qingnian yanjiu*, 17 (1982). Another common problem cited by informants is the tendency to fill out questionnaires in a random manner, not taking them seriously. On methodological problems more generally, see Rosen and Chu, *Survey Research*.

5. Zhang De and Zhou Liangluo, "The Ideology and Special Characteristics of Contemporary University Students," *Qinghua daxue jiaoyu yanjiu*, no. 2 (1986): 35–47. Despite these responses, over 60 percent of the sample expressed an interest in joining the party.

6. Tao Chounian, Sun Binggang and Yu Chunxian, "What Are University Students Thinking?" *Wengao yu ziliao*, no. 3 (1985): 29–34. This is a publication of the Shandong provincial party committee school.

7. Song Daoquan, "Several Factors Not Conducive to the Study of Mao Zedong Thought," *Weidinggao*, no. 6 (1986): 20–24. For a translation, see Stanley Rosen, ed., "Youth Socialization and Political Recruitment in Post-Mao China," *Chinese Law and Government* 20, no. 2 (Summer 1987): 18–28.

8. Yang Dongping, "Contemporary Chinese University Students: A New Epoch," *Shijie jingji daobao*, December 23, 1985, 12 (trans. in *Chinese Law and Government* [Summer 1987]: 9–17). On the privatization of youth values, see Stanley Rosen, "Prosperity, Privatization and China's Youth," *Problems of Communism* (March 1985): 1–28.

9. Commentator, "Institutions of Higher Learning Should Focus Their Attention on Education and Teaching." *Guangming ribao*, April 3, 1987 and Robert Delfs, "A Lesson for Students," *Far Eastern Economic Review*, May 14, 1987, 16. It had been common before the 1985 and 1986 student demonstrations to deemphasize political study. For example, Beijing University, faced with student apathy, cut the number of hours

for political study in half in 1985. See Joint Publications Research Service [hereafter *JPRS*], China, U.S. Govt. Publications 85, no. 67, JPRS-CPS-85-067 (July 3, 1985), 103–4 (AFP, June 7, 1985). For additional data on the conservative backlash in 1987, see Stanley Rosen, "Students," in *China Briefing 1988*, ed. Anthony J. Kane (Boulder, Colo.: Westview Press, 1988), 79–105.

10. Several sections of the survey will be translated in Stanley Rosen, ed., "Research on Ideological and Political Education in Beijing," *Chinese Education* (Summer 1989).

11. Li Gui, Ren Yuan, and Yau Hongling) "An Investigative Survey of Conditions Among Middle School Ideological and Political Workers in Beijing Municipality," *Gaojiao yanjiu* (Beijing), no. 1 (1988): 74–80.

12. Kang Qing, "Why Is the Percentage of Young Party Members Getting Smaller and Smaller?" *Zhongguo qingnian bao*, July 5, 1984, and *People's Daily* publishes an editorial stressing the relationship between absorbing large numbers of progressive youth to the party and the party's life, *Zongguo qingnian bao*, August 28, 1984.

13. "Party Membership Among University Students," *Jiaoyu tongxun*, no. 42, October 21, 1983, 6.

14. Calculating the number of student party members can be tricky. For example, many older students who entered in the first post-Cultural Revolution classes of 1977–78 were party members. But after they graduated, the nationwide percentage dropped from 3.8 percent to below 1 percent. Moreover, another set of figures for 1983 shows that there were 30,000 party members among the 1.2 million college students (2.5 percent). This is highly misleading, however, because twenty thousand of the thirty thousand were in special college classes for cadres, and were not "regular" students. On party building in post–Mao China, see Hong Yong Lee, unpublished manuscript, unnumbered chapter.

15. See, for example, the surveys on party recruitment of young intellectuals and university students in *Chinese Law and Government* 20, no. 2 (Summer 1987).

16. Li Yongjin, "Stress Recruitment of Party Members among University Students," *Gaojiao yanjiu*, no. 2 (April 1985): 87–93 (trans. in *Chinese Law and Government*, 20 no. 2 (Summer 1987): 67–84).

17. Research Group on Youth Education, Guangdong Glass Factory, "Pay Great Attention to Recruiting Outstanding Youth into the Party," *Qingnian tansuo* (Guangzhou), no. 4, 1984, 25, 16 (transl. in *Chinese Law and Government* 20, no. 2, (Summer 1987): 97–101).

18. Li Yongjin, "Stress Recruitment."

19. Sources for this and the following paragraph include Foreign Broadcast Information Service *Daily Report* (hereafter *Daily Report*) China, U.S. Govt. Publications 89, no. 62 (April 3, 1989), 52 (*Jiefangjun bao*, March

24); *Daily Report*, February 28, 1989, 45–47 (*Renmin ribao*, February 20); *Daily Report*, March 2, 1989, 47–50 (Zhongguo tongxun she, March 1); *Daily Report*, March 14, 1989, 34 (*Hong Kong Standard*, March 13); *Daily Report*, December 14, 1988, 29–30 (*Jiefangjun bao*, November 27); *Daily Report*, June 2, 1988, 52–57 (*Jiefangjun bao*, May 17); *Cheng Ming* (Hong Kong), December 1988, 27.

20. Zhang Wenrui et al., "The Great Changes and New Characteristics in the Composition of our Troops," *Qingnian yanjiu*, no. 6 (June 1986): 19–23; (trans. in *Chinese Law and Government* 20, no. 2 (Summer 1987): 102–17.

21. The "primary motive" for enlisting of 95 percent of the recruits had been "to defend the motherland" and "fulfill one's duty," but the researchers had wisely asked for a secondary motive, thus eliciting the more personal—and credible—responses.

22. Zhu Minghe and Liao Youlin, "The Influence of Economic Prosperity on Soldiers from the Countryside," in *Nanjing junqu zhuanji, 1984 budui qingnian yanjiu lunwenji* [A Collection of Research Articles on Youth in the Military, 1984], 205–14.

23. *Daily Report*, September 20, 1988, 45–46 (Xinhua, September 17).

24. *Daily Report*, October 25, 1988, 38–39 (Xinhua, October 22, citing *Liaowang*.

25. Yang Xingnan, "Rejection of Female College Graduates Must Be Stopped," *Zhongguo funubao*, February 27, 1985, 1.

26. Chen Ziju, "What Is the Reason and Solution for the Disproportionate Enrollment of Male and Female Students at Shanghai Teaching and Vocational Schools?" *Qingnian bao* (Shanghai) September 14, 1984 and interviews at vocational schools in Beijing and Shanghai.

27. Zhuang Jianguo, "An Investigation and Analysis of Employment Questions Among Young Women Waiting for Work in Shanghai," *Laodong kexue yanjiu ziliao*, no. 21 (November 5): 1985.

28. For examples, see Wu Jikang, "Why Don't Young Women Want to Enter Textile Mills?", *Qingnian yanjiu*, no. 5 (1986); Zou Naixian, "Survey of Changes in Young Female Textile Workers' Demands on Life," *Qingnian yanjiu*, no. 10 (1985); Youth Work Group under Wuxi Textile Industry Bureau, "Preliminary Study of the Question of Providing Special Education to Young Women Textile Workers," *Shanghai qingshaonian yanjiu*, no. 8 (1984). These surveys are all translated in Stanley Rosen, ed., "Chinese Women (3)," *Chinese Sociology and Anthropology* 20, no. 2 (Winter 1987–88).

29. Wu Jikang, "Why Don't."

30. Zou Naixian, "Survey of Changes."

31. Youth Work Group, "Preliminary Study."

32. Zou Ping, "Survey of Abortions among a Portion of Single Young Women in Beijing," *Qingnian yanjiu*, no. 10 (1985) 57–61; translated in "Chinese

Women (3)," *Chinese Sociology and Anthropology* 20, no. 3 (Spring, 1988).

33. James L. Tison, "China Tries To Shore Up Education," *Christian Science Monitor*, March 6, 1989.

34. "Chicken Feed," *The Economist*, November 26, 1988, 36.

35. Stanley Rosen, "Recentralization, Decentralization and Rationalization: Deng Xiaoping's Bifurcated Educational Policy," *Modern China* 11, no. 3 (July 1985): 301–46; Rosen, "Restoring Key Secondary Schools in Post-Mao China: The Politics of Competition and Educational Quality," in David M. Lampton, ed., *Policy Implementation in Post-Mao China* (Berkeley: University of California Press, 1987), 321–43.

36. *Daily Report*, September 1, 1988, 24–25 (Xinhua, August 31).

37. *Daily Report*, June 6, 1988, 43 (Xinhua, June 2).

38. Zong Xian, "Is It Worth It to Quit School to Engage in Business?" *Qingnian bao*, December 21, 1984, 5.

39. Xu Zhaoming, "Is It True That the Richness of Spiritual Life Is Inseparable from Money?" *Qingnian bao*, July 12, 1985, 5.

40. BBC Summary of World Broadcasts, FE/0420, March 29, 1989, p. C1/1 (Peking Television, March 24).

41. Li Yuanchao, "The Rural Communist Youth League Should Lead Youths to Become Rich," *Nongcun qingnian*, no. 3 (November 1984): 5.

42. Rosen, "Prosperity, Privatization."

43. Susan Shirk, *Competitive Comrades* (Berkeley: University of California Press, 1982) and Stanley Rosen, *Red Guard Factionalism and the Cultural Revolution in Guangzhou* (Boulder, Colo.: Westview Press, 1982).

10

"PERFECTING" THE PLANNING MECHANISM: THE POLITICS OF INCREMENTAL REFORM IN THE GDR

Thomas A. Baylis

Three propositions concerning economic reform in Eastern Europe have been so widely shared by Western analysts and many East European reformers that they can be said to constitute the conventional wisdom on the subject. The first holds that the economic problems of Eastern Europe are deep-seated and cannot be resolved without the implementation of basic reforms. The second argues that genuine reform must go far beyond institutional tinkering; it requires the replacement of central planning and bureaucratic controls by market forces as the primary determinants of economic outcomes. The third insists that economic reforms cannot succeed unless they are accompanied by fundamental *political* reforms.

The second proposition has been put succinctly by the Hungarian economist János Kornai in a recent extended assessment of the Hungarian New Economic Mechanism. "We reserve the term reform," he says, "for the change in a socialist economic system, provided that it diminishes the role of bureaucratic coordination and increases the role of the market."[1] The economist Jan Prybla goes further: "For reform of a centrally planned economy to deserve its name, the market and private property must become the dominant determinants of production, investment, and the distribution of income shares in the system."[2] The Hungarian sociologist (now in the West) Iván Szelényi is one of the many who have enunciated the third proposition: "No significant economic reform is possible

This is a revised and expanded version of "East Germany's Economic Model," by Thomas A. Baylis, which appeared in *Current History* in November 1987.

in Soviet-type societies without a major political reform, and no real self-management is possible without political self-determination and vice-versa."[3] Perhaps the most celebrated recent advocate of the third proposition, however (as well as the first as applied to the USSR, and now of important elements of the second) is the Soviet general secretary, Mikhail Gorbachev.

The conventional wisdom is not wrong simply by virtue of being conventional. But the experience of the German Democratic Republic (GDR) suggests that the three propositions above are not beyond challenge and deserve more critical scrutiny than they have normally received. The GDR is easily the most prosperous of the East European states, and, while East-West comparisons of living standards are problematic, the GDR's estimated GNP per capita substantially exceeds those of Britain and Italy.[4] During the first half of the 1980s, the GDR weathered the effects of the second "oil shock" and the Eastern European liquidity crisis more easily than its CMEA allies, sharply reducing its hard currency debt and reporting a solid rate of produced national income (PNI) growth for the period.[5] Unlike several of its neighbors, the GDR has been able to maintain its side of the "social contract" with its citizens, increasing pensions, continuing its ambitious program of housing construction, and maintaining its costly subsidies of consumer essentials.[6] Yet, except for a brief and—at least according to the current official assessment —unsuccessful experiment with reform in the 1960s, the GDR has repeatedly proclaimed its loyalty to the precepts of the centrally planned and directed economy.[7] The term "reform" vanished from the vocabulary of the SED (Socialist Unity Party) after the 1960s; when it reemerged in a February 1988 speech by Erich Honecker, it was used to characterize the GDR's ostensibly consistent policy since 1971, the year Honecker became SED First Secretary.[8]

In the current, Gorbachev-inspired reform discussions in Eastern Europe, the GDR, in the dubious company of Romania, appears rapidly to be becoming the odd man out. The GDR's leaders reject the search for a "new model of socialism" undertaken with some enthusiasm in the USSR, Hungary, and Poland, considerable ambivalence in Bulgaria, and obvious reluctance in Czechoslovakia.[9] While conceding that perestroika may well be necessary to cure the ills of the Soviet economy, SED officials argue that it does not correspond to their own country's conditions. The GDR, they claim, has already carried out significant measures of economic reorganization, which it characterizes (following pre-Gorbachev Soviet terminology) as the "perfecting [*Vervollkommnung*] of the planning mechanism." "Perfecting," they grant, is not a one-time undertaking but an ongoing process of adaptation to changing economic circumstances which will always be necessary in a dynamic socialist system; thus the GDR follows attentively the experiments of its allies with an eye to their possible usefulness in the GDR.[10] But the principle of central planning remains sacrosanct, and the unbridled introduction of devices borrowed from market economies unacceptable. The very success of the GDR's economy, they assert, demonstrates that the country would be ill-advised to risk dramatic changes in its economic strategy. In an interview with a West German magazine, the veteran Politburo member Kurt Hager expressed the official SED position in a now celebrated, rather condescending simile: "If your neighbor chooses to repaper the walls of his house, would you feel obliged to do the same?"[11]

USSR officials, for their part, have explicitly praised the GDR economic example, particularly the development of industrial *Kombinate* (combines).[12] Gorbachev himself singled out the GDR for praise in speeches in the Soviet Union in mid-1985 (although interestingly enough these flattering references were eliminated in the version published in book form) and during his appearance at the SED's eleventh Congress in 1986.[13] Some Western commentators contended that the initial version of Gorbachev's own economic reforms was much closer to the GDR "model" than to, say, the Hungarian one.[14] GDR economists have expressed some resentment that the GDR's economic course has aroused so much less interest in the West than the Hungarian reforms.[15]

What particularly distinguishes the GDR's position from reform discussions in the USSR, Hungary, and elsewhere, is the complete absence of any mention of political or social reforms as necessary to economic restructuring. The concept of glasnost, for example, has been ignored by the GDR, except for the backhanded acknowledgement reflected in the banning of the German-language Soviet magazine *Sputnik* and a number of recent Soviet films. Ordinary East Germans, to be sure, remain well-informed about glasnost through

Western radio and television reports. Gorbachev's speech at the January, 1987, CPSU Central Committee plenum, with its proposal for competitive intraparty and local governmental elections, appeared only in summary form in *Neues Deutschland;*[16] the June 1988 CPSU Conference received somewhat greater coverage coupled with the comment that no party possessed "a prescription appropriate for all."[17] The GDR has similarly ignored Soviet proposals for greater enterprise democracy.[18] Erich Honecker has warmly endorsed Gorbachev's foreign policy initiatives, but has largely passed over his domestic proposals and stressed that each socialist society must act in accordance with its own distinctive needs and stage of development.[19] In December 1988, however, he permitted himself the comment that Western suggestions that the GDR emulate Soviet reforms were a counsel to "march into anarchy."[20]

The questions I want to address in this chapter, then, are three. First, is there something we can call a "GDR model" of economic planning and management? Second, can it be viewed as a reform, or at least as a viable alternative to the Hungarian or other schemes as a means by which Eastern European regimes can address their economic difficulties? Third, has the GDR succeeded in devising a viable economic course that can be kept free of implications for political change? The third question is, I think, pivotal for understanding the GDR's choice of economic strategy, as well as the theoretical options open to other economically advanced Communist systems; I will give it special attention in the concluding sections of this essay.

THE "NEW ECONOMIC SYSTEM" AND THE PROBLEM OF POLITICS

The East German view of proposals for economic reform is colored by its experience as a pioneer of such reforms in the 1960s. In the fall of 1962 the SED's First Secretary Walter Ulbricht encouraged GDR economists and functionaries to take up the discussion of the reform proposals of Evsei Liberman then underway in the Soviet Union. In January 1963 the SED's Sixth Congress endorsed the principles of reform, and by June the party had issued a set of directives for the "New Economic System of Planning and Management" (NES).

Circumstantial evidence suggests that the reforms—the first in Eastern Europe—were introduced on the urging of the Soviet Union, which was anxious to use the GDR as something of an experimental laboratory before embarking on a similar course at home.[21] Whatever the origins of the NES, many GDR citizens and officials welcomed it enthusiastically, in part because they believed its impact could not be restricted to the economic sphere. "Everyone there, writers, scientists, white-collar employees, workers, all look with fascination to the new economic policy," wrote a West German journalist. "The one group hopes that it will bring more flexibility (or better, less dogmatism), the other that it will make their regime more proficient and thus more popular."[22]

Indeed, the introduction of the NES was followed by a brief thaw in the cultural sphere and by the emergence of a significant literature of what Peter Christian Ludz called "institutionalized revisionism."[23] In this literature a handful of philosophers and social scientists utilized the inspiration provided by the NES to publish relatively adventurous proposals that extended openly or by implication into the political sphere. Georg Klaus, the GDR's preeminent philosopher of cybernetic systems theory, cautiously sought to apply cybernetics concepts to questions of Marxist ideology, to the problems of the role of the state in society, and questions of economic regulation, implying over the long run an enhanced self-regulation of society's subsystems, presumably at the expense of detailed central steering.[24] The economist Günther Kohlmey went still further, constructing a cybernetic model of a centralized system of economic planning, which he contrasted favorably to the traditional centrally planned version.[25] Uwe-Jens Heuer, a legal theorist, used a cybernetic framework to advocate a far-reaching decentralization and democratization of the GDR's political as well as its economic system. In his emphasis on the importance of the conflict of group interests in the GDR Heuer appears to have been influenced by the simultaneous discussion in Czechoslovakia.[26] All three writers were subsequently criticized, and retreated to somewhat safer ideological redoubts, but they remained important figures in GDR philosophy and social science—Klaus until his death in 1974 and Kohlmey and Heuer up to the present.

The NES reforms were never pursued as far as their more enthusiastic advocates would have liked—they were subsequently eclipsed by the Czech reform proposals and by the Hungarian New Economic Mechanism—and it seems apparent that one reason was the fear of the SED's leadership that they might bring undesirable political consequences. Ulbricht stressed from the beginning that the reforms were meant to *strengthen* democratic centralism by relieving the central authorities of the tasks of "petty tutelage," just the reverse of what "certain revisionist elements once wanted."[27] In 1964 and 1965, SED leaders criticized excessive displays of autonomy and "egoism" by the party's specialized Bureaus of Industry and Construction, enterprise associations (VVBs), and factories; they attacked the alleged "economization" of party work and the consequent neglect of ideology. The suicide of the planning chief and NES architect Erich Apel in December 1965—apparently in protest against a long-term Soviet-GDR trade agreement that frustrated the desire of some officials to shift much of the country's trade to the West—provided another warning against the political hazards of reform. Finally, the cautionary example of Czechoslovakia, where proposals for economic reform had gone hand-in-hand with political liberalization, furnished a powerful argument to Politburo critics of economic experimentation.

There were a number of cogent economic reasons for the modification of the reforms in 1967–68 and their final abandonment in 1970,[28] capped by a "growth crisis" aggravated by unfavorable weather conditions in 1969–70. There is little doubt, too, that many of the optimistic expectations that accompanied the introduction of the reforms reflected a naivete born of inexperience with the problems of doing so in the context of an entrenched system of centralized economic control. But the larger reason for failure probably lies in the political constraints and fears, underscored by the Czech events, that kept the NES reforms from becoming fully effective, in spite of initially encouraging results. A comparison of the GDR decision to abandon the reforms with the Hungarian decision to initiate a bolder reform program in 1968 in spite of the Czech developments, and then to "reform the reforms" in the middle of an economic crisis at the beginning of the 1980s, may be instructive. In the GDR in 1970, no broad and coherent set of proposals for expanding the reforms seems to have existed—reflecting the absence of an open and freewheeling debate among economists like that which seems to have characterized Hungarian reform discussions from the beginning. The GDR's leaders, many of whom had harbored serious doubts about the reforms since their inception (the East German "reform party," while well represented on the Central Committee and in state organs, never captured many seats on the SED Politburo or Secretariat), were forced to choose between the abandonment of reform and the highly uncertain alternative of expanding it; in any event, it does not seem surprising that they chose the former. The decision to return to a highly centralized planning system preceded by only a few months the replacement of Ulbricht by Honecker as SED First Secretary. Not inappropriately, since the new party leader has never been counted among the supporters of reform,[29] his regime was identified with the restoration of economic orthodoxy and acquired something of a vested interest in at least outwardly maintaining it.

THE "PERFECTED" GDR ECONOMIC SYSTEM: AN ALTERNATIVE MODEL?

The present "perfection" of the GDR economic system centers, first, on the creation of industrial *Kombinate* as the pivotal units of economic management and coordination, and, second, on the revision of success indicators and the expanded use of other indirect monetary "levers" in the hope of stimulating more rational economic behavior. Party leaders have also ventured lesser but still significant changes in the agricultural pricing system, foreign trade arrangements, the system of transportation charges, and elsewhere. Finally, they have placed an overarching emphasis on the stimulation of scientific and technological innovation and its rapid application in production.

The latter is hardly unique, given the long-standing rhetorical attention that ruling parties have devoted to accelerating the "scientific-technological revolution" (STR) throughout the bloc, but it is, I think, of peculiar importance to the GDR. Overall, the GDR is the most advanced of the CMEA countries technologically, but much of its plant and equipment is outmoded and it suffers from a severe labor shortage and a weak natural resource base. It is the leading supplier of machine tools, computers, and other advanced products to the Soviet Union, which has repeatedly pressed for improvement in the quantity and quality of GDR deliveries and would seem likely to do so even more in the face of the decline in its own sources of hard currency for the purchase of Western technology.[30] In Western markets, the GDR finds it increasingly difficult to compete with the Newly Industrializing Countries (NICs) in the sale of many products; in the vital category of machine tool exports, it is also experiencing a decline in its Western market share.[31] It is thus imperative that it raise its own technological level in order to maintain its exports to (and thus imports from) the West as well as to satisfy its obligations to the USSR. Centrally planned economies, however, are notorious for their resistance to innovation,[32] and one of the primary objectives of the GDR's organizational modifications has been to overcome such resistances.

Thus a pre-eminent element of the *rationale* supporting the creation of the *Kombinate* was the need to link research more closely to production. The 127 centrally directed industrial *Kombinate*[33] — which Honecker has called the "backbone" of the GDR's economic system — are supposed to be distinguished from their predecessors, the VVBs, by their emphasis upon "vertical" as well as horizontal integration. That is, in addition to monopolizing the production of a particular class of goods, they seek to combine under their authority all phases of the production process, from research and development through the production of important inputs to sales. The directors of the *Kombinate* are also supposed to be more directly involved in production than the heads of the old VVBs, and thus better aware of technological needs; in the preferred type of *Kombinat*, management is simultaneously responsible for directing the combine's "lead enterprise."

In so far as possible, the regime has sought to make the combines autarkic units. Not only are they responsible for most of their own research (some of which may, however, be carried out on a contract basis with universities and divisions of the Academy of Sciences), but they are expected to fabricate their own "means of rationalization," where possible. Increasingly, investment is expected to come from the *Kombinat's* own or borrowed resources—not state grants. Sixteen selected *Kombinate*, the Politburo announced in July 1987, would pioneer in the "comprehensive" financing of their own means of production; the principle is to be gradually extended to all of them. A novel policy that constrains capital goods-producing *Kombinate* is the expectation that they manufacture a range of final products that includes consumer goods. In general, the—apparently all but intractable—problems of coordination and cooperation across combine boundaries are to be reduced by minimizing the need for them. The result are giant monopolies, which presumably encourage economies of scale as well as offering the advantages already listed, but which one might also think would bring with them some of the classic disadvantages of monopoly in capitalist systems. This process of industrial concentration—also evident in the ballooning size of enterprises *within* the combines—stands in sharp contrast to the tenor of recent Hungarian discussions, but has been criticized only cautiously and indirectly in the GDR.[34]

The authority granted to the combine general director looks formidable from the perspective of the component enterprises—even though these are supposed to retain some legal autonomy—but rather less so when viewed from above. The general director allocates resources and tasks among the combine's component enterprises and other units, and can shift them from one enterprise or unit to another. He appoints enterprise managers, and can create new enterprise sections. He can centralize certain tasks (e.g., research) and decentralize others. He is responsible for the combine's plan and carries out certain planning functions that previously were assigned to the ministries—e.g., material balancing within the combine. Some combines have heightened responsibilities for trade and intra-CMEA cooperation and some are authorized to sign export contracts with foreign firms.

The superordinate ministry retains extensive powers of intervention, and the general director must continue to act within a dense thicket or plan indicators and "normatives." He has little power over such crucial matters as investment, product assortment, and the determination of prices and wages. He has only limited discretion over the use of the combine's profits and its various "funds," and none (with the exceptions noted below) over its foreign currency earnings. The incentive structure for vigorous entrepreneurial performance thus seems rather weak.[35] On the other hand, the combine's monopoly position undoubtedly strengthens the general director's bargaining position with higher authorities. No domestic competitors and few other reliable yardsticks exist for evaluating the information he provides, in spite of the regime's attempts to strengthen control mechanisms.[36]

The GDR introduced significant changes in its palette of "economic levers" in 1982 and 1983. The traditional indicator of gross output—"industrial goods production"—was downgraded in favor of four "primary indices": net profit, net production, consumer goods and services, and export. The first two were intended to stimulate the more efficient use of energy, materials, and labor, with net profit also expected to heighten attention to marketing. The second index, net production, has in practice become the most important one; statistics for net profit, by contrast, are not published in the annual plan fulfillment report. In 1988, net production in industry is said to have risen by 7 percent, while the "production of goods" rose by only 3.7 percent.[37] Although similar measures are used elsewhere in the bloc,[38] the calculation of net production is difficult and prone to a number of distortions.[39] The continued absence of "scarcity prices" (in spite of some recent administrative pricing changes) also mitigates the usefulness of both net production and net profit results. And it remains the case that *Kombinat* and plant directors have a total of over two hundred indexes they must give at least passing attention to; the number has actually increased in recent years.[40]

Another new economic lever, the "contribution to the social funds," was introduced at the beginning of 1984. It is, in effect, a stiff 70 percent tax on payrolls, intended to force combines and enterprises to shed excessive workers. As a transitional measure, the state agreed to reduce the required payments or to provide temporary subsidies to firms finding it difficult to meet the new requirements. GDR budgetary data indicate that collections from the new charge amounted to 20.1 billion marks in 1984 and rose to 34.0 billion by 1986, while state deductions from net profit fell by 15 billion marks in 1984 and remained roughly at that level through 1986. Subsidies amounted to 17.0 billion in 1984, but virtually disappeared by 1986.[41] Their disappearance suggests that price adjustments have made it easier for firms to pay the tax. Published sources do not reveal whether it has succeeded in significantly reducing the inefficient use of labor; informal indications are that it has not.

The SED has developed or refined several other levers intended to stimulate cost-saving, quality, and innovation in the last several years. The *Produktionsfondsabgabe* (production funds levy), an annual charge on capital surviving from the original NES reforms, was revised in 1982–83 to reward investment projects completed ahead of schedule and to penalize delayed completion or underutilization of plant and equipment.[42] Producer (though not consumer) prices have been regularly revised since 1976 and pricing formulas introduced that are designed to provide firms a higher return on new and high quality products and a lower return on older, substandard ones.[43] In 1986 the party announced the creation of a new *Kombinat* and enterprise "investment fund," whose size is dependent on profit levels. It may be used for investment in the modernization of production facilities and the improvement of working and living conditions, and appears modestly to expand *Kombinat* discretion in these areas; its use for investment not carried out with internal resources is subject to higher approval, however.[44]

The SED has sought to improve its agricultural performance not through market-oriented reforms on the Hungarian or Chinese models but through manipulation of its system of prices and subsidies. No major organizational changes have been undertaken, although the SED appears for the moment to have suspended its efforts to move toward the "industrialization" of agriculture.[45] At the beginning of 1984, subsidies for agricultural inputs were slashed in the hope of persuading producers to use them more efficiently. In exchange, prices paid to farmers for their products were increased by 52 percent. In order to keep consumer prices at their unchanged, low levels, the state had to increase its subsidies at the retail level from 12.1 billion marks in 1983 to 20.6 billion in 1984 and 27.6 billion in 1985.[46] Thus, substantial incentives to lower production costs were purchased by perpetuating incentives for wasteful consumption. Farmers responded by bringing in record harvests in 1984 and 1985 and lowering the GDR's dependence on fodder imports.[47] To be sure, record harvests in the Federal Republic were recorded in the same years, leaving the efficacy of the GDR's pricing and subsidy reforms unclear; GDR agricultural productivity continues to lag behind the Federal Republic's.[48]

The GDR's foreign trade system underwent modification as part of the *Kombinat* reform; the purpose was to involve combines and enterprises more directly in foreign sales while retaining the state's foreign trade monopoly.[49] To this end, twenty-one "foreign trade enterprises" (AHBs) were placed within individual combines; additional AHBs attached to industrial ministries were assigned to service several combines at once. The AHBs' directors, however, remained simultaneously subordinate to the Foreign Trade Ministry. In certain cases, export-oriented combines can sign export treaties themselves, but the main purpose of the new arrangement appears to have been to involve the *Kombinate* in foreign marketing and to link production more closely to the needs and demands of foreign customers. The elevation of exports to one of the four chief performance indicators under the plan presumably gives the general directors reason for being attentive to such requirements. In the past, as Melzer notes, "the incentive for combines to increase exports [were] very limited as long as they [did] not share in foreign currency earnings," and thus could not purchase imports on their own. In 1987, however, the sixteen *Kombinate* singled out for broadened self-financing were granted permission to retain a portion of their foreign exchange earnings for the purchase of imports.[50] The GDR still appears to lag behind most of its CMEA partners in developing other measures to promote expanded economic relationships with capitalist states; as of this writing, for example, it is the only CMEA member not to have sanctioned joint ventures with Western firms, and it ranks close to the bottom in other forms of "cooperative relationships."[51]

Taken as a whole, what does the GDR's "perfected" system of economic planning and management amount to? Is it a "reform"—albeit, in the words of Doris Cornelsen and her colleagues, a "reform in small steps?" Is is a stable and coherent package of measures that can be commended to other Communist regimes unwilling to undergo the risks of drastic market-oriented reform? Does it contain within it any inherent logic of further development—toward a more fundamental, market-based reform, or in some other direction?

It is perhaps important to stress what the GDR model does *not* do, compared to the Hungarian and other East European reforms or to some of the proposals of Gorbachev. It does not reduce the importance of or simplify central planning, nor does it narrow the scope of central bureaucratic control; if anything, the web of controls has become still thicker. Detailed decisions on investments, material balancing, prices, and foreign trade continue to be made by the planning commission and state ministries and committees, within a framework approved by the SED Politburo. There has been no substantial expansion of the private sector or legalization of the "second economy."[52] There have been no initiatives toward—or even public discussions of—subjecting the prices of certain goods to market determination, countenancing bankruptcies or open unemployment,[53] expanding the discretion and independence of state banks, permitting worker participation in the selection of management or other significant economic decisions, or applying for membership in the IMF or GATT.

As it stands, the GDR's system is dotted with inconsistencies and ambiguities, many of them acknowledged by GDR economists and other specialists. Direct administrative controls and subsidies exist alongside indirect, parametric steering devices, with the effectiveness of the latter in danger of being impaired by the working of the former. Prices, while all determined administratively, are set according to several inconsistent criteria, e.g., actual production costs, the quality and age of products, the degree to which they reflect innovation and "intensification," capital costs, world market prices.[54] The demarcation of authority among ministries, the *Kombinate*, and individual enterprises is elusive. Western critics have no difficulty in identifying elements of, e.g., the *Kombinat* reform that would appear inimical to the GDR's goals of technological innovation and enhanced efficiency, such as their daunting size and their monopoly position.

The "GDR model," then, does not represent a coherent vision of the economy as a whole, but rather a series of *ad hoc* decisions reflecting a variety of influences. East German officials themselves now stress that their economic system is by no means "closed," but may be expected to undergo continuing modification as economic conditions change.[55] Whether for ideological reasons or simply in order to discourage excessive expectations, the regime has decided to emphasize for the present the fundamental ideal of a rationally planned economy under the centralized direction of the party. But this principle is joined somewhat awkwardly to elements (and slogans) borrowed from the New Economic System, policies imitating Soviet precedents (e.g., "counterplans"), and pragmatic responses to the exigencies of the credit crunch of the early 1980s and to the GDR's labor shortage and difficult energy and raw materials situation—more generally, to the pressures of both the international economic system and those arising within the CMEA.

Yet, the GDR "model" works, at least for the moment, and by the standards of the East bloc indeed appears to work reasonably well. Whether it deserves to be called a "reform" is largely a matter of definition and taste. To limit the application of that term to the dramatic expansion of the role of market forces, however, seems to me to make an essentially ideological statement, one which denies the possibility that even far-reaching structural changes in a bureaucratic system of economic management can significantly influence its performance.[56]

It is useful to remember that *no* economic system in the real world is an integrated, logically consistent whole. All involve mixtures in varying proportions of market influences and planning, of bureaucratic regulation and individual initiative, of monopoly and competition. So long as the GDR economy performs satisfactorily, the present pattern of tinkering with important details of the system is apt to persist. Should the economy falter, as it now shows some signs of doing (and especially if that should coincide with the continuing pursuit of more radical reform in the USSR and/or with the retirement of Honecker), the present system could serve as a transitional stage on the way to more radical measures.

Such a transition would not be easy, however. The present monopoly position of the *Kombinate* would be likely to undermine any attempt to introduce market-determined prices, a measure probably indispensable to a far-reaching reform. Creating a measure of domestic competition would require a drastic reorganization of East Germany industry away from the *Kombinat* structure in which the SED has so large a material and ideological investment. In this respect the GDR's present economic model is something considerably less than a halfway house between the command economy and market socialism.

ECONOMIC REFORM AND POLITICAL CHANGE

To the GDR's leaders, one of the attractions of its present economic system is unquestionably its apparent lack of utility as a lever for promoting political change. They are undoubtedly conscious of the presence in the GDR of most of the elements that could coalesce into a broad movement for political reform, a possibility more disconcerting in the context of the inter-German treaty and warming inter-German relations. Such well-publicized phenomena as the autonomous peace and ecology movements with their close ties to the East German Evangelical Church, the persistent unrest and the constant testing of limits among prominent intellectuals, the rise of a youth "counterculture," and the continuing reports of a sizeable number of GDR citizens who have applied for exit permits must also be viewed in conjunction with the diminishing capacity of the regime to control them. Its characteristic balancing of repressive measures with quiet concessions no longer seems able to contain public discontent and the open advocacy of political liberalization. What is still lacking, however, is any linkage of the incipient emergence of an East German "civil society" to demands for economic changes such as those that played so important a role in Czechoslovakia in 1968 and in Poland in 1980 and later.

The logic that leads from market-oriented economic reforms to pressures for fundamental political change has more often been assumed than carefully spelled out in the literature. Let me therefore briefly enumerate five categories of possible political consequences that may flow from such reforms:

1. Perhaps the most compelling argument against economic reform to East European party leaders is that strengthening the hand of factory managers, workers, consumers, and the market will *weaken if not undermine the leading role of the party*. On one level the concern is that of lower- and middle-level officials (of both party and state) who fear that the loss of their right to intervene in economic matters will erode their power base;[57] it is the resistance of

such officials that has been repeatedly cited as a major obstacle to reform in the Soviet Union. On another level the concern is with the influence of the party as an institution in society at large; much of its traditional importance has been based on its role as economic manager, personnel recruiter, and mobilizer, all of which market-oriented reforms would at least sharply reduce.

2. In Yugoslavia, Hungary, Czechoslovakia, Poland, and now the USSR itself, pressures for economic reform have brought with them demands for an expansion of *workplace democracy*—if not full self-management, at least some form of election of managers and participation in other decisions. To be sure, there would seem to be no inherent connection between market-oriented reforms and workplace democracy; capitalist market systems, at least, have had little difficulty in avoiding the latter. One mechanism at work in Eastern Europe is undoubtedly the concern of economic reformers to allay worker (and union) skepticism toward reform (see below) with the promise of participation. It does seem clear that, once the desirability of workplace participation is conceded, the principle quickly spills over into the political sphere proper, e.g., into support for competitive local elections, the extension of genuine powers to parliaments, and so on.

3. The development of some sort of system of *interest representation* in the political sphere is sometimes said to be another natural concomitant of economic reform. Once enterprises, private businessmen, peasants, and other are granted broader economic opportunities and face more genuine economic risks, their incentive to organize for their own political advantage grows.[58] This tendency is apt to join with independent pressures on behalf of some sort of "socialist pluralism."[59]

4. Successful economic reform, it is widely held, cannot proceed or win broad support in the absence of a *broad, freewheeling public debate* over its components and likely benefits and disadvantages—both among specialists and representatives of those most likely to be affected by them. Such a debate—and Hungary is the most compelling example of it to date—can hardly be expected to leave the political system untouched, nor is it likely to coexist easily with rigid censorship of critical social or cultural perspectives.[60]

5. Finally, market-oriented economic reform is said to have a

number of at least short-term *negative social effects,* and these effects bring with them political consequences. In Hungary, the attribution of growing wage differentials and social inequalities to reform measures has provoked wide discussion and provided useful arguments for conservative politicians. Kornai is doubtful that such inequalities do necessarily follow from reform, but admits that advocates of reform were in the past often insensitive to the issue.[61] The fear of unemployment, or at least of wrenching job changes, has accompanied reform proposals in almost every East European state. Gorbachev, in his speech at the June 1987 CPSU Central Committee plenum, felt obliged to take account of it,[62] and the Hungarian leadership has accepted a rate of joblessness of up to 2 percent and instituted a program of unemployment payments as part of the price for their most recent round of reforms.[63] Other possible social consequences of reform include hardships brought about by inflation, increased corruption,[64] widespread "moonlighting" with its attendant impact on family stability, and even the expansion of the second economy, which reform is often meant to curtail.

The GDR has not been able to avoid many of the negative social consequences listed under category 5 in its own economic model. Indeed, the need for a highly differentiated system of economic rewards is openly proclaimed,[65] and the spectre of unemployment raised by the introduction of the "contribution of social funds" and calls for greater adaptability on the part of the work force have not been fully exorcised by regime protestations.[66] The unabashed advocacy of expanded two- and three-shift work—in spite of its effects on health and family life—in order to better utilize production facilities has long been a staple of official rhetoric. In general, official emphasis on the STR and on economic growth at all costs carries with it a willingness to tolerate social and environmental costs as well as awkward ideological problems no less severe than (and sometimes no different from) those implied by market reform.[67]

On the other hand the SED has been able thus far to resist any serious erosion in its own dominating position in East German life, has met pressures for "socialist democracy" with transparent tokenism, has restricted the development of a system of interest representation (in spite of some cautious scholarly discussion of the topic),[68] and has kept explicit debate over economic as well as political reform out of the official media.[69] Glasnost, as noted earlier, has yet to make its appearance in East Berlin.

CONCLUSIONS

To date, then, the SED has been notably successful in carrying out enough changes in its economic system to permit it to adapt to changing technologies and international circumstances without unleashing irresistible pressures for fundamental political change. How long it will be able to continue to do so is less clear. The political and economic equilibrium that the GDR has attained strikes the observer as incomplete and unstable. It is not hard to cite a number of difficulties the GDR will have to face if it is to maintain this equilibrium, although we must be careful not simply to assume that they are insurmountable or to underestimate the adaptibility of the SED leadership—mistakes made often enough by Western analysts in the past.

First, internal pressures for political change may be generated by the logic of the GDR's system just as they are elsewhere by radical market reforms. The position of the general directors of the *Kombinate*, particularly such large and influential ones as Karl Zeiss Jena, suggests the possibility of a shift in political power relationships—although not necessarily "democratization"—as these pivotal figures seek to build coalitions and to overcome bureaucratic obstacles in the struggle for scarce resources. More broadly, the SED's commitment to the STR, and especially to future-oriented "key technologies," can probably not be implemented without a sustantial opening up of its heretofore tightly controlled information system—a point often discussed with respect to the USSR but perhaps still more significant for the GDR, given its comparatively high level of development.

Second, Western critics have argued—and some GDR economists agree—that the GDR's economic successes in the early 1980s have depended heavily on the short-term benefits of *Kombinat* formation, one-time measures (e.g., the installation of insulation) taken to curb the wasteful use of resources, and an export strategy (emphasizing refined oil products) that is no longer viable. Sustained growth, it is argued, will require measures going beyond those contained within the present system and will inevitably entail broader political consequences. The significant decline in the GDR's growth rate for 1987 and 1988 and persistent reports of consumer good shortages lend some support to this argument.[70]

Third, the GDR now must face significant external pressures issuing from the introduction of both economic and political reforms elsewhere in the East bloc, above all in the Soviet Union. Mikhail Gorbachev has denied the intention of imposing his reform program on other bloc members, even while his advisers have asserted that the restructuring of socialism is an "international process."[71] He can in fact have little interest in risking political unheaval in a country whose economy is still the most successful in the bloc and whose reliable economic performance is vital to his plans for his own country. On the other hand, his interest in promoting fuller CMEA integration, including some form of currency convertibility, is likely to remain unrealized so long as the GDR resists following the reform course of its neighbors.[72]

Moreover, the GDR's long devotion to the Soviet example will make it difficult for it to proceed as the single bastion of the centrally planned economy in Eastern Europe while detailed Western reports on Soviet reforms and their echoes elsewhere in the bloc enter East German living rooms each evening. The pending decision over the succession to General Secretary Honecker—he is now seventy-six, and for the first time questions are being raised about his health[73]—might also enhance the chances for political change. Even while the SED leadership visibly hardened its resistance to reform in late 1988, reports of discontent among the party rank and file and of an active interest among GDR social scientists in reform proposals grew. They suggest that a candidate for the succession advocating perestroika might find a welcoming constituency.

POSTSCRIPT, FEBRUARY 1990 *

The collapse of the Honecker regime in October 1989 and the virtual disintegration of the ruling party that followed it dramatically altered the context of discussions of economic policy in the GDR. The

* The preceding essay was completed in February 1989 and has not been changed.

goals of the peaceful East German revolution of October and November were, to be sure, primarily political ones, and the leaders of the fledgling opposition groups had no clear economic agenda when they unexpectedly found themselves at the head of an extraordinary mass uprising. The new GDR government under Hans Modrow revealed a level of previous mismanagement and corruption in the economy that surprised even Western observers, and the architect of the GDR's economic model, Günter Mittag, was expelled from the Politburo and the party and subsequently imprisoned. Nevertheless, the Modrow government's initial economic program was a cautious one: it promised to legalize joint ventures and to increase the use of market mechanisms, but at the same time to retain central planning. It seemed to imply that the faults of the GDR's economic system lay less in the inherent character of the incremental model than in the arrogance and dishonesty of its chief administrators. Reform Communists and opposition figures alike expressed their intention of preserving the GDR's system of social benefits and of preventing the GDR from being turned into a poor economic appendage of the Federal Republic.

The GDR might thus have continued to offer an example of incremental reform contrasting sharply with the drastic measures introduced in Poland or the faltering Soviet program. But by early February the rapidly accelerating drive toward German unification, motivated in part by the continuing exodus of young East Germans to the West and by warnings of impending East German economic or political collapse, had been reinforced by the exigencies of inter-German electoral politics. It now appeared that the GDR's future economic course might well be decided in Bonn, where most economists and politicians counselled a quick transition to a full-scale market system. Calls for the prompt implementation of a German currency union, criticized by economists and bankers but seized upon by the Kohl government and some East German politicians, further enhanced that possibility.

Even in the event of rapid reunification, however, the GDR's economic system will undoubtedly leave its legacy for the future economic development of the territory it presently occupies and perhaps even for the German West. While inefficient *Kombinate*, for example, will undoubtedly be broken up, others, perhaps joined to leading West German firms, may become formidable players in the European Community. The past importance of the GDR as a supplier of machinery and other goods to the Soviet Union might strengthen still further "all-German" economic—and political—links to that country. But the likelihood that East Germany will continue to offer an alternative reform model to the rest of Eastern Europe and the USSR is greatly diminished. Given the still tenuous prospects that successful market economies can be created in the former Soviet bloc, the disappearance of the GDR's incremental alternative may not be an entirely fortunate development.

NOTES

This chapter is a revision of a paper delivered at the 1987 Annual Meeting of the American Political Science Association, Chicago, Illinois; a condensed earlier version was published as "The East German Economic Model" in *Current History* 86 (November 1987): 377–81, 393–94.

1. János Kornai, "The Hungarian Reform Process: Visions, Hopes, and Reality," *Journal of Economic Literature* 24 (December 1986): 1691.
2. Jan Prybla, "China's Economic Experiment: From Mao to Market," *Problems of Communism* (January–February 1986): 22.
3. Iván Szelényi, "Socialist Opposition in Eastern Europe: Dilemmas and Prospects," in *Opposition in Eastern Europe*, ed. Rudolf L. Tökes (Baltimore: Johns Hopkins University Press, 1979), 206.
4. According to Paul Marer's calculations, the GDR's per capita GNP was $5,910 in 1980; second-place Czechoslovakia's was just $4,740. Marer, "Economic Policies and Systems in Eastern Europe and Yugoslavia," in *Ninety-ninth Congress, Second Session, Joint Economic Committee, East European Economies: Slow Growth in the 1980s*, v. 3 (Washington: U.S. Government Printing Office, 1986), 607. Another 1980 estimate gives the GDR's real GDP per capita (at 1975 prices) as $5,532, Czechoslovakia's as $4,908, Britain's as $4,990, and Italy's as $4,636. R. Summers and A. Heston, "Improved International Comparisons of Real Product and Its Composition, 1950–1980," *Review of Income and Wealth* (June 1984), as cited in Francis G. Castles, "Whatever Happened to the Communist Welfare State?" *Studies in Comparative Communism* 19 (Autumn/Winter 1986): 217.
5. See my "Explaining the GDR's Economic Strategy," *International Organization* 40 (Spring 1986): 381–420. Many Western economists believe that PNI figures seriously overstate the GDR's actual growth, ow-

ing in part to concealed inflation. Michael Keren has estimated GDR inflation figures for 1973–1977 at 2.8 percent and 1977–1983 at 2.7 percent, reducing NMP growth figures for these years by more than half. Keren, "Consumer Prices in the GDR Since 1950," *Soviet Studies* 39 (April 1987): 263–65.

6. On December 1, 1989, minimum pensions were to be raised by between 30 and 100 Marks, depending on the number of years worked. "Pensions in the GDR," *Informationen*, no. 24, December 23, 1988, 10–12. The cost to the GDR's budget of subsidizing consumer essentials reached 49.8 billion Marks in 1988. *Neues Deutschland*, January 19, 1989.

7. See Günter Mittag, "Management, Planning, and Economic Cost-Accounting in the GDR Economy," *Einheit* 41, no. 10 (1986): 876–83.

8. "Erich Honecker before SED *Kreis* First Secretaries," *Deutschland Archiv* 21 (May 1988): 557.

9. See Otto Reinhold, "The Program of Our Party Has Proven Itself in Life," *Neues Deutschland*, December 3–4, 1988, 5.

10. Reinhold notes that an institute for examining developments in other socialist countries has been established in the SED's Academy for Society Sciences. Ibid., 5.

11. Barbara Donovan, "Honecker Continues to Reject Reforms," *Radio Free Europe Research* [hereafter *RFER*], BR/77, May 8, 1987.

12. See Ed A. Hewett, *Reforming the Soviet Economy* (Washington, D.C.: Brookings Institution, 1988), 300–301.

13. Walter Süss, "No Model for GDR? The SED's View of Soviet Reform Efforts," *Deutschland Archiv* 19 (September 1986): 985.

14. Philip Hanson, "The Shape of Gorbachev's Economic Reform," *Soviet Economy* 2 (October–December 1986): 318, 322.

15. See, e.g., Wolfgang Heinrichs, "Comments," in "Symposium on the German Democratic Republic," ed. Irwin L. Collier, Jr., *Comparative Economic Studies* 29 (Summer 1987): 55–56.

16. E. Kautsky, "Gorbachev's Reforms and the GDR," *RFER*, BR/32, March 6, 1987.

17. Michael Shafir, "From Sofia to Beijing: Reactions to the Nineteenth Soviet Party Conference," *RFER*, BR/133, July 15, 1988, 4–5.

18. See Joel C. Moses, "Worker Self-Management and the Reformist Alternative in Soviet Labor Policies, 1979–1985," *Soviet Studies* 39 (April 1987): 205–28; Russell Bava, "On *Perestroyka*: The Role of Workplace Participation," *Problems of Communism* (July–August 1987): 76–86.

19. See Erich Honecker, "The Tasks of Party Organizations in the Further Realization of the Decisions of the 11th SED Congress," *Neues Deutschland*, February 7–8, 1987, 3–11.

20. "From the Politburo Report Presented by Erich Honecker," *Neues Deutschland*, December 2, 1988, in Foreign Broadcast Information Ser-

vice, *Daily Report—Eastern Europe* [hereafter *Daily Report*], December 14, 1988, 13.

21. See my *The Technical Intelligentsia and the East German Elite* (Berkeley: University of California Press, 1974), 234–35; also Gert Leptin and Manfred Melzer, *Economic Reform in East German Industry* (Oxford: Oxford University Press, 1978), chap. 1.

22. Marion Gräfin Donhoff, Rudolf Walter Leonhardt, and Theo Sommer, *Reise in ein fernes Land* (Journey to a Distant Land) (Hamburg: Die Zeit Bücher, 1964), 24.

23. Peter Christian Ludz, *The Changing Party Elite in East Germany* (Cambridge: MIT Press, 1972), 325–407.

24. George Klaus, *Kybernetik und Gesellschaft* (Cybernetics and Society) (Berlin: VEB Verlag der Wissenschaften, 1964); see also Ludz, 397–400; Steffen Werner, *Kybernetik statt Marx?* (Cybernetics instead of Marx?) (Stuttgart: Verlag Bonn Aktuell, 1977).

25. Werner, *Kybernetik*, 61–67.

26. Uwe-Jens Heuer, *Demokratie und Recht im neuen ökonomischen System der Planung und Leitung der Volkswirtschaft* (Democracy and Law in the New Economic System of Planning and Management of the Economy) (Berlin: Staatsverlag der Deutschen Demokratischen Republik, 1965), Ludz, *Changing Party Elite*, 404.

27. Baylis, *Technical Intelligentsia*, 245.

28. These are outlined in Manfred Melzer, "The GDR—Economic Policy Caught Between Pressure for Efficiency and Lack of Ideas," in *The East European Economies in the 1970s*, ed. Alex Nove, Hans-Hermann Höhmann, and Gertraud Seidenstecher (London: Butterworths, 1982), 45–49.

29. See Peter-Claus Burens, *Die DDR und die "Prager Frühling"* (The GDR and the "Prague Spring") (Berlin: Duncker & Humblot, 1981), 115, 121, 125–28.

30. Between 1986 and the end of 1988, however, the quantity of GDR machinery and equipment exports to the Soviet Union dropped by nearly 20 percent. It is unclear to what extent this decline reflects Soviet dissatisfaction with the quality and assortment of the East German products, and to what extent an East German desire to take advantage of its improved terms of trade with the USSR to utilize more of its machinery domestically. Pieter A. Boot, "The GDR Economy Between East and West: Problems and Opportunities," in *Studies in GDR Culture and Society* 6, ed. Margy Gerber, et al. (Lanham, Md.: University Press of America, 1986), 21; "East German Foreign Trade Performance During 1980–86," *PlanEcon Report* 3, nos. 47–48 (November 26, 1987): 16; "Recent Developments in East German Foreign Trade," *PlanEcon Report* 4, nos. 44–45–46 (November 25, 1988): 1, 37.

31. Wolfgang Stinglwagner, "The GDR in Technological Competition,"

Deutschland Archiv 20 (May 1987): 503; Pieter Boot, "East-West Trade and Industrial Policy: The Case of the German Democratic Republic," *Soviet Studies* 39 (October 1987): 651–57.

32. See Raymond Bentley, *Technological Change in the German Democratic Republic* (Boulder, Colo.: Westview, 1984).

33. In addition, there are ninety-five regionally directed industrial *Kombinate* and 105 additional ones in construction, transport, and other fields. *Statistisches Taschenbuch der Deutschen Demokratischen Republik 1987* (Statistical Pocket Book of the German Democratic Republic 1987) (Berlin: Staatsverlag der Deutschen Demokratischen Republik, 1987), 29.

34. Franz Rudolph, "Developmental Tendencies of the Socialization Process and Its Formation According to Plan in the Combines," *Wirtschaftswissenschaft* 34 (July 1986): 973–89; Heinz-Dieter Haustein, "Role and Functioning of Industrial Enterprises in the German Democratic Republic," in Economic Commission for Europe, *Symposium on Economic Reforms in the European Centrally Planned Economies*, Vienna November 24–29, 1988, 88–89.

35. See Wolfgang Seiffert, "Is the GDR a Model?" *Deutschland Archiv* 20 (May 1987): 471. Boot argues that "there is a 'top ten' of privileged combines, which have many opportunities to influence construction tasks," but that "especially in the light industries, the industrial ministries have maintained a firm grip on the development and production profile of the enterprise." Boot, "East-West Trade," 665.

36. See Doris Cornelsen, Manfred Melzer, and Angela Scherzinger, "The East German Economic System: Reform in Small Steps," *Vierteljahreshefte zur Wirtschaftsforschung*, no. 2 (1984): 200–220.

37. *Neues Deutschland*, January 7–8, 1989, 1.

38. See Ian Jeffries, "Introduction and Summary," in *The Industrial Enterprise in Eastern Europe*, ed. Jeffries (Eastbourne, East Sussex: Praeger, 1981), 26.

39. Doris Cornelson, "On the Position of the GDR Economy at the Turn of the Year 1986–87," *DIW (Deutsches Institut für Wirtschaftsforschung) Wochenbericht* 54 (January 29, 1987): 57–59.

40. Kurt Erdmann, "Suppressed Changes in Combines in the GDR," in Forschungsstelle für gesamtdeutsche wirtschaftliche und soziale Fragen, *Glasnost und Perestroika auch in der DDR?* (Glasnost and Perestroika in the GDR too?) (Berlin: Berlin Verlag Arno Spitz, 1988), 160–63.

41. Heinz Vortmann and Ulrich Weissenburger, "The State Budget of the GDR 1980–1985," *DIW Wochenbericht* 53 (October 16, 1986): 534; *Statistisches Jahrbuch der Deutschen Demokratischen Republik 1987* (Statistical Yearbook of the German Democratic Republic 1987) (Berlin: Staatsverlag der Deutschen Demokratischen Republik, 1987), 262–63.

42. Phillip J. Bryson, "GDR Economic Planning and Social Policy in the 1980s," in Collier, "Symposium" 28; Cornelsen, Melzer, and Scherzinger, "East German Economic System," 210; Haustein, "Industrial Enterprises," 85.
43. Cornelsen, Melzer, and Scherzinger, "East German Economic System," 212; Haustein, "Industrial Enterprise," 85–86.
44. Cornelsen, "On the Position . . . 1986–87," 63; Haustein, "Industrial Enterprise," 87.
45. Horst Lambrecht, "GDR Farm Policy Bets on High Producer Prices," *DIW Wochenbericht* 54 (February 12, 1987): 98.
46. Ibid., 94.
47. Doris Cornelsen, "On the Position of the GDR Economy at the End of the Five-Year Plan 1981–85," *DIW Wochenbericht* 53 (January 30, 1986): 63.
48. See *Materialien zum Bericht zur Lage der Nation im geteilten Deutschland 1987* (Materials for the Report on the State of the Nation in Divided Germany 1987) (Bonn: Bundesministerium für innerdeutsche Beziehungen, 1987), 440–43.
49. See ibid., 209–11; Manfred Melzer, "Combine Formation and the Role of the Enterprise in East Germany," in Jeffries, *Industrial Enterprise* 109–10; Maria Haendke-Hoppe, "Foreign Trade and Foreign Trade Reform—Restructuring without Openness," in *Glasnost und Perestroika*, 71–76.
50. Doris Cornelsen, "The GDR Economy in the First Half of 1987," *DIW Economic Bulletin* 24 (October 1987): 10.
51. See "Joint Ventures in Eastern Europe," *RFER*, April 10, 1985; "Joint Economic Ventures with the West," *RFER*, July 18, 1986; Haendke-Hoppe, "Foreign Trade," 80.
52. Private businesses—most of them in crafts, repair services, or the operation of small restaurants—produced 2.8 percent of the GDR's net product as of 1985. Since 1976, such services (along with the sale of produce and animals from private agricultural plots, not included in the 2.9 percent figure) have enjoyed more official favor than in earlier years, and additional measures to support them were announced in 1988. Reportedly, the number of such businesses began modestly to increase in 1986, after many years of decline. See *Materialien 1987*, 170; Maria Haendke-Hoppe, "Private Trades in the GDR," *Deutschland Archiv* 20 (August 1987): 843–51; Hans Schilar, "Planned Economy in the German Democratic Republic—Foundations and Changes," in Economic Commission for Europe, *Symposium*, 30.
53. Indeed, regime ideologists have argued energetically (and with scarcely concealed allusions to Hungary) that unemployment is inconsistent with socialism. See Reinhold, "The Progress of Our Party," 5.
54. See Manfred Melzer and Arthur A. Stahnke, "The GDR Faces the Eco-

nomic Dilemmas of the 1980s," in *East European Economies* 3, 155–58.

55. See, e.g., Helmut Koziolek and Lothar Beyer, "An Efficiently Performing Socialist Planned Economy: The Basis of Our Dynamic Societal Development," *Einheit* 42, no. 7 (1987): 600–609.

56. See Hewett, *Reforming the Soviet Economy*, 10–14.

57. See John B. Hall, "Reform-Bargaining in Hungary: An Interview with Dr. János Mátyás Kovács," *Comparative Economic Studies* 28 (Fall 1986): 25–42.

58. See Bálint Balla, "Obstacles on the Path of the Hungarian Economic Reform: A Sociological View," *Osteuropa* 36 (October 1986): 870–71.

59. See Timothy Garton Ash, "The Opposition," *New York Review of Books*, October 13, 1988, 3–6.

60. See Marer, "Economic Reform in Hungary: From Central Planning to Regulated Market," in *East European Economies* 3, 284.

61. Kornai, "Hungarian Reform," 1724–25. Empirical evidence on the point is unclear. See Henryk Flakierski, "Economic Reform and Income Distribution: A Case Study of Hungary and Poland," special issue of *Eastern European Economics* 24 (Fall–Winter 1986).

62. *New York Times*, June 26, 1987, 1, 7.

63. See Karol Okolicsanyi, "CC Endorses Drastic Economic Proposals," *RFER*, Hungarian SR/11, August 5, 1988, 4–5.

64. See Prybla, "Thrust into an Economic Experiment," 38. "Thrust into a market environment, bureaucrats tend to behave not like capitalists, but like black marketeers, lining their pockets, stealing, and generally acting not according to the rules of the market, but according to the street-smart, corrupt codes of the underground economy." One might remark that recent American experience suggests that even a long-established "market environment" can foster similar behavior.

65. See Ulrich Busch, "Socialist Performance Principle, Money Income, and the Production of Consumer Goods," *Wirtschaftswissenschaft* 35 (March 1987): 355–73.

66. See Günter Schneider and Kurt Völker, "Scientific-Technical Progress and Work in Socialism," *Sozialistische Arbeitswissenschaft* 28 (January–February 1984): 26–38.

67. See the suggestive article by Eckart Förtsch, "The Sciences and Technology Policy in the GDR: Some Consequences and Acceptance Problems," *GDR-Monitor* (Winter 1986/87): 85–104.

68. See, e.g., Gerd Quilitzsch, Dieter Segert, and Rosemarie Will, "Interest Conflicts and the Political System: For Uwe-Jens Heuer in Honor of his Sixtieth Birthday," *Staat und Recht* 36, no. 8 (1987): 656–63. This significant article amounts nearly to a full rehabilitation of Heuer's 1965 book (see 26), which at the time was sharply attacked. I am grateful to Hartmut Zimmerman for calling my attention to this article.

See also Heuer's own recent article, "On the History of the Marxist-Leninist Concept of Democracy," in *Politische Theorie und soziale Fortschritt,* ed. Karl-Heinz Röder (Political Theory and Social Progress) (Berlin: Staatsverlag der Deutschen Demokratischen Republik, 1986), 182–206.

69. In the summer of 1988, several articles in the journal *Deutsche Zeitschrift für Philosophie* examining reforms in other socialist states seemed to suggest their relevance for the GDR. See especially Alfred Kosing, "The Dialectics of the Further Development of the Developed Socialist Society," *Deutsche Zeitschrift für Philosophie* 36 (1988/7): 577–87. An article by the Dresden SED First Secretary Hans Modrow published in July praised reforms in China; see Barbara Donovan, "SED Regional Leader Praises Chinese Economic Reform," *RFER,* BR/142, July 26, 1988. The work of Uwe-Jens Heuer and his associates cited above (nn. 24 and 68) has consistently implied the need for political and legal reform; see also Heuer, Gerd Quilitzsch, and Dieter Segert, "Socialist Policy as the Subject'of Comparative Science," *Deutsche Zeitschrift für Philosophie* 36 (1988/10): 900–908.

70. E. Kautsky, "GDR's Satisfaction about Foreign Policy but Concern about the Economy," *RFER,* BR/243, December 21, 1987, 2–3; *Neues Deutschland,* January 7–8, 1989, 1; *Financial Times,* February 3, 1989, 2. Honecker himself has cited baby pacifiers as an item in short supply. "From the Politburo Report," 26.

71. *New York Times,* November 5, 1987, Al, A14; Oleg Bogomolov, "The Socialist World on the Path to Restructuring," *Kommunist,* no. 16 (1987) as translated in *Problems of Economics* 31 (July 1988): 6–8.

72. The GDR has opposed currency convertibility in the CMEA, but in July 1988 agreed to a vaguely worded declaration of the organization committing it to work toward a "unified market." Vlad Sobell, "The CMEA's Goal of a 'Unified Market,' " *RFER,* BR/130, July 12, 1988.

73. See *Die Welt,* February 2, 1989, 1, *Daily Report,* February 3, 1989, 12–13.

11

THE LIMITS OF REFORM: THE POLITICAL ECONOMY OF "NORMALIZED" POLAND

Jack Bielasiak

The economic reform conceived in 1981, in the midst of severe economic chaos and social tensions, was perceived by most sectors of society as a necessary step in the resolution of the Polish crisis. At the end of the 1980s, the reform is viewed generally as a failure. The reason for change is due not to altered material conditions, which still necessitate a major restructuring of the economy, but to the different political environment created by the "state of war" on December 13, 1981. Quite simply, a reform shaped in the Solidarity period could not be successfully implemented in the very different atmosphere of normalization. Despite the government's commitment to economic reform under General Jaruzelski, the post-1981 consolidation precluded success in altering the economy without changes in the polity.

Over the past decade, the Polish leadership has faced two extreme problems: a major economic crisis and an overt state-society conflict. The attempt to reform the economy has been severely affected by both these factors. On the economic front, the government experienced dilemmas that are evident throughout the socialist world but are especially difficult to resolve in the chaotic economic conditions of Poland. Here, as in the Soviet Union, China, or Hungary, restructuring has been accompanied by the entrenchment of central ministries, bargaining for special treatment by enterprises, and growing consumer dissatisfaction. In addition to these economic dislocations, the Jaruzelski regime had to deal with a hostile political environment. During the course of normalization, an alienated public and a vocal opposition have been suspicious of the government's commitment to reform, and have demanded political guarantees in return for their cooperation in the economic reconstruction. More than anywhere else in the socialist community, the road to reform in Poland has depended both on the resolution of the dilemmas associated with economic innovation and the reversal of the political stalemate between the rulers and the ruled.

The original 1981 reform blueprint was exceptional for it was designed in dialogue between the authorities and independent social forces, and contained both economic and political proposals. It was the culmination of a wide debate over different designs drawn up by official commissions, expert groups, and independent bodies associated with Solidarity.[1] The drafts proposed by the government emphasized a Hungarian-type regulated market economy, while the ones advanced by Solidarity, the Network of self-management, and economic institutes stressed also provisions for labor-managed enterprises. Differences in the proposals were significant, centering on the structural features of the new economic system and the process of reform implementation. As with many other issues during the 1980–81 period, sharp conflicts emerged which culminated eventually in compromise. Already the *Directions of Economic Reform* approved by the Ninth Extraordinary Polish United Workers' Party (PUWP) Congress in July 1981 contained provisions for a regulated market economy.[2] The two bills passed at the end of September 1981, the State Enterprise Law and the Law on Workers' Self-Management,[3] embodied both the concepts of (1) economic and political change and (2) governmental and social participation in reform implementation.

This dual "dialectic" was critical for the success of the economic innovation. While political change and social participation may not be necessary conditions for reform of the economy in actually existing socialism, both factors were indispensable in Poland during the course of renewal. This was a reflection of the dichotomy of the 1980–81 political system, between the official sphere and a newly self-organized society.[4] Mass aspirations for participation in policy formulation were fulfilled by the self-management features of the reform. These provisions were an indispensable condition for the mobilization and support of society for a new economic design would, it was hoped, safeguard against political forces opposed to economic remodeling.

The military intervention of December 13, 1981 drastically altered the situation. The primary intent of martial law was to suppress self-organized, independent groups, and Jaruzelski's first actions involved the suspension and then the dissolution of civil organizations, including Solidarity.[5] These acts of political normalization signaled the separation of the reform into political and economic components. While the commitment to reform in the economy remained operative, the sociopolitical aspects were eradicated through martial law. The concept of reform was altered fundamentally from one involving a design negotiated with society to one steered exclusively by the authorities and executed by the bureaucracy.[6] In short, the dualities of the blueprint were uncoupled: political changes were eliminated from the reform plan, and social participation was excluded from the process of implementation. A reform conceived as a broad change in economic management and social governance was reduced to a more technical plan for decentralization and enterprise autonomy.

This narrowed perspective placed the direction of economic policy in contradiction to political normalization. For the recovery program, even confined to production and consumption, was predicated on introducing economic efficiency by means of decentralization and quasi-market relations. Such a devolution in the concentration of economic power went against the main thrust of political consolidation, the elimination of autonomous social organizations and the restoration of centralized, monopolistic power over society. The success of the plan depended on implementing divergent policy goals in the economic and political spheres. However the possibility of relegating the autonomous, decentralizing features of the reform exclusively to the economy while concentrating on political centralization is extremely difficult under any circumstances, and particularly so in conditions of normalization when political instruments of control are the prevailing foundation of systemic stability.

THE REFORM BLUEPRINT

The reform introduced in January 1982 was outlined primarily in the July 1981 *Directions for Economic Reform* and the laws on enterprises and self-management of September 25, 1981. The documents reflected the ideas proposed during the 1980–81 renewal, concentrating on managerial decentralization reminiscent of the Hungarian New Economic Mechanism and on self-management mechanisms evident in the Yugoslav system.[7] The recovery program focused on enterprises as independent units in economic and sociopolitical decision-making, as expressed by the 3S, (*samodzielnosc, samofinansowanie, samorzadnosc*) of independence, self-financing and self-management.

The primary aim of the design was to improve the efficiency of the economy by transforming the traditional command system into a mixed economy combining central directives with market mechanisms.[8] To attain that aim the institutional structure of the command economy had to be dismantled in favor of a decentralized administrative set-up substantially enhancing the prerogatives of the basic economic units vis-à-vis the political and economic center.

Institutions associated with the latter, such as the planning commission and the financial and branch ministries, were to be concerned primarily with macroeconomic, long-range issues. Enterprises could then operate more freely and attain command over microeconomic decisions. The self-financing feature of the blueprint placed the primary emphasis for the behavior of the enterprises on financial considerations of profitability. To this end fiscal discipline was to be introduced by eliminating the "soft budget constraint" that made enterprises dependent on subsidies from the central economic authorities; instead bankruptcies were to be a feature of the new economic system.

Administrative directives were to give way to financial levers, such as prices, taxes, and interest rates that would allow the center to regulate the economy by means of parametric guidelines. To that end it was vital to establish uniform rules for all enterprises, preventing the resurgence of bargaining for special dispensations characteristic of the centrally planned economy. Since the idea was to establish market equilibrium, flexibility in price setting was a critical element in the new economic program. To assure price determination in a competitive environment, the reform emphasized the need to expand the private sector through new forms of cooperative and private ownership.

Implementation was to be assured through the introduction of enterprise self-management. This provision, however, was the most controversial aspect of the reform blueprint. The Network, an association of self-management activists close to Solidarity, proposed a version based on "social enterprises," placing the means of production in control of the workforce, and on workers' councils empowered to make managerial decisions, including appointment of the enterprise director.[9] The governmental plan opposed both these features, seeking to retain the concept of "state enterprise" and the selection of managerial personnel by the ministries.

The end result was a compromise. Employee councils were to be elected by the entire workforce of an enterprise, and to have the right to make decisions concerning the plan, the wage fund, investment, profit sharing, and social expenditures. The enterprise director was accountable to the council, which could overrule him, although he also had a veto over certain decisions of the council. The system thus devised shared authority for enterprise activities between management and the labor force.[10] While the latter had a right to select the director in most cases, a list of excluded enterprises of "national importance" provided the power of appointment in these instances to the founding organ, i.e., the ministry.

Since the scheme called for shared power in the enterprise, it was described as a substitute for the institution of political democracy.[11] It was to be reinforced by the "socialization" of the planning mechanism, that is, by allowing open debate on the central plan, including a consultative role for a variety of independent societal organizations.[12]

These "social participation" aspects of the reform program were also meant to serve an economic and political mobilizing function. The assumption was that participation in enterprise affairs would motivate the workers toward greater economic effort. While the Yugoslav experience may cast doubt on the economic efficiency of self-management, there was no reason to suppose that its imposition in the chaotic conditions of Polish enterprises would not improve economic performance. Most important was the role of self-management as a mobilization device in support of the reform scheme. There were two aspects to this role. First, the reformers viewed self-management as a political counterweight to vested interests working to maintain the old type of command system.[13] Second, self-management had an important function as assurance for enterprise autonomy within the new economic system. This is because, as an organization of the basic economic units, self-management would naturally focus on the welfare of the enterprise against centripetal tendencies. In a way self-management was the culmination of the entire reform process, for by safeguarding enterprise autonomy against centralist forces it enhanced the provisions of a regulated market economy.

The extensive role of self-management in the design for economic improvement was necessary to obtain the support of society for the reform package. Participation in management by the workforce was a natural extension of the social self-organization prevalent in Poland during the renewal course. It had the merit of providing the working class with an institutionalized mechanism of influence and control over enterprise affairs, and through it over broader economic issues. In this manner, self-management was a political channel guaranteeing society's participation in public choices. Most significantly, it replaced the adversarial relationship between the authorities and Solidarity within a new framework for workforce involvement in decision-making.

LIMITING REFORM: NORMALIZATION

The spirit of the reform adopted during the course of the state-society dialogue of renewal was altered by martial law. Surprisingly, despite the abandonment of most renewal programs, the economic design was implemented on schedule on January 1, 1982, although most of its social, self-management provisions were suspended. At the time, General Jaruzelski depicted his concern with the welfare of the nation as an integral part of normalization.[14] The rapid introduction of the reform was to serve as the most visible sign of the government's program of recovery.

Economic welfare, however, did not constitute the entire agenda

of the state of war. After all, General Jaruzelski did not activate
military power with the sole aim of introducing economic reform.
Rather the foremost intent of normalization was to stabilize the
domestic political situation by reasserting state control over society,
mainly through the elimination of independent social organizations
formed during the Solidarity era. The government hoped that improved material conditions would facilitate societal acceptance of
the new political reality, and foster long-term political stability.
Indeed the Polish government sought to use the economic card to
attain popular support, openly identifying the 1982 reform with the
ideas of renewal and proclaiming its support for the continuity of
the reformist course initiated during the 1980–81 period.

Nonetheless, the official rhetoric was careful to distinguish between the substance of the reform and the methods of its formulation and implementation. To the authorities, normalization meant
that social forces could not inhibit the policy preferences of the
ruling elite, as was the case during the 1980–81 interlude. On the
contrary, the aim was to eliminate such practices in favor of centralist, monopolistic norms in the exercise of power, and thus to deac-
tivate Solidarity and other independent organizations.[15] However,
these steps had the effect of alienating the population from any
government policy, including that of economic reform.[16] The social
and political demobilization of society through martial law made
impossible the channeling of popular will even to such a worth-
while project as economic recovery. Depriving the 1982 reform of
its sociopolitical components relegated the blueprint for change to
the official sphere, stripping it of the legitimacy acquired through
the provisions for social participation and self-management.

The historical record of socialist states offers ample testimony to
the difficulty of separating economics from politics. The problem
has been ascribed as the "fused" nature of Soviet-type societies,[17]
derived from the ideological premises of state ownership of the
means of production and the communist party's vanguard role in
the construction of socialism. One-party rule and central economic
command form a complex administrative structure responsible for
the distribution of economic resources and political privileges. The
tasks of this administration, including the coordination of material
allocation and the reconciliation of conflicting interests, serve si-

multaneously as the integrators of the system. Political authority is dependent on this network of hierarchical decisions and controls, signifying both the concentration and interlocking of political and economic power.

Precisely for that reason, reform attempts become a problem not only of management in the economy but also of governance in the polity.[18] In particular, the authorities' concern is that the infusion of decentralization and autonomy in the economic realm may result in a similar diffusion of political power from the regime to autonomous social forces. They fear for political stability, and this often leads to a backlash by vested interests against the idea of reform, even one restricted to the introduction of partial autonomy in the economy. The consequence is a de-emphasis in reform implementation, leading to a decline in commitment to the changeover.

One of the distinguishing characteristics of the Solidarity period in Poland was that the interlocking nature of the system seemed to favor the introduction of a reform program. This situation was derived from the already changed nature of the political life in the country, when independent mass organizations challenged the political power of the bureaucracy. Since the diffusion of political power had already taken place, the task of restructuring the command economy was a natural concomitant with the political transformation. The social provisions of the economic design were thus in alignment with the established social and political reality. Furthermore, since political and administrative authority was already severely circumscribed by society, the implementation of the reform could be pursued without the extensive roadblocks usually engineered by interests associated with the political and economic command system.

The drastic alteration of the political and social reality by martial law altered the environment receptive to reform. Not only did normalization attempt to eradicate the groups that had grown during the period of renewal, it sought to establish new political controls that would integrate the social forces into the political system sponsored by the regime. The policies initiated by the government thus proceeded from the suppression of independent organizations to the establishment of new, "authorized" public associations.[19] The incorporation of such organizations into the official political process became the essence of normalization. Unlike the groups formed during the renewal period, the new public institutions explicitly recognized the leading role of the party and administrative obligations to the construction of socialism, i.e., the normalized society. Such a political strategy sought to replace the former social self-organization and collective group solidarity with corporate-style integration from above, by means of vertical linkages and social atomization.

However, the absence of social participation in the reform process had its effect on policy implementation, by eradicating the social backing necessary to safeguard the application of reform principles in the economy. There remained no substantial independent force capable of counteracting the interests of the political and administrative elite in favor of centralized and bureaucratic controls in the economy.[20] Furthermore, without the institutional mechanism of self-governance and self-management, the advocates of reform lacked the means to mobilize societal interests as supports for economic reconstruction.

The policy of depoliticization went beyond the suppression of channels for mass influence to the deliberate encouragement of political and social apathy.[21] The ensuing passivity went beyond the political arena to include withdrawal from greater economic efforts, at substantial costs to productivity and efficiency. The popular perception was that the regime's effort was but another "reform from above" with little value to society. For example, a 1984 poll of workers in Warsaw enterprises found that a large majority of the respondents saw no evidence of reform within factories (57.9 percent); another significant portion evaluated the impact of reform negatively (11.3 percent), or were ambivalent toward reform (9.6 percent). Only a small minority of workers (13.2 percent) were positive about the impact of reform. These generally negative assessments reemerged in a nation-wide poll which found that by February 1988, only 16 percent of the sample were hopeful about their future. In the early 1980s, 60 to 75 percent of a nationwide sample had been optimistic about the reform and economic improvements.[22] These attitudes have reinforced the workers' unwillingness to tolerate the negative consequences of economic rationalization, such as price increases or potential unemployment. The authorities' fear that economic restructuring may thus lead to renewed social tensions and disturbances had led them to mitigate the positive consequences of productive rationality. The best example of such a spiral are the various compensation and wage schemes offered to counter the consecutive price increases, which add more fuel to the inflationary gap and market disequilibria.

Such an approach signified the subservience of economic performance to the overreaching goal of normalization cum stabilization. The regime's primary concern remained the maintenance of political controls; in case of a compatibility problem between political normalization and economic reformation, the choice fell on limiting the economic changeover.[23] The pattern throughout the reform period after January 1982 was to steer the economy through constant administrative regulations and directives, such as special operational programs and purchasing orders, that interfere with the working of the economic system. These ad hoc measures serve to reinforce the hierarchical interactions in the economy, restrict the choices available to enterprises, and constitute an ever-growing number of exceptions to the principles of the reform.

The systemic pressures of fusion, the policy choices of normalization, and the operational programs activated in the name of these policies have conspired to produce an economic situation overburdened with administrative regulations and bureaucratic fiat; a system that is far removed from the reform blueprint envisaged in 1981. Above all, normalization meant a social and political environment suspicious of all innovations. Therefore, despite the official desire to institute reform in the economy while containing the spillover effects in the political arena, reform could not thrive in the normalized world of post–1981 Poland.

THE REFORM IN PRACTICE

After its implementation in January 1982 the reform agenda was severely curtailed. In the first instance, this was accomplished through special provisions associated with martial law. Once these were suspended, in December 1982 and then lifted in July 1983 the reform process was restricted by procedures governing "the period for overcoming the socioeconomic crisis." The latter was a special circumstance, under the existing conditions in Poland, allowing the authorities to impose extraordinary legislation and restricted socio-political rights for the duration of the crisis.[24]

These practices had an overwhelming impact on the reform design formulated in 1981, distorting the features of both the intended regulated market economy and the self-management mechanism. For example, the period since January 1, 1982, has been overburdened by an overwhelming number of legal and administrative acts in the economic sphere. In the first three years of the reform, some 330 laws and over 12,000 administrative directives were passed. These have peppered the economic system with extraordinary regulations often at odds with the provisions established by the reform, e.g., the law governing the financing of state enterprises was encumbered by 36 administrative directives that made difficult the "self-financing" provision of the "3-S" reform.[25] Many of these regulatory restrictions were created as political and economic emergencies of martial law, and were intended as temporary measures. Since then they have achieved a more permanent status, and have been justified by the continuing economic shortages and social tensions. In fact the evocation of "operational programs" to large sectors of the economy, of administrative controls and governmental contracts, has had the effect of retaining many features of the CPE in the postreform economy. In addition, overregulation has produced extensive uncertainty among managers as to the rules of economic behavior, since legal and administrative directives often reinterpret the rules of the game—at substantial cost to economic stability.[26]

The regulatory power reinforced the position of the central and intermediary economic apparatus.[27] For example, while the number of branch ministries has been reduced, this restructuring did not significantly diminish the scope of economic power exercised by the ministries through control over resource allocation, enterprise organization, or personnel appointments and rewards. Similarly, the influence of the functional ministries and commissions has expanded. While this may be a positive development, since these institutions have a nationwide perspective and are involved in parametric regulation, the primary agency remains the Planning Commission—the paramount example of a command structure operating by administrative means. At the mid-point of the organizational chart, a level that was to be eliminated under the new system, the administrative structure has been recreated in a new guise. The old trusts (*zjednoczenia*) have been replaced by new associations (*zrzeszenia*) of enterprises, which despite a voluntary status have been compulsory since they provide access to material and financial resources. Therefore, about 90 percent of all enterprises have regrouped in these associations, which act as transmission belts from the economic center to the individual firms.

The tendency toward renewed organizational concentration since 1981 is corroborated by developments on the personnel front. After an initial decline in the staff of the central economic agencies, since 1984 a resurgence in the personnel employed in the central economic apparatus has taken place.[28] This propensity toward organizational and administrative expansion explains why the frequency of commands from the central agencies to the enterprises has been the same in the pre- and post-reform periods.[29] Yet, since the economy has been an amalgam of traditional CPE and reform-type provisions, the enterprises have obtained greater room for bargaining and formation of informal coalitions to appeal administrative directives. The increased room for maneuvering does not, however, mirror the behavior of competitive market units but signals more informal lobbying within the command administrative structure.

Indeed the economic system has continued to limit enterprise autonomy and managerial independence.[30] The government's "operational programs" and extensive purchasing orders translate into direct production tasks and targets which limit much of the enterprise's ability to decide on output, prices, and employment. Administrative agencies establish prices through bureaucratic intervention rather than reliance on flexible market-type adjustments. The result is the freezing of contractual prices, established on a cost-plus basis, that perpetuate economic distortions. This is reinforced by the disregard of the self-financing reform postulate, so that the "soft budget constraint" remains operational, enabling enterprise bailout through special tax exemptions, subsidies, or the allocation of foreign exchange.[31] While the provision for bankruptcies of unprofitable enterprises remains active in principle, it is difficult to apply and bankruptcies have been virtually unknown under the new system.[32] Without adequate financial discipline, there is no incentive to introduce cost-saving measures to replace the traditional forms of financial support. These economic practices yield inadequate measures of profitability and efficiency, and thus contribute to continued market disequilibria for both producers and consumers.

The coexistence of both command and reform principles, especially under continuing crisis conditions, has facilitated discrimination among enterprises, through such devices as taxation and credit terms, subsidies, and personnel appointments. In this manner, the government is fostering a particularism that determines economic behavior on the basis of specific dispensations. The individual firm does not gain from independent, self-financing behavior, but through successful administrative relations with the allocating bureaucratic centers and intermediary organizations.[33] In short, the enterprise does not function in the intended market-type environment. In remains essentially a component in the administrative network where commands and regulations dominate, and where economic activity is equated foremost with political and bureaucratic bargaining.

The degeneration of the reform from its intended course has been even more marred, of course, with respect to social participation. The deliberate official policy to foreclose institutional means for mass expression reined in the institution of self-management.[34] The apparent fear, at the time martial law was imposed, was that activation of self-management organs on January 1, 1982, would lend a channel for political expression to Solidarity activists opposed to the new situation. For that reason, the laws on self-government and enterprises were first of all suspended for the duration of the state of war. With the lifting of martial law, the statutes of September 25, 1981, were modified through the elimination of certain of their provisions, and by the introduction of new articles and executive acts.[35] The net effect of the legal action was to reduce self-management to consultation, with workers' councils subservient to enterprise management. Most extreme was the special legislation of July 21, 1983, for the period of overcoming the socioeconomic crisis, which permitted suspension and dissolution of self-management organizations.

The provisions for the reactivation of workers' councils enacted in July 1983 redefined the institutional capabilities of self-governance. Most significant was the legal exclusion from self-management rights of enterprises of national importance affecting some three million workers. These were in most instances the largest enterprises in the country, accounting for the bulk of industrial output in Poland. Clearly, the authorities deemed these firms as potentially unstable, with sociopolitical conditions inappropriate for the formation of workers' councils. Self-management was allowed in smaller, less vital enterprises encompassing 5.5 million employees.[36] However while self-management organs were established in these firms, only a small number are active as self-governance agencies (about 15 to 20 percent of such organs). The remainder lack autonomy and vitality in the face of the legal and institutional limitations imposed by the state. Equally telling is the prohibition against horizontal linkages among the self-management bodies, in contravention to article 35 of the law. Despite repeated attempts to establish such links, for example by the Elena factory in Torun, a hotbed of the horizontalist party movement in 1981, the government has intervened consistently to prohibit such horizontal initiatives.[37] Apparently the authorities' fear was that grass root, spontaneous processes outside the control of the party or state posed the danger of workforce mobilization that may revert into actions against the regime.

The councils' policy competencies were extensively altered as well. Particularly important was the downgrading of their powers in personnel selection, which were deliberately shifted away from the workers' councils. Thus the list of enterprises of national importance in which the councils have no rights of selection expanded from an original 200 to over 1,400 factories. Moreover, in the remaining enterprises not on the exclusion list, the self-management units were precluded from determination concerning managerial job descriptions or salaries.[38] The principle of nomenklatura was safeguarded through these restrictions, largely disenfranchising the councils as self-management organizations.

In effect, the decision-making role of the councils declined in favor of a consultative role to management. The latter's rights to overrule the decisions of the workforce were expanded, and restrictions mounted in areas of the councils' jurisdiction. For example, council jurisdiction shifted from the vital areas of profit sharing and wage structure to more marginal concerns, such as the use of enterprise reserves or social funds.[39] Even in this last area, the trend has been to circumvent the councils' prerogatives by providing the official trade unions with veto powers over social expenditures. Recent surveys on enterprise affairs demonstrate that the vast majority of decisions are made by an informal "collective" consisting of the director, the party secretary, and the heads of the factory trade union and self-management organizations—with the role of the enterprise director most extensive, followed by that of the party cell. Self-management organs have thus been increasingly deprived of decision-making power by the expanding activity "from above" of management, and the "from below" actions of other social and political organizations.[40]

The changes severely limited the council's governance potential, redirecting their work to an intermediary between management and the workforce that often approaches the traditional role of "transmission belts" between the authorities and the workers. Self-management had been thus deprived of its participatory, democratic forms to take on a more instrumental character.[41] In this role the workers' councils have provided bargaining leverage to management in the latter's dealings with authorities outside the enterprise, or have acted as a conduit for the mobilization of workers to enhance production efforts, or have served as agents for the other social and political organizations which use the institution of self-management to strengthen their own status in the factories.

As in past instances of self-management in Poland, the ideal of workers' power in the enterprises was circumvented by the requirements of politics. In this respect self-management is but a reflection of the overall national political and economic conditions, which continued to place political requirements above other endeavors. After 1982 normalization meant a predominant concern with the consolidation of political power against a society perceived as entranced with the ideas of self-organization and independence. Institutions approaching those ideals were viewed by the regime with suspicion and concern. Self-management proposals had to fall into line with the overall policy of the government, a strategy to instill economic recovery within a monocentric sociopolitical system. Without autonomous self-governance in the enterprises, however, the reform lost credibility with the working class; and without the support of society the reform design fell victim to inertia.

THE SECOND STAGE OF REFORM

The distortions evident in the application of the 1982 reform were bound to affect the performance of the Polish economy. The initial improvements in the material sphere, due to martial law "order," gave way to growing difficulties in the establishment of an economic balance. The immobility of the reform process and the stalemate in economic progress provided the impetus for a major economic campaign, "the second stage of reform," during 1987.

The call for renovation was first issued at the Tenth Congress of the PUWP in June 1986. In his speech, General Jaruzelski argued that the continuing problems of the economy could not be resolved without a reexamination of the reform process.[42] These remarks signaled the party forum's demand for a comprehensive review of the economic situation and renewed efforts for material recovery. The deliberations at the congress initiated an important change in the regime's perspective, departing from the claim that the reform was proceeding along the lines of the 1982 blueprint and recognizing instead that the reconstruction design had not really been implemented, and that bold innovations were necessary to move further along the road of recovery.

The official demand for the second stage of reform was a recognition of the severe crisis prevailing in the economy and of the growing popular doubts about the government's commitment to a reformist course. It was clear by the mid-1980s that a severe imbalance in the economy persisted, characterized by continuing shortages of industrial and consumer products, and a deterioration in the standard of living. The economy continued to be plagued by the dramatic production decline experienced between 1979 and 1982, and production growth rates in subsequent years did not compensate for the loss. While net material production grew by 5.6 percent in 1984, 3.4 percent in 1985, and 5.0 percent in 1986, it remained well below the 1978 level, particularly on a per capita basis. The recovery record was marred by the increasing debt to Western countries: the hard currency debt rose from $25.5 billion in 1980 to $33.5 billion in 1986. This despite cuts in imports from the West that aggravated the shortage of materials and parts needed for domestic production. The result was a severe downturn in consumption, triggered by high price increases and inflation rates (20.3 percent in 1986 and 26.3 percent in 1987). Thus, the real income of the population decreased by 25 percent over the last seven years.[43]

No wonder that the economic situation gave way to the widespread perception that the government was incapable of managing the economy. Official opinion polls showed a steady decline in the number of people who believed that the resolution of the country's economic problems was possible. In 1985, close to 50 percent of a national sample held that the authorities did not undertake actions to overcome the economic crisis, and 64 percent believed that the economic program did not contribute to the resolution of the economic problems. At the end of both 1985 and 1986, about 12 percent of the population evaluated the economic situation as "good" or "somewhat good," but by mid-1987 that proportion had declined even further to 8.6 percent of the respondents. The deterioration in public opinion was even more striking in regard to evaluation of the future: at the end of 1986, 17 percent believed that the next year will be worse and 33 percent believed it will be better; one year later, in expressing their expectations for 1988, almost 50 percent of the population saw things as getting worse and only 17.4 percent as getting better. There was also a growing feeling that social tensions were more pronounced, with 80 percent of the population in 1987 seeing the likelihood of severe social conflicts as a distinct danger in the near future.[44]

The authorities' proposal for the second stage had to take into account both these factors, the reality of material life and society's attitude toward reform. The work on the renewed design was undertaken by the Commission for the Economic Reform, which issued in April 1987, the 174 "Theses on the Second Stage of the Economic Reform."[45] The thrust of the proposal aimed at reestablishing the principles of the 1982 reform, admitting that they had been severely weakened by many discretionary and temporary decisions. The rectification sought to impose a more radical approach by emphasizing four "main lines of systemic changes:" strengthening the provisions for enterprise autonomy, diversifying economic activity through changes in ownership forms, increasing the role of the market, and reforming the administrative structure.[46]

While proponents of the second stage looked upon those proposals as an important "radicalization" in the economic approach of the government, the extensive and prolonged debate following the publication of the "Theses" suggested that many experts had reservations about the innovative nature of the program.[47] In their evaluation the problem was not so much with the principles of economic reconstruction as with the failure to apply those plans following the initiation of the 1982 reform. The problem of inaction on the economic front, the criticism continued, was unlikely to be resolved through the April "Theses," since those were only vague reaffirmations of well-known principles and did not provide specific remedies for the institution of a meaningful reform. For example, the "Theses" discussed the need to provide for better channels of popular participation only by referring once again to the necessity of strengthening the self-management features of the Polish economy.

The second stage did affirm the necessity for combining economic and political reform and societal and governmental cooperation through policy guidelines and legislative acts adopted to implement the new economic model. But even here, in a series of speeches and documents in October and November 1987, the authorities remained vague as to the specific content and process of both linkages.

The flurry of activity in the autumn of 1987 sought to create the conditions necessary to launch in practice the second stage of the reform. The most concrete steps were taken at the October 23–24 Sejm sessions, which enabled fifteen laws to provide the legal basis for the reform.[48] The legislation recognized that a difficult period of adjustment was inevitable in order to bring the economic crisis to an end, and called for the strengthening of enterprise autonomy, the formation of a properly functioning market, the development of a competitive banking system, the improvement of social services and insurance, the restructuring of the economic center, and a readjustment of prices.

The Sejm's timetable, while very general, did provide for "an essential change in the functional scope and organizational structure of the central economic administration" in 1987 and "a palatable step forward in balancing the Polish economy and increasing the

role of the market" in 1988. The first of these goals, undertaken at
the October 1987 session, was to streamline the economic administration. The process resulted in a decline in the number of ministries from twenty-six to nineteen. The effectiveness of the action,
however, remained in doubt as the change provided for reassign-
ments of administrative personnel, rather than dismissal of central
personnel, and only mentioned a future alteration in regional administration.

As concerns the second item in the timetable, the balancing of
the Polish economy, progress could not occur without significant
changes in prices. The program thus recognized that a readjustment
in the price structure had to occur soon, designating early 1988 for
a rise in the prices of important consumer items. While some of the
increase was to be matched by compensations through raises in
wages and welfare grants, the price increases would nonetheless be
extensive, averaging some 40 percent in 1988, to be followed by
further increases in 1989 and 1900. The perspective of the second
stage of the reform was therefore that an austerity period was inevitable in order to overcome the crisis, and had to be implemented
through the termination of price subsidies.

The problem for the authorities was to render the austerity measures acceptable to the population. The general public lacked confidence in the government's ability to improve the economy and the
standard of living. Past experience certainly has shown that reform
programs faltered through bureaucratic inaction and governmental
retreat. For the public, reform was associated with price increments
and little else. Society's disbelief in reform in turn translated into
an unwillingness to support austerity as a prelude to a revitalized
economy.

The task of the political leadership was to mobilize popular support for the second stage, both to assure society's acceptance of the
difficult period ahead and to use social forces to counter antireform
vested interests. To succeed in this task, the authorities had to
overcome their persistent concerns that social mobilization would
enhance society's political aspirations for autonomy. The regime's
concerns with such sociopolitical repercussions of reform were evident throughout the course of the second stage campaign, but the
severity of the economic situation seemed to push the leadership

toward an opening of the political arena so as to provide for social participation in the reform process.

In this manner, political reform and popular involvement emerged as a component part of the second stage. The renewed linkage between the economic and political arenas took three distinct forms. The first was the government's call for the revitalization of the self-management features present in the original reform design, stressing their importance for both enterprise and local administrative activities. With regard to enterprises, the authorities once again defined self-management as an essential factor in assuring the autonomy of enterprise and the decentralization of economic activity. The renewed stress on improving the efficiency of self-management institutions was a recognition of the ongoing failure to establish workers' councils as important partners in enterprise management. The second stage of the reform thus appealed for an increase in the powers of the councils and for "real self-management of work establishments." To facilitate this task, Premier Messner promised that "the list of enterprises of fundamental importance for the national economy will be reduced from 1,300 down to a mere 400."[49] Such a measure, if carried out, would lift the prohibition against self-management in the major industrial enterprises, heretofore a critical barrier to the power of workers' councils in the Polish economy. As concerns territorial self-government, the proposed measures sought to increase the activities of people's councils in administration and provide local government with the rights of communal ownership.[50] Altogether the intent was to facilitate the decentralization and demonopolization of the Polish economy by enhancing the powers of individual enterprises and local administrative units.

A second aspect of the economic-political linkage concerned the expansion of "socialist pluralism." The program aimed at opening channels of participation to broad sectors of society to engage social forces in the reform process and induce their support for economic restructuring. Socialist pluralism was presented at the democratization of governance and management through the inclusion of social strata and groups previously excluded from the system. The political leadership emphasized this more inclusive vision throughout the second-stage campaign, including appeals by General Jaruzelski for the "broad appointment of non-party people to managerial and

responsible posts."[51] Moreover, the participation of previously un-
tapped forces in the reform process was depicted as a test of "various persons and milieux" to commit their resources to the recovery
course, so that "everyone who wants to act constructively in this
field may find a proper place for himself."[52] This willingness to go
beyond a strict interpretation of political loyalties revealed the authorities' need to mobilize society in support of the economic reform, and their realization that without societal participation the
program of recovery was once again in danger.

Mobilization of popular support, however, depended upon the
opening of political life in the country. While there were some small
steps in the expansion of the participatory process during the second-stage campaign, the Polish authorities remained cautious in the
application of "socialist pluralism." A "secret" document drawn up
by members of the political leadership in September 1987 did envisage an extensive restructuring of the political system, even considering limitations of the party's monopoly in public life and discussions with a "socialist opposition."[53] By the time of its public
appearance as a revised report of the PUWP's Politburo on November 18, the document was significantly weakened in its commitment
to political reform.[54] Instead the report reverted back to proposals
within "the program of socialist renewal," an official stance adopted
in 1980 to contain the self-organization movement. While the report
appeared tolerant of a "socialist and constructive opposition" and
autonomous public organizations, these provisions were curtailed
by the continuing emphasis on "the leading role" of the party in
society and on "the constitutional foundations" delimiting public
activity. Even this perspective was diluted further in the discussion
of the report at the November 25 Central Committee plenum, whose
thrust was to restrict the potential political opening encompassed in
the "socialist pluralism" formula.[55] The political establishment once
again proved averse to the risks perceived in the unfolding of the
economic and political processes associated with the reform.

Instead the regime preferred to rely on a third element in the
economic-political and state-society linkage: a national referendum
to pass on the issues contained in the second-stage proposals. First
announced at the October 8, 1987, Central Committee meeting, the
referendum was depicted as providing society with the opportunity

to debate the state of the economy and the means necessary to improve material conditions in the country. Most significantly, the act was praised as a primary example of "direct democracy . . . and decision-making by the whole of population," as well as a "big conversation with society."[56] In this manner, the referendum was meant to reflect all the merits of public participation in governmental policy, and to symbolize the democratization process associated with the second stage of reform.

From the point of view of the political establishment, the referendum had considerable advantage over more permanent forms of socialist pluralism as a mechanism for popular expression. Foremost, the referendum was a massive, direct form of popular participation that could not be institutionalized as a permanent feature of the political system. In addition, the referendum by its very nature had to be written in general and vague terms, so that specific provisions could not be imposed upon the authorities. Instead, the intent was to obtain support for the reform package while allowing the government to determine the concrete policies and implementation measures. Even here, public officials made clear from the start that the referendum was a consultative device concerning not the actuality of the reform but only its intensity, scope and timetable. "The nation . . . will either decide to sharpen economic rigors and to proceed faster so that tomorrow is better or it will resolve that it had better move at a slower pace, resigning itself to a prolongation of the strenuousness of today."[57]

The first question posed in the referendum sought approval for a "radical economic improvement . . . knowing that it will require going through a very difficult period of two or three years."[58] While there followed a brief supplementary explanation to the question, the measures enumerated were vague. The one item covered in more detailed concerned the end of government subsidies and "beginning early in 1988, very considerable price increases of many items." The thrust of the referendum, clearly, centered on obtaining society's approval for an economic recovery which necessitated an initial period of severe austerity, including successive price rises over the next three years. Apparently in return for society's acceptance of such an economic plan, the government was willing to tolerate a greater opening in the political arena. The second referendum question thus asked, "Are you in favor of the Polish model of a thorough democratization of political life, with the objective of strengthening self-management, extending human rights and increasing the participation of citizens in management of the country?" In this section too the supplementary explanation did not provide many concrete examples of the proposed "democratization," but limited the proposed opening by the requirements of "socialist renewal."

The questions revealed the intent of the referendum. The government realized that the second stage could not succeed without the cooperation of the populace, specifically in regard to the transitional period of austerity, and to attain society's support, the authorities were willing to initiate procedures to foster popular participation in the reform process. The referendum itself was depicted as the first step in this process, as a dialogue between the state and society. However, the ambivalence of the reform program, as exemplified by the vague wording of the referendum, resulted at best in ambiguous reactions on the part of society. Some people viewed reform as essential, and were apparently willing to accept even a partial, unclear recovery blueprint. Others rejected the government's claim that the referendum signified the public's ability to influence policy issues, and pointed out instead that the referendum restricted society to a reactive role without the capability of influencing the content of the reform. Thus, the Solidarity leadership, reflecting the prevailing ambiguity between the necessity of reform and the uncertainty of the government's plan, first called for a boycott of the vote by the population, but then downgraded its opposition toward ignoring the referendum.[59]

The voter turnout on November 29, 1987, was the lowest in the history of People's Poland, with about sixteen million people, or 67.2 percent of the eligible voters, turning out to cast ballots. Since by Polish law a referendum must be approved by at least 50 percent of all eligible voters, the high rate of absenteeism helped to defeat the proposals. While of those actually voting, a majority approved the referendum questions, of the total eligible voters only 44.3 percent favored the question on economic reform, and 46.3 percent the question on democratization.[60]

The defeat of the referendum, however, did not resolve the ambiguity surrounding the reform. On the one hand, government spokesmen depicted the vote as a great lesson in democracy, and pointed out that a sizable portion of the Polish population approved measures to undertake a radical reconstruction of the economy, including the austerity program. On the other hand, Solidarity pointed out that the vote was certainly an expression of the public's opposition to those in charge of the reform process, if not of the need for reform.

There is no doubt that the results expressed public distrust of the authorities' program, particularly of the methods selected to involve social forces in the process. Throughout the course of the second-stage campaign, there were few actions that demonstrated the government's willingness to institutionalize forms of public participation in the reform design and its execution. Instead the emphasis on the referendum as the primary instrument of government-citizen consultation reflected the continuing commitment of the regime to limiting the influence of social forces in the determination of the reform agenda. The leadership's awareness that reform could not succeed without a measure of public involvement conflicted again with the establishment's fears that democratization of political life would undermine the fragile political stability of the post-1981 normalization.

The dilemma of reform continued to define the post-referendum situation in Poland.[61] In the aftermath of the November 29 vote, the government reaffirmed its commitment to the second stage. However in recognition of the outcome, but consistent with the prior official interpretation that the vote concerned the pace and not the content of economic reconstruction, the implementation of the second stage was modified and slowed. In particular, price increases were staggered and lowered. Beyond this adjustment the reform continued to be defined by generalities and lack of concrete measures to initiate action. Political disagreements between moderate and hard-line party factions emerged at the Central Committee meeting of December 15, 1987, and culminated once again in a vague program of "profound economic and political changes," without offering further instructions for the implementation of the reform, or enacting new procedures to carry out the tasks associated with the second stage.[62]

Yet, the leadership was well aware of the need to introduce political reforms in order to attain its economic goals. The connection between the two realms was readily acknowledged in official pronouncements, as was the need to "gain public support" to secure the outcome of the reform. The rapid deterioration of the economic situation finally led the regime in the fall of 1988 to move beyond such rhetorical statements to acquiesce to a political program of reconciliation. The leadership was forced into action by an ever intensifying economic crisis. Global and per capita production in 1988 was still lower than ten years earlier, the debt mounted to $38 billion, and estimates for the future were not encouraging. Most dramatic was the situation in consumption, with price increases fueling rampant inflation, which reached a rate of 55 percent in 1988. Despite compensatory wages, salaries could not keep pace with the inflationary spiral.[63] Faced with such economic hardship, the public became even more pessimistic in its assessment of the national economic condition. Since late 1985, national polls had revealed systemic increases in the proportion of the population assessing the economy as "bad" or "very bad"—reaching the over 60 percent mark in mid-1987. Even more remarkable was the fact that 86 percent of respondents at the end of 1988 felt that their buying power had declined throughout the year, and that 96 percent held that their income did not cover the price increases. Only 1.3 percent of the respondents believed decisively that the reform was likely to continue and succeed.[64]

The intensity of popular discontent translated once again into action in two strike waves during May and August 1988. The latter embraced some thirty-thousand workers seeking not only an improvement in living conditions, but demanding also the relegalization of Solidarity. The workers' protest sent a shock wave throughout the system, and the government moved in September to open negotiations with Solidarity at a roundtable to resolve the economic and political stalemate. The leaderships' initiative was not welcome by all sectors of the political establishment, as the conservative *apparat* resented the prospective opening of the political process to the "opposition."

CONCLUSION

Reform has become the primary currency of political discourse in most of the socialist world during the 1980s. The focus on reform has been generated by growing concerns with economic growth, productivity, and technological innovation. The emerging consensus, in the USSR, China and Eastern Europe, is that extensive reformation of the CPE is necessary.[65] Structural change to replace command directives and bureaucratic intervention with market relations and parametric mechanisms has become acceptable. There is also growing evidence that the leaders of the socialist countries committed to reform are well aware that revision of the economy is tied to alterations in the political practices of socialism, and that the relationship must be overtly recognized by introducing elements of political reform alongside the economic reconstruction. Of course the nature of the sociopolitical innovation is still delimited, but earlier attempts to insulate political change from economic transformation have given way to simultaneous advocacy of reform in the economy and the polity. By embracing this viewpoint, the leaders of the Communist world appear to have learned, even if unconsciously, the lessons of the Polish reform.

The Polish case is extreme, both as to the depth of its economic crisis and political upheaval and the pattern of political and economic response to the crises. Perhaps for that very reason, the Polish experience provides a series of lessons concerning the course of reform under socialism. These affect foremost our understanding of the dialectic between economic and political change, and while the lessons may be obvious, they are not necessarily trivial.

In the first place, the reform course in Poland demonstrates the critical need for consistency in economic and political strategies of change. The reform designed in Poland during the 1980–81 renewal contained extensive provisions for a regulated market economy and for self-management of enterprises, a reflection of the major political and social changes evident at the time in the formation of independent, self-governing organizations. The economic project was thus a natural outgrowth of the broader societal transformation. The activation of political normalization in December 1981, however, produced a major discord between an economic policy aimed at reform and a political policy aimed at consolidation. An economic design framed through a dialogue between the state and society could not be successfully implanted in an environment characterized by the suppression of society by the state. This situation in Poland was dramatically different from the post-1956 process in Hungary.[66] There the issue of economic change was debated within the context of political normalization, when both economic reform and social dialogue were part of the same approach towards a reconciliation between the regime and society. The case of the German Democratic Republic illustrates the same point concerning consistency, in that the steadfast elite emphasis on central and administrative controls in both economic and political spheres accounted for the continued resistance to the reform impulse in the GDR.[67] In contrast, the incongruence evident in the case of Poland created continued difficulties for the success of either policy, economic reform, or political stability.

The necessity for strategic consistency demonstrates that a linkage exists between economic reform and political change in socialist countries. The Polish experience illustrates well the interrelationship.[68] During the renewal period, it was difficult to separate economic policy from innovations in the sociopolitical arena, even despite the reluctance of Solidarity to assume economic responsibilities. In the ensuing period, the political demands of consolidation forced a redefinition of the reform closer to the post-martial law realities. The important issue evident here concerns the nature of the linkage between the economic and political spheres and the possibility of imposing some boundary upon the crossover. While the linkage is clearly present, more uncertain is the direction and strength of the relationship.

There is no doubt that when economic reform is instituted, it is often the product of a perceived crisis in economic growth or of a threat to social stability. Such situations activate proposals for change on the part of reform oriented leaders. The latest round of such proposals in the socialist community has made explicit the linkage between politics and economics. In China, the extensive decentralization and market-exchange evident in the productive sector has engendered revisions in the functions of the Communist party and state institutions. In the Soviet Union, General Secretary Gorbachev has tied his calls for "radical reform" in economic production with advocacy of "democratization" in politics and self-management in the workplace. After prolonged experimentation with economic change, the Hungarian leadership too has recently emphasized the need for social and political reform as a component in the continued reconstruction of the economy. These developments are testimony to the fact that the political leaders seem to be aware of the interrelationship between economic and political process of transformation, leading to the recognition that economic change most be accompanied by some social and political reform.

This realization constitutes the third lesson of the Polish reform course, the need to provide for "social participation" in the reform design and implementation. Such channels for public debate and mass involvement in economic affairs serve foremost as mobilization for support of the proposed changes. These are important to overcome the initial costs of economic reformation, including price increases and employment dislocation, and to neutralize political opposition to economic change on the part of vested interests. In this sense, provisions for social participation take on an important political task in lifting the constraints on reform. The deactivation of this feature in the 1982 Polish economic program was substantially responsible for the derailment of the reform.

"Social participation" brings us back to the issue of the relationship between economic and political change. For the activation of participatory channels to aid the economic process may impose severe constraints upon the policy preferences of the leadership, initiating in turn a countermove to safeguard the elite's prerogatives. Indeed the permeability of the boundary from economic to political change often brings a backlash aimed at reversing the course of social participation and political "democratization." The warnings about the dangers of "spiritual pollution" in spreading bourgeois ideology in China are a case in point. The recent "nationalist" demonstrations in the Soviet Union are a similar warning about the dangers of reform. And the prolonged reluctance of the Polish government to open institutional channels of social participation, despite pressing need for reform in the economy, reflected their awareness that such actions have severe political consequences.

Poland, of course, is an extreme case. The experience of the

Solidarity period has infused a consciousness of self-organization and independence among large sectors of society that remains part of the political landscape. In these conditions social participation mechanisms revived the specter of social rebellion against the regime.

NOTES

1. *Reforma Gospodarcza: Propozycje, tendencje, kierunki dyskucji* (Warsaw: Panstwowe Wydawnictwo Ekonomiczne, 1981).
2. Kierunki Reformy Gospodarczej, *Trybuna Ludu*, July 1981.
3. "Ustawa o Samorzadzie Zalogi Przedsiebiorstwa," *Trybuna Ludu*, September 29, 1981.
4. For discussions of various issues concerning the 1980–81 period, see Jack Bielasiak and Maurice D. Simon, eds., *Polish Politics: Edge of the Abyss* (New York: Praeger, 1984).
5. Jack Bielasiak, "The 'Normalization' of State Socialism: The Reorganization of Political Power in Poland" (Paper presented at the Annual Meeting of the American Political Science Association, New Orleans, September 1985).
6. Zbigniew M. Fallenbuchl, "The Present State of the Economic Reform," in *Creditworthiness and Reform in Poland*, ed. Paul Marer and Wladyslaw Siwinski (Bloomington: Indiana University Press, 1988), and Witold Morawski, "Reforma Gospodarcza w Polsce," *Studia Socjologiczne*, no. 2 (1984).
7. Stainislaw Gomulka and Jacek Rostowski, "The Reformed Polish Economic System 1982–83," *Soviet Studies* 36, no. 3 (July 1984): 386–87.
8. For extensive discussion of the reform, see Fallenbuchl "Present State," Gomulka and Rostowski, "Reformed Polish Economic System"; and Morawski, "Reforma Gospodarcza."
9. Henry Norr, "Solidarity and Self-Management, May–July 1981," *Poland Watch*, no. 7, 97–122.
10. Witold Morawski, "Employees' Self-management and Economic Reforms," *Polish Sociological Bulletin*, nos. 1–4 (1982): 173–98; and David Holland, "Workers' Self-Management Before and After 1981," in Marer and Siwinski, *Creditworthiness*.
11. Witold Morawski, "Reformy Gospodarcze i Polityczne jako Czynniki Przezwyciezania Kryzysu," in *Zasppkajanie Potrzeb w Warunkach Kryzysu*, ed. Jerzy J. Wiatr (Warsaw: Uniwersytet Warszawski, 1986), 42–92.
12. Gomulka and Rostowski, "Reformed Polish Economic System," 388.
13. See Holland and Morawski, "Reformy Gospodarcze."

14. Wojciech Jaruzelski, speeches of December 13, 1981 and January 25, 1982, in *Selected Speeches* (Oxford: Pergamon Press, 1985), 28–34 and 35–44.

15. Bielasiak, "The 'Normalization' of State Socialism."

16. Stefan Nowak, "Postawy, Wartosci i Aspiracje Spoleczenstwa Polskiego," in *Polskie Systemy Wartosci i Modele Konsumpcji,* ed. Renata Siemienska (Warsaw: Uniwersytet Warszawski, 1984), 13–67.

17. See, for example, Alec Nove, "Socialism, Centralized Planning and the One-Party State," in *Authority Power and Policy in the USSR,* ed. T. H. Rigby, Archie Brown, and Peter Reddaway (New York: St. Martin's Press, 1980).

18. On the relationship between economic and political reform, see Wlodzimierz Brus, "The Political Economy of Polish Reforms," *International Praxis* 5, no. 2 (July 1985): 195–208; idem, "Political Pluralism and Markets in Communist Systems," in *Pluralism in the Soviet Union,* ed. Susan Solomon (New York: St. Martin's Press, 1983).

19. Bielasiak, "The 'Normalization' of State Socialism."

20. See George Blazyca, *Poland to the 1990s: Retreat or Reform?* (London: The Economist Intelligence Unit, 1986), 42–43.

21. For the most recent survey of the attitudes of Polish citizens, see the extensive study by Wladyslaw Adamski, Krzysztof Jasiewicz, and Andrzej Rychard, eds., *Raport z Badania Polacy '84* (Warsaw: Uniwersytet Warszawski, 1986), and Krzysztof Jasiewicz, *Raport Wstepny z Badania Opinie Polakow-Jesien 85* (Warsaw: Uniwersytet Warszawski, 1986).

22. Wieslawa Kozek, "Zalogi Przemyslowe Wobec Reformy Gospodarczej," in *Gospodarka i Spoleczenstwo,* ed. Witold Morawski (Warsaw: Uniwersytet Warzawski, 1986), 99–128; and OBOP data cited in Jane L. Curry, "The Psychological Barriers to Reform in Poland," *East European Politics and Society* 2, no. 3 (Fall 1988): 489.

23. For an extensive evaluation of the reform, see Blazyca, *Poland to the 1990s* and Fallenbuchl, "The Present State of Economic Reform."

24. *Rzeczpospolita,* July 1983.

25. Fallenbuchl, "Present State," 118.

26. Ibid., 117–27.

27. Blazyca, *Poland to the 1990s* 39–41, and Fallenbuchl, "Present State," 16–19.

28. Wlodzimierz Pankow and Michal Fedorowicz, "Samorzad w gospodarce Polskiej 1981–1985," *Kontakt,* no. 11 (November 1986): 38–52.

29. Janusz Beksiak, "Enterprise and Reform: The Polish Experience," *European Economic Review* 31 (February–March 1987): 122–24.

30. Blazyca, *Poland to the 1990s* 41–42, and Fallenbuchl, "Present State," 10–29.

31. Gomulka and Rostowski, "Reformed Polish Economic System," 389–90.

32. For an announcement of the first bankruptcy in Poland, see "The First Bankrupt," *Polish Perspectives*, no. 4 (Autumn 1986): 60.

33. Beksiak, "Enterprise and Reform," 122–23.

34. Morawski, "Reforma Gospodarcza," 26.

35. An official report of the Polish Sociological Association on the question of self-management appeared in 1986. For excerpts of the report, see Pankow and Fedrowicz, "Samorzad."

36. Pankow and Fedorowicz "Samorzad," 44–45.

37. Blazyca, *Poland to the 1990s*, 41.

38. Pankow and Fedorowicz, "Samorzad," 41.

39. Holland, "Workers' Self-Management."

40. Pankow and Fedorowicz, "Samorzad," 48.

41. Witold Morawski, "Demokracja Przemyslowa a Politika Gospodarka," 129–46, and "Samorzad Pracowniczy: Wizja i Realia," in *Gospodarka i Spoleczenstwo*, ed. Witold Morawski, (Warsaw: Uniwesytet Warzawski, 1986).

42. Trybuna *Ludu*, June 30, 1986.

43. Zbigniew M. Fallenbuchl, "The Polish Economy in the Year 2000," *The Carl Beck Papers*, no. 607 (September 1988): 1–29. See also Ewa Morawska, "On Barriers to Pluralism in Pluralist Poland," *Slavic Review* 47, no. 4 (Winter 1988): 629.

44. Ryszard Bugaj, "Dlaczego Kryzys sie Przedluza," *Tygodnik Powszechny*, January 5, 1986; Jerry Baczynski, "Obnizka Przed Podwyzka," *Polityka*, January 9, 1988; and Centrum Badania Opinii Spolecznej (CBOS), "Opinie o Sytuacji Gospodarczej i Politycznej w Kraju," September 1987.

45. "Theses on the Second Stage of Economic Reform," *Reforma Gospodarcza*, no. 102, supplement to *Rzeczpospolita*, April 17, 1987.

46. Marian Wozniak, "Second Stage of the Economic Reform," *Contemporary Poland* 20, nos. 7–8 (July–August 1987).

47. For example, Mieczyslaw Mieszczankowski, "A Short History of Reform," *Zycie Gospodarcze*, May 10, 1987, and Tomasz Jezioranski, "The Second Stage," *Zycie Gospodarcze*, July 12, 1987.

48. *Rzeczpospolita*, October 24–25, 1987.

49. *Rzeczpospolita*, October 12, 1987.

50. *Rzeczpospolita*, October 24–25, 1987.

51. *Trybuna Ludu*, May 8–9, 1987.

52. *Rzeczpospolita*, October 10–11, 1987.

53. Abraham Brumberg, "Poland: The New Opposition," *New York Review of Books*, February 18, 1988.

54. *Trybuna Ludu*, November 18, 1987.

55. *Rzeczpospolita*, November 26, 1987.

56. Wojciech Jaruzelski, *Rzeczpospolita*, October 10–11, 1987.

57. Ibid.

58. For the text of the referendum, see *Rzeczpospolita,* October 24–25, 1987.

59. J. B. De Weydenthal, "Uncertainty Continues in Poland," Radio Free Europe, *Background Report/202,* October 28, 1987.

60. *Rzeczpospolita,* December 1, 1987.

61. See, for example, Tomasz Jezioranski, "Support and Concerns," *Zycie Gospodarcze,* December 6, 1987; Zdislaw Sadowski (interview), "I Do Not Accept the View That the Majority Rejected the Program," *Polityka,* December 12, 1987; and Irena Dryll, "Referendum and After," *Zycie Gospodarcze,* December 13, 1987.

62. *Rzeczpospolita,* December 16 and December 17, 1987.

63. *Zycie Gospodarcze,* December 25, 1988; Bugaj, "Dlaczego Kryzys," and Wieslaw Krencik, "Karuzela Kreci sie Nadal," *Polityka,* September 29, 1988.

64. CBOS, "Opinie o Sytuacji," and Marek Henzler, "Poczucie Czasu," *Polityka,* December 24, 1988.

65. For a theoretical discussion of reform, see Tadeusz Kowálik, *On Crucial Reform of Real Socialism* (Vienna: The Vienna Institute for Comparative Economic Studies, 1986). For the individual countries, see Timothy Colton, *The Dilemma of Reform in the Soviet Union* (New York: Council on Foreign Relations, 1986); Gail W. Lapidus, "Gorbachev and the Reform of the Soviet System," *Daedalus* 116, no. 2 (Spring 1987): 1–30; Elizabeth Perry and Christine Wong, eds., *The Political Economy of Reform in Post-Mao China* (Cambridge: Harvard University Press, 1985); Dorothy J. Solinger, "Industrial Reform: Decentralization, Differentiation, and the Difficulties," *Journal of International Affairs* 34, no. 2 (Winter 1986): 105–18; and Charles Bukowski and Mark A. Cichock, eds., *Prospects for Change in Communist Systems* (New York: Praeger, 1986).

66. Ellen Comisso and Paul Marer, "The Economics and Politics of Reform in Hungary," *International Organization* 40, no. 2 (Spring 1986): 421–54.

67. Thomas A. Baylis, "Explaining the GDR's Economic Strategy," *International Organization* 40, no. 2 (Spring 1986): 381–419.

68. Waclaw Wilczynski, "Polish Economic Reform and the Economic Theory of Socialism," *Oeconomica Polona* 13, no. 1 (1986): 47–69.

INDEX